FROM BLENHEIM
TO CHARTWELL

FROM BLENHEIM TO CHARTWELL

The Untold Story of
Churchill's Houses & Gardens

STEFAN BUCZACKI

UNICORN

First published by Unicorn
an imprint of the Unicorn Publishing Group LLP, 2018
5 Newburgh Street
London
W1F 7RG

www.unicornpublishing.org

This book is based on a revised and updated version of *Churchill & Chartwell*
by Stefan Buczacki published by Frances Lincoln in 2007.

© Stefan Buczacki, 2018

10 9 8 7 6 5 4 3 2 1

ISBN 978-1-911604-23-5

Cover design Unicorn Publishing Group
Typeset by Vivian@Bookscribe

Printed and bound in Spain

CONTENTS

$\mathscr{F}$OREWORD
by Randolph Churchill

As one of the most significant and most studied individuals in our history, my great-grandfather's life has been raked over countless times by historians and biographers. It might seem in consequence that there is nothing new to discover. However, when Stefan Buczacki began what was planned to be a study of Chartwell and its garden and discussed the project with my great-aunt, Mary Soames, she urged him to widen his brief. No one had previously studied the many other homes and their gardens that Churchill and his wife Clementine bought and sold over the years, the residences that culminated in their ownership of the great house of Chartwell itself.

The resulting story is the product of years of painstaking research, of uncovering scarcely known facts and scarcely known houses – including one that Churchill bought almost by mistake. Through his thorough research Stefan portrays the full breadth of Churchill's homes with insight and detail that helps us understand Churchill, both statesman and family man. We are indebted to Stefan for his scholarship and vivid account.

It has been a fascinating revelation, even for my own family.

Introduction

In his highly praised biography *Churchill*, the late Roy Jenkins wrote that he did not claim to have unearthed many new facts about his subject. He said that with published sources about him on their existing scale, this would be almost impossible and concluded that there are 'no great hidden reservoirs of behaviour to be tapped'. In as much as Churchill is probably the most biographed man in history whose letters and papers have been raked over by two or three generations of researchers, that is probably true and the interest and significance of most published Churchill study today lies in the interpretation of what are essentially irrefutable facts. But there is a significant aspect of Churchill's life that has never been examined in detail. Most biographers have overlooked much of the private, domestic existence of this very public man.

Whilst it is generally known that Winston and Clementine Churchill owned a property called Chartwell and it was their home for forty years, the fact that they also owned, rented or borrowed many other houses is largely unappreciated. When I first set about researching what I expected to be 'the Chartwell story' therefore, it soon became evident that I too needed to know what had gone before and who and what had influenced them. Then, in turn, many other questions arose. Why did they move home so often and sometimes own two or three properties at the same time when at others they owned none? Who and what were the driving forces in deciding where they would live? How were the houses paid for? Why and when did Churchill take up farming and equestrian enterprises? And how did the family's pattern of domestic life relate to Churchill's political career?

It also became evident that while much of the information I needed was certainly in the pubic domain at the Churchill archives, it had in large measure remained hidden because the bits that interested me were those that other biographers had ignored. And they were usually the bits that had been left out when the documents and letters were published.

I soon reached three decisions therefore. First, I would read all the relevant Churchill papers as original documents; second, where I had unavoidably to rely on secondary information, I would be circumspect in trusting any facts or comments that were neither in the late Sir Martin Gilbert's official biography nor written by members of the Churchill family; and third, I would endeavour to visit all the Churchills' homes, official and private, long and short term, owned and rented as well as those of significant friends who influenced them.

I had two significant pieces of good fortune. I located a small but highly important collection of unpublished papers of the Chartwell architect Philip Tilden and I was allowed access to a critical group of closed papers in the Churchill archives relating to Churchill's farms.

I had thought that being a lifelong admirer of Churchill might prove a handicap as I unfolded, layer by layer, a side to the man that was essentially unknown. Would I be disappointed and discover private feet of clay as this greatest of world statesmen dealt with estate agents, managed his mortgage, kept an eye on the grocer's accounts, chose wallpaper, argued with architects, hired and fired servants, developed his garden and haggled with builders? On the contrary, I discovered an unexpected humanity and whilst through his letters I certainly came to know the Churchill the world knows, a man born to lead, an ever impatient and often intolerant man aware of his own destiny, a driven politician with an ego the size of a tank, I also found a gentler individual with human frailties and a measure of insecurity, an always loving – if not always caring – husband and above all, a man of total integrity. To my surprise, in the house-owning, home-making, garden building Churchill of my study I found a bit of everyman.

Author's Acknowledgements

Throughout my research and writing I have been deeply grateful for the kind support and interest of the late Lady Soames, the last surviving child of Winston and Clementine Churchill. She patiently responded to those queries to which only she could possibly know the answers and I was greatly touched by her kind welcome on my visits to her home. Nonetheless any errors of fact or interpretation about her parents' lives that may remain are my responsibility. Lady Soames also generously gave permission for some important collections of closed papers in the Churchill Archives relating to the Churchill farms and farm accounts to be opened for my study.

I am greatly appreciative of the interest shown in my work by Churchill's great grandson Randolph who has most kindly written a Foreword to this new edition.

Many archivists and librarians have been helpful to me but none more so than Allen Packwood and his staff in the Churchill Archives at Churchill College, Cambridge where I buried myself for a year. They were unfailingly efficient and displayed a pleasance, warmth of welcome and interest in my work not always to be found in such institutions. It was greatly appreciated.

Having set myself the goal of visiting all the Churchills' homes, and those of many of their friends, I cannot express too highly my gratitude to the present owners, occupiers and tenants who have made this possible. They have opened doors, given personally guided tours, plied me with coffee (and in some instances served the most splendid lunches in the most splendid surroundings) and generously loaned precious and personal photographs and documents. In order to protect their privacy, however, I have not linked any of their names with their properties.

I am especially grateful to the owners of a collection of unpublished papers of the architect Philip Tilden which were made freely available to me and without which my study of the redevelopment of Chartwell would have been immeasurably less complete. Among others who loaned documents, I wish particularly to thank John Julius Norwich who generously gave me access to unpublished material that he later used in his autobiography.

I am also grateful to my son Brig Julian Buczacki who read the script with military precision, pointed out a few matters of military and historical inconsistency and took a special delight in questioning one or two examples of his father's syntax.

The staff of the National Trust have been supportive and helpful throughout and I was hugely grateful to Carole Kenwright, lately Property Manager at Chartwell, for giving me free rein to explore the house and grounds at my leisure while Jon Simons, lately Head Gardener at Chartwell and his staff kindly and patiently responded to my queries, both horticultural and historical. While I was revising my script Katherine Barnett and Tim Parker, respectively Project Curator and Collections Manager and Gardens and Countryside Manager at Chartwell were unfailingly helpful in supplying me with up to date information.

At Unicorn Publishing Simon Perks and his colleagues have been understanding and supportive and I have been especially appreciative of their empathy with the author's point of view.

The persons named below are too numerous to thank individually but all have made essential and invaluable contributions to my study in countless different ways and I am grateful to them all. I apologise if inadvertently any names have been omitted.

The late Hon Edward Adeane (Dean Trench Street); Verity Andrews (Reading University Archives); Toby Anstruther (Hoe Farm and Sir John Lavery); Christopher and Primrose Arnander (Gertrude Jekyll); The Viscount and Viscountess Asquith; Viscount Astor; Maj and Mrs Joe Aylward (Overstrand); Stuart Band (Devonshire Collection, Chatsworth); James Bettley (Philip Tilden); Ashish Bhatt (Ditchley); Cherie Blair; Rita Boswell (Harrow School Archives); William Bradfield (Overstrand); Nathalie Brassington and Staff (St George's School, Ascot); Anthony Brookes and Bob Shearer (Harold Swithinbank and SY Venetia); Fay Brown (Ventnor); Jane Brown (Gertrude Jekyll); Prof Michael

Brown (Downing Street); Mike Buffin (National Trust gardens); Tim Butler (National Trust); Elizabeth Buxton (Philip Tilden); His Excellency Rene J. Mujica Cantelar (former Cuban Ambassador in London); Howard Charman and Rémy Saget (Cannes); Brig Christopher Galloway (Ditchley); Pamela Clark (The Royal Archives); Sarah Clarke (Imperial War Museum); David Coffer; Neil Cooke; David Coombs (Churchill's paintings); Myrna Corrie (Belted Galloway Society); Raoul and Gyll Curtis Machin (Lullenden garden); Peter Day (Carpenters); Mary Digby (Chartwell garden); Ron and Daphne Dilley (Carpenters); Gina Douglas (Linnean Society); Doris Edleston (Albert Hill); Jeremy Edmond (Port Lympne); Michael Edwards (Hoe Farm); Marjorie Farley (Hyde Park Gate); Dr Martin Farr (Reginald McKenna); David Fenwick (crocosmias); Matthew and Sally Ferrey; Elizabeth Finn (Sevenoaks Library); Peter Fitt (Breccles Hall); Donatella Flick; John Forster (Blenheim); Michael and Ellie Foster; Sue Geddes (Downing Street); the late Sir Martin Gilbert; George Goring (Goring Hotel); Pam Greening (Royal College of Veterinary Surgeons); Joanne Grenier-Morton (Imperial War Museum); Helen Hamilton (Ian Hamilton and Belted Galloway cattle); Ian Hamilton; Jane Haries (Downing Street); Ray Harlow (Sandwich); David Hatter (Chartwell Visitors' book); Lady Heseltine; Allyson Hayward (Norah Lindsay); Nickie Holding (Carpenters); Maurice Hollows (Overstrand); Bridget Howlett (London Metropolitan Archives); Jilly Humm (Downing Street); Christopher Jerram (Mells); Anna Johns (Blickling Hall); Paul Jordan (Brighton History Centre); the late Clinton Keeling; Paul Kendall (Royal Botanic Gardens, Kew); Alison Kenney (Westminster City Archives); Rev Helen Kendrick (Sutton Courtenay); Stephen King; Ann Laver (Godalming Museum); Ivor Lee (The Labour Corps); John and Celia Lee (Hamilton and Churchill families); Barbara Leigh (Seal Library); Jill Leney (Templeton); Ruth Longford (Morpeth Mansions and Frances Stevenson); The Earl and Countess of Lytton; Rusty MacLean (Rugby School Archives); Alison MacPherson; Rt Hon Sir John Major; Dame Norma Major; His Grace the late 11th Duke of Marlborough; Hugh McCalmont (Banstead); Claire McKendrick (Glasgow University Library); Alan McLeod; Rodney Melville (Chequers); Patricia Methven (Kings College, London); Elizabeth Milner (National Gardens Scheme); Capt J. R. F. Mills (Anglesey); Philip Mitchell (Juddmonte Farms); Hugo Morriss (Banstead); Anthea Morton-Saner; Rebecca Ockwell (National Trust); Pat O'Connor; John Julius Norwich; The late 2nd Earl of Oxford and Asquith; Derek Paul

(Overstrand); Berit Peterson (Royal Entomological Society); Jan Potter; Phil Reed (Imperial War Museum); Margaret Richardson (Gertrude Jekyll); Nicholas Robinson (Fitzwilliam Museum); Judith Seaward (Chartwell); Julian Seymour; Caroline Shaw (Rothschild Archive Centre); Peter Sheppard; Roz Sherris (Museum of London); Angie Sidebotham (Juddmonte Farms); Jon Simons (Chartwell garden); Linda Sinclair (Arlington Street); Alf Smith (Downing Street and Admiralty House); Yvonne Spencer-Churchill; Richard Spoors (narrow gauge railways); Paul Stamper (English Heritage); Ian Stanley; Peter Stanley; John Steer (Frinton-on-Sea); June Stubbs (Thorney Island Society); Sue Sutton (Seaford Museum); Nigel Talbot-Ponsonby; Trish Tippett (Hyde Park Gate); John Vincent (Victor Vincent); His Grace the 9th Duke of Wellington; Robert Welsford (Corporation of the Sons of the Clergy); Dr Margaret Whalley (Anglesey); Jean Wickham (Overstrand); Tom Williamson (University of East Anglia); John and Gina Wilson; Sebastian Wormell (Harrods); David Yaxley (Houghton Archives).

Rosetta Cottage, Cowes, Isle of Wight where Churchill's parents first met and the plaque at Rosetta Cottage commemorating the meeting during Cowes week 1873.

The hastily prepared room at Blenheim Palace in which Winston Leonard Spencer-Churchill was born on 30 November 1874.

CHAPTER 1
*E*ARLY INFLUENCES

When the sun rose over Blenheim Palace in Oxfordshire on the morning of Monday 30 November 1874, the great house had one more resident than when it had set the previous evening; one who by intention, should not have been there. At half past one in the morning, Jennie, the American born wife of Lord Randolph Churchill, Member of Parliament for the Borough of Woodstock and the second surviving son of the house's owner, the 7th Duke of Marlborough, had given birth to her first child. He would be christened Winston Leonard Spencer-Churchill and baptised in the Blenheim chapel a month later.

Lord Randolph Churchill,
Churchill's father.

Jennie, Lady Churchill (Lady
Randolph), Churchill's mother.

There had been no expectation that Winston Spencer Churchill – as he chose to be known, in due course dropping both the hyphen and the Leonard – would be born in the ancestral mansion. His parents happened to be staying there between homes and his birth was two months premature; so unexpected in fact that he was born in a temporary bedroom made ready in great haste. Lord and Lady Randolph – as they were generally known – had taken a three month let for

£200 on a house at No 1 Curzon Street in London's Mayfair. This arrangement had ended in July and the intention was that their first child would be born at a new London home nearby, a distinctive early Georgian house at 48, Charles Street into which they were due to move at the start of their tenancy in January.

No 48 Charles Street, Churchill's first childhood home.

No 48 Charles Street was a fine town house, one of the most attractive small town houses in London, but it was certainly no Blenheim. Churchill returned to the old palace countless times during his life, and family gatherings there, especially at Christmas, were always precious to him. From an early age, he also came to appreciate the setting of Blenheim, its gardens, grounds and the rolling park landscaped by Lancelot 'Capability' Brown. His parents' various town houses had little if any garden and he would be over forty before he had a proper one of his own. As early as spring 1882, at the age of seven, Churchill wrote several letters from Blenheim to his father telling him he had collected a basket of primroses and some 'wild hyacinths' [bluebells] and that there were violets and daisies in the Blenheim gardens. He touchingly told the distant and austere Lord Randolph in April that year how much he preferred walking in the gardens at Blenheim to Green Park or Hyde Park.[1] Naturally the young Churchill visited and stayed with friends, some of whose homes had fine gardens and grand estates but it was Blenheim that played a critical and early part in shaping his love of gardens, of flowers and of the natural world.

Churchill's ancestor, John the 1st Duke of Marlborough was granted the

Manor of Woodstock by Queen Anne on 17 February 1705 as a gift from a grateful country in recognition of his services during the war against the French. The architect John Vanbrugh and his assistant Nicholas Hawksmoor were entrusted with creating an appropriate house, to be called Blenheim after the battle site at Blindheim in Bavaria where Marlborough and his Austrian ally Prince Eugene of Savoy had defeated the French. Marlborough wanted his house, the Palace as it became, to be something like the home that Vanbrugh and Hawksmoor had built for the 3rd Earl of Carlisle at Castle Howard, a house Marlborough greatly admired. The construction at Woodstock began in the summer of 1705 but it proceeded unhappily. Sarah, the Duchess of Marlborough unfortunately fell out of favour with the Queen and then the funding dried up under the incoming Tory government. The builders sued the Duke, who was obliged to dip deeply into his own purse, then the Duchess argued with Vanbrugh who left, taking Hawksmoor with him. How Churchill, in the summer of 1923 must have felt the historical resonances as he tangled with his own architect at Chartwell; although his battles and his budgets were on a rather smaller scale, something for which he must have been immensely grateful. And he did not have an interfering wife.

The Marlboroughs finally moved into Blenheim in 1719 but the Duke was not to enjoy his home for long. He died in 1722 leaving his widow to continue directing the work on the estate. Who, among Vanbrugh, the Duke himself or Henry Wise, master gardener to the Queen was responsible for the overall plan of the grounds at Blenheim is not known. But self-evidently, the scheme was to be formal, its scale was vast and it was altered several times at the Duchess's bidding before her own death in 1744. It was not until twenty years later, under the 4th Duke of Marlborough that the grounds at Blenheim acquired essentially the appearance with which Churchill grew up and that is familiar to visitors today. The Duke engaged the designer Lancelot 'Capability' Brown to transform the entire park of 2,500 acres into a unified semi-natural landscape. It is widely considered a masterpiece. Entering from Woodstock through Hawksmoor's Triumphal Arch, Churchill saw as we do, how Brown integrated what Hawksmoor and Vanbrugh had left as individual pieces – the palace itself, the bridge, the scattered plantings and rides – into one magnificent entity. He created the Great Lakes and an artificial river, cascades, carriage drives and discrete and ingenious positioning of groups of trees. Although in time, Churchill himself was to create lakes and plant trees, it is hard to believe even he felt he was truly emulating Brown but being so familiar throughout his life with a landscape of trees, contrived vistas and water, it is hard to believe too that the germ of his ambition was not sown in his childhood; at the garden he so much admired, a garden where '...there is no violent contrast, no abrupt dividing line between the wildness and freshness of the garden and the pomp of the architecture'. But no garden ever stands still. Gardening is the four-dimensional art and it changes by the day under the influences both of nature and man. Even as Brown was completing his involvement in the late eighteenth century, William Chambers and others were creating small temples within the Pleasure Grounds close to the house, one of which, the Temple of Diana on a particularly prominent point overlooking the lake was Chambers' own work and was to feature significantly in Churchill's personal life. Each owner of Blenheim, each successive Duke, has made his personal mark and the development of the gardens is a story that has itself filled books. Using some of the vast wealth that his American first wife Consuelo Vanderbilt brought to the Blenheim coffers the 9th Duke, Churchill's

Charles (Sunny), 9th Duke of Marlborough, Churchill's cousin

cousin, changed much of the area close to the house during his lifetime. He engaged the French designer Achille Duchêne to create new formal gardens and most conspicuously transformed an old shrubbery on the western side into spectacular water gardens in the French style, a project not completed until 1930. For eight years between 1902 and 1910 the three acre Great Court was a mess as Marlborough swept away Brown's lawns to return it to its original gravelled and cobbled form and the estate was in constant turmoil as in the course of little more than the first two decades of the twentieth century, he planted almost half a million trees. On the eastern side of the Palace, Henry Wise's flower garden, installed for the 1st Duchess, had fallen into a parlous state by the late nineteenth century and Duchêne redesigned this too. As a young man visiting and staying at Blenheim, Churchill would have seen many of these upheavals, the building sites that ensue when gardens are created or altered, a situation that nonetheless clearly did not put him off his own landscape gardening for it was a scene that was to become all too familiar in the nineteen twenties at Chartwell.

Number 48 Charles Street, Churchill's first London home, was then the heart of fashionable Mayfair and was one of the group of streets around Berkeley Square laid out about 1675. Lord Randolph's home at No 48 is one of the more distinguished houses with two attractive white obelisks in front of its arched doorway. The arrangement of its rooms is typical of houses of the period and, give or take variations in size, it set a pattern that was to be followed throughout Churchill's life. A rather grand staircase ascended from an elegant entrance hall off which the reception and dining rooms were generally situated, the withdrawing rooms and library were on the first floor, the bedrooms on the second and third and the servants' quarters at the top. A rear stairs gave the servants access to the rest of the house and to the kitchen and service rooms in the basement.

Because he died within the memories of many people alive today, it is easy to forget that Churchill was a Victorian; yet he was born shortly after the middle of Queen Victoria's sixty-three year reign. Victorian values, Victorian standards and Victorian practices were part of his growing up. And because he became a man of the people and spent his political life in the House of Commons not the House of Lords, it is easy to forget too that he was an upper class Victorian. Churchill's young life was peopled with servants and in due course he employed them himself. Seven or eight domestic staff was the usual quota for town houses of the size of No 48 Charles Street and for a family of the Churchills' standing. The servants lived on the top one or two floors, gaining access by the back stairs to their work places, tending the family's rooms or in the basement where the kitchen and stores were situated.

Among the first servants Lord and Lady Randolph employed at Charles Street was a woman who was to be central to the early years of Churchill's life: his nurse Elizabeth Everest to whom he became devoted. She took him on holiday and corresponded with him at school; once, in fine nanny fashion, she called him

Elizabeth Everest ('Woom'), Churchill's nanny.

'a naughty little boy' for not writing to his parents. He was eighteen years old at the time. She taught him about flowers and the countryside and shared with him early attempts at smallholding. Elizabeth Ann Everest was born in Chatham and thought Kent the centre of the world. Its capital she said was Maidstone and all around grew strawberries, cherries, raspberries and plums. 'Lovely' said

Churchill, 'I always wanted to live in Kent'. Elizabeth Everest spent her life in service and before Lady Randolph appointed her, she had been working for a vicar in Cumberland but for so pivotal a figure in Churchill's upbringing, she is imbued with a curious enigma. Churchill and his brother called her 'Woom', 'Woomany' or sometimes 'Oom'; 'Woom' was how she signed herself when writing to them. Formally, she was Mrs Everest to everyone although the reality is that she was unmarried and there is no real clue to why the fiction was perpetuated although nannies were sometimes called 'Mrs' regardless of their marital state. The one person who seems to have disliked her was Churchill's grandmother, Frances the 7th Duchess of Marlborough ('Duchess Fanny') who called her 'that horrid old Everest'[2] although Churchill's cousin Shane Leslie said this was because Woom did not like cold and draughty Blenheim. She would keep Churchill in London and away from his grandmother because she thought the palace unhealthy. Ironically, in 1891 when the boys were old enough for Lady Randolph to have no further need of her services, Elizabeth Everest went to work for the old Duchess at her London house in Grosvenor Square. She was eventually dismissed (by letter) in October 1893, an episode that caused Churchill much distress.

Churchill's childhood days at 48 Charles Street were brief, thanks to an ill-judged intervention by his father in the private affairs of his friend the Prince of Wales. The Prince was away in India during the winter of 1875–6 while his friend and companion the Earl of Aylesford was embroiled in rather complex divorce proceedings in which Lord Randolph's elder brother the Marquess of Blandford was cited as co-respondent. Lord Randolph threatened to make public a bundle of intimate letters written by the Prince of Wales to Aylesford's wife some years previously. It was a bad move. The Prince was most extraordinarily cross. There was talk of a duel. Lord and Lady Randolph went to America in the summer of 1876 hoping that things would cool down and Lord Randolph apologised but it was clear he needed to be out of the way for rather longer to stand any chance of restoring his favour at Court. A neat solution was therefore proposed by Lord Beaconsfield (the Conservative Prime Minister, Benjamin Disraeli). The Duke of Marlborough should be appointed Lord Lieutenant (Viceroy) of Ireland and take his son Lord Randolph with him as his unpaid private secretary – unpaid because this would avoid him having to give up his seat in the House of Commons. All that was necessary was to nudge aside the existing Viceroy, the

Duke of Abercorn, a move neatly achieved without bloodshed. So it was that in early January 1877 after only two years in his parents' Mayfair home, young Winston and Mrs Everest and most of the Churchill family were on the boat to Ireland.

The Vice-regal lodge in Phoenix Park, Dublin, now called Áras an Uachtaráin and the official home of the President of Ireland, is a bit like a scaled-down White House. It was designed in the mid-eighteenth century by an amateur architect named Nathaniel Clements and a short distance away was The Little Lodge, 'a long, low white building with Green shutters and verandahs'.[3] This was the residence of the Private Secretary, Churchill's father, and it was to be their home for the next three years.

The most important event of young Winston Churchill's stay in Ireland was the birth of his one and only sibling to whom he remained close throughout his life.

No 29 St James's Place, Churchill's second childhood home.

John Strange Spencer-Churchill, always known as Jack, was born in Phoenix Park in Dublin on 4 February 1880 shortly before his parents returned to England in time to take part in the general election in April. His penance done – although it would be some time before he was properly welcomed back into the Prince of Wales' circle – Lord Randolph retained his seat at Woodstock but Disraeli's government fell to Gladstone's Liberals and the Duke of Marlborough's tenure as Viceroy was at an end. Lord Randolph had sub-let the Charles Street house and was therefore in need of an alternative London home so he moved his family across Piccadilly to the secluded and fashionable Georgian haven that is St James's Place. He took a lease on No 29, a compact five-storied house where he at least knew his neighbours. Next door at No 30 was Sir Stafford Northcote, sometime Liberal but by then Conservative MP for North Devonshire and until recently Chancellor of the Exchequer in Disraeli's government. He was the man who had taken over from Disraeli as Conservative leader in the House of Commons on the Prime Minister's elevation to the peerage as the 1st Earl of Beaconsfield in 1876.

At St James's Place a first glimpse is seen of the servants who were sharing young Churchill's life. In addition to the redoubtable and enigmatic Mrs Everest, there were Amelia Legge, the cook, Sarah Mitchell, the housemaid, Rebecca Secret, the lady's maid, Charles Howard, butler, Frederick Martin, footman and seventeen year old Jane Clark, the kitchen maid. But by late 1882, after less than three years in St James's Place, they were on the move again. The family needed

more room but this necessitated parting company with their distinguished address and taking a larger house in an area frequented by those whom today would be called the nouveau riche. The area was Tyburnia, centred on the site of the infamous Tyburn gallows on the edge of Hyde Park. Lord Randolph took a lease on No 2 Connaught Place, at the corner with Edgware Road, a tall five-storied stuccoed house built around 1810 with its principal rooms facing south across Hyde Park to benefit from the view and like its neighbours, accessed from a private road at the back. Many burials from public executions had taken place in the area and it is said that a mass grave was found beneath No 2 not long after

No 2 Connaught Place, Churchill's third childhood home.

the Churchills moved in at the end of 1882. In consequence, the house was said to be haunted and perhaps in further consequence, and probably at Lady Randolph's instigation, electricity was installed in No 2 Connaught Place which thus became one of the first houses in England to be so illuminated. The young man who installed it was called Samuel Mavar – some fifty years later, Clementine Churchill met him while she was returning to England from New York on the RMS *Berengaria*. He had emigrated to become a successful mining engineer.

The Connaught Place house was notionally Churchill's home for the next nine years. He had never lived in one place for so long but for much of the time he was an unhappy and absentee resident. At the beginning of November, just before the family left St James's Place and shortly before his eighth birthday he was sent away to school. The school was St George's in Wells Lane, Ascot where he spent nearly two hateful years with around thirty-five other unfortunate inmates under the exceedingly grim regime of the Reverend Herbert Sneyd-Kynnersley and his wife Flora. The boys were allowed some freedom – Churchill wrote of going fishing one Saturday – but despite the fact that the school had every modern facility (like 2 Connaught Place, it was also illuminated by

St George's School, Ascot, Churchill's first school (anonymous watercolour, probably late 19th century).

Nos 29–30 Brunswick Road, Hove, the site of the Misses Thomsons' school.

electricity, 'then a wonder' Churchill later wrote),[4] it also had the most fearsome flogging regime he ever encountered and it was with much relief that he was taken away at the end of the summer term of 1884. It is possible he was moved when Mrs Everest spoke to Lady Randolph after seeing the after-effects of his birchings but for whatever reason he was sent to a more benign establishment at Nos 29 and 30 Brunswick Road, Hove, owned by two young unmarried women, Charlotte Thomson and her younger sister Catherine. The school was formed from two early Victorian terraced houses in the typical Hove bow-fronted style close to fashionable Brunswick Square on the south side of the town. The sea was not far away down a steep hill. The school was large enough to accommodate up to twenty-two pupils with a matron, cook and four servants and a tiny rear garden provided the opportunity for the children to partake of fresh air but the Thomsons' regime clearly extended to taking their young charges into the countryside because it was while in Hove in September 1886 that Churchill first wrote of his pleasure at collecting butterflies. In the following year, he wrote to his mother 'I am never at a loss to do anything while I am in the country for I shall be occupied with 'Butterflying' all day (I was last year)'.[5] There was clearly official encouragement too: seventy years later he said 'When I was a small boy at school we were given nets and encouraged to massacre butterflies. When they were caught they were pinned on a board, and boys competed with boys in the number of species on their board. There were Tortoiseshells and Red Admirals and Peacocks'.[6] At Hove too, he was able to play cricket and to ride three times a week and in January 1885, there is a mention of a bowl with two goldfish, the first reference to creatures that were to hold a life-long fascination for him.

In 1885, the political career of Churchill's father was reaching a climax. Gladstone's Liberal administration lost a vote in the House of Commons, Gladstone resigned and the Tory leader Lord Salisbury was invited to form a government. Although Lord Randolph had never held office, he was the supreme orator, the talismanic figure who could influence the electorate and he presumed to tell Lord Salisbury that he would not serve in his government if his former neighbour Sir Stafford Northcote was Leader of the Commons. He got his way, Sir Stafford went to the House of Lords and Lord Randolph became a Privy Councillor and a minister for the first time – Secretary of State for India in Lord Salisbury's caretaker government. In November, an election was called, Lord Randolph won South Paddington but Gladstone's Liberals had the largest number of seats while the Irish Nationalists held the balance of power. The situation was unsatisfactory and early the following year, Salisbury resigned and Gladstone was back as Prime Minister. He lasted until June, another election was held in July, the Tories triumphed and Lord Randolph, who was seen as the architect of victory was rewarded by Salisbury in being appointed both Chancellor of the Exchequer and Leader of the House of Commons. His rise had been meteoric. Young Churchill at school in Brighton was now being asked for his father's autograph. But the glory was short-lived. An ill-judged speech in the autumn of 1886 followed by an inability to push through his budget were to cost Lord Randolph his job. He resigned and Lord Salisbury was never to forgive him. The meteoric rise was followed, like the path of all shooting stars, by a fall to earth.

In March 1888, Churchill passed the entrance examination to Harrow and with two fellow pupils from Brighton started there the following month in Mr Henry

Davidson's Small House. His time there and the chimera of his achievements in the various subjects are well known. His letters home are full of measles, toothache, shortages of money, school reports both good and indifferent, lack of parental visits, rifle shooting and his prospects for admission to Sandhurst which he eventually achieved, at the third attempt, in August 1893. Although his marks were not good enough to gain him admission to the infantry, as his father had wished, they were good enough for the cavalry and in due course he was gazetted in the 4th Hussars as a second lieutenant in February 1895.

Churchill's boyhood summer holidays were generally spent well out of his parents' sight at the seaside with Mrs Everest. In 1885 for instance, he went to Cromer although Ventnor on the Isle of Wight was a particular favourite. It was the home of Mrs Everest's' sister Mary – her husband John Balaam was at one time a warder at Parkhurst Prison and their son Charles was the same age as Churchill. Winston first went to Ventnor at the age of three in March 1878 by when John Balaam was superintendent of the Ventnor Gas and Water Company.

No 2 Verona Cottages, Ventnor (now 28 Mitchell Avenue) where Churchill spent boyhood holidays.

He stayed at his home, a house called Flint Cottage perched high on the slope above the gas works from which the smell of gas must have been extremely intrusive. There was a steep path from the house down to the sea and during a walk along the cliffs, young Winston recalled seeing the training ship *Eurydice* in full sail off-shore. Then a sudden squall caused them all to dash home and on his next walk along the same cliff path, there were three masts protruding from the water, masts that betrayed the last resting place of the ship which had been sunk in that same squall with the loss of over three hundred lives, one of the worst British shipping tragedies. Seeing boats bringing corpses ashore made a lasting impression on Churchill; it was the first time – the first of many throughout the next ninety years – he had personally experienced death at such close quarters.

Flint Cottage (arrowed) above the former Ventnor gasworks where Churchill spent boyhood holidays (early 20th century).

In 1888 by when John Balaam was semi-retired and working as a rates collector, Winston and Jack made a visit – possibly one of several – to stay with the family at a newly built house, No 2 Verona Cottages in Newport Road high above the town. The boys enjoyed picking raspberries and gooseberries from the Balaams' garden which had distant views out across Ventnor to the sea.[7] The local belief is that in all Churchill made five visits to Ventnor, staying also at a lodging house 2 Hambrough Road and at a house in Alma Road just off the Esplanade although there is no obvious reason why he should have visited the town and not stayed with the Balaams. But if there was one truly important place in addition to Blenheim that helped shape young Churchill's love of the great outdoors, it was Banstead Manor, set in the lovely rolling countryside to the south of Newmarket.

Banstead Manor and the then vast Cheveley Estate on which it stands were owned by Harry McCalmont, the son of a London barrister. By dint of a peculiar family will, he inherited £4 million from an unmarried relative who had made his

The old house at Banstead Manor (early 20th century), rented by Lord Randolph for holidays.

Harry McCalmont, the owner of Banstead Manor.

fortune in banking (the McCalmonts were then the most important financiers in the City after Barings) and he used it to indulge in a prodigious spending spree. He bought an estate in Hertfordshire, a house in St James's Square and a yacht, as well as the Cheveley Park Estate which at first he leased and then bought from John Manners, the 7th Duke of Rutland. In the summer of 1890, Lord Randolph was becoming increasingly interested in horse racing (he had already won the 1889 Oaks with a jet black filly called L'Abbesse De Jouarre) and in Harry McCalmont he could not have found better inspiration as he was also spending part of his vast wealth on the turf. McCalmont may in turn have benefited from the political influence that accrued from Lord Randolph's friendship – five years later he himself entered Parliament as Conservative member for East Cambridgeshire. McCalmont owned some remarkably successful horses including one of the greatest of all English thoroughbreds, Isinglass. Another of his horses, St Maclou was to beat Bob Sievier's Sceptre in the 1902 Lincolnshire. As McCalmont lived in the main house at Cheveley, the agricultural estate of Banstead Manor was available to let and Lord Randolph and his mother, Duchess Fanny took a joint lease on it; and then in January 1891, Lord Randolph took over the entire let himself.[8] Churchill and Jack with other family members and friends' children spent perfect schoolboy holidays there.[9] The teenage Churchill built a den, a large mud and wooden hut, constructed with the help of some estate workers. Around it he and Jack, together with their cousins Shane Leslie and Hugh Frewen, a boy named Christopher, the son of John Ranner the gardener from nearby Dover Cottage and other children from the estate built fortifications and a defensive catapult. Stories persist locally of Churchill's boyish mischief at Banstead and no window was considered safe from his catapult while Tom Bell, the farm bailiff's son was lured by the future Prime Minister into falling down a trap door in the stable hay loft.[10]

It was at Banstead too that Churchill and his brother began small-holding, keeping chickens, ferrets, a guinea pig and rabbits although the modest returns he made from selling the eggs would not, Mrs Everest told him, even pay the labourer's wages; so setting a financial pattern that was to continue throughout Churchill's farming life.[11] In the bitterly cold Christmas holidays of 1890 they killed rabbits for the pot, had fun in the snow and skated on the pond. At Banstead, there were kittens and puppies to play with and, in the summer, fresh fruit and vegetables from the garden and Mrs Everest's home-made jam. It was all, Mrs Everest said, 'so much better for them than London'.[12]

But all good things must come to an end. In the summer of 1892, Lord Randolph Churchill was finding his finances unduly constrained and he decided to give up his London house 2 Connaught Place and then in October relinquished Banstead Manor too. The Churchills left their mark at Banstead nonetheless. Lady Randolph had never taken kindly to washing her hair in the hard Suffolk water and so had a large rainwater tank installed in the attic. Unfortunately the house was badly built and with inadequate foundations and shortly after the McCalmont family sold the property in 1927, the rafters finally gave way under the tank's weight and thanks to Lady Randolph's concern for her coiffure, the entire house was wrecked leading to its subsequent demolition.[13]

Back in 1892, and potentially homeless, Lord Randolph turned for family help as his son was later to do many times himself. His mother Duchess Fanny had been widowed by the death of her husband, Churchill's grandfather, John the 7th Duke of Marlborough in July 1883 and had a large Georgian house at fifty, Grosvenor Square. The house dated from around 1746 although it had an early Victorian exterior and the two families decided to move in together and this remained what was in effect Churchill's home until shortly after the death of his father, probably from syphilis, after a long period of illness at the end of January 1895. The house disappeared during the wholesale redevelopment of Grosvenor Square in the early twentieth century.

No 35a Great Cumberland Place, Lady Randolph's London house.

Lord Randolph Churchill bequeathed many things to his son – a famous name, a powerful oratory and the fact that politics coursed through his veins. But he also bequeathed something much more tangible. After some bequests to Lady Randolph, his modest residual wealth was left in Trust for the benefit of his two children – a statement dated 1908 indicated the value of shares and other holdings to be worth then just under £42,000 – and Churchill was therefore able to approach the Trustees on a regular basis for many decades to come to obtain loans to finance his house purchases.[14] Lady Randolph, the Duke of Marlborough and Viscount Curzon were the original Trustees although Winston himself and Jack were later also appointed. It was an arrangement that was born out of pure pragmatism and there is never a hint of any stigma being attached to him having to go at frequent intervals, more or less cap in hand, to his cousin and younger brother, as the other Trustees.

The year 1895 was in many ways a turning point in Churchill's life. He now had a career, but he had lost his father and in the course of the succeeding months, he would also lose his grandmother Jerome and, in July, old Mrs Everest at the age of only sixty-two. For many years after her death, Churchill's accounts contained regular invoices from Collins, a florist in Manor Park in East London for flowers to be placed on Elizabeth Everest's grave. In 1895 too, and much to his relief and contentment, Churchill had a new home. In the autumn, his mother moved out of Duchess Fanny's house and in to one of her own, a tall Georgian property at 35a Great Cumberland Place, on the corner with Upper Berkeley Street and just a few strides from Marble Arch.

In the autumn too, there are real signs from his letters that Churchill was coming of age – precociously – as an observer of the political scene. He was coming of age in the army also and the 4th Hussars were making preparations for their posting to India the following year. There was leave available and Churchill took advantage of the opportunity to make his first significant overseas journey and see some action. For these were peaceful times and as he himself observed '…scarcely a captain, hardly ever a subaltern, could be found throughout Her Majesty's forces who had seen even the smallest kind of war'.[15] Instead of joining his colleagues chasing foxes, therefore, he planned to sail with his army friend Reginald Barnes to New York then on to Cuba where Spanish troops were endeavouring to put down a local guerrilla rebellion. He had more or less official backing from the British Army authorities to obtain military information while he was there and, setting a pattern that was to become familiar over the coming years, persuaded the *Daily Graphic* to pay him 5 guineas a time for regular reports that he would write on the action. He and Barnes sailed on the Cunarder RMS *Etruria* from Liverpool on 1 November, arrived in New York on the 9th and then after a thirty-six hour train journey to Florida, sailed from Key West to Havana on a small steamer, the SS *Olivette*, on the 20th. It was his first experience of a land totally different from his own. '…the temperate yet ardent climate, the abundant rainfall, the luxuriant vegetation, the unrivalled fertility of the soil, the beautiful scenery…' created a deep impression. Accompanying the Spanish troops he came under fire for the first time: 'I heard enough bullets whistle and hum to satisfy me for some time to come…' he later wrote.[16] But it was only a brief encounter with beautiful scenery and bullets and in under a month, the adventure was over. Churchill and Barnes returned to New York and sailed for home on the Etruria in mid-December. Back in England in January, having brought cigars, coffee and guava jelly to stock his mother's cellars in Great Cumberland Place, Churchill enjoyed a few months of polo and social life and then, in September, sailed with his regiment to India.

RMS *Etruria*, the Cunard liner that took Churchill from Liverpool to New York and back.

SS *Olivette*, the American steamship on which Churchill sailed from Key West to Cuba.

Endnotes

[1] CHAR 28/13/8. WSC to Lord Randolph Churchill, 10 Apr 1882.

[2] Leslie. A. *The Fabulous Leonard Jerome,* p. 56.

[3] Churchill, W. S. *My Early Life; A Roving Commission,* p. 19.

[4] Churchill, W. S. *My Early Life; A Roving Commission,* p. 23.

[5] CHAR 28/13/93. WSC to Lady Randolph Churchill, 7 Sep 1886.

[6] Moran, Lord. Churchill. The struggle for survival 1940/65, p. 659.

[7] CHAR 28/15/24–25. WSC to Lady Randolph Churchill, 3 Aug 1888.

[8] CHAR 1/4/2. Elizabeth Everest to WSC, 21 Jan 1891.

[9] Hugh McCalmont, personal communication, 30 Nov 2005.

[10] Hugo Morriss, conversation with the author, 30 Nov 2005.

[11] CHAR 1/4/7. Elizabeth Everest to WSC, 24 May 1891.

[12] Blenheim Papers. Cited in Churchill, R. S. and Gilbert. M. *Winston S. Churchill.* Vol. 1. P. 139. Original not seen. Elizabeth Everest to Lady Randolph Churchill, 1 Jan 1891.

[13] Hugo Morriss, personal communication, 14 Nov 2005.

[14] CHAR 1/79/5. Will of Lord Randolph Churchill 25 July 1883 Copy and Statement of Funds dated 23 March 1908.

[15] Churchill, W. S. *My Early Life; A Roving Commission,* p. 88.

[16] Churchill, W. S. *My Early Life; A Roving Commission,* p. 94.

CHAPTER 2
*I*NDIA AND AFRICA

For anyone with even a passing interest in wild life and natural history, whether as collector, hunter or observer, the first experience of the Tropics, especially the lush, humid Tropics, takes away your breath and challenges your senses. And although Churchill had already felt the warmth of Cuba, there will have been no less of a thrill in his heart, eyes and nostrils when the SS *Britannia* docked at Bombay on Friday 1 October 1896. The eager anticipation of danger, excitement and adventure for the young subaltern was mixed with at least an outline knowledge of the prodigious natural treasure that was the sub-continent. But despite the British having had a significant presence in India for over two hundred years, its plant and animal life was still not properly chronicled. While today's traveller to almost any part of the world can find at least a modest local field guide, reference books were sparse and expensive in 1896. Churchill had none.

Although the rainy season was coming to an end, the aroma of spices and of strange and unfamiliar vegetation still hung heavy in the air as Churchill and his

SS *Britannia* on which Churchill sailed with his regiment
to India.

companions passed beyond the city on the train that weaved its way 600 miles south through Poona and Hubli to their new garrison home in Bangalore. The British had been in Bangalore for many years and had maintained a permanent garrison there since 1831. It was one of the most important of the southern military outposts of British India and whilst lacking the high altitude cool of the northern hill stations, it was a reasonably attractive posting. Bangalore is '… usually considered an agreeable place to soldier in' Churchill had written to his grandmother two days before leaving England.[1] Then, as now, it offered a fine environment for growing plants and is sometimes called the garden city of India. Roses have always grown well there – and today are raised commercially – and on his arrival, Churchill thought the climate excellent and noted how it encouraged a lush profusion of flora and fauna. 'The roses of Europe in innumerable large pots attain the highest perfection of fragrance and colour. Flowers, flowering shrubs and creepers blossom in glorious profusion. Snipe (and snakes) abound in the marshes; brilliant butterflies dance in the sunshine, and nautch-girls by the light of the moon'.[2] There were English girls also among them and Churchill struck up friendships with two whom he christened The Plum and The Peach.

When did Churchill first acquire his apparently improbable life-long fascination with butterflies? Perhaps he watched them as a young child in the grounds at Blenheim; perhaps he was even fortunate enough in those halcyon lepidopterous days of the late nineteenth century to have seen the large tortoiseshell in its old Oxfordshire haunts. Or perhaps it was at the age of eleven when he had 'massacred' them (plus at least one 'Dragon-Fly') at school in Brighton.[3] Whether he caught and released any or skewered them all to a board he didn't reveal but by the time he arrived in Bangalore ten years later, he certainly had had plenty of experience in forming a collection and was well versed in how to kill, set and mount his specimens. There was every incentive. When half a dozen different modestly coloured insects in an English garden on the same day would be a matter of some remark (even in the eighteen-nineties), the bounteous richness of the butterfly life of southern India must have been paradisiacal.

Bangalore stands at the corner of a 900-metre high plateau with rocky outcrops, wooded hills, valleys and patches of jungle nor far away. Around 150 species of butterfly occur – or used to occur – in the area and it is possible to imagine some of those Churchill would have seen in his garden in the October of 1896.[4] When he wrote to Jack, he told him the garden was full of rare and beautiful

Indian Lime Butterfly, which Churchill may have mistaken for a White Admiral.

insects including purple emperors, white admirals and swallowtails – remembering species he knew from home.[5] Among the local swallowtails, he must have seen the abundant common mormon and the black and white lime butterfly. Perhaps he mistook this insect for a white admiral which it rather resembles and his 'purple emperor' may have been a fine butterfly called the great eggfly which is especially common in Bangalore after the rains.

Clearly entranced, Churchill asked his mother to send him one small collecting box, two large collecting boxes, five assorted setting boards, one net, one box of pins and one killing tin, for which he enclosed 'a cheque for a fiver'. There were, he told her, so many beautiful and rare butterflies in the garden that he would be able in a few weeks to make a collection without any difficulty. But Lady Randolph appears to have had better things to do; her letters were full of political news and accounts of her social activities and a visit to the local supplier of naturalist's requisites does not seem to have held much appeal. Undeterred, Churchill improvised some equipment and was soon building up his collection. Then disaster struck. In early December he wrote to Jack reporting that the collection had been destroyed by a rat, a malevolent creature that crawled into the specimen cabinet and ate the lot. The only consolation was that Churchill caught the miscreant and set Winston his terrier to dispatch him. Although Churchill told Jack he had begun again, sadly, nothing more is heard of the collection; polo and soldiering took over both his time and his correspondence. It was claimed that Churchill later said he whiled away the hours watching butterflies in the exercise compound at the State Model Schools in Pretoria where he was imprisoned in 1899 during the Boer War, but no more appears of them in his own writings until he visited East Africa in 1908 and it was to be nearly half a century before the passion for Lepidoptera was renewed actively.[6]

The subalterns in Bangalore were accommodated in a clutch of ample single-storied bungalows around the cavalry mess, each in their own walled grounds

Cavalry bungalows in Bangalore with large pots of roses. The figure
seated at the rear of the carriage is believed to be Churchill.

with gardens although their location within the city can't now be identified.
Churchill shared his 'palatial' pink and white bungalow, 'wreathed in purple
bougainvillea', with two fellow officers Reginald Barnes, who had accompanied
him to Cuba and Hugo Baring and they inherited an established rose garden
from the previous occupant, replete with a hundred and fifty standards including
such nineteenth centuries splendours as 'Gloire de Dijon', 'La France' (the first
ever Hybrid Tea, bred in France in 1854) and 'Maréchal Neil' [*sic*]. Churchill
was delighted by it and a passion for gardening had taken an early hold. Writing
to his mother on the long train journey to Bangalore after visiting the Calcutta
races, he told her how much he was looking forward to getting back to his
ponies and roses and then a week later, he asked her to send a few English
seeds – wallflowers, stocks, even tulips – the horticultural learning curve hadn't
yet reached the point of discovery that tulips are better grown from bulbs.[7]
Once again, there is no suggestion that Lady Randolph had either the time or
inclination to oblige but six weeks later, the garden had evidently expanded and
Churchill was reporting enthusiastically on his achievements, in between the all
important absorbing of English history: 'The garden is getting on well, though
water is badly needed. I have 250 rose trees & 70 different sorts so that every
morning I can cut about 3 great basins full of the most beautiful flowers which
nature produces. I am half way through Macaulay...'[8]

When two months later Churchill reviewed his stay in India, he concluded that he had 'not been unhappy, though occasionally very bored, and I contemplate without repugnance returning to my books, my butterflies & my roses…'[9] And a year later he was in even more reflective mood, drawing example from nature in concluding that sanctity of life was entirely a human concept: 'You may think of a beautiful butterfly – 12 million feathers on his wings, 16,000 lenses in his eye – a mouthful for a bird…'[10] He never forgot his formative time in Bangalore and retained not only his passion for roses and butterflies but also a fondness for his old servant Munuswamy and for the last fifteen years of the old man's life before his death in 1959, Churchill sent him £5 a year.

Churchill remained at least notionally in India until the spring of 1899, having in the meantime managed to become attached as a war correspondent to Sir Bindon Blood's expeditionary force to subdue Afghan tribes on the North-west Frontier and then obtained a temporary attachment (thanks to the intervention of Lady Randolph and her friend Lady St Helier) again as a correspondent, to the 21st Lancers under Kitchener in the Sudan where he famously took part in the blood bath of Omdurman, one of the last regimental cavalry charges in British military history. But it was politics not soldiering that were truly taking a hold and starting to shape his destiny so shortly afterwards he resigned his commission. Reflecting a few years later, he felt the army was a poor profession although 'I got all the fun of it for I was in active service nearly all the time…'[11]

Churchill arrived back in London via Cairo in late April and took up his room again at his mother's' house in Great Cumberland Place with the advantage, as he recognised, that his expenses would be small. The house then provided the base for his first electoral foray: to fight the two member seat of Oldham for the Conservatives at a by-election following the death of one of the sitting members in June. He came a creditable third with the two Liberal candidates occupying the first two places.

But by the autumn, two powerful forces were again pulling Churchill away from domestic life: adventure and the prospect of significant earnings. The long-running tension between Britain and the South African Boer Republics finally came to a head in open conflict in October; even though, as Churchill observed 'Nearly fifty years had passed since Great Britain had been at war with any white people…'[12] Almost as the British forces mobilised, the Morning Post hired him as its principal war correspondent at £250 a month plus expenses. The

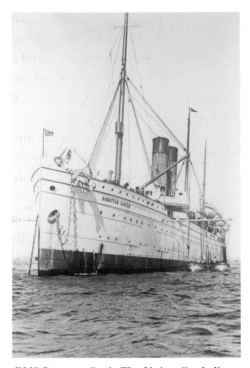

RMS *Dunottar Castle*, The Union Castle liner on which Churchill sailed on his fateful journey as a war correspondent to South Africa.

first sailing to South Africa was by the 5,625 ton Union Castle liner *Dunottar Castle* from Southampton on the 11th; and Churchill was on it.

Churchill's South African adventures are well chronicled, most memorably and with the most splendid understatement by Churchill himself in his book *My Early Life*, and his famous capture by the Boers and subsequent escape are as familiar as any *Boy's Own Paper* tale. What is less well remembered is that he was in South Africa at the same time as two people who loomed large in his domestic life. Sir Ian Hamilton, whom Churchill first met on a ship in the middle of the Indian Ocean, was there as a brigade commander. He had been born into an army family and was destined to become a committed professional soldier, reaching the rank of Colonel at a younger age than any other serving officer. Hamilton was tall, skeletally thin and intuitively brave – he had two recommendations for the Victoria Cross turned down, the first on the grounds that he was too young and the second to avoid creating a precedent by awarding it to a General who had personally led his men in battle. In due course, he would become a trenchant critic of Churchill's method of growing potatoes. Churchill's second companion in South Africa was rather more unexpected. In January 1900, his mother turned up.

The previous autumn, Lady Randolph had gathered around her a group of like-minded American women in Britain to raise funds for equipping a hospital ship, to be despatched to South Africa 'for the relief of the sick and wounded soldiers'. She convinced an American shipping millionaire named Nadel Baker to loan an old cattle boat called the *Maine* which was duly converted. It sailed on Christmas Day, 1899, under British and American flags, with Royal blessing and with Lady Randolph herself on board. Much to her subsequent consternation, her younger son Jack sailed two weeks later, Churchill having obtained a lieutenancy for him in the South African Light Horse. The *Maine* made stops on her way and was overtaken by Jack who met his mother at Capetown. They then sailed on together to Durban where Churchill himself was waiting for the family reunion. But Lady Randolph's joy with her sons was to be short. Jack was wounded in the calf during a skirmish and became his mother's first casualty aboard her floating hospital.

The *Maine* lay at Durban for two months tending the wounded and then Lady Randolph and her ship returned to England, arriving at the end of April. Churchill stayed on, experiencing much danger and joining Ian Hamilton's march through the Orange Free State to the Transvaal and Pretoria before finally leaving Capetown on 7 July in the same Union Castle liner, the *Dunottar Castle*, that had taken him to South Africa little more than seven months earlier. Churchill arrived back at Southampton on Friday 20 July 1900 although there was to be no maternal greeting. Lady Randolph was by then taken up with the arrangements for her marriage to the new man in her life, Captain George Cornwallis-West, which was to take place the following Saturday at St Paul's, Knightsbridge. Churchill dutifully attended his mother's wedding but almost immediately found himself homeless because Lady Randolph Churchill, now as Mrs Cornwallis-West, had decided to let 35a Great Cumberland Place and after her Scottish honeymoon, intended renting Salisbury Hall, at Shenley near St Albans. It is easy to see the attraction of this solid-looking and rather imposing moated brick house. It was based on one built early in the sixteenth century by Henry VIII's treasurer, Sir John Cuttes on what was already an historic site. Nell Gwynne once lived in a cottage on the estate, a feature that may have had a particular appeal to the adventurous Lady Randolph. It has been said that Salisbury Hall was Lady Randolph's first home with sufficient land for a garden; and that Churchill helped her to decide which flowers to grow and where to plant them, although this seems improbable.[13]

For Churchill's own immediate housing needs in 1900, his cousin Sunny Marlborough came to the rescue. He had two years remaining on the lease of a flat at 105, Mount Street, Mayfair, just off the east side of Park Lane. Mayfair was rich Marlborough territory but Mount Street was not quite as grand as the streets where his father had owned houses. It was a mixed residential and business

The Mount Street apartment block containing Churchill's first flat No 105 (1886).

street and No 105 was part of an assertive red brick and terracotta block in a style called French Flamboyant designed for the developer William Warner by Ernest George and Peto in 1886, the year before Edwin Lutyens became their pupil. The block overlooks St George's (Hanover Square) Gardens to the rear and was built in two different halves by two different builders. For the only time in his life, Churchill had commercial neighbours. They occupied the ground floors of his first independent home and were a motley if rather up-market assortment – Henry Tessier, court jeweller, Frances Stocks, court milliner, a wedding present shop, the London and Westminster Coal Company and at the far end, close to St George's and in the other half of the block, the extensive offices of J. Andrews, the builder who built this eastern section. Churchill wasted little time moving in and was living there by the beginning of September. He had a small amount of work undertaken at the flat by Andrews – mainly plumbing improvements, but as the properties were only fourteen years old, little else was needed. The flats or 'chambers' were 'ranged round an amply lighted court of white glazed brick' and obtained 'excellent light at the back as well as the front'.[14] They were 'fine rooms' and he was much more comfortable than he had been at Cumberland Place Churchill told his Aunt Leonie; and it was to her rather than his mother, who was rather busy being newly wed, that he turned for advice on furnishings. He bought a few things from the fashionable store of Maples but was sure his rooms were capable of some more improvement although that kind of material arrangement irritated him. As long as his table was clear and there was plenty of paper, he said, like many a bachelor before and since, he didn't worry about the rest. But added that of course he realised he could no longer live for nothing.[15]

As a twenty-six-year-old aspiring politician, it was time to pay his way in the world. Although he had lost in his first attempt to enter Parliament, he was now looking for another opportunity; although that in itself would not pay for the flat – Members of Parliament received no salaries until 1911 when they were allowed to receive £400 from the public purse. A General Election was looming in October, and the Oldham Tories wanted him back. He stood, and scraped second place in the two-member constituency after little more than a week's campaigning; an ostensibly unremarkable moment in the electoral life of the nation but one that presaged almost sixty-five momentous and unparalleled years for Churchill as a parliamentarian. A lecture tour of England in November helped to raise some capital and at the beginning of December, Churchill sailed from Liverpool for New York in the Blue Riband Cunarder *Lucania* for more lectures in the United States and Canada before the new Parliamentary session in February 1901. By the time the SS *Etruria* brought him home, he had a fairly healthy bank balance and the means to live reasonably comfortably and entertain at his bachelor apartment.

RMS *Lucania*, the Cunarder on which Churchill travelled to New York on a lecture tour.

While Marlborough gave his cousin the remains of the lease, Churchill himself later renewed it and remained at Mount Street until the end of 1905. His five-year tenure of the flat was a formative time both for the young politician and the nation. It was a period in which Queen Victoria died and Lord Salisbury (Robert Cecil) resigned as Prime Minister in favour of his nephew Arthur Balfour; hence, possibly, the saying that it is easy to become Prime Minister when 'Bob's your uncle'. In 1901 Churchill made his maiden speech in the House and espoused the Free Trade cause, then became increasingly isolated in the Conservative Party and dramatically crossed the floor in 1904 to sit next to Lloyd George on the Liberal benches – resulting in his removal from membership of the Carlton Club in the following April.

Churchill also discovered the by-products of a public life. He was attracting volumes of correspondence – invitations to address gatherings of free-traders and others were flooding in – and he needed a secretary. In the short term, he asked his mother to find him a 'compendious cabinet' with drawers and holes to file his growing mountain of papers but relief was at hand. After he had engaged some temporary secretarial help, Lady Randolph obliged with her own secretary, a woman named Annette Anning who was born in India and had previously worked for Arthur Balfour the Prime Minister. She was twenty-five when she began her employment with Churchill in November 1902 and was to remain with him until 1909, her handwritten letters distinguished by a neat careful script to which Churchill added his signature. She was the first of a long line of faithful and reliable Churchill secretaries, official and private, who were to serve him for the rest of his life.

The lease at Mount Street was due to expire and it was now proving itself inadequate for Churchill's needs. This was hardly unexpected. There is a time in most young professionals' lives when they start to feel confined by a flat and aspire to a house. So late in 1905 he began to look for a property convenient for Westminster. The search didn't take him long and by December – even before receiving a survey – he had agreed to purchase for just over £1,000 the lease of a modest, neat, terraced house a short walk away, just off Piccadilly.

Bolton Street runs north-west from Piccadilly to Curzon Street where Churchill's parents were living shortly before his birth and only one street away from his own first childhood home in Charles Street. In 1708 it was being described as the end of London to the west, there being no more houses before Knightsbridge. Churchill's old house, No 12 is on the east side with front rooms that, at least upstairs, would catch the evening sun. It lies a few metres from Piccadilly itself,

No 12 Bolton Street, Churchill's first house.

far enough in 1905 to be cushioned from the bustle and noise of what, since the end of the eighteenth century, had become one of the most fashionable and busy streets in the capital. Although much of the traffic was still horse-drawn and rurally aromatic, motor taxis had arrived a couple of years earlier and the first motor buses too were becoming familiar. It was only a few strides from one of the grandest new buildings in London, the Ritz Hotel, which after only a year's construction was nearing completion, ready for its opening on 24 May 1906. The hotel was a venue that in the years ahead was to become a favourite for members of the Churchill family, their friends and guests.

By a curious quirk of historical coincidence, Bolton Street thus because home for the second time to a politician who served both as First Lord of the Admiralty and Prime Minister. The Whig Prime Minister George Grenville, who had briefly been First Lord, moved to Bolton Street after losing the premiership to Lord Rockingham in July 1765 and remained there until his death in 1770. Neither his nor Churchill's residences are marked by blue plaques, however, and the only plaque in Bolton Street (brown not blue and one of the earliest in London, erected by the Royal Society of Arts in 1885) is on No 11, next door to Churchill's house and marking it as the one time home of the novelist and diarist Fanny Burney (Madame d'Arblay).

No 12 Bolton Street is built on four floors with a basement, although no garden. In 1905 it was already well supplied with electricity as well as gas, was fully plumbed and had sufficient bathrooms, lavatories and other rooms for a young man about town to accommodate himself and his servants and to entertain. Despite the changes that a century of owners and tenants have wrought, its basic layout and character remain and, now a suite of offices, it is still an elegant house. A spacious entrance lobby opens into a narrow hallway from where an even narrower staircase leads down to the basement and via a passage to where Churchill had a scullery, pantry, kitchen, small lobby, toilet and wine cellar.

The ground floor was occupied by the dining room and library with a small drawing room at the front on the first floor, bedrooms for himself and a guest room for Jack on the second and third, with the servants, as was customary, at the top. A survey of the property had been arranged by Lumley & Lumley, Churchill's solicitors, and this was ready for him on his return to London from Christmas at Blenheim. It had been a difficult few weeks. In November, he had been unwell and receiving attention for being, almost literally, 'tongue-tied' – a speech problem caused by a 'ligament that nobody else has' and which was to plague him throughout his life. He was treated by a masseuse and also by the distinguished laryngologist Sir Felix Semon and a local speech specialist Harry White who taught him to lip-read. Churchill received widespread sympathy although his cousin and close friend Sunny Marlborough wondered rather uncharitably if the illness was brought on by listening to Sir Henry Campbell-Bannerman's speeches, some bad champagne or 'the efforts of too frequent visits to the vicinity of Marshall and Snelgrove'.[16] Moreover, following a summons to the home of the Prime Minster in Belgrave Square on Saturday 9 December, Churchill had also just received his first ministerial appointment, as Parliamentary Under-Secretary for the Colonies under the biblically bewhiskered Lord Elgin, a 'rugged old Thane of antique virtue and simplicity';[17] and a man with a frugal charisma. Elgin, grandson of the well known collector of Greek marbles, had been a rather effective Viceroy when Churchill was in India ten years earlier.

It was therefore already a distracting time to be thinking about moving house. And having left the Conservative Party, Churchill had been encouraged to run as a Liberal in North-West Manchester, a city centre constituency with strong business and Jewish elements; an ideal platform for a free-trader. Parliament was due to be dissolved on 8 January, the new session was to begin on 13 February; and North-West Manchester would be one of the first to vote, on 13 January. (Elections and voting dates in Britain were then staggered). He issued a long election address on 1 January highlighting his defence of the Free Trade cause in the city in advance of his planned visit there three days later with his new private secretary Edward 'Eddie' Marsh.

Eddie Marsh had joined the Colonial Office in 1896, served as an Assistant

No 16 Arlington Street, home of the
Duke and Duchess of Rutland.

Private Secretary to Joseph Chamberlain and by 1905 was a First Class Clerk in the West African department. Churchill's own new appointment as Under-Secretary for the Colonies led to an invitation for Marsh to join him. He and Churchill had first met briefly at a Christmas party the previous year given by Sir John Dickson-Poynder and his wife at their home at Hartham in Wiltshire. They met again at Hartham in the summer and the acquaintance was renewed on the evening of Tuesday 13 December during a small gathering at 16, Arlington Street, St James's, the London home of the artist Violet Lindsay, Marchioness of Granby (soon to become Duchess of Rutland). Among the other guests was Churchill's aunt (Lady Randolph's sister) Mrs Jack Leslie, who knew Eddie Marsh reasonably well and seems to have bent Churchill's ear on his behalf; although the original suggestion for the approach probably came from Churchill's long-time friend and sometime love Pamela Lytton. Marsh was sent for the following morning but was uncertain about accepting. After a day thinking over matters and seeking advice from Pamela Lytton's mother who had also been at the party promoting his cause, he and Churchill dined alone together at 105, Mount Street in the evening. Marsh came away late, reassured that the post was the right one for him – 'Such an excitement. I *must* tell you…' he wrote to Mrs Leslie.[18] It was initially for six months but in the event, he was to work with Churchill at no fewer than eight government departments and remain his friend and confident, and later that of Clementine too, until his death in 1953. Marsh was a constant source of support and advice, not only in professional but in domestic matters also and his presence was to loom significantly during the traumas of the early days at Chartwell, then nearly twenty years away.

Eddie Marsh was no ordinary civil servant and although he never reached a career height of any dizziness, his reputation endures as a man of the arts.

He was also the author of one of the wittiest and most entertaining autobiographies ever written. He obtained a double first in Classics at Trinity where the philosophers Bertrand Russell and G. E. Moore were among his close friends. An early interest in the work of English water-colourists including Paul Sandby and John Sell Cotman led to him becoming a significant patron of young British artists (John Currie, Mark Gertler, the Nash brothers and Stanley Spencer among others) and within a few years he had 'the nucleus of what became one of the most valuable collections of modern art in private hands'...one that 'covered

Edward 'Eddie' Marsh, Churchill's long-time devoted secretary.

every inch of wall space in his apartments at 5, Raymond Buildings, Gray's Inn...'.[19] He befriended and supported poets and writers too and his apartment became a 'virtual second home for Rupert Brooke'. He never married and although his biographer Christopher Hassall is discreetly silent on the matter he was 'the centre of a large homosexual artistic community'.[20] The Churchill correspondence too is all but silent on his private life although Clementine – who came greatly to like him – touched on the subject in later years when describing to Churchill a dinner party she had given and referred judgmentally to '...Bohemian couples, poets, artists etc of the 'Eddie' school some of whom have neglected the formality of a visit to Church or indeed Registry'.[21]

It was against a hectic professional and personal background therefore that in the afternoon of Monday, New Year's Day 1906 – no New Year Bank Holiday in England until 1974 – Churchill visited the Bolton Street house with his architects and builders to assess what works needed undertaking and to decide how much of the previous tenant's furniture he might wish to purchase at valuation. Churchill still had accounts outstanding with J. Andrews, the builder from Mount Street – these remained unpaid in May 1906 – and a different builder, W. Turner Lord & Co, also based in Mount Street was engaged for most of the work in the Bolton Street house. Fortunately, maternal help and guidance were at hand; Lady Randolph Churchill accompanied her son that Monday afternoon and they/she immediately took the decision to effect a number of alterations and redecorate the house from top to bottom.

Churchill then returned to political matters, caught the train north with Eddie Marsh on 4 January and after eight days hectic campaigning captured North-West Manchester for the Liberals and played a pivotal part in the sweeping aside of long-held Tory redoubts across the city. He continued to rally support for the party and assist what became a comprehensive national Liberal victory that brought Campbell-Bannerman to Downing Street. Churchill finally returned to London at the end of the month in time for the new parliamentary session.

Lady Randolph and the builders hadn't been idle during Churchill's absence and a comprehensive quotation from Turner Lord was awaiting him on his return. The decoration was to be undertaken in the simple elegant style that was to become a hallmark of all his homes. Ivory white woodwork, papered white ceilings, polished mahogany handrails to the stairs with the beautiful cast iron banisters painted gold bronze, dado rails grained and varnished in the fashion of the time, tile paper in the toilets and pantry. Outside the woodwork was washed down and painted. Druce & Company of Baker Street, well known for their fine mahogany supplied the bedroom furniture. Resources would not however extend to new furnishings all round and so Churchill brought some from Mount Street with the result that the carpets were rather a rainbow mixture – red on the stairs, blue in his bedroom, green and 'sickly looking' in Jack's room.

The two real extravagances were the dining room at the front on the ground floor and the library. For the dining room, Churchill had a splendid carved wood chimneypiece and overmantel designed with reeded cheeks. A new marble surround was made for the hearth, white plaster cornices were installed, the existing gas fittings were stripped out to be replaced with a better electricity supply, and the gracious white room was furnished with a specially made oval mahogany dining table, opening to nearly 9 feet by 4 feet to seat twelve guests in cane-backed armchairs with leather seats. The whole was finished with silk curtains and valances. Almost certainly, most of this taste was Lady Randolph's and she took a close and continuing interest in her son's homes until her death. Her own houses were always light and airy, in marked contrast to the heavy browns that were the late Victorian tradition.

For many years, a licence was required to employ male servants. It was referred to as 'keeping', rather like slaves, and the tax was paid (cost £1 10s 0d in 1906) on the same Inland Revenue licence as dogs, cars, carriages and armorial bearings; female servants attracted no such obligation. Churchill had a licence for two male servants at Bolton Street and there is reference in a hand-written note concerning his room requirements to '2 servants (3)' but only one is known: George Scrivings to whom he became devoted. George's parents, William and Emma Scrivings came originally from Devonshire – Scrivings with various spellings is a West County name – but had settled in Prittlewell near Southend-on-Sea in Essex where George was born and his father worked as a jobbing gardener. George Scrivings' first employment was in Essex as an architect's clerk but he came into contact with the Churchill family when he served as a steward aboard Lady Randolph Churchill's Boer War hospital ship *Maine*. By 1901 he was working back in Essex as a shipping clerk although it is possible he worked at Mount Street too as Eddie Marsh said that ever since the Maine adventure he had been Churchill's 'stand-by and faithful friend'. At Bolton Street, Churchill also engaged George's wife as his cook/housekeeper. A housemaid was employed too and the Scrivings had at least two children although Mrs Scrivings' mother seems to have had charge of them and they do not appear to have lived at Bolton Street. Before long however the Scrivings family was to feature in one of the early tragedies of Churchill's private life.

The house was extremely well equipped and Mrs Scrivings can have had little complaint about her working conditions. Everything necessary was obtained, usually from Harrods which since its opening in 1902, had become very much the smart person's shop. The kitchen equipment included such essentials as an asparagus kettle and even stretched to an early refrigerator for which Churchill paid £4 3s 6d. The housemaid was also spared the washing – a Mrs Thornley collected it and brought it over regularly from her laundry in Earlsfield.

Following the London Colonial Conference in April 1907, attended by the Dominion Heads of Government, and at some time in the early summer, Churchill decided to make a visit during the forthcoming parliamentary recess to the Mediterranean islands and on through the Suez Canal to East Africa. It is not clear why or how the idea came to him but it was to be part private, part political (although Marsh called it an 'official tour') – he was after all, Under-Secretary for the Colonies and his Secretary of State Lord Elgin encouraged it: '...it will I am sure be of the greatest advantage that you should have seen the country'.[22] He asked Eddie Marsh if he would like to accompany him ('Will a bloody duck swim?' was the response[23]) and initially also invited his cousin Freddie Guest but at the last minute he was unable to come because his wife Amy was imminently due to give birth – to a young son who was to be christened Winston Churchill Guest. Guest's place was taken by Colonel Gordon Wilson who was married to Churchill's aunt. He also took his reliable servant George Scrivings although he had been warned of the dangers he faced. Thomas Walden, who for many years was butler to Lord and Lady Randolph Churchill, and was later found war time employment as a porter at the Home Office, told George to keep off the drink which would be fatal in such a hot climate. Walden predicted that he would never return and when Scrivings, with £10 in his pocket, took leave of his family to travel with Churchill to France, it would indeed be the last time they saw him; although something more insidious than the demon drink would be responsible.[24]

Before departing, there was however the small matter of money to consider. Churchill could not afford to leave Bolton Street empty during his absence – it was costing him nearly £20 a month in ground rent, rates and fuel, apart from the servants' wages. The house would have to be let and so when Churchill departed for a month on the Continent to observe French army manoeuvres and then visit Italy and Moravia en route to the East African tour, he left his mother and Jack to find someone. It was to be no easy matter. September is not a good month as many people are still away, Lady Randolph told him.[25] She and Jack tried everything. They asked their friends. They in turn asked all their friends. The agents sent people to look. But all to no avail. Then, after six weeks, Jack wrote to Churchill. The letter reached him in Valetta in late September where he and Scrivings rendezvoused with their prospective African travelling companions. He read, first the good news: 'A tenant has arrived for Bolton Street'. Then the bad: 'But what do you think? Mr Bob Sievier....'[26] Churchill was incensed; and little wonder.

Robert Standish Sievier was one of the seriously infamous rogues of the day, euphemistically referred to as a 'character of the turf' but in reality an inveterate gambler and womaniser who constantly sailed close to the wind. He was a man who was seldom out of the newspapers and was himself the publisher of a scurrilous rag called The Winning Post in which he libelled his racing rivals and published stories that, in the context of their time, were frankly obscene. He always claimed to have been born in a London hansom cab and, like Churchill, as a young man he too had been an adventurer. At the age of sixteen, he sailed to South Africa to enlist in the Frontier Armed and Mounted Police, saw conspicuous action there, was ship-wrecked on the way back, eventually returned to gain work in Ireland and England as a jobbing actor, became a bookmaker, sailed to Australia, married, divorced, returned home, was declared bankrupt, began play-writing, married again, took up the training of horses, separated... the whole roller-coaster saga peppered by frequent brushes with the Law.[27]

Robert Standish 'Bob' Sievier who rented 12 Bolton Street.

Robert Sievier's compelling claim to racing immortality is that for a time he owned Sceptre, one of the most famous fillies in the history of the British turf, having paid 10,000 guineas for her at the Eaton Hall sale of the late 1st Duke of Westminster's yearlings in 1899. Sievier ran his horses hard, as he ran his life, and Sceptre was once entered for five big races in a fortnight. She won four of the five classics for him in 1902 but missed out on the Derby, thanks it was always said to her jockey Herbert Randall making a dog's dinner of the race and in the following year Sievier sold her to Sir William Bass for £25,000.

By 1906, however, in his mid-forties, Sievier's fortunes were passing through a trough and he was in need of some temporary accommodation.

Remarkably, Sievier was for some years a close friend of the barrister F. E. Smith (later the 1st Earl of Birkenhead), who was elected as Tory MP for the Walton Division of Liverpool in 1906 and soon afterwards became an associate, close friend and confidant of Churchill himself. By intriguing coincidence, 'F. E.' had been with Churchill observing the French Army only a few days before Lady Randolph Churchill's letter arrived.

Sievier offered 10 guineas a week rent for the Bolton Street house for twenty-one weeks. Lady Randolph Churchill tried to push him further but he would not budge and she concluded that £250 was worth having. Sievier had his own servants but Lady Randolph wanted Churchill's housemaid to remain to keep an eye on things while Mrs Scrivings would be found another position. Nonetheless, after Churchill had discussed this with Scrivings in Malta, it was decided his wife should stay on at Bolton Street instead and in recompense, she would have a holiday later. Churchill expressed strong misgivings about dealing with 'such a ruffian' as Sievier and wrote to Jack saying he hoped all papers and personal effects had been made secure. Jack reassured him that every paper and photograph had been removed, and pointed out that Churchill himself had had social contacts with financiers no less shady – and with Mrs Scrivings on hand, any irregularities would be swiftly reported.

The African tour party travelled from Malta to Cyprus then on through the Suez Canal to Aden in the second class light cruiser HMS *Venus*, made available by the Admiralty. After a stop at Berbera they arrived in Mombasa at the end of October and thence inland by special train which stopped whenever requested. The journey took them to Nairobi and then by steamer across Lake Victoria to Entebbe in Uganda, to Kampala and on to Jinja where they embarked on a memorable trek into the bush. Eddie Marsh loved every minute of it – '...we are on 'safari'...there are ten of us and we have 350 native porters!' he wrote to Lady Lytton.[28]

HMS *Venus*, the cruiser made available by the Admiralty for Churchill's 'safari' visit to East Africa.

Kenya and Uganda in the early years of the twentieth century offered a compelling wildlife experience. The populations of big game were still vast and Churchill was entranced both by the abundance and richness of the vegetation and the astonishing quantity and diversity of the wild animals which from the carriage windows of their Uganda Railways train appeared as if an entire zoological gardens was disporting itself. He watched wild ostriches walking sedately in two and threes, herds of antelope and gazelles numbering as much as five hundred each and zebras that came close enough to enable him to see their individual stripes. But Churchill was a man of his time and a born hunter. He had stuck pigs in India and chased foxes at home and it was only to be expected that he would kill the big game of Africa too. When their personal train stopped in the bush, Churchill and Wilson would shoot more or less whatever was nearby. A favoured method was to prowl among the undergrowth of a dry river bed looking for shaggy, dark brown water-buck or other large antelope, although the rhinoceros hunt was undertaken in the open where the method of killing was found to be crudely simple. First find your rhinoceros, walk towards it, from any direction other than the windward, and shoot it in the head or the heart. If you hit it anywhere else, just shoot again.

Churchill was not however just another white man in Africa with a blood lust. In war, he observed, there is the hope of glory but at the end of the rhinoceros hunt, there is only a hide, a horn, a carcass and the vultures. Nonetheless, his bag was considerable and a quantity of skins was shipped back to the leading London taxidermists, Rowland Ward of Piccadilly. By the following March, Wards had mounted rhinoceros, zebra, wildebeest, Grant's and Thomson's gazelles and warthog among others. The wildebeest was equal to the largest they had ever measured. It is not apparent however what happened to the trophies and there must be a suspicion that Clementine would not give them room in the marital home because three years later, Churchill was paying handsomely for their warehousing and they were still in Ward's store in 1914.

East Africa moreover gave Churchill a perfect opportunity to renew his passion for butterflies. The butterfly fauna of Africa extends to over two and a half thousand species and apart from the low altitude rain forests of West Africa, the forest areas of Uganda offer as rich a variety as can be seen anywhere on the continent. 'Never', he wrote, 'were seen such flying fairies'.[29] They flaunted their splendid liveries in inconceivable varieties of colour and pattern. Many reminded him of the peacocks, orange tips and small tortoiseshells he knew from home but many more were quite unfamiliar and entranced him in their appearance and behaviour. He was no doubt as thrilled as any visitor from temperate regions to see such rich and gorgeous insects as the swallowtails, the red and orange acraeas and the great blue-winged assemblages that make up the species of Charaxes. Churchill was fascinated however that such beautiful insects could exhibit such strange and dirty habits, feeding on the ground on patches of putrescent and odorous filth and so engrossed in their activity that he was able to pick them up and examine them gently in his fingers. But he was struck too by their contrariness. Having found it impossible to resist the temptation to form a collection, he had no sooner made himself a net from telegraph wire and mosquito curtain, than the butterflies vanished. Whether this was truly from their perversity or simply the fact that he had left the deeper recesses of the forest, Churchill was unsure. He nonetheless carried with him the notion that the butterflies of Uganda represented an unrealised opportunity and a few years later, told the story when he was visiting Wilfrid Scawen Blunt.[30] It appears that Blunt had cases or frames of mounted butterflies on the chimney pieces of his house, Newbuildings Place and like Churchill seems to have had a personal interest in them. His library contained two sumptuous multi-volume nineteenth century illustrated books that Churchill must have admired – Humphreys and Westwood's Butterflies of Great Britain and Donovan's Insects of India. The only butterfly book Churchill ever owned was Ford's King Penguin edition published in 1951 and that would have cost him a few shillings.

Churchill did however collect giant orange tips and other species which he shipped home and showed with some pride a few years later to his young nephew Johnny when he shared with him his own delightful version of lepidopterous biology. Caterpillars can be either good or bad, went Churchill's thesis. The bad ones are greedy and never stop eating and are therefore punished in their next world when they become drab meadow browns and common heaths who live miserable lives for a day or two. If the caterpillar however is good and not greedy, it will emerge in due course as a gorgeous painted lady, swallowtail or Camberwell beauty which will live for many days and may even hibernate to appear again the following spring.[31]

At Fajao, close to the Murchison Falls on the Victoria Nile in Uganda, George Scrivings sprained an ankle which meant he had either to be on his back or in a chair for nearly three weeks during the safari, carried by coolies, taking no exercise but eating abundantly. It was Churchill's view that he thus became fat and flabby and therefore was in no condition to resist 'the bacteriological poison' when he was struck down by what was diagnosed as choleric diarrhoea. As he had eaten the same food as the rest of the party, there seemed to Churchill no other explanation. Eddie Marsh told him Scrivings was seriously ill when they arrived at Khartoum by steamer on 23 December. Churchill found him 'in a condition of prostration with a strange blue colour under his skin'. Although taken to a hospital with English doctors, he deteriorated during the night and died at ten the following morning. After a 'miserable day', Churchill buried him in the evening in the local cemetery and, thanks to the band and men of the Dublin Fusiliers who were stationed locally, he was interred with full military honours 'as he had been a yeoman'. 'The day after the battle of Omdurman it fell to my lot to bury those soldiers of the 21st Lancers who had died of their wounds... Now after nine years... I had come back to this grim place where so much blood has been shed, and again I found myself standing at an open grave, while the yellow glare of the departed sun still lingered over the desert, and the sound of funeral volleys broke its silence'.[32]

The death of George Scrivings came as a huge shock to Churchill and the family. Jack said he would never 'get so faithful a slave again'.[33] Lady Randolph Churchill described him as 'such a faithful devoted servant & a good fellow'. Although the death merited barely half a page in his published account, Churchill was later to say it 'cast a gloom over all the memories of this pleasant and even wonderful journey',[34] and he telegraphed the news to his mother who in turn telegraphed it to Jack who was at Blenheim for Christmas. Lady Randolph Churchill also telegraphed Mrs Scrivings and prepared to go from Blenheim to see her in London on Christmas morning, an astonishing gesture for an Edwardian woman of her standing to undertake for her son's housekeeper; although having received no reply, she was forced to abandon the idea.[35] The following day, she did hear from Mrs Scrivings who was in Scotland visiting her mother and then sent a series of telegrams gradually revealing the story of George's illness but left it to her own mother to break the final fatal news. Churchill meanwhile wrote to Jack with a full account asking him to read as much of it to Mrs Scrivings as he thought fit and saying he would arrange for a monument to be erected over the grave and for it to be photographed for her.[36]

Churchill was also anxious she was told not to worry about her future and that as far as his 'limited means' allowed, he would endeavour to look after her and her children. He was true to his word and paid her a quarterly allowance and arranged pension provisions. Some five years later, in 1911, Mrs Scrivings wrote to Churchill asking if he would give a lump sum payment in lieu of her allowance and so enable her to set up a small business. Churchill considered the request carefully but declined on the grounds that the funds were insufficient and because 'women with small sums of money of this kind are very liable to be taken in by designing persons'.[37] When Mrs Scrivings then decided to emigrate with her children and live with a married sister in Seattle, Churchill contributed £25 towards the expenses of her journey, in addition to her pension. The annuity was finally exchanged for a lump sum of £105 in 1921. Nor did Churchill neglect Scrivings' mother. He paid her an quarterly allowance until her death, also in 1921.

From Khartoum, Churchill travelled up the Nile to Alexandria, leaving there on 9 January and was met by Sunny Marlborough at Naples and eventually arrived back in England on 17 January 1908, Jack having accompanied him on the last part of the journey from Paris. Bob Sievier was still in residence at Bolton Street – he was due to leave on 24 February and despite the efforts both of Jack and of Churchill's agents Mabbett & Edge, he could not be persuaded to go any earlier. Sievier did say the house was open to Churchill at all times until he finally left, but clearly the notion of cohabitation didn't appeal and would have done the junior minister's reputation no good whatsoever. Churchill had in consequence anticipated a month's stay at the Ritz and asked his mother to make the arrangements. His friend F. E. Smith had offered his house at 70 Eccleston Square but in the event, and setting a trend that was to continue for many years, the family helped. Lady Randolph took maternal charge and accepted an invitation for her

No 10 Carlton House Terrace, the home of Churchill's cousin Rosamond Guest.

son to stay with Churchill's cousin Rosamond Guest and her husband Matthew, Lord Ridley who had offered him a large sitting room and bedroom and the use of the downstairs dining room of their huge and opulent home at 10 Carlton House Terrace, on the edge of the Duke of York's steps, as they would be away for a fortnight. 'The house will be practically yours,' she told him. He would have servants and a cook and he could dine and lunch at the Ritz; it would be much less expensive than staying there.[38]

The coming year was to be eventful on all fronts. The ailing Prime Minister, Henry Campbell-Bannerman resigned on 3 April and died three weeks later to be succeeded by H. H. Asquith and there was a general expectation – not least from Churchill's quarter – that he would be in the new Cabinet. So it proved and he accepted the Presidency of the Board of Trade in what was to be one of the most distinguished and talented of all British Cabinets.

By a curious and archaic piece of legislation, in statute until 1926, MPs elevated to become Ministers were obliged to seek re-election by their constituents. Although often a formality, to the extent of the Opposition not even putting up candidates, the Tories of North-West Manchester saw it differently and the floor-crossing Churchill would not be given an easy passage. William Joynson-Hicks, whom Churchill had seen off in 1906, gained his revenge and Churchill lost. Unabashed and undaunted, he headed north and was embraced by the Liberal voters of Dundee where there was to be a by-election in May as a result of the sitting member being elevated to the peerage. Churchill romped home and the general perception was that he had the seat for life. Hardly anyone then noticed Edwin Scrymgeour, the candidate who trailed in a bad fourth on a prohibition ticket. But his time would come. The fact that Dundee was over ten hours by train from London and Churchill never found it a particularly convenient journey would take its toll. People in Dundee today have said to me 'Churchill never even came here'; an exaggerative untruth but old legends die hard.

Endnotes

[1]   [Cited in Churchill, R. S. *Winston S. Churchill Comp. Vol. 1*. Original not traced]. WSC to The Duchess of Marlborough, 8 Sep 1896.

[2]   Churchill, W. S. *My Early Life; A Roving Commission*, p. 119.

[3]   CHAR 28/13/93. WSC to Lady Randolph Churchill, 7 Sept 1886.

4   Yates, J. A. The butterflies of Bangalore and neighbourhood. *Journal of the Bombay Natural History Society,* 36, 450–459, 1932.

5   CHAR 28/22/14. WSC to Jack Churchill, 15 Oct 1896.

6   Newman, L. H. *Butterflies – Wings for Sir Winston.* Country Life, 3 December 1987.

7   CHAR 28/23/8–9. WSC to Lady Randolph Churchill, 7 Jan 1897.

8   CHAR 28/23/18–19. WSC to Lady Randolph Churchill, 18 Feb 1897.

9   CHAR 28/23/18–19. WSC to Lady Randolph Churchill, 18 Feb 1897.

10 CHAR 28/24/13–16. WSC to Lady Randolph Churchill, 10 Jan 1898.

11 Wilfrid Scawen Blunt papers FM 9–1975, 5 Sep 1909.

12 Churchill, W. S. *My Early Life; A Roving Commission,* p. 249.

13 Martin, R. *Lady Randolph Churchill. A Biography. Vol 1, 1854–1895.*

14 The Builder, 15 May 1886.

15 Stour Papers. [Cited in Churchill, R. S. *Winston S. Churchill Comp. Vol. 1.* Original not seen]. WSC to Mrs Jack Leslie, 8 Sep 1900.

16 CHAR 1/50/53. Duke of Marlborough to WSC, 1 Dec 1905.

17 Marsh, E. *A Number of People,* p. 150.

18 Hassall, C. Rev. Pottle, M. *Edward Marsh,* Oxford DNB.

19 Hassall, C. Rev. Pottle, M. *Edward Marsh,* Oxford DNB.

20 Plummer, D. *Queer People,* p. 124.

21 CHAR 1/125/20–22. CSC to WSC, 18 Aug 1918.

22 CHAR 10/25. Lord Elgin to WSC, 5 June 1907.

23 Marsh, E. *A Number of People,* p. 155.

24 CHAR 1/66/77–78. Lady Randolph Churchill to WSC, 30 Dec 1907.

25 CHAR 1/66/10–12 Lady Randolph Churchill to WSC, 22 Aug 1907.

26 CHAR 1/66/30. Jack Churchill to WSC, 24 Sep 1907.

27 Welcome, J. *Neck or Nothing. The Extraordinary Life & Times of Bob Sievier.*

28 Hassall, C. *Edward Marsh. A Biography,* p. 138.

29 Churchill, W. S. *My African Journey,* p. 89.

30 Wilfrid Scawen Blunt papers FM 9-1975, 5 Sep 1909.

31 Churchill, J. S. *Crowded Canvas,* p. 37.

32 Churchill, W. S. *My African Journey,* p. 117.

33 CHAR 1/66/75–76. Jack Churchill to WSC, 27 Dec 1907.

34 CHAR 28/152B/210–213. WSC to Jack Churchill, 28 Dec 1907.

35 CHAR 1/66/77–78. Lady Randolph Churchill to WSC, 30 Dec 1907.

36 CHAR 28/152B/210–213. WSC to Jack Churchill, 28 Dec 1907.

37 CHAR 1/99/18. E. Marsh to A. Scrivings, 3 Apr 1911.

38 CHAR 1/72/7. Lady Randolph Churchill to WSC, 03 Jan 1908.

CHAPTER 3
CLEMENTINE

One evening in the March of 1908, Churchill was a guest at a dinner party at 52 Portland Place, the home of Lady St Helier, a friend of his mother and a London hostess of some renown. He had been reluctant to go and did so only at the urging of Eddie Marsh who reminded him how helpful Mary St Helier had been in using her influence to assist his going to Egypt ten years earlier. Churchill relented, went to the party but arrived late. Punctuality was never his greatest virtue. He was placed at the table next to a young woman who had also been reluctant to attend but as the dinner was being given by her aunt, who had accorded her many kindnesses, she too had bowed to pressure from her mother to go. The young woman was the twenty-two-year-old Clementine Hozier. Her mother was Lady Blanche Ogilvy, the eldest daughter of the 10th Earl of Airlie; Lady Blanche's husband was Colonel Henry Hozier, also of Scottish descent, a man who had followed a dazzling military career by becoming a pivotal figure at Lloyds. He was not however Clementine's biological father. Blanche Hozier was famously promiscuous and of the various candidates rumoured to have fathered Clementine, much the most likely is a man named Bay Middleton who led a dashing life in the army and the hunting field before he was killed when he broke his neck in a riding accident in 1892. Mary Soames refers to one direct and one oblique mention by Wilfrid Scawen Blunt in his infamous diaries of Blanche Hozier confiding Middleton's name to him; and there is in fact a third.[1] Blunt, who had himself been one of Blanche Hozier's lovers, wrote in 1908: 'Clementine & Kitty who died, are both Blanche told me long ago, her daughters by Bay Middleton who I believe was a charming man, but I never saw him. It is much wiser for a woman, who has an inferior husband, to choose a suitable sire for her children and both these girls were delightful, refined & superior in every way'.[2]

Churchill and Clementine Hozier had met once before some four years earlier at a ball given by Lord and Lady Crewe at their home Crewe House in Curzon Street. On that occasion, he had barely seemed to spare her a glance although his mother was later to say that he did think he fell in love with her then.[3] This time however he was transfixed.

Clementine Hozier was beautiful, gracious, elegant and well-bred. She was not however rich and she had no property endowments. Winston Churchill was young, dashing, a rising star of the political stage and also well bred. He too however was not rich and his property was a small terraced house. Material impediments nonetheless did not stand in the way of a whirlwind romance or of encouragement by both their mothers – like Lord Randolph, Henry Hozier was also dead. Following a number of meetings at social gatherings over the next few months, Churchill arranged for his cousin, Sunny Marlborough to invite Clementine to join a small party at Blenheim in August. His affection for Blenheim was deep and enduring and he told Clementine he wanted to show her the house with a promise that in the gardens, they would find 'lots of places to talk in & lots of things to talk about'.[4] He promised her 'pools of water, gardens of roses, a noble lake surrounded by giant trees...'.[5] On the evening of Monday 10 August, the house party assembled and before retiring, Churchill arranged to meet Clementine in the rose garden the following morning. Despite Churchill once again being late, the tour of the rose garden was made. It is a classically English rose garden of a kind that was Clementine's passion and for which she was to hanker for years. Circular with internal paths between the beds and a massive looped iron perimeter framework from and over which climbers cascade, it was redolent with fragrance on that summer morning as the enclosed structure trapped the aroma of the countless glorious Victorian and Edwardian shrub roses. Churchill's passion was rising with the perfume and they walked again in the Blenheim grounds in the afternoon. It was a fine day but a shower prompted them to shelter in the small Temple of Diana that William Chambers had built to overlook the Great Lake and it was there that a proposal of marriage was

The reconstructed rose garden at Blenheim Palace.

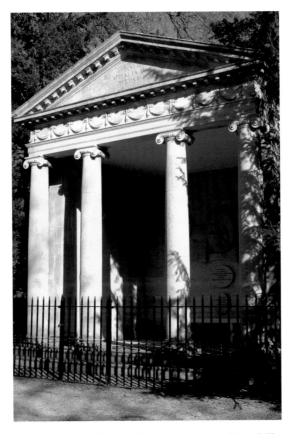

The Temple of Diana, Blenheim, where Churchill
proposed to Clementine.

made and accepted. The rest of the party was soon privy to the joyous news. Churchill had found a partner, companion, confidante and love who would unswervingly devote the rest of her life to supporting him and yet was, in doing so, embarking on one of the most difficult and challenging tasks that can have faced any young wife in twentieth century Britain.

The young couple exchanged notes the following morning, and another rose garden meeting was arranged for after breakfast. Churchill said he would pick a bunch for Clementine before they started.[6] They travelled to London the same day to obtain Clementine's mother's blessing and then all three returned to Blenheim and the engagement was made public the following Saturday when they were at Salisbury Hall with Lady Randolph.

SIR WINSTON
LEONARD SPENCER
CHURCHILL

NEJVYZNAMNĚJŠÍ EVROPSKÝ STÁTNÍK
20. STOLETÍ NAVŠTÍVIL HRAD
VEVEŘÍ V SRPNU 1906, ZÁŘÍ 1907
A SE SVOU PANÍ CLEMENTINE
POTÉ I V ZÁŘÍ 1908.

THE MOST SIGNIFICANT EUROPEAN
POLITICIAN OF THE 20TH
CENTURY VISITED THE CASTLE
OF VEVEŘÍ IN AUGUST 1906,
SEPTEMBER 1907, AND AFTERWARDS
WITH HIS WIFE CLEMENTINE IN
SEPTEMBER 1908.

Plaque at Veveri Castle, now in the Czech Republic, where Churchill and Clementine spent part of their honeymoon.

It was a time of much happiness in the Churchill household as Churchill's brother Jack had married Lady Gwendeline Bertie, the daughter of the Earl of Abingdon on 7 August. Their marriage was at the Register Office in Abingdon as the bride, always known in the family as Goonie, was a Roman Catholic. Churchill and Clementine in their turn were married at St Margaret's Westminster on Saturday 12 September, Clementine staying the previous night with Lady St Helier in Portland Place. It was a great social occasion. Wilfrid Scawen Blunt arrived late and had to sit in the family pew where Lady Blanche mischievously placed him next to yet another of her former lovers, Hugo Elcho, later Lord Wemyss.[7] The bride carried a bouquet of white tuberoses but real roses were present too – the five bridesmaids carrying pink rose bouquets. In his sermon Churchill's former Harrow headmaster Bishop Welldon said with remarkable prescience 'The influence which the wives of our statesmen have exercised for good upon their husband's lives is an unwritten chapter of English history, too sacred to be written in full…'[8] After a few days at Blenheim following the wedding, Churchill and his bride departed for their honeymoon in Italy and Austria.

Lady Randolph took it upon herself to prepare the Bolton Street house for the newly-weds' return: 'No easy matter I can tell you!' she wrote to them.[9] The honeymoon was, as it should have been, a joyous time together during which they 'loitered and loved – a good & serious occupation for which the histories furnish respectable precedents'[10] but when they returned home in early October, Clementine was to find her bedroom given an Edwardian makeover by Lady Randolph who, to her rather puritan consternation, had bedecked it with bows and trimmings. Throughout their marriage, Churchill and Clementine had separate bedrooms, a custom that seems strange to most modern couples but has long been a feature of life for the English upper class.

But makeover or not, it was time to move on. Within a month of their return, and despite their separate bedrooms, Clementine was pregnant and Bolton Street was just too small for a young family so by the end of 1908, the Churchills were looking for somewhere larger; and for a purchaser to take over the remaining eight years of their existing lease. There was no shortage of interest in No 12 and Churchill's agents showed the property to many potential clients, several no doubt put off by the fact that as early as January, and even before he had found anywhere to move to, Churchill had already dismantled the fittings in the drawing room. The eventual purchaser, a local GP named Harold Spitta, who took it March 1909 at £250 a year, wrote to the agents that he was not prepared to offer any premium as the house was in such bad condition.

The Churchills thought of a move to Bloomsbury but nothing came of it[11] and then at the beginning of March they found what they were looking for in Eccleston Square in the heart of Pimlico. The square was created in 1835 by Thomas Cubitt who took a lease from the Duke of Westminster to provide rather grand neo-classical houses for the aristocracy and the successful professional classes. It took its name from the Cheshire village of Eccleston, also part of the Duke's Grosvenor empire. Most importantly, it was close enough to Westminster still to be fashionable; 'For heaven's sake, my dear, don't let him take you anywhere beyond Eccleston Square!' Trollope had written only forty years earlier.[12] Although there were no private gardens, Cubitt compensated, as in many other London squares by providing a fine communal garden in the centre. The houses, especially on the fashionable West side, were designed to essentially the same plan, and largely for ease of entertaining with a dining room and morning room on the ground floor, an elegant L-shaped first floor drawing room with a high ceiling, a rear conservatory and double French windows leading on to a front balcony overlooking the Square's gardens. The principal bedrooms were on the second and third floors with servants' quarters on the fourth. The lower ground floors were occupied by the kitchen, servants' hall, coal cellars and the all-important silver vaults. For £200 a year and an option to purchase a 65 year ground lease for £2,000, Churchill took on the lease of No 33 and although basically in good repair, the house had fallen behind the times in its facilities and needed more bathrooms and 'water closets'. So some work and certainly some redecoration were needed. Lady Randolph did not need prompting.

No 33 Eccleston Square, Churchill's second London house.

She was not ready just yet to let go her influence on her son's tastes and in April she arranged a meeting with Mr Baxter from Maples to choose the paper for Churchill's bedroom, the colour of the front door and other details. Clementine's response is not recorded although she did have her own way in most of the house which was decorated in her 'lovely, unaffected taste',[13] though uncharacteristically letting herself go for her own bedroom where among shades of orange, brown and green, the walls were appliquéd with a design of a large fruit-laden orange tree.

Churchill also proposed changing the disposition of the rooms and adding a new dining room at the rear because he needed to make space for a library on the first floor. Churchill was an inveterate buyer and reader of books and at that time, as he was building up his library of English literature and history, regular bills from London booksellers accounted for a significant part of his spending. At Eccleston Square he also re-laid the entrance hall with striking black and white marble. His survey revealed some evidence of settlement and 'two rather important cracks' at the front[14] – no surprise as the square was built on an old swamp, the Bulinga Fen which had been drained some three hundred years earlier by James I. The settlement however proved no deterrent to Churchill but having agreed the purchase and with a few weeks of building work to take place, they were potentially homeless because Dr Harold Spitta was moving into 12 Bolton Street. So, once again, the family helped and they found sanctuary at 22 Carlton House Terrace with Freddie and Amy Guest – and their son young Winston Churchill Guest. At different times, the Churchills had relations and friends living in several houses of this most gracious of London terraces. The old Carlton House, the London residence of the Prince Regent, was built at huge cost on part of the former royal garden of

Churchill with his cousin Freddie Guest (1921).

St James's Palace by John Nash in the late eighteenth century. Once the Prince ascended the throne as George IV, however, he lost interest in the property and it was demolished in 1827. Nash replaced it with Carlton House Terrace and Carlton Gardens to provide houses for 'persons of the highest social rank' – but also, unfortunately, with rather more wealth than the Churchills themselves could ever muster. They have fine gardens and unusually for significant London houses, no mews at the rear so as to preserve the views of St James's Park. After a short stay in this gracious home, the Churchills moved into the more modest Eccleston Square in May.

They had barely settled before Churchill and Jack were in Oxfordshire for the annual camp of the Oxfordshire Yeomanry, Clementine staying with their friends the Liberal politician Lewis 'Loulou' Harcourt and his American wife Mary at Nuneham Park, a rambling Oxfordshire mansion famously described by Fanny Burney in 1786 as 'straggling, half new, half old, half comfortable, half forlorn, begun in one generation and finished in another'.[15] Sadly Clementine was too late to see the landscape that Horace Walpole in 1780 called the most beautiful in the world; although it was still better in 1909 than it is today.

Goonie Churchill gave birth to her first child on 31 May and Clementine followed suit, her daughter Diana being born on 11 July. She then spent some time at Carpenters, a small single-storey house on Wilfrid Scawen Blunt's Newbuildings estate in Sussex. Blunt kept few servants and seemed to prefer

Carpenters, the wooden bungalow on Wilfrid Scawen Blunt's estate where the Churchills stayed (early 20th century).

accommodating his visitors in this little wooden bungalow a few miles away from the main house.[16] The extraordinarily hirsute poet, diarist, politician, anti-colonialist, Arab horse breeder and hedonist Blunt was one of the more colourful members of the Churchills' social entourage. He was a compulsive womaniser and having once conquered Clementine's licentious mother Blanche Hozier he remained her close friend and confidant; in truth their correspondence reveals them both as inveterate gossips and Lady Blanche would motor over to Newbuildings from Glynde Place where, like Clementine, she sometimes stayed with her stockbroker friends the Beckwith Smiths who rented it. The social web was moreover far-reaching. Blunt knew Lord and Lady Randolph well and was a close friend of Churchill's cousin Shane Leslie and many others either in or on the periphery of the Churchill circle. He married the extraordinarily tolerant Lady Anne Isabella Noel King, the grand-daughter of Lord Byron and their

Newbuildings Place, West Sussex, the home of Wilfrid Scawen Blunt.

daughter Judith was linked by her first marriage both to Edwin Lutyens and Churchill's first real love, Pamela Lytton. Blunt came from a long line of Sussex landowners and was related to the Wyndhams who owned Petworth where he was born. He had two major estates, the ancestral family home of Crabbet Park at Horsham which he and his wife restored and where he built up his Arab stud and Newbuildings Place nearby at Southwater, a delightfully cosy red brick house with twin curved gables in the Dutch style, built around 1680. Blunt and Churchill greatly enjoyed each other's company, Blunt believing that despite their political differences, he had influence on him and on some of his policies. They visited each other's homes, Churchill cheerfully downing large quantities of Blunt's old Madeira and both he and Clementine joined their host in wearing Arab robes when they were at Newbuildings. Having conquered her mother, Blunt was besotted with Clementine and every mention of her in his diaries is accompanied by highly approving remarks on her appearance. 'She is the most beautiful of women, splendidly beautiful, and I found her affectionate and kind as very beautiful women are to very old men' he was later to write.[17] And on

Wilfrid Scawen Blunt (right) with guests in the garden at Newbuildings Place.

one mischievous occasion, he flirted with her quite unashamedly at one of their 'fancy dress' dinners in the intimate panelled dining room at Newbuildings. He wrote '…Clementine this time in a kind of mermaid's dress which looked as if she had no clothes at all underneath her outer sheath of crimped silk. She whispered to me that it was almost so, when I remarked about it. She is certainly a lovely woman…'[18]

On her visit in summer 1909 Clementine was entranced by the untamed informality – on this occasion of the garden at Carpenters, rather than her host. 'It is quite wild, savage & altogether delightful here – the house is quite as rough as the shanty in *The Admirable Crichton* – it is painted green & just peeps out of a mass of undergrowth…'[19] Newbuildings itself was also renowned for its unkempt beauty and also its fragrances, of '…jasmine at the front door; Persian roses at the back door and in potpourri all over the house; wood smoke'.[20] Later that year, when the Churchills were returning the hospitality, Blunt was treated to another view of the proud parents' first-born: 'Went to lunch with Winston and Clementine. The baby Diana was brought in with the coffee, and Winston got up and kissed it and was delighted when it laughed'.[21]

Wilfrid Scawen Blunt (oil painting by Neville Lytton – detail).

Clementine's next visit was one of her regular sojourns with her Cheshire cousins. The Stanleys are a large and exceedingly complex family with many branches but the 'Stanley cousins' to whom Clementine often referred and to whom she was very close, were the Stanleys of Alderley Park in Cheshire, more specifically Sylvia and Venetia the daughters of Edward Lyulph Stanley, 4th Lord Stanley of Alderley and his wife Maisie. As with Clementine herself, however, stories circulated about Venetia Stanley's parentage and Blanche Hozier mischievously re-told a story that Venetia's father might not have been Edward Stanley but George Howard the 9th Earl of Carlisle who was married to Stanley's sister Rosalind: 'On dit that she was George Howard's daughter but somehow I never thought that George and Maisie quite passed the rubicon' she wrote.[22]

The original Stanley home, the Jacobean Alderley Hall near Wilmslow in Cheshire was destroyed by fire with its contents in 1779. The family then moved

Venetia Stanley (*c.* 1914), Clementine's
cousin, portrait by Bertram Park.

Alderley Park, Cheshire, the family home of Venetia Stanley.

into the Bailiff's house which they progressively enlarged and it was here that Clementine and Churchill stayed. It was largely pulled down in 1933 by Edward John Stanley, the dissolute 6th Lord Stanley of Alderley who then sold off the remains in 1938. Mary Soames has said that Venetia Stanley was the greatest influence on Clementine's gardening interest and activities and Alderley Park where Venetia grew up had fine gardens although there is little record of them.[23] Venetia Stanley's real gardening opportunity came however after 1915 when she married the Liberal politician Edwin Montagu and converted to his Jewish faith. It was a surprising and fairly loveless marriage punctuated by Venetia's many indiscretions. It was also one that devastated H. H. Asquith whose close and intimate confidante she had been for several years. And just as her own parentage has been called into question, so there is a compelling evidence that Venetia's only daughter Judith was fathered not by her husband but by Eric Ednam, later the 3rd Earl of Dudley. In 1916, the year after his marriage, Edwin Montagu bought Breccles Hall near Attleborough in Norfolk and it was there that Venetia's gardening skills flourished. Breccles Hall was and is a truly beautiful red brick house with wonderful walled gardens. Although partly altered and disfigured in the nineteenth century, and then altered again by Detmar Blow in the early twentieth, it remains true to its Tudor origins.

The walled south garden at Breccles Hall, the home of Edwin and Venetia Montagu (*c.* 1936); assistant gardener Billy Dove mowing.

Interior of Breccles Hall, oil painting by Winston Churchill (1920s).

The tomb of Edwin Montagu and Venetia Stanley in the woods behind their home at Breccles Hall, Norfolk.

Following the General Election in the spring of 1910, Asquith appointed Churchill to the Home Office. Churchill had in fact earlier written to him asking that he be considered either for that post or for the Admiralty[24] – and by the next autumn, he had had both. As Home Secretary, despite being the Principal Secretary of State, Churchill had no official residence and so he continued to live and entertain at 33 Eccleston Square. His annual income, however, took a leap – from £2,000 to £5,000 a year[25] and on the strength of this, he decided to press ahead with his new dining room and instructed Maples accordingly. But leopards don't change, economies were still having to be made and Churchill took the momentous decision to do away with two of his telephone extensions in order to save £3 a year. Eddie Marsh thought it a bad idea – 'Do keep them – it is not much money and it will be bloody if no one can telephone to you without you coming down to the hall!'[26]

The Eccleston Square house featured in one of Churchill's more outrageous exploits for it was to there that he returned on Tuesday evening 3 January 1911 following his role in the so-called Siege of Sidney Street. In December, a gang of burglars had been discovered attempting to tunnel into a jeweller's shop at Houndsditch in the East End and in the course of the episode three policemen were shot dead. (Clementine asked Churchill if he planned to go to the funeral and wondered if she should send a wreath.)[27] In early January, the gang was cornered by police and troops in Sidney Street in Stepney and Churchill made a dramatic and controversial personal intervention of a kind typical of him but unprecedented for a Home Secretary before or since. In the course of the episode two of the burglars were killed.

On 28 May of that year, 1911, Clementine gave birth at Eccleston Square to her second child and only son, Randolph – known to his parents as the Chumbolly – but almost immediately afterwards, Churchill left for Blenheim; to attend another of the regular camps of the Oxfordshire Yeomanry rather than as a family guest at the Palace. There is no doubt the Churchills entertained royally at 33 Eccleston Square but the Blenheim camp seemed to offer an opportunity to render this rather more literal because it was from there on 6 June that Churchill wrote to tell Clementine that the previous afternoon he had been for a long drive and walk with the King – George V who had succeeded to the throne on the death of his father Edward VII in May of the previous year. Churchill thought him 'a charming boy' – although in truth the King was seven years his senior – and told Clementine that His Majesty wanted to come and dine at Eccleston Square 'and meet a few men'. 'You could receive him on a sofa in the Library & then go up again to bed – if you felt well enough….' he said.[28] Friday 16 June was suggested but it came and went because the King was at Ascot all week. The following week he was engaged with his Coronation and there is no evidence from his diaries that the Churchills ever hosted a private dinner party for him, at Eccleston Square or anywhere else.[29]

Later that year, and walking back from a rather uncharacteristic visit to a golf course, Churchill was asked if he would like to move from the Home Office to the Admiralty. He and Clementine were staying with Asquith at Archerfield House on the Firth of Forth, a fine Adam residence with its own links that Asquith rented as a retreat for several years while Prime Minister. Churchill wrote of how he responded to Asquith's question with 'Indeed I would'.[30]

It is not easy from the perspective of the early twenty-first century to appreciate the significance of the post of First Lord of the Admiralty in the early years of the twentieth. The British fleet, its size, strength, management and disposition

Archerfield House, North Berwick, rented by Prime Minister H. H. Asquith.

was pivotal to European and global power and during his years in the Cabinet, Churchill had played a major role in the arguments over the appropriate number of British Dreadnoughts and other battleships needed to maintain superiority over the German Navy; just as he was to argue about aircraft numbers in the nineteen thirties. And, appropriately, whereas the position of Home Secretary at that time attracted no official residence, the First Lord was provided both with Admiralty House and the use of the Admiralty yacht HMS *Enchantress.* Churchill took up the latter facility with alacrity but was more reticent about a move from his own home in Eccleston Square and for the time being, the new First Lord's family stayed put in Pimlico. At least they had the use of the communal garden for which privilege they paid £2 6s 0d a year with the threat that the key to the garden would be forfeited if it was 'transferred or used at any time to admit persons not entitled to admission'.

The reason Churchill did not immediately move to Admiralty House in 1911 was probably one of austerity – it was far bigger than his own home and would need more servants. Mary Soames wrote that it required twelve, considerably more than 33 Eccleston Square.[31] The number of servants Churchill employed at any one time however is something of a mystery. Never a man to spend more on anything than was necessary, he was paying insurance at Eccleston Square in 1909 for seven full-time domestic servants, apart from a governess and this seems strange if he was not employing them.[32] In April 1913, he took out a licence for three male servants although whether for Eccleston Square or Admiralty House is not obvious. It is true that until he moved to Admiralty House, where he would be charged a modest rent of £500, he would retain his full £5,000 First Lord's salary – double his emolument at the Board of Trade – but he did not have much spare capital. An additional explanation for the delay in moving might simply be that he knew he would be away from hearth, home and young wife for some while, lured by the seductive appeal of the fittingly named *Enchantress.*

The HMS *Enchantress* that took Churchill to sea was one of a lost breed of ocean-going splendours, a steam yacht. They were glorious craft that with their slim and elegantly raked funnels, bowsprit and sumptuous polished wood and brass, epitomised late Victorian and Edwardian style and grace. In 1911, the navy had two – the twin-funnelled Royal yacht *Victoria and Albert III* and the single funnelled *Enchantress* with a complement of 196 officers and ratings which was at the disposal of the Commissioners of the Admiralty, and especially of the First

HMS *Enchantress,* the Admiralty yacht.

Lord. And no First Lord took greater advantage of her than Churchill. He had only been in post for about a few weeks before he was on board; and between his appointment as First Lord in late 1911 and the outbreak of war, he was on *Enchantress* for a total of about eight months; indeed during some months, such as November 1911, he was seldom away from her.[33] Much of this time he was visiting ships, dockyards and other naval installations although the First Lord was a generous host and Clementine and other family members and friends were often invited to share the pleasures of life afloat.

In 1914, *Enchantress* served as a field hospital for officers but was then laid up until recommissioned in January 1919. She was ultimately broken up early in 1935 when Churchill was asked if he would like to have the pane of glass from the ship that had been engraved with his coat of arms.[34] He declined, saying he had nowhere to hang it.[35]

In late February 1912 at Eccleston Square, Clementine suffered a miscarriage and despite appearing to recover fairly swiftly, she was not well when she returned to London in April after a stay in Paris with Churchill's cousin Rosamond Guest and her husband Lord Ridley. Churchill again was away and she wrote to him plaintively as she lay in her room at the front of the house, gazing at the 'sooty tops' of the plane trees in the Square outside. Clementine remained in poor health for some months and so sadly was not able to join her husband on the *Enchantress* to view – and hear – the spectacle of the Review of the Fleet at Spithead by George V on 9 July 1912, when Churchill took the precaution of buying ear plugs for each member of his party.[36]

Throughout her married life Clementine Churchill was never anything less than Winston Churchill's support. She was the archetypal understanding woman behind the strong man and she devoted immense time and energies to being the wife of the supreme politician. She never had her own career and although she pursued with great vigour some charitable works, especially in wartime, Mary Soames has made it clear that everything, even her children, took second place in Clementine's life to supporting her husband. But as the mother of her family she did recognise many of their needs. There had been too much absentee parentship in both her own and Churchill's childhoods for Clementine to make all the same mistakes. Like other mothers, then as now, the summer holiday was important to her. Every year, Clementine had at least one holiday, usually staying with family or friends, resting, relaxing and, like other wives before and since, gathering and gleaning ideas for her own home. In the summer of 1911 she played safe and took Diana and the month-old Chumbolly, Randolph, to somewhere she knew already – Seaford, on the Sussex coast between Brighton and Eastbourne. She had fond memories of her own holidays there in the late eighteen nineties[37] when she, her sister Nellie, their mother and a French governess Mlle. Gonnard stayed for several months in furnished lodgings with two spinster sisters, Caroline and Emily Rolles at Nos 9 and 11 Pelham Place, an imposing terraced row that was part of a local attempt to regenerate Seaford into a second Brighton. The houses where they stayed received an almost direct hit from a bomb in November 1942 with five fatalities.

Pelham Place, Seaford (1909), a favoured holiday location for Clementine as a child.

In 1911, a few days after the Coronation in June, Clementine rented a distinctly more modest abode – a then fairly new but singularly undistinguished semi-detached house called 'Rosehall' in Sutton Park Road, a stiff walk up the long hill from the sea. One afternoon she motored over from Seaford to Glynde Place, an imposing grey flint and stone Elizabethan house to visit the Beckwith Smiths, great friends of her mother's, who were renting it from its owner Admiral

Rosehall, Sutton Park Road, Seaford; now Rose Lodge, Avondale Road
where Clementine stayed in 1911.

Brand. Mrs Beckwith Smith 'a nice little Irish woman' had something Clementine so admired. 'She has made such a lovely rose garden at Glynde; every rose in the world, looking as if they grew wild & in the middle of it a divine little bronze statue of a beautiful young man which she found & bought in Italy'.[38] Churchill visited the family in their humble lodgings at Seaford as frequently as he was able but it was a stressful time abroad as Germany was already flexing its military muscle and so he had sound enough excuse for his absence.

Then in July 1912, as Clementine gained strength again after her miscarriage, came the first of what might almost be counted a proper family holiday with at least modest interventions from her husband and the father of her children.

Glynde Place, East Sussex, where Clementine admired the rose garden.

Ironically it was at the home of a woman with whom Churchill was almost never to see eye to eye, of whose position in politics he disapproved and with whom he had one of the most widely quoted – if just possibly apocryphal – exchanges following a weekend's argument: 'Winston, if I was married to you, I'd put poison in your coffee'. 'Nancy, if I was married to you, I'd drink it'.[39]

Churchill had known Waldorf and Nancy Astor since at least 1907 and he and Clementine were regular visitors to their homes at Hever and Cliveden, and the Astors to Blenheim where the oft-quoted exchange is said to have taken place. The friendship between Churchill and Nancy Astor was odd but not untypical of the man – 'a long, sometimes stormy and always uneasy relationship between two people neither of whom seemed to understand the other, or to have made much effort to do so, and yet who could not resist a measure of mutual attraction'.[40] Whilst Hever, just down the road from Chartwell is a magical place, a beautiful and historic castle that was the childhood home of Anne Boleyn and changed little since the Middle Ages, Cliveden is pure nineteenth century opulence. It stands on high ground overlooking the Thames near Taplow and the original

Cliveden Mansion, south front (1916), home of the Astors.

house had some features in common with Blenheim. It was built in 1666 with avenues and perambulations designed by Bridgeman but the house and grounds the Astors owned had been created by Sir Charles Barry around 1850. The garden was the mixture of Italianate and much else that was the fashion of the time; the Villa Borghese gardens in Rome contributed a balustrade. There seems no record of what the Churchills thought of it.

In 1911, the Astors commissioned Nancy's brother-in-law, the English architect Paul Phipps to build them a house on the new Sandwich Bay estate in Kent. Nancy Astor named the house Rest Harrow after the small, hairy, scrambling plants that grow on the sea-shore nearby – the property is only narrowly separated from the shingle of the shoreline. Clementine and the children were loaned the house in July, other members of the family, including Churchill himself, coming and going from time to time. They bathed in the sea and enjoyed local sightseeing but can have gained little inspiration from the house itself, a vast red brick pile (which Nancy Astor herself was predictably to call 'a sea-side cottage'[41]) and, being barely two years old, had no garden, no roses to delight Clementine;

Rest Harrow, Sandwich (early 20th century), Nancy Astor's seaside house where the
Churchills stayed.

merely a two acre plot of grass and scrubby tamarisk fenced from the sea.

In December that year, Churchill had a considerable amount of work
undertaken at 33 Eccleston Square[42], perhaps because he was thinking of staying
but more probably because he had by then made the decision to move to
Admiralty House and realised that to obtain a tenant paying a good rent, some
upgrading was necessary. The heating and electricity supply were improved,
much redecoration done and the carpets cleaned, repaired and re-sown – some
had come with them from Bolton Street where they were already second-hand
so must by then have been almost threadbare. Any worthwhile tenant would
expect better. And the tenant they found was certainly worthwhile: Churchill's
Cabinet colleague and Randolph's godfather, the Foreign Secretary Sir Edward
Grey who was in need of a London house. Later in the year, while Churchill was
away, Clementine had lunch with him in the house and enviously admired the
way the library had been filled with roses brought from Fallodon, his country
seat in Northumberland.

Finally, in the first week of April 1913, the family made the move to Admiralty
House, or at least Clementine and her children made the move to Admiralty
House. Churchill was at Portsmouth with his *Enchantress* and he left Clementine

to take charge. Maples came to move the furniture but Mrs Churchill was not enjoying the experience. 'House moving is going on & there is no resting place for the soles of my feet' she wrote, 'I am now sitting in a desolated library (ink-pots and pens gone)…'.[43] Nonetheless, with a generosity of spirit and an informality not seen in later twentieth century Prime Ministers, H. H. Asquith and his daughter Violet picked her up on the Saturday morning and they drove to their newly rebuilt riverside house The Wharf at Sutton Courtenay in Oxfordshire. 'Leaving a house where one has lived nearly 4 years' Clementine wrote, 'is as much an event in a Kat's life, as changing from Home Office to Admiralty for a Statesman!'[44]

The Wharf, Sutton Courtenay, H. H. Asquith's house, often visited by the Churchills.

Today, Sutton Courtenay keeps its head down in the shadow of the cooling towers of Didcot power station but has nonetheless retained much of the Thames-side charm that endeared it to the Society set in the early years of the twentieth century. The ancient Manor House in the centre of the village and its chatelaine, Norah Lindsay were the focus of social life. The Prince of Wales

The Manor House, Sutton Courtenay (1924), home of Norah Lindsay.

was a frequent visitor and the Asquiths were among those who had come to share an appreciation of the village's charms and location, conveniently close to Oxford. Through the facility of Margot Asquith's private allowance, they owned a complex of riverside buildings at the northern end of Sutton Courtney. Margot converted an old barn at the water's edge for her personal use while behind it, facing the main street, the arts and crafts architect Walter Cave built them The Wharf, comprising a new building he created on the site of the old Queen's Head pub together with an adjoining brick-built property called Walton House. The Churchills were regular guests.[45]

The party spent a relaxing weekend, played some golf and on the Monday morning, Clementine caught the early train to Paddington and took up residence at Admiralty House, 'our Mansion' as she called it. Mansion? Perhaps. Admiralty House is certainly an imposing building. It was designed in 1786 by Samuel Pepys Cockerell, pupil to the Admiralty architect Sir Robert Taylor at the request of the then First Lord, Earl Howe who found his accommodation in the Admiralty itself a little crowded – it was full of clerks and also occupied by the other Lords of the Admiralty and their families who lived cheek by jowl. The house lies discretely hidden adjacent to the main Admiralty building in Whitehall and overlooking to the south-west Horse Guards Parade and St James's Park. There is no significant way in from Horse Guards Parade at the back but the colonnaded entrance in Whitehall is grand and impressive.

Admiralty House resonates with reminders and relics of the triumphs and tragedies of the Royal Navy over two centuries. It 'casts into mortifying shade all the other Governmental residences' said Christopher Hussey.[46] This may be so and it might be magnificent for formal entertaining but it is hardly a cosy family home and after the relative intimacy of Eccleston Square, it is easy to see how it daunted poor Clementine. It is in truth, less of a residence and more a State cave with huge echoing rooms on three floors, servants' quarters in the roof and service rooms in a warren of a basement with passageway doors left over from a destroyer. The great rooms have disproportionately tiny fireplaces and the thought of heating it must have been terrifying. It is small wonder that Churchill was reputedly tempted to try lighting the infamous Admiralty House stove, a large and extraordinarily ugly construction in the second entrance hall, a copy in cast iron of the marble *columna rostrata* in Rome. It is said the ensuing smoke, flames and noise put the fear of God into all within sight and hearing and the experiment has never been repeated.

Clementine decided that by sealing off and by-passing the first floor, she could run Admiralty House with only nine servants and although the property was largely furnished by the Government, she was at least able to choose furnishings for the bedrooms, sitting rooms and nurseries – albeit from a 'grim catalogue'.[47] It probably was not as grim as some of the furniture in the rest of the house. The so-called 'fish furniture' in the official dining and drawing rooms was a gift in the nineteenth century by the executors of one John Fish to the memory of Lord Nelson. It is not readily described but the arms and backs of the chairs are carved so as to resemble dolphins. They might easily frighten small children. Around 1960, it was removed, more appropriately, to the Royal Pavilion in Brighton.

Earlier First Lords at least had the benefit of a fine official garden along the north side of Horse Guards Parade but this was swept aside when the much maligned extension to the Admiralty building rose in its place at the beginning of the twentieth century. Only scattered fragments of the garden remain – a temple with Doric columns and a sundial are at Althorp in Northamptonshire while a summerhouse with four caryatids by William Kent is at Buckingham Palace.

There was no formal family seaside holiday in 1913 but while Churchill was away on *Enchantress* early in the year, Clementine continued with her social calls. She spent time at The Wharf with the Asquiths and with Freddie Guest and his wife at the country house they were renting from the Finch family: Burley House at Burley-on-the-Hill in Rutland. The Guests' vast wealth was derived from the Dowlais Ironworks in Merthyr Tydfil, founded by an ancestor in the nineteenth century. Their name survives today in the industrial conglomerate Guest, Keen, Nettlefold (GKN). The family never did things by halves and their homes were all imposing. The setting of Burley is splendid and it had been considered as a site for the Duke of Wellington's new house before he was given Stratfield Saye. The house at Burley was designed in prematurely Palladian style by the architect John Lumley with a fifteen bay front and sweeping colonnades. 'Many a ruler of a minor state in Germany would have been proud of such a palace' said Pevsner. It had been the scene of one of Clementine's early traumatic Churchill experiences. In August 1908, Winston was staying there shortly before he proposed to her when a fire broke out and waiting at Blenheim she heard confusing accounts of the happenings and was greatly anxious for his safety. In the event, no-one was injured and Churchill himself played a significant part in rescuing works of art from the flames. Although Clementine did not really like the Guests, their houses were always large enough for her to escape from them and they generally had interesting gardens. Those at Burley were certainly intriguing; at one time, they extended to over 250 acres and included an early 17th century avenue and bowling green and extensive formal gardens. Humphry Repton worked there around 1795.

Despite the lack of a seaside holiday in 1913, Clementine did have some opportunities to join Churchill afloat. The Asquiths came with them on *Enchantress* for a Mediterranean cruise in May and then in August, there was a family party, including Lady Blanche and Nellie, for a cruise from Chatham round the coast of Scotland, Churchill visiting naval establishments and the others enjoying the sea air and the scenery.[48]

Endnotes

[1]   Soames, M. *Clementine Churchill. 2nd. Ed.* p. 6

[2]   WSB FM 395–1975. Diary 14 Aug 1908.

[3]   WSB FM 395–1975. Diary 14 Aug 1908.

[4]   CSCT 2/1/10–11. WSC to CSC. 7 Aug 1908.

[5]   CSCT 2/1/8–9. WSC to CSC. 8 Aug 1908.

[6]   CSCT 1/1/5. WSC to CSC. [?] Aug 1908.

[7]   WSB FM 395–1975. Diary 14 Aug 1908.

[8]   Soames, M. *Clementine Churchill, 2nd Ed.*

[9]   CHAR 1/72/95. Lady Randolph Churchill to WSC, 29 Sep 1908.

[10] CHAR 28/27/86A. WSC to Lady Randolph Churchill, 20 Sep 1908

[11] CSCT 1/3/27–28. CSC to WSC, 16 Oct [1909].

[12] Trollope, A. *The Small House at Allington.*

[13] Soames, M. *Clementine Churchill, 2nd Ed*, p. 102.

[14] CHAR 1/89/19–20. Maple & Co. – surveyors' report for Lumley & Lumley, 13 Mar 1909.

[15] Burney. F. *The Diary and Letters of Madame d'Arblay, Vol. 1*

[16] The Earl of Lytton, conversation with the author, 27 April 2006.

[17] WSB FM 436–1975. Diary 16 Sep 1917.

[18] WSB FM 12–1975. Diary 19–20 Oct 1912.

[19] CSCT 1/3/14. CSC to WSC, 29 Aug 1909

[20] WSB 190–1975. Diary 28 Nov 1917.

[21] WSB FM 12–1975. Diary 25 Nov 1909.

[22] WSB FM 15–1975. Diary 3 Jun 1915.

[23] Mary Soames, Conversation with the author, 15 January 2004.

[24] CHAR 2/45/11. WSC to H. H. Asquith, 5 Feb 1910.

[25] CHAR 1/96/13. Note Inland Revenue to Edward Marsh, 5 May 1910.

[26] CHAR 1/96/4. Edward Marsh to WSC, Mar 1910.

[27] CSCT 1/2/21–22. CSC to WSC, 19 Dec 1910.

[28] CSCT 2/4/9–10. WSC to CSC, 5 June 1911.

[29] RA, Diaries of King Edward VII, 1911.

[30] Churchill, R. S. and Gilbert. M. *Winston S. Churchill.* Vol. 2, p. 536.

[31] Soames, M. *Speaking for Themselves. The Personal letters of Winston and Clementine Churchill.* p. 58.

[32] CHAR 1/89/50. Policy from Central Insurance Co. Ltd., 6 Jul 1909.

[33] Churchill, R. S. and Gilbert. M. *Winston S. Churchill.* Comp. Vol. II Pt 2, pp. 1371–1373; Vol. II Pt 3, 1580–3; 1704–9.

[34] CHAR 2/235/37. Sir Vincent Baddeley to WSC, 17 Apr 1935.

[35] CHAR 2/235/43. WSC to Sir Vincent Baddeley, 24 Apr 1935.

[36] CHAR 1/106/41. Account from Gieve, Matthews & Seagrove, 1 Aug 1912.

[37] Soames, M. *Clementine Churchill. 2nd. Ed.*, p. 83.

[38] CSCT 1/5/28-30. CSC to WSC, 4 July 1911.

39   Sykes, C. *Nancy. The Life of Lady Astor,* p. 127.

40   Sykes, C. *Nancy. The Life of Lady Astor,* p. 107.

41   Sykes, C. *Nancy. The Life of Lady Astor,* p. 138.

42   CHAR 1/110/37–40. Account from Lapthorne & Co. [?], Dec 1912.

43   CSCT 1/6/17. CSC to WSC, 4 Apr [1913].

44   CSCT 1/6/18–19. CSC to WSC, 6 Apr [1913].

45   Soames, M. *Clementine Churchill. 2nd Ed.,* p. 104.

46   Hussey, C. *Country Life,* 24 Nov 1923.

47   Soames, M. *Clementine Churchill. 2nd Ed.,* p. 101.

48   Soames, M. *Speaking for Themselves. The Personal letters of Winston and Clementine Churchill.* p. 76.

CHAPTER 4
NORFOLK AND THE DARDANELLES

One day in August 1883, the *Daily Telegraph*'s theatre critic, the writer and lyricist Clement Scott, took advantage of the new railway link from London to find himself in Cromer in north-east Norfolk but with nowhere to stay. Walking eastwards along the coast soon brought him to the cliff-top village of Overstrand where he was found accommodation for a few days in a local miller's cottage. That visit changed the life of Overstrand for ever and brings this delightful but obscure Norfolk fishing village into the Churchill story. So entranced was Scott by what he found that he wrote a series of articles for his paper extolling the virtues of the locality which, owing to the profusion of red field poppies growing locally, he called Poppyland. The rich and famous of London society followed Scott in droves and the fishermen's cottages were soon interspersed with the newcomers' grand and opulent houses. Some have since been demolished and

Overstrand, Norfolk; the beach.

some fallen victim to the retreating east Norfolk coastline but among the most notable and remarkable of those that remain are two by Lutyens – Overstrand Hall built in 1899 for the banker Lord Hillingdon and even more astonishing, The Pleasaunce, adapted in 1897–9 from two existing houses for Lord Battersea, formerly the Liberal MP Cyril Flower who had been a whip in Gladstone's government of 1886.

Those who could not afford to build in Overstrand were content to visit and stay with those who could; and among them were the Churchills. The Norfolk coast was an area already familiar to Winston because in the summer of 1885, at the age of ten, he had been sent for some weeks with Mrs Everest to Cromer, staying first at the very fashionable sea-front Tuckers Hotel and afterwards at the then new Chesterfield Lodge in West Street. Tuckers was where the titled and crowned heads of Europe came and the Duchess of Marlborough was a frequent visitor. Local tradition, inevitably, is that at some time the Churchills visited almost every big house in Overstrand but what is certainly true is that Clementine, by then five months pregnant, took Diana and Randolph there with their nanny and a maid early in the July of 1914. They were accompanied by Goonie and her children Johnny and Peregrine and for at least part of the time, Jack was there too. Clementine rented a house called Pear Tree Cottage from the Battersea Estate[1] – Lord Battersea himself had died in 1907 and The Pleasaunce, a few minutes walk away, was by then the home of his widow, the philanthropist Constance Flower (née Rothschild). Clearly her philanthropy did not extend to the Churchills, because Winston himself was later to ask Clementine to keep a close eye on the outlay that the stay at Pear Tree Cottage was costing him.[2]

Like other 'cottages' in the Churchills' lives, Pear Tree Cottage was in truth a decent sized house with at least six bedrooms. The eponymous pear tree was espaliered along one wall and among the house's charming features was a pantry lined with some striking De Morgan tiles left over from the building of The Pleasaunce. It lies in what in 1914 was the only route from the main part of the village to the cliffs and the sea, a pleasant narrow lane called The Londs. Five minutes walk took the Churchills to the fishermen's stalls and lobster pots and to the steps at the top of the cliffs which afford beautiful views along the coast. The house had been completely re-built in about 1890 from an ancient fisherman's cottage and rope store and the Churchill children must have loved the Victorian rustic summerhouse in a corner of the garden as much as their mother was

Above: Pear Tree Cottage,
Overstrand (1905) where the
Churchills stayed in 1914.

Right: The Londs, Overstrand
(*c.* 1905).

Jack Churchill at Beehive
Cottage, Overstrand (1914).

frustrated by her condition from indulging herself on the private tennis court at the side. The servants were installed in another property, The White House to the rear while Goonie and her family were a few minutes walk away at Beehive Cottage. No such name exists today and a long-standing local belief that it was actually a house called Beckhythe Cottage elsewhere in the village is belied by a rare photograph of Jack Churchill standing in front of what is clearly a different building and by Johnny Spencer-Churchill's reference to it being 'at the other end of the lawn'. The most likely candidate seems to be a cottage in the Londs only some 30 metres from Pear Tree Cottage that is today called Woodthorpe.[3] Like Pear Tree Cottage it too was formerly part of the Battersea estate.

Churchill saw the family installed in Overstrand during the weekend of 4 and 5 July and then caught the train back to London. Although there was a direct service to Liverpool Street in 2 hours and 18 minutes, it speaks volumes of his need to have life filled at every moment that Clementine was concerned over his possible indignation at having to wait five minutes at the station.[4] On Wednesday, he embarked again on *Enchantress* but was soon back in Norfolk because the following weekend she dropped anchor off Overstrand for the First Lord to be rowed ashore. After spending time together, Churchill then returned to his floating office on Sunday evening, leaving Pear Tree Cottage as a 'happy, sunlit picture' in his mind's eye and watching forlornly as his family climbed the zigzag steps up the cliffs back to the Londs. He mused that he must try and get a little country house for them 'for always',[5] the first hint of what was to become a lifetime's passion, although the first inkling too that houses would be of his choosing, not his wife's.

Telephones were scarce in rural Norfolk in 1914. Pear Tree Cottage certainly was not so blessed and one of the few phones in Overstrand was at Sea Marge, a massive half-timbered house built a few years earlier for the German Jewish financier and Liberal Party supporter, Sir Edgar Speyer, a man Clementine was later to refer to as 'notorious'.[6] He fell from favour because of accusations relating to his German background and possible wartime disloyalty and his British citizenship and membership of the Privy Council were revoked in 1921. Not until 2004 when such action was apparently considered against Clare Short was the withdrawal from an individual of Privy Council membership to be contemplated again. During the war, many stories circulated around Overstrand concerning Speyer's possible liaison with German spies. In 1914, however, he was on good and amicable terms with Churchill and allowed the family to use his phone. Clementine took advantage of the facility to make several calls to Churchill in London but in view of Speyer's German origins it is a notable irony that it was on his phone in Overstrand that a particularly significant call was made by Churchill himself.

He had travelled to Overstrand on the afternoon of Saturday 25 July, with Europe 'trembling on the verge of a general war'.[7] The British fleet had just taken part in a review by the King at Spithead but the ships had not immediately been dispersed. So in between doing fatherly things like playing with the children on the beach and damming the little rivulets in the sand, he used the phone to keep in touch with the Admiralty. He rang the First Sea Lord, Prince Louis of Battenberg at nine on the Sunday morning to be told there were no new developments so he went with the family to the beach. 'It was a very beautiful day. The North sea shone and sparkled to a far horizon'.[8] Churchill then returned to Sea Marge at mid-day to await a return call from the Admiralty. There was no great change in the various news items but all were '...tending to a rise in temperature'.[9] This was enough. Churchill's family holiday and the idyll of Pear Tree Cottage were over for him, he said his goodbyes and caught the afternoon train back to London.

Clementine, Goonie and the children stayed on in Norfolk, enjoying the last few weeks of peace, and sightseeing. They went one day to Blickling Hall near Norwich, a property Clementine was to visit again in later years to admire its Norah Lindsay garden. And they continued to give Churchill anxiety about the costs, both of Pear Tree Cottage and Admiralty House; 'Rigorous measures will have to be taken' he wrote at the end of July.[10] Five days after he sent this letter, Britain was at war with Germany.

Clementine had the family car with them at Overstrand. It was a 15 h.p. Napier Landaulette for which Churchill had paid over £600 in 1911 but it was notoriously unreliable and cost him a small fortune in repair bills.[11] 'The motor is a lame duck till Wednesday at least', Clementine wrote on 8 August, 'so I hope the Germans won't arrive before that date…We are telegraphing to Napier's for a new cylinder & the best motor firm in Norwich is to send a man to put it on etc'.[12] The unreliability of the car notwithstanding, they stayed until late August but then the holiday was finally over, the family was together again at Admiralty House and Clementine, while looking forward to the birth of her new baby (Sarah was born on the 7 October), was faced with arranging their domestic life through the hostilities. There was still a widely held belief, as there is with most British wars, that it would all 'be over by Christmas' and at that stage, no-one anticipated the task would occupy the next four years. But at least Clementine had companionship because in September, Goonie accepted Churchill's offer to stay with them at Admiralty House, shutting up her own home in Cromwell Road and sending the children initially to her father's house at Brackley.[13]

The Dardanelles episode in early 1915 was a collective tragedy; a tragedy for the forces involved, a tragedy for the nation and a personal tragedy for Churchill. The plan had seemed simple enough – a British and French naval force was to bombard Turkish coastal forts, penetrate the Dardanelles Strait into the Sea of Marmora and so gain access to Constantinople and force Turkey to negotiate a surrender while the army was to take and hold the Gallipoli Peninsula. The military commander was Churchill's old friend Major-General Sir Ian Hamilton and among those now serving on Hamilton's staff was Churchill's brother Jack. As First Lord of the Admiralty, Churchill had backed the enterprise to the full but was deeply to suffer personally when it failed. Although the British and French ships attacked the Turkish forts in early March, no real account had been taken of the extent of German mine-laying activities or the ability of the Turkish forts to hit back and two capital ships were sunk. The British naval commander Vice-Admiral John de Robeck withdrew and notwithstanding Churchill's every persuasion, no reinforcements were sent. On the Gallipoli Peninsula, British and Anzac troops became pinned down and suffered massive casualties at the hands of the Turkish forces who occupied the higher ground. Despite originally supporting the plan and supporting Churchill, Lord Fisher the First Sea Lord, a man who, judged by his letters alone, was permanently in the later stages of insanity, turned against them both and then, at a critical moment in early May when things were going from bad to worse, resigned.

Churchill was the political victim. Arguments over his relative culpability for the venture have provided historical scholars with fertile ground but it is ineluctable that the failure of the Dardanelles operation was the final straw for the viability of Asquith's Liberal Government at a time when many other aspects of the war were also going badly. One of the conditions of the coalition agreement struck between Asquith, Lloyd George and the Conservative opposition leader Andrew Bonar Law, was that Churchill be removed from the Admiralty.

Mary Soames has written that the Dardanelles saga formed a sombre background to her parents' lives for a very long time and her mother Clementine said she thought Churchill would never get over it – 'I thought he would die of grief'.[14] Although Churchill was still in the Cabinet as he had accepted the token post of Chancellor of the Duchy of Lancaster (replacing Edwin Montagu), he was out of his home at the Admiralty. The machinery of Government and the Civil Service has little room for sentiment and in 1915, conspicuously unlike 2006, Cabinet Ministers relieved of their departments had barely time to pack their bags. But there could be no return to Eccleston Square as Lord Grey was still in residence so with literally, no roof over their heads, the Churchills were again rescued by the wider family and were relieved to be able to stay for a few weeks with Lord Wimborne – formerly Sir Ivor Bertie Guest and married to Churchill's aunt Lady Cornelia Spencer-Churchill. He was the father of Churchill's close friend and cousin Freddie (Frederick Edward Guest), who also took his turn from time to time at helping the housing crisis. The Guest seniors' property was at 22 Arlington Street, next door to The Ritz on the south side of Piccadilly but in 1913, they bought the adjoining property No 21, adding two additional floors and it was this house they made available to their homeless relatives. Goonie too

No 21 Arlington Street, Lord Wimborne's house where the Churchills stayed in summer 1913.

was homeless so the two families pooled their resources and she moved into Arlington Street with them, collecting her children who with their nanny had been living during the winter with Lady Randolph at her house in Brook Street.

The Churchills were together at 21 Arlington Street from May until late July and although undoubtedly convenient, the arrangement cannot have entirely suited Clementine with her 'general antipathy towards the 'Guest tribe'[15] but it did give them chance to take stock. And there were compensations although the house itself must have prompted them to wonder if they could ever afford anything comparable. Even before the Guests' addition, it was one of the finest town houses in the West End, built in 1740 by James Leoni for Richard Boyle, later to become the 2nd and last Viscount Shannon, MP and Commander in Chief of the Irish military forces under George II. Later owners included George Granville Leveson-Gower, the first Duke of Sutherland who was born there, as was his son Francis, the 1st Earl of Ellesmere. The merchant and banker Joshua Bates refurbished it in 1851 at a cost of £20,000. Not least among its desirable features is a splendid terraced garden overlooking Green Park. During the eighteenth century, the residents of the Arlington Street houses constantly enlarged their gardens by encroaching on Green Park and by 1796 this had reached such alarming proportions that George III granted them a lease of land on the east side of the Park to fix the boundaries permanently.

Fortuitously, the Churchills also had an important bolt-hole available in the country because while Churchill was still expecting to remain at the Admiralty, they had found a house to rent for the summer: Hoe Farm, in the village of Hascombe near Godalming in Surrey. Mary Soames called Hoe Farm 'a true haven'[16] after the Dardanelles and it is easy to understand why. It is a splendid 15th century farmhouse, significantly altered in the 17th century and then worked on by Lutyens in 1890–1 when he added a dining room wing and created a charmingly intricate staircase with two arms which meet at a half-landing and then separate again. Even more than most Churchillian 'cottages', it is a substantial property and in 1915 had around ten bedrooms and several bathrooms. The renting was shared with Goonie Churchill and her children (Jack was still in Gallipoli) and both families and their servants spent most weekends there.

It is a mystery how the Churchills knew about Hoe Farm as it certainly is not a place to be tripped over by accident, lying secluded at the end of a well-concealed lane. The house was part of the Park Hatch Estate owned by a

Hoe Farm, nestling in a fold of the Surrey hills, Churchill's retreat after the Dardanelles disaster.

Hoe Farm, photographed by Gertrude Jekyll c. 1905.

Joseph Godman, local landowner and hunting friend of Lutyens' father, Charles Lutyens and the fourth in a line of Joseph Godmans who had held the estate. It was an earlier Hoe Farm tenant, Robert Evelyn Hay Murray, (a member of the Duke of Atholl's family and private secretary to Lord Rosebery), who had engaged Lutyens to undertake the alterations. Murray however died in 1910 and although there is no documentation to link Churchill with any particular local resident, Hascombe lies in the heart of wealthy west Surrey and there must have been a number of friends or acquaintances in the area who could have alerted him to the possibility. One likely candidate is Sir Charles Archer Cook, the Chief Charity Commissioner who lived at Sullingstead House on the hill overlooking Hoe Farm.[17]

Not the least intriguing feature of Hoe Farm is that it was not only worked on by Lutyens, as were many houses in the area, but it also lies in the heart of Gertrude Jekyll country. In 1915, the grandest of gardening grandes dames was living only a few miles up the road at Munstead and this in itself raises the fascinating possibility that she and Churchill met. If so, it can surely only have been by accident although Lady Randolph did know Agnes Jekyll, Gertrude Jekyll's sister in law, while Agnes's daughter Pamela was married to Churchill's political sparring partner Reginald McKenna. Even so, while both politically Liberal, the two families were hardly natural bedfellows. Tantalisingly Gertrude Jekyll did take two photographs of Hoe Farm that have only recently been identified. It appears however that in the early 1890s she photographed several of Lutyens' early Surrey buildings: Hoe Farm, Crooksbury, Winkworth Farm, the Park Hatch Lodges and his shop at Shere and often these are juxtaposed in her photograph albums with older vernacular buildings. She did design the gardens at Crooksbury but almost certainly not at Hoe Farm, possibly because it was created early in Lutyens' career before their collaboration developed.[18]

Hoe Farm not only gave Churchill a post-Dardanelles haven in the summer of 1915, it also launched him on a life-time's passion and one that was to provide him with an ever-enduring escape. For it was in the garden at Hoe Farm that Churchill took up painting. The story is well known: Goonie Churchill enjoyed painting and was working with water colours in the garden one day in June (her son Johnny Spencer Churchill later said the paints were his[19]). Churchill borrowed them to try for himself and then, for reasons not altogether clear, decided he wanted to experiment with oils instead. Clementine went to Godalming to buy some for him and he produced the first of more than five hundred paintings that were to flow from his brush over nearly sixty years. Once he was back in London, Churchill opened an account with Roberson's, the artists suppliers in Long Acre and was soon making regular purchases of paint, turpentine, canvasses, easels and other artists' materials. Among their London friends and neighbours were Sir John and Lady Lavery, both painters of note and Hazel Lavery drove down to Hoe Farm to give Churchill his first lesson in oils – 'Splash into the turpentine, wallop into the blue and white….'[20] The Laverys were a continuing encouragement to him and he was later to spend much time working in John Lavery's studio at 5 Cromwell Place.

Above: Sir John Lavery who with his wife Hazel taught Churchill to paint at Hoe Farm.

Left: 5 Cromwell Place, Sir John Lavery's studio.

Among the visitors to Hoe Farm was Wilfrid Scawen Blunt who came with his long-time nurse/ companion Elizabeth Lawrence. On Saturday 14 August, he spent the day with Churchill and his family, having driven from his home at Newbuildings Place, to be met half way by the Churchills' car. Clementine, Nellie and Lady Blanche were there with Goonie and the children, Peregrine, Johnny, Diana, Sarah and Randolph. He found them all gathered beneath an old yew tree where Churchill was sitting and '...attempting to paint Nellie's portrait an impossible sketch in oils of a childishly elementary kind which they were admiring with splendid courage'.[21] (The painting seems to have vanished; perhaps painted over as Churchill tended to do with failures.)[22] Blunt recalled Churchill, deeply in his post-Dardanelles despond, telling him 'There is more blood than paint upon these hands. We thought it would be a little job, and so it might have been if it had been begun in the right way and now all these lives lost'.[23] Blunt reflected 'Poor Winston! He has certainly been through a furnace of political affliction and I imagine that but for his wife's devotion and his domestic happiness with his children and the support of a few relatives, he might have gone mad...'[24]

The Churchills continued to visit Hoe Farm until October but away from the peace and escapism of the Surrey countryside, the political situation was deteriorating fast. The landings in Gallipoli staggered from disaster to disaster and Ian Hamilton was never again to hold a military post of significance. By the autumn Bulgaria had entered the war on the side of Austria and Germany and in November, the Coalition Cabinet was reorganised and slimmed down. Churchill was not in it. He had had enough, resigned from the Government and in mid-November went to France with the express wish of serving at the Front.

Clementine and Goonie stayed on at Arlington Street but before going to France, Churchill moved out. He needed an escape from five extremely lively children, their nannies and a nurse in a house which although seemingly large, appeared to shrink before his eyes. For a time he addressed his correspondence from the Liberal Party Headquarters at 19 Abingdon Street opposite the Houses of Parliament, an area that today is open space, but to escape the overpowering domesticity, he did what many another man in the same position has done and moved in with his mother. She was living at 72 Brook Street, a tall, gracious Georgian house with charmingly curved heads to the lower windows. It was a house about which Goonie Churchill had waxed lyrical when she was entertained there to 'a seven course dinner, beautifully served'. The dining room walls were decorated with fine pictures and after dinner they had sat in 'a 'pickled' [bleached] oak room, beautifully lighted in the cornices by invisible electric Lights & filled with lovely bibelots, furniture, rugs, flowers…'[25] Thickly carpeted stairs led up to a green painted drawing room with wonderful lighting and bedecked with tapestries, and then on to a silver bedroom, a white bathroom and a blue dressing room. Like all Lady Randolph's homes, it was ravishingly appointed. Clementine Churchill later said 'She really has a genius for house decoration'[26] and her grandson wrote that buying houses, doing them up and selling them again was one of Lady Randolph's few really profitable ventures.[27]

No 72 Brook Street, Lady Randolph's house where Churchill stayed in 1915.

In early October, Clementine, Goonie and the children left Arlington Street and moved in to Jack and Goonie's own house at 41 Cromwell Road. Churchill did not join them until just before his departure for France in November when he persuaded his mother to let the Brook Street house and move to Cromwell Road herself.

After they married, Jack and Goonie had lived for a few months with Lady Randolph and George Cornwallis-West at Salisbury Hall which Goonie disliked, perhaps because it was reputedly haunted, and their first married home together was 10 Talbot Square, just off Sussex Gardens. This however had been sold in either 1911 or 1912 when they bought the Cromwell Road house, a much larger

No 41 Cromwell Road, Jack and Goonie Churchill's house.

and grander property on the corner with Queensbury Place and almost opposite the Natural History Museum.

With Churchill and Jack away Clementine continued to live with Goonie at 41 Cromwell Road, Lady Randolph helping them out by contributing £40 a month towards the running costs before she moved in herself at the beginning of December.[28] The house was even more chaotically crowded than Arlington Street as there were by then five adults, five children (although the older children were away at boarding school for some of the time) and nine servants. Churchill came home for a brief Christmas weekend before returning to France. The two young families, like millions of others throughout the country were, for the time being, fatherless. Clementine however kept herself busy during Churchill's absence – she had taken much interest in supporting the work of the YMCA in running workers' canteens – and as usual, stayed regularly with friends. She visited the Stanley cousins at Alderley and in mid-February 1916 she was at Walmer Castle the residence of the Lord Warden of the Cinque Ports, a position Churchill himself was later to occupy with much pride and pleasure. The then warden, Lord Beauchamp, had loaned the castle for the weekends to H. H. Asquith and Clementine was there as his guest. She took delight in finding on that bright warm winter's weekend, a pink rose, a white violet and a sprig of cherry pie, more than she would have in any garden of her own for a long time.[29]

Churchill had a period of leave in March 1916 when he met Clementine at the Lord Warden Hotel in Dover. During his stay in England, he spoke in the Naval Estimates debate but blundered badly at the end of his speech in urging the return to the Admiralty of the ridiculous Lord Fisher. He then went back to France having decided to come home permanently at the earliest practical opportunity in order to take up a strong Opposition role in the House of Commons. He was eventually able to take leave of his battalion and return to London at the beginning of May; initially to 41 Cromwell Road which was soon to be a silent witness to one of the more dramatic moments of the First World War.

The early summer of 1916 was proving a time of personal stress and political impotence for Churchill. He did not get the job he wanted as Air Minister and he was being taunted and tormented by reminders of the Dardanelles. On 4 June he and Sir Ian Hamilton were working in Churchill's study in Cromwell Road on evidence to counter the arguments they anticipated Kitchener, as Secretary of State for War, would put forward at the forthcoming Dardanelles enquiry. There was a commotion in the road outside and the sound of someone calling out Kitchener's name. Churchill threw open the window and an uncouth looking newsboy was selling his wares to the accompaniment of a momentous announcement. Kitchener was dead, drowned when the cruiser HMS *Hampshire* on which he was sailing from Scapa Flow to Russia had struck a mine and gone down with almost all hands.[30] A month later, Asquith filled Kitchener's job at the War Office by moving Lloyd George from the Ministry of Munitions. Churchill wanted to fill the Munitions vacancy; but again, he wanted in vain.

The domestic scene was stabilising however as with Lord Grey's lease on 33 Eccleston Square expiring in late 1916, the Churchills were now able to reclaim their London home while their tenant 'retired to brood in the North'.[31] Goonie let 41 Cromwell Road for the remainder of the war to Constantia the wife of Sir Herbert Beerbohm Tree – who was confined to a nursing home – and in good Churchill fashion, wandered from house to house, staying with friends for some three years. After the war, she and Jack returned to Cromwell Road and stayed there until 1933 or 1934 when they bought 42 Chester Terrace and also Holworth House at Ringstead Bay in Dorset.[32]

But whilst Clementine and Churchill would always need and would always have a London base, there was a drawback. Town houses were fine but many of them, and certainly those the Churchills had owned, lacked something significant. They lacked land. Their friends had country homes and Clementine especially wanted one of her own, with a garden. A rural cottage she thought would have been ideal. Churchill had certainly promised her a country house when she was on holiday at Pear Tree Cottage and earlier in that same summer of 1914, while staying with her sister Nellie at her mother's home, St Antoine on the Rue des Fontaines in Dieppe, she had written to Churchill telling him that whenever she saw an empty cottage in the country, she wanted to buy it at once – and would have bought one on the nearby cliffs had not the agent – 'luckily for you' – been on holiday. It was, she wrote, the twentieth time she had found 'the cottage of her dreams'.[33] The reality, however, was that whilst cottages, even fairly big ones, were adequate for the summer holidays, permanent residence – not to say their status in society – demanded something rather more substantial and Churchill never succumbed to Clementine's chocolate box fantasies. What he did find for her was altogether different and not for the only time in their lives, his house buying was to land them in financial straits.

Knowing almost nothing about farming, the Churchills were about to buy a fairly decrepit mediaeval farmhouse with no modern amenities together with a sixty-seven acre mixed farm in a run down state with all the exigencies that the war imposed. It was a recipe for more than a little tribulation.

Endnotes

1 W. Bradfield, conversation with the author, 1 Sept 2005.
2 CSCT 2/7/19–20. WSC to CSC, 31 July 1914.
3 W. Bradfield, personal communication, 10 Jan 2007.
4 CSCT 1/8/4-6. CSC to WSC, 6 July 1914.
5 CSCT 1/8/5–6. WSC to CSC, 15 July 1914.
6 CHAR 1/125/20–22. CSC to WSC, 18 Aug 1918.
7 CSCT 2/7/17. WSC to CSC, 24 July 1914.
8 Churchill, W. S. *The World Crisis*, Vol. 1, p. 197.
9 Churchill, W. S. *The World Crisis*, Vol. 1, p. 198.
10 CSCT 2/7/19–20. WSC to CSC, 31 July 1914.
11 CHAR 1/101/47. Account from S.F. Edge Ltd., 11 Aug 1911.
12 CSCT 1/8/11. CSC to WSC, 8 Aug 1914.
13 C. Lee, personal communication, 19 Sept 2006.
14 Soames, M. *Speaking for Themselves. The Personal letters of Winston and Clementine Churchill*, p. 108.
15 Soames, M. *Speaking for Themselves. The Personal letters of Winston and Clementine Churchill*, p. 654.
16 Soames, M. *Speaking for Themselves. The Personal letters of Winston and Clementine Churchill*, p. 110.
17 M. Edwards, conversation with the author, 3 Sept 2005.
18 M. Richardson, personal communication, 17 Nov 2005.
19 Churchill, J. S. *Crowded Canvas*, p. 31.
20 [Churchill, W. S. *Painting as a Pastime*], cited in Coombs, D. *Sir Winston Churchill's Life through his Paintings*, p. 54.
21 WSP FM 15–1975. Diary 14 Aug 1915.
22 D. Coombs, personal communication, 12 Feb 2006.
23 WSP FM 15–1975. Diary 14 Aug 1915.
24 WSP FM 15–1975. Diary 14 Aug 1915.
25 Goonie Churchill to Jack Churchill, 1 Sept 1914. [Cited in Churchill, P. and Mitchell, J. *Jennie: Lady Randolph Churchill*, p. 250; original not seen].
26 CHAR 1/139/14–15. CSC to WSC, 10 Feb 1921.
27 Churchill, P. and Mitchell, J. *Jennie: Lady Randolph Churchill*, p. 21.

28   CSCT 1/9/7–10. CSC to WSC, 28 Nov 1915.

29   CHAR 1/118A/68–69. CSC to WSC, 13 Feb 1916.

30   Hamilton, I. *Listening for the Drums,* p. 56.

31   WSB FM 320–1977. CSC to Wilfrid Scawen Blunt, Easter Monday [1917/1918?].

32   C. Lee, personal communication, 19 Sept 2006.

33   CSCT 1/8/36. CSC to WSC, 5 June [1914].

CHAPTER 5
ℒULLENDEN

Churchill had so far always placed his faith in the same Estate Agents, a firm called Lofts and Warner whose business had grown from one started in Mount Street by William Warner, the developer who built Churchill's first Mount Street flat and it was Lofts and Warner who let 33 Eccleston Square for him. What brief Churchill gave them in his search for a country house can only be guessed at but in the autumn of 1916 they directed him towards south-east Surrey and a draft contract was drawn up in October for an ancient timber-framed farmhouse called Lullenden near Lingfield. If Churchill had really been motivated in his purchase by the fact that his friends had country houses, it was a quite extraordinary choice. No one he knew owned anything like Lullenden and although Edwin and Venetia Montagu did have a fine red-brick Elizabethan house in Norfolk it was many miles, literally and metaphorically, from this ancient edifice.

Lullenden farmhouse (*c.* 1910).

The house is a low, irregularly shaped and graceful building. There is a 1694 date carved on one of the fireplaces but the property had been considerably altered even then and was undoubtedly much earlier, probably fifteenth or even fourteenth century. It lay 'in a remote and intricate piece of hill country at the point where Sussex, Surrey & Kent meet; the house being in Sussex and the fields the other two counties',[1] and although run more or less as a working farm, it was essentially a hobby for the previous owner who had restored it in 1907; a notable music teacher and professional violinist called Percy Sharman; 'Firm bowing, perfect phrasing, and exquisite tone production characterised his performance…'[2] Sharman had decided to sell mainly because his wife, an asthma sufferer, found the place unhealthy.[3]

On a bright summer's day, Lullenden looked glorious. Now, over a hundred years later, restored and with modern amenities, it is glorious. On a cold wet winter's day in 1916, it was quite extraordinarily depressing. That is not to say the potential was not there. Although altered, it retained many original and beautiful features: a large dining room, another, smaller dining room, a good-sized drawing

Percy Sharman and his wife at the rear of Lullenden (*c.* 1910), the house Churchill bought in 1917.

room and a truly beautiful hall with a crown post and double height ceiling that Sharman used as his music room. There was a study, eleven bedrooms and three bathrooms and in addition, a capacious barn with much potential.

Lullenden, the barn, as restored.

Lullenden, the music room (early 1920s).

Lullenden also had around six acres of garden, fourteen acres of woodland, sixteen of arable land and forty of pasture and rough grazing. The farm offered some reasonable rough shooting for pheasant and partridge. The position was private and secluded, lying down a winding drive and the house was invisible from the nearby lane. There was a small, more recently built one-bedroomed lodge at the entrance, and two cottages. The site was sheltered from the worst of the north and north-west wind and the soil was an acidic clay loam – the locals used to say, with some exaggeration, that it would grow oaks and rhododendrons but not much else. There was however no mains water and no electricity. There were no farm buildings, no hay, no manure, no stock and the fields were overgrown. And as this was still the middle of the war, labour was short and materials scarce or unavailable.

Lullenden garden (1920s).

As usual, Churchill approached the Trustees of Lord Randolph Churchill's estate to fund the purchase and the survey report prepared by Lofts and Warner was good enough to persuade them that the Lullenden lease was worth the asking price of £5,500 – although even then, Churchill was being told by knowing friends that the sum was excessive[4] and he seems to have been circumspect in discussing the real cost. Wilfrid Scawen Blunt for example was told they only paid £4,000.[5]

The purchasing arrangement was that £250 would be paid as a deposit in October, a further £1,750 in December and the balance of the purchase money would remain on mortgage for ten years at 4½ per cent interest. The lease was in Clementine's name although they were jointly responsible for the ground rent. Contracts and conveyances were duly signed and completion was agreed for 8 February 1917. In the following August, Churchill also bought Lullenden Lodge for £1,500 to complete his holding. But there was also a matter that was undoubtedly a novelty to the town house owning Churchills – the tithe. Originally, a tenth part of the produce of agricultural land sold to support the local church, tithes in their final form became tithe rent charges before they were abolished in 1936 but in 1917, they were still a component of a land-owner's outgoings and were archaically linked to the annual price of corn. In the year Churchill purchased Lullenden, he became liable for a tithe of £7 4s 2d.

At the beginning of December 1916, Asquith's ability to hold his government together was faltering and then, with ministers resigning all around him, he too tendered his resignation on 5 December. Although the King invited Bonar Law to form a government, he was unable to do so and the same evening, Lloyd George became Coalition Prime Minister. But Churchill was still out in the cold. There was no sign of the Air Ministry he so badly wanted and with the Conservatives standing firm against any involvement by Churchill, Lloyd George, in his turn, felt unable to offer him a job.

There was nonetheless plenty to occupy him at home as the purchase of Lullenden from Percy Sharman proceeded over the winter. However, although Sharman may have been a fine musician, he and Churchill certainly weren't singing from the same hymn sheet when it came to property negotiations. After completion of the purchase in February, there followed a long-running dispute over who owned a quantity of old oak timber on the property. Churchill wanted it for his planned building works – in due course he converted the old barn into a day nursery – but Sharman claimed it was his. A further dispute related to the ownership of some dog kennels and it was over a year later, in March 1918, that the matter was finally settled, Churchill agreed Sharman owned both the oak and the kennels, paid for some of the timber and bought the rest of his oak elsewhere. Any dogs presumably went homeless.

In March 1917, Churchill arranged for the firm of Elliott Son & Boyton to carry out a survey to look at the potential for developing the garden and for installing a tennis court and in April work was begun on laying a water main. Then, in an attempt to try and make some headway on the land, he employed three German prisoners of war called Nicholas, Bernheim and Rosenburg for four months at 25s a week on drainage work and on 'trenching a field for potatoes'. Bernheim was lean and short, Nicholas was fat and rather jolly while Rosenburg struck the children as positively evil-looking. The nurses were suspicious about them all and when one of the children fell ill, Rosenburg was accused of trying to poison the drinking water, possibly they thought with the intention of murdering Churchill himself.[6] He was therefore removed and as all of them were fairly ineffective and the neighbours objected to Germans being in the village, Churchill abandoned the scheme. He then tried with little success to employ local labour but was only able to muster a gardener, one 'very old and crippled man' named Robert Leigh whom he inherited from Sharman, and two boys; not enough manpower or expertise even to take in a hay crop – the small amount they were able to cut rotted on the ground. He did however buy six bullocks which he put out to graze and they survived.[7]

In the early summer of 1917, Churchill and Lloyd George were drawing closer together and the Prime Minister began taking him increasingly into his confidence. Churchill was entrusted with a personal mission to France to appraise the timing of the new Allied offensive and then, finally, in mid-July, came what he had wanted for so long. He was asked to take over from Christopher Addison as Minister of Munitions. As was customary with a ministerial appointment, he had to offer himself for re-election and at the end of the month was returned by the voters of Dundee with a majority of 5,266 although on a reduced poll. He was at least close to the centre of power, and he had a war department. He spent time in France, offered advice to everyone around him, whether they wanted it or not, and saw the first use – at Cambrai in November – of the tanks he had so strongly championed.

One lovely warm day in September while Churchill was in France, Clementine had a visitor. The aging Wilfrid Scawen Blunt drove over and spent the day with her, lunching in the garden. She told him how happy Churchill was with his home and that he intended to stay there all his life. Blunt found Lullenden a place of enchantment and stole a kiss from Clementine in the barn before he left. But by the following spring, when he learned of her latest pregnancy, the old man was fantasising. He mischievously thought that stolen kiss entitled him to consider Clementine's new baby to be 'in some sort' spiritually his.[8]

Thrilled as Churchill was to be a Minister again, he was also undoubtedly thrilled at finally being a member of the land-owning fraternity and to being, almost, a proper farmer. But whilst he forged ahead politically, the practical realities of his agricultural situation were catching up with him. He did everything possible to try and make some progress on the farm in the first year although in truth he was going from one crisis to another. And there was worse to come. In February 1918, the local Godstone District War Agricultural Committee took it upon themselves to inspect Lullenden.[9] For a man who had done his best, their report made utterly depressing reading and it certainly was not what Churchill needed as a distraction from the pressures of office. They found Lullenden in a very poor and derelict state and said they understood it had been in a very bad condition when Mr Churchill purchased it. Their careful inspection did not reveal any material improvement. The presence of general neglect was in fact increasing. They pointed out that the hedges required trimming and cutting back, the ditches needed clearing, and a number of the fields were full of brambles and thorn bushes...

'The even mead...
Wanting the scythe, all uncorrected, rank,
Conceives by idleness, and nothing teems
But hateful docks, rough thistles, kecksies, burs...'

Churchill, ever the keen theatre goer, must have felt an empathy with the Duke of Burgundy after Agincourt. It was a grim indictment and although Churchill claimed with fair reasoning that the neglect was due to a shortage of labour, the worthies of the Godstone District War Agricultural Committee were unmoved: '...we should have thought that Mr Churchill would have been in a position to obtain all the labour required in the way of German prisoners'.[10]

Then there was more. A week later, another letter arrived, having followed Churchill to Lullenden from Eccleston Square; although not from his own house at No 33 but from No 86 on the opposite side, the offices of the imposingly named Surrey War Agricultural Committee. James Murray, chairman of the said

Lullenden, the fields that Churchill was required to cultivate in 1918.

committee, acting under the powers invested in him by Regulation 2M of the Defence of the Realm (Consolidation) Regulations 1914, Cultivation of Lands Order, 1918 slapped on the Minister's desk a demand that within fourteen days 11.755 acres in two fields at Lullenden be broken up and cultivated properly as arable land with essential food crops.[11]

The Cultivation of Lands legislation stemmed from a campaign for increased food production that the Government had introduced in December 1916 and is of interest to agricultural historians as an early attempt at State control. It used the premise that arable farming could provide food for four times as many people as could be obtained from grass – by raising livestock. Administratively it worked through decentralisation from the Board of Agriculture to local committees – hence the Surrey War Agricultural Committee. The powers were draconian. Where the Committees considered it necessary for increased food production, they could – as at Lullenden – require land to be ploughed or enter the land and plough it themselves. Failure to comply rendered occupiers liable to fines or imprisonment. There was no right of appeal. Churchill was understandably totally frank. 'I am quite willing to have the two fields specified... broken up and cultivated. I have, however, neither labour, horses, nor implements for this purpose, and no knowledge of what should be done'. He said he had been advised it would be better to leave the fields in grass for stock feeding during the summer and then ploughed twice in the autumn as this would help eradicate the infestation of wireworm. He said he would do all that was possible as means allowed and ended on an uncommonly plaintive note. 'I cannot, however, undertake any work of personal supervision as I am scarcely ever able to leave my official work in London as Minister of Munitions'.[12]

Churchill was nonetheless not a man to be cowed by civil servants, regulations or wireworms and he set about his task with renewed vigour. He attempted to obtain more prisoner of war labour but was unsuccessful so turned instead to the British Army. Throughout the war the loss of agricultural workers to the armed forces put a great strain on the country and as a result soldiers stationed in Britain could be used on farms during harvest time. But in May 1916 the army decided that men who were under orders to go overseas or being trained for drafting abroad could no longer undertake this work so the following year, a decision was made to form Agricultural Companies made up of men who would not be fit to serve overseas, the Officers being men who were similarly no longer fit for front line service or were retired. In July of 1917 it was decided that these Companies should have a strength of 500 other ranks and that the Board of Agriculture should decide where the men were to be employed. In December 1917, 694 Company was formed and it was that company who came to Churchill's rescue. Five men, Privates 540820 R. S. Hunt, 154121 W. G. Fielder, 529040 A. B. Ward, 530627 F. J. Morbey and 530640 J. Holt were sent from Guildford at the end of April by command of Capt. Halliwell Hollis to work for Churchill at Lullenden.

With their assistance, things moved on. By July, he had built a cowshed and pigsty, with two more planned, bought ten more bullocks, a horse and cart and two sows. He managed in the second summer to take a small hay crop and build a manure heap. The vegetable garden was enlarged and planted and three quarters of an acre dug and planted with potatoes. He undertook a considerable amount of fencing and other maintenance. He bought a Jersey cow and calf from his farming neighbour Graham Partridge at Gotwick Manor. In total, he spent about £1,000 of his capital towards food production and hoped in the circumstances that the authorities would not insist on the two fields being ploughed up. He said 'The difficulties and expenses entailed upon the owner of a small property without farm buildings, cottages or farm implements in ploughing approximately

15 acres of ground are very formidable; the prospect of a crop doubtful; the prospect of financial loss certain'.[13] Herbert Cooke, Executive Officer of the Surrey Agricultural Executive Committee relented. After he and James Murray had visited the property and noted the improvements, the ploughing notice was withdrawn.

The Lullenden horse and cart were essential, not least for transporting coal and other goods from Lingfield station, but were none too reliable. The horse was an old war horse that had seen service in France and on being driven by Clementine to the railway station one day early in August, took fright on seeing a steam roller. Clementine thought it must have mistaken the machine for a German tank because it charged. 'I do not think she should be decorated, as at this period of the war, courage should be accompanied by judgement' she later wrote.[14] Although the horse was unhurt, the cart was damaged, as was Clementine's knee and she was anxious lest her unborn baby (she was five months pregnant with Marigold) be disturbed from its broodings and 'should come out & see what the matter was'. In the event, all was well.

It seems to have been some time late in 1917 that Churchill took the decision to look for another London home even though they still had a long lease on 33 Eccleston Square. Possibly the house was simply no longer big enough; Clementine referred to it as 'our own little home'.[15] However, now owning Lullenden with its attendant outlays, 33 Eccleston Square really had to be sold before Churchill could contemplate another purchase. Fortunately interest in the property was not long in coming; but from an unexpected quarter.

At its meeting on 9 January 1918, the Executive Committee of the Labour Party had resolved to look for suitable premises to combine administrative accommodation with two separate board rooms and on 13 February, its secretary Arthur Henderson reported that together with Messers Goaling and Bowerman, representing the Parliamentary Committee of the Trades Union Congress, he had 'visited premises in Eccleston Square and strongly recommended that the Party should take up a tenancy provided the Parliamentary Committee and the Trades Union Congress were agreeable'.[16] At the monthly joint meeting of the Parliamentary Committee of the Trades Union Congress and the Executive Committee of the Labour Party at the House of Commons the same afternoon, a committee was set up to report on 33 Eccleston Square and the neighbouring house No 32 which was also available. The reports proved favourable and the 'present tenants' [*sic*] were even willing to sell the Labour Party the carpets in the library and dining room for £50.[17] The Committee agreed to this with alacrity. But there was a last minute hitch. The Labour Party nominated Arthur Henderson as their proposed assignee of the lease with Ramsay Macdonald joining him if necessary. Churchill was advised by his solicitors that it was 'desirable to have men of substance' and said that Arthur Henderson alone would be perfectly acceptable[18] but the solicitors for Churchill's landlord, a Mr Steward, who held the lease, were unhappy with Arthur Henderson's references, and they weren't particularly keen about the use of the house as political offices. Churchill was not at all pleased. 'It would be most unfortunate if, after having incurred heavy expense in vacating my house and fitting it up for occupation by the new tenants, any impediment were to arise' he wrote.[19] In the event, the Duke of Westminster as owner of the freehold raised no objection so the argument was over-ridden and in late May the Labour Party paid Churchill £2,350 for the lease and £50 for his carpets.

Churchill was then living at the Ministry of Munitions and each weekend when he was not in France he took his work to Lullenden but there is some mystery about exactly where in London he lodged. The Ministry had its headquarters and several departments in Whitehall Place but also occupied buildings at 28 Northumberland Avenue, 6 Whitehall Gardens, 17 Cockspur Street and elsewhere in and around Westminster. It seems likely that Churchill stayed in one of a terrace of Georgian houses that formerly existed adjacent to the Munitions Ministry with their frontages on Whitehall Place and their gardens on Great Scotland Yard.[20] Sir Robert Peel had lived in one of these houses and could walk through his garden to a building which was the first Metropolitan Police Headquarters. The Georgian terrace was badly damaged in World War II and an extension to the Ministry building – by then the Ministry of Agriculture, Fisheries and Food – was built in their place. Because of the absence of a London home in 1918 for Clementine and the children however, they first borrowed the Horner's town house in a Georgian terrace at 16 Lower Berkeley Street (now Fitzhardinge Street) and then the wider family as usual came to the rescue and Churchill's Aunt Cornelia (Lady Cornelia Spencer-Churchill, the widow of Sir Ivor Bertie Guest) loaned them her London house 3 Tenterden Street (since demolished), just off Oxford Street and close to Oxford Circus.

In the summer of 1918, things were certainly looking up at Lullenden.

No 16 Lower Berkeley Street (now Fitzhardinge Street), the Horners' London house which the Churchills borrowed in summer 1918.

Churchill contemplated purchasing the lease of the farm and Lullenden Lodge from his father's Trustees but changed his mind although the farm was gradually starting to look and function like one. More horses arrived as 'remounts' from No 2 Remount Department, Woolwich, a department that arranged for surplus army horses to be loaned to farmers although Churchill didn't fare too well, acquiring a mare called Maggie who was too light for farm work and a stallion called Duke with a farcy leg. A new cow and calf arrived from Sunny Marlborough at Blenheim but despite the best endeavours of Holden, the local cowman, she didn't take kindly to being milked and Clementine was brought face to face with some of the realities of farming. She was concerned that the cow suffered great physical pain when she was milked. 'This is all becos' this is her first experience of marriage & child bearing under the heel of man!... Farming is really a very brutal occupation. One is always killing some animal or mating it without consulting its inclination, or separating it from its child, or putting a ring in its nose, or clipping its wing...'[21]

Churchill was spending a great deal of time in France and on the afternoon of Thursday 8 August, flew there with the intention of watching the new British offensive in which it was anticipated a significant role would be played by his tanks. When he wrote to Clementine two days later from the Chateau Verchoq near St Omer, which the Commander in Chief of the British Forces, Douglas Haig had provided as his base, he told her their flight had taken them close to Lullenden.[22] But Clementine was not at home to offer a wave. On the Friday, she had embarked on a rather circuitous tour to see friends and in the evening arrived to stay with Goonie in Sutton Courtenay in Berkshire, and found her in 'a dreamy haven of peace lapped by the waters of the Thames'. She was 'leading a quiet hammock life, visited & courted by all those who visit The Wharf & the Manor House.'[23] Clementine's letter was addressed from 'Brookside' but I have been unable to identify a house of this name. The word Brookside appears on old maps of the western end of Sutton Courtenay, close to Ginge Brook, but there is no trace of a building, either on the map or in reality. The area is however only a few hundred yards from The Wharf but on this occasion, Clementine found Sutton Courtenay unusually quiet. The Asquiths were away at Archerfield and the blinds were drawn on The Wharf while the Manor House was let. She planned to come back in September when life had returned.

On the Monday Clementine drove on to Somerset to stay with her friend Frances, Lady Horner at her beautiful home, Mells Manor, near Frome. The Horner family had owned land in the area since the sixteenth century and Mells Manor was built on the foundations of the old monastic ruins following the dissolution. It was and is essentially an Elizabethan house. Originally H-shaped, it is now half its former self as in the early eighteenth century, one of the Horner family married into money and built a new house nearby in Mells Park, pulling down the North wing of the Manor for its stone. This apparent act of vandalism was however put pragmatically into context by Lady Horner's grandson, Julian,

Mells Manor, Somerset (mid 20th century), the home of Frances, Lady Horner.

Mells Manor gardens.

the late Second Earl of Oxford and Asquith, when he showed me with some satisfaction how it had opened up a magnificent view of the adjoining St Andrew's Church. The Horners' other house at Mells Park was badly burned in 1917 and Frances Horner showed Clementine the ruins which reminded her she said of the palaces at Messina after the 1908 earthquake.[24]

In 1895, Frances and her husband Sir John Horner, newly appointed Commissioner of Forests and Woods, were in need of a London home and came into contact with Edwin Lutyens. The route was circuitous but inevitable – Frances Horner's sister Agnes, an old friend of Lady Randolph Churchill, was married to Herbert Jekyll, brother of Gertrude Jekyll, Lutyens' gardening friend. So it was that Lutyens was invited to Mells in October 1896 to see if he could assist the Horners – which in due course he did. They bought a London house at 9 Buckingham Gate where Lutyens helped Frances Horner change and improve the rooms.[25]

Frances Horner's mother died in 1900 and the family decided to let Mells Park and move back to the Manor House: more intimate, more friendly and more manageable. Lutyens was invited to make some alterations to the house and some minor changes to the garden. It was the first of many marks he was to make on the local community and the entire village is now imbued with a Lutyens aura – several monuments, including the village war memorial are his, as is a rather claustrophobic double avenue of Irish yews in the churchyard.

The approach to Mells Manor in 1918, along a short curving drive, was past a beautiful planting of pleached limes, now grossly overgrown. Then as now, it promised much and although Clementine had been there previously, she had forgotten the charm and beauty of the place and this visit whetted even more her wish for a home and garden of comparable tranquillity, one that perhaps could be metamorphosed from the run-down grounds of Lullenden.

Mells has a garden of around four acres, on a free-draining chalky soil, exposed but benefiting from intimate walled enclosures, and it was the closest of these, on the South side of the house, that particularly entranced Clementine with its central sundial and three warm pink brick walls. In the nineteen twenties, Lutyens transformed an old covered veranda to create an extension to the Manor which now forms a happy continuation of the northern boundary of this garden. But in 1918, the veranda was still there and the delicious fragrance of stocks, nicotianas, lavender and roses drifted into the house on the warm

August evening when Clementine arrived. She was captivated and the following day wrote a eulogy to Churchill while the impressions were fresh in her mind. Two days later, she wrote again: 'This is a delicious place where in to rest and dream & I feel my new little baby likes it – Full of comfort, beautiful things, sweet smelling flowers, peaches ripening on old walls, gentle flittings & hummings & pretty grandchildren'.[26]

Clementine was also much taken at Mells Manor with the latest '*en-tous-cas*' all-weather tennis court and the 70 by 30 feet open air swimming pool surrounded by roses and purple clematis but importantly, she noticed, sited well away from trees which would shed their leaves and spoil the limpid water. She filed away such practical touches in her mind and thought that when they were rich it was something they might have at the bottom of the hill at Lullenden where the stream could run through it. Little could she know then how water running both in and out of garden pools was to dominate her life, though not at Lullenden, nor indeed when they were rich, but in the financially constrained times at Chartwell, not so many years distant.

But Mells was not all fragrances, tennis and limpid swimming pools. Clementine took advantage of a visit to the home farm and its Jersey herd to pick up tips for her new role as a farmer's wife. She learned the intimacies of bull keeping – that you only keep a bull for two years and must then sell him because, 'of course, a bull must not marry his own daughters'.[27] The investment however could be rewarding and she wrote to Churchill that the Horner's own private bull, 'very good looking with a curly fringe' had cost only 3 guineas at three days old but was by then worth perhaps £100. Her husband's pulse must have quickened, and no doubt he too stored up the information for future use by his alter ego, the gentleman farmer.

Although Clementine wrote to Churchill about Mells Manor in a tenor that suggested he was unfamiliar with the place, this was evidently not the case. There is a puzzle about when and how often he was there but at least one occasion is known. It is referred to in Frances Horner's autobiography where she describes him staying with them in Somerset for a few days in June 1911[28] although her memory played her false and the visit actually took place in the middle of August. Clementine was on holiday in Bavaria with her cousin Venetia Stanley where they were joined by Jack and Goonie. Churchill himself had intended going but duties were too pressing and instead he went alone to Somerset for a few days and later recalled that he could think of nothing else but the peril of war. Sitting on a hilltop in 'the smiling country which stretches around Mells', his head was filled with A. E. Housman's lines from *The Shropshire Lad*:[29]

'*On the idle hill of summer,*
Sleepy with the sound of streams,
Far I hear the steady drummer,
Drumming like a noise in dreams.

Far and near and low and louder,
On the roads of earth go by,
Dear to friends and food or powder,
Soldiers marching, all to die.'

Mells, however, was before long to be seared in Churchill's memory for a quite different reason. It was while staying with Lady Horner at Mells on 29 May 1921 that his mother slipped as she descended the irregular old stairs, a fall that resulted in her left leg being broken, leading to gangrene, amputation and her death a month later.

Churchill may moreover have been to Mells Park during its later occupancy by Reginald McKenna. McKenna, married to Sir Herbert Jekyll's younger daughter Pamela, and often at loggerheads with Churchill in Government, preceded him as First Lord of the Admiralty and so his family preceded the Churchills as occupants of Admiralty House. The McKennas took a fifteen year lease on the ruined Park House at a nominal rent from Sir John Horner in 1924 on the condition that they would rebuild it.[30] Under McKenna's instruction, Lutyens produced a massive, four-square and extremely severe design, essentially the house that is there today. He also produced a similarly massive four square monument beneath which Reginald McKenna now lies in Mells churchyard.

Endnotes

[1]   WSB FM 436-1975. Diary 16 Sept 1917.

[2]   *Yorkshire Herald*, 11 April, 1902.

[3]   CHAR 1/133/7-10. WSC to Ian Hamilton, 24 May 1919.

[4]   HP Ian Hamilton to [?] Wood, 15 Nov 1923.

[5]   WSB FM 436–1975, 16 Sept 1917.

[6]   Churchill, J. S. *Crowded Canvas*, p. 36.

[7]   CHAR 1/131/35–37. WSC to Surrey War Agricultural Committee, 15 Mar 1918.

[8]   WSB FM 436–1975. Diary 12 May 1918.

[9]   CHAR 1/131/16. Report by Godstone District War Agricultural Committee, 27 Feb 1918.

[10] CHAR 1/131/16. Report by Godstone District War Agricultural Committee, 27 Feb 1918.

[11] CHAR 1/131/25–29. Surrey War Agricultural Committee to WSC, 13 Mar 1918.

[12] CHAR 1/131/21–24. WSC to Surrey War Agricultural Committee, 11 Mar 1918.

[13] CHAR 1/131/73–76. WSC to Surrey War Agricultural Committee, 17 July 1918.

[14] CHAR 1/125/16–19. CSC to WSC, 15 Aug 1918.

[15] WSB FM 320-1977. CSC to Wilfrid Scawen Blunt, no date.

[16] LP Executive Committee Minutes, 13 Feb 1918.

[17] LP Executive Committee Minutes, 10 April 1918.

[18] CHAR 1/130/29. Lumley & Lumley to WSC, 8 Apr 1918.

[19] CHAR 1/130/48-49. WSC to Lumley & Lumley, 19 May 1918.

[20] N. Cooke, personal communication, 7 Nov 2006.

[21] CHAR 1/125/20-22. CSC to WSC, 18 Aug 1918.

[22] CSCT 2/8-2/12. WSC to CSC, 10 Aug 1918.

[23] CHAR 1/125/6-10. CSC to WSC, 11 Aug 1918.

[24] CHAR 1/125/11-15. CSC to WSC, 13 Aug 1918.

[25] Horner, F. *Time Remembered*, p. 202.

[26] CHAR 1/125/16–19. CSC to WSC, 15 Aug 1918.

[27] CHAR 1/125/11—15. CSC to WSC, 13 Aug 1918.

[28] Horner, F. *Time Remembered*, p. 102.

[29] Churchill, W. S. *The World Crisis*, Vol. 1, p. 65.

[30] Brown, J. *Lutyens and the Edwardians*, p. 156.

CHAPTER 6
ℋOUSE HUNTING

By late summer 1918, as work at Lullenden progressed, furniture was still being moved down from Eccleston Square, having been stored at various London addresses. During the summer, while Churchill had been living at the Ministry of Munitions, Clementine spent more time on the farm with the children who loved it there. Randolph Churchill has written of playing a game of 'bear' in the garden in which his father hid in a tree while the children searched for him; a zoological variant of the 'gorillas' at Hoe Farm. Goonie too moved down with Johnny and Peregrine and all the elder children went by pony and trap to school in Dormansland, the nearby village – Churchill once said he thought children should be collected and carried to school to escape the danger of the road and what he called 'the motor car tyranny'.[1] At Lullenden, however, the children were also safe from the Zeppelin air raids in London. The first Zeppelin raid,

Dormansland School, near Lullenden (1922) which the Churchill children attended.

on the East Coast, had been in January 1915 – not far from Overstrand – and then, from May onwards, Zeppelins attacked London and other targets about twice a month. From 1917, they were gradually replaced by heavy bombers and the last air-ship raid was on 5 August 1918, by which time they had taken part in about fifteen raids on London and around forty elsewhere, and killed over 500 civilians. In World War II, Clementine was adamant that the Churchill family should sit out the hardship with the rest of the population and she vetoed Sally Churchill, Winston's great-niece, being evacuated to Canada. In 1918 however, when air raids were still a terrifying novelty, she had no compunction about moving the family out of London.

Clementine began entertaining and giving dinner parties, her cousin Madeleine Whyte moved down for a month and rented a cottage from Graham Partridge their farming neighbour at the bottom of the hill. But what she wanted above all was her garden. She wanted roses. Despite having at last found her a country home, Churchill however felt unable in wartime to devote labour and money to any gardening other than vegetable growing. His paintings of the garden at Lullenden reveal a few poppies and other apparently self-sown flowers although nothing planned or organised. But at least a gesture could made towards something ornamental and Clementine asked Churchill to take her to Cheals' nursery at Lowfield Heath two miles north of Crawley, about ten miles away where she wanted to buy some small rock plants to fill the cracks and crevices. The family firm of Cheals was a long established retailing business that moved into horticulture in the mid nineteenth and set up a plant nursery in 1871. By 1918 it was vast, and had an almost unrivalled reputation. It was also ideally placed to serve the head gardeners of the notable houses of the area and beyond. Trees and shrubs were always their strength although alpines and other hardy plants were well represented and they owned their own quarry near Haslemere to supply stone for building rock gardens. Throughout the Edwardian period they designed and created gardens at many properties but none finer and more spectacular than that at Hever Castle for Waldorf Astor which the Churchills knew well. Although Clementine knew her alpines could not be planted until the autumn, she hoped to see them in bloom first so she could gauge the overall effect.[2] It may have been the first time she had ever been to a plant nursery – at least with the intention of buying anything. It was certainly the first time she had anywhere to put them.

Hever Castle, (mid 20th century), Waldorf Astor's house.

By the autumn of 1918, more prisoner of war labour (the Huns as Clementine called them) had been organised and despite the neighbours' lack of enthusiasm, they were set to work on fencing although unlike the British soldiers, they could not of course be left unsupervised. Then, with the Armistice in November came major changes in the family's life. On 15 November, just four days after the Peace was signed, their fourth child Marigold was born at 3 Tenterden Street; she was to be called the Duckadilly by her parents in the best traditions of Churchillian pet-names.

Immediately after the Armistice, Lloyd George opted to dissolve Parliament and call a General Election, the first since 1910. Churchill had to absent himself from his wife and new daughter to campaign vigorously in Dundee and when the results of the poll were announced at the end of December (delayed to allow soldiers' votes to be included) the Coalition was triumphant. Churchill himself was re-elected with a massive majority. Lloyd George offered him the choice of the Admiralty or the War Office. As a long-time champion of the role of aircraft, he accepted the latter as Secretary of State for War and Air – but one without a proper London home because after renting 16 Lower Berkeley Street and 3 Tenterden Street in the autumn, organising a London base was proving a tricky matter. Clementine had thought she had it all planned. She and Winston with Marigold, Sarah, Diana and Randolph would spent Christmas at Lullenden together with Goonie and her two boys. Then, in the New Year, Goonie and her family would return to Lady Blanche Hozier's house at 41 Bloomfield Terrace

No 41 Bloomfield Terrace, Lady Blanche Hozier's London house.

while she and Winston would rent her sister Nellie Romilly's little red brick house round the corner at 15 Pimlico Road for two or three months, leaving the family at Lullenden with the nurses and visiting them at weekends. She even decided what rent they would pay – four guineas a week seemed about right.[3]

No 15 Pimlico Road, Nellie Romilly's London house.

Nellie however had other ideas and the carefully laid plan did not materialise. Churchill had to act quickly and settled on renting 1 Dean Trench Street, a small but neat corner house just off Smith Square and within striding distance of the Houses of Parliament. There seem two possible ways in which Churchill may have known of the property. It could, as usual, have been a family connection. The owner of the house was the Hon Victoria Adeane, the widow of Captain Henry Robert Augustus Adeane who was killed in action with the Coldstream Guards in 1914. He was a descendant of the 1st Baron Stanley of Alderley and therefore a distant cousin of Clementine. Victoria Adeane, who also lost her only brother

No 1 Dean Trench Street (as rebuilt after World War II), which the Churchills rented in 1918.

in action in 1915, was then spending most of her time living with her father and the house was therefore empty and available.[4] It is also possible however that the father may have been Churchill's contact as they were well acquainted: Arthur John Bigge, the 1st Lord Stamfordham, was Private Secretary to the King, having earlier been Private Secretary to Queen Victoria.

Back at the Lullenden ranch, staffing at all levels was a continuing headache and in January 1919, it became apparent that old Robert Leigh was too infirm to continue. Churchill had always taken great care of his employees (he was still paying an allowance to the mother of his servant George Scrivings who died in Africa in 1907) and so he approached Leigh's original employer Percy Sharman with a view to sharing with him the payment of a pension until he became eligible for a state pension in six years time. The old age pension had been introduced for those aged seventy and over by Asquith's government – and announced by Churchill himself – in 1908 and the qualification age was not reduced to sixty-five until twenty years later. Churchill and Sharman reached an agreement by which they would each pay half – 3s 9d a week.

In March, a successor to Leigh was found and he breezed into Lullenden like a white tornado. His name was Jeffrey and he came with a considerable family, some of whom also gained employment on the land or in the house. Clementine appointed him, subject to Churchill's endorsement, as gardener/bailiff and then stood back as he leapt into action, first moving the greenhouse, then shifting the whole garden, then taking on three labourers for three months to motor-plough two of the most unkempt fields before sowing them with corn. He was an accomplished carpenter, knew how to concrete, demanded an electric engine to saw wood, made decisions and seemed very knowledgeable. Clementine took the view that he would either make or break Lullenden and that if they did have to sell, they could pass on 'this tyrant' with it.[5]

A start was made on the construction of Clementine's longed for all weather *en-tous-cas* tennis court, like the one she had admired at Mells. However, apart from her rock plants which she had been allowed to squeeze in to the crevices, the garden was still not much more than a vegetable patch and it was beginning to dawn on them both that, in buying Lullenden – and Jeffrey notwithstanding – they had bitten off more than they had time and resources to handle. The property was costing Churchill £350 a year plus £40 for water and £60 in taxes; and he was responsible for four employees. To compound matters, commitments in London meant he and Clementine were rarely able to be there – they had owned Lullenden for over six months before Clementine stayed for more than a weekend. They just were not getting value for money. The possibility of disposing of it began seriously to be discussed. Then, by thoughtful planning or serendipity they invited Sir Ian Hamilton and his wife for lunch on Sunday 16 March having already intimated to them that they were thinking of selling.

Sir Ian Hamilton's career had effectively come to an end after Gallipoli – he was given no more military responsibilities and was appointed lieutenant of the Tower of London in 1918 and created GCMG the following year. He had been a brilliant and brave soldier but ultimately 'He lacked mental

Sir Ian and Lady Hamilton.

toughness, basic common sense, and sufficient ruthlessness to dismiss an incompetent subordinate... and he underestimated the enemy...'[6] Despite this sad end to a fine career, he evidently retained much charm and good humour and few men emerge so personably from their letters. His wife Jean was the daughter of a successful Glasgow business man and extremely wealthy but although Churchill and Hamilton were long-standing and close friends, and Clementine liked the old General, the two wives never really hit it off; and Jean Hamilton was ambivalent about Churchill. 'We know we don't like each other' she once confided to her diary, adding that Churchill always had a hostile schoolboy manner with her. 'I try to be myself and talk to him – he does not try and is himself, which is generally very rude but sometimes disarmingly naïve and simple'.[7] In truth, Jean Hamilton had a general antipathy towards all the Churchills. She felt sorry for Goonie, 'exquisite Goony' [sic] for marrying Jack but thought it 'would be awful, utterly unthinkable to be married to either of these two Churchills, though of the two men I would prefer Jack to live with, though Winston's career would be a compensation...'[8]

On that chill March day in 1919, she was dreading the lunch. She was cold when they arrived, having driven down from London in their open car and found Churchill difficult. She feared the meal would be impossible. But at least the white dining room was happy and delicious 'with the lovely boy, Randolph, sitting at the head of the table with his governess'. She thought Lullenden messy, full of clay and mud and with an untidy garage and outhouses but nonetheless she could see the potential and particularly liked the rocks and little pool at the side of the house. There was clearly much to ponder on the drive back to their London home in Hyde Park Gardens.[9]

The Hamiltons had been looking at another property, a large house in Essex called Coopersale which unlike Lullenden, already had a beautiful garden. Jean Hamilton had fallen in love with it but a few days before the Lullenden lunch had learned that the religious order who owned it had decided after all not to sell immediately (it was in fact sold the following year). Lullenden was worthy of serious consideration therefore and the following week, Hamilton wrote offering to rent the house for a year. Churchill felt that three years should be the minimum. He would charge about £500 a year rent with no additional burden or responsibilities and Hamilton as tenant could buy all he wanted of the vegetables, poultry, dairy products and wood fuel with Churchill taking the surplus. Churchill would also take care of all the tenant's carting and coal at the usual rates and spend £50 a year on the flower garden, including the replanting of the herbaceous border, something he had never offered to Clementine.[10] But what Churchill really needed was a sale. Hamilton told his wife he was frightened about the commitment to buy outright and really did only want to take it for a year. They were invited down again for a few days in mid-April to consider things further. Clementine unfortunately was confined to London with flu so Jean Hamilton had undiluted Churchill to cope with. This was the great post-war flu epidemic that was sweeping Europe but at least the children were there with their nurses, although all of them, Marigold, Sarah, Diana, Randolph and the servants had it and were suffering in the barn. Only a few days previously, and unbeknown to the children, Isabelle, the Churchills' much loved Scottish nurse had died of flu and Churchill had had to move temporarily out of the Dean Trench Street house while it was disinfected. And it poured with rain and the roads were flooded. It was hardly a jolly stay. But against all the odds, Lullenden was growing on Jean Hamilton. 'I love it,' she wrote, ' and want it for my own, and would like to plunge and buy it and set to work at once to fashion one or two things more after my heart's desire… it's the sort of romantic place I long to have – it's a snuggy place with rocks, pools, trees and streams such as my childish soul loved, and still loves – unluckily it's clay soil, very damp, cold, chill clay soil all around, though the house is dry and smells dry'.[11]

At home in London, the Hamiltons could think of little else except Lullenden and over dinner one evening, Sir Ian, no doubt now with some urging and without giving too much thought to what he was saying, told his wife he would buy it outright and pay Churchill £10,000 if he would include all the livestock.

Then, no doubt after slightly more reflection, he said he would pay what Churchill himself had paid plus the expenses he had subsequently incurred. Jean Hamilton took him at his word although by the time the contents and stock had been valued and added in, the negotiated price came to £9,800, a figure that Lady Hamilton unfortunately failed to convey to her husband. Four years later, Hamilton was still unaware of this and admitted he was 'rather shocked' when the facts were brought to his attention by the District Valuer. 'The purchase of Lullenden by my Wife from Mr Winston Churchill was entirely unbusinesslike and had no relation to any real value' he wrote. 'Mr and Mrs Winston Churchill are among our oldest and most valued personal friends. I wanted a place in the country and I heard they were desperately anxious to get rid of theirs as quickly as might be Mr Churchill then informed me that he had bought Lullenden for £5,000 although he had been blamed by his friends who thought it greatly in excess of its value. Still, he took a fancy for it and paid what was a fancy price even during boom times. Had Lullenden belonged to anyone else but Mr Churchill or some of the two or three equally great friends I have, I would have waited for the auction and bought it, very likely, for £3,000.'[12] Hamilton could only conclude that Churchill had incurred far more expense than he imagined in turning the old pasture into poor quality plough land. 'I remember also,' he wrote, 'that there was a very heavy items [*sic*] for wages of German prisoners who were employed on these very expensive agricultural activities by Mr Churchill, whose ideas on the culture of potatoes and wheat were somewhat original.'[13]

The Hamilton's offer really did provoke some serious thinking and on balance the Churchills felt they should probably accept but nonetheless kept them waiting. There had also been some interest in a possible purchase from a couple named Vogt so Clementine – as owner of the lease – wrote a letter in early May accepting the Hamilton's proposal although she could not immediately bring herself to post it and kept it in her private box at Dean Trench Street while they thought further. Then her antennae picked up a rumour. She heard that Jean Hamilton had gained an impression that they intended to stay at Lullenden after all and so the Hamiltons were looking at an alternative house. She used her initiative and took the plunge, 'cutting the Golden Knot' as she put it, and sending Ian Hamilton 'the fateful letter'. 'He who hesitates is lost but he who goes on hesitating loses both Vogts and Hamiltons' she wrote to Churchill.[14] The deal was done, Clementine selling her lease to Jean Hamilton although initially agreeing to keep it a secret lest Lady Hamilton's mother, living alone in Scotland, gained the impression she might never see them again. 'Our pleasure at the idea of possessing Lullenden is very much tempered by our regret that you should have to leave it' wrote Hamilton, blissfully unaware of what it had cost him. 'I simply hate the idea that you should lose this pleasure and Diana and Randolph I am afraid, will never forgive us.'[15] The Hamiltons were back at Lullenden in the pouring rain for Sunday lunch on 20 July with Violet and Maurice Bonham-Carter and Sir Ernest Cassel. Jack Churchill drove them down from London and Jean Hamilton was in a more charitable mood. Jack she thought was 'a comfy creature' and 'the great Winston' that day was charming. Lady Hamilton even felt sorry for him as he so obviously loved Lullenden but had been forced to sell for want of money.[16]

The Churchills' belongings being moved out through the front porch, Lullenden.
The painting is the Sir John Lavery portrait of Churchill in uniform now at Chartwell.
(November 1919; annotated photograph pasted in Lady Hamilton's diary).

As the Lullenden adventure seemed to be drawing to a close, the matter of finding another town house became ever more critical. It was well over a year since the Churchills had completed the sale of the lease of 33 Eccleston Square and since Clementine had tried, in vain, to interest Churchill in an old vicarage on the corner of Buckingham Palace Road and Pimlico Road. The vicar of St Michael's had found it a bit big and was thinking of moving. Clementine persuasively described it as two-storied but it was a vast rambling pile on three floors and unsurprisingly there was the customary lack of response from her husband.[17] It was eventually demolished in 1932 to give way to a block of flats.

St Michael's Vicarage, Buckingham Palace Road (shortly before demolition, 1932) and which Clementine tried to interest Churchill in buying in 1919.

Renting was clearly no long term solution. Accommodating four children, domestic staff and wanting space for the social and political entertaining that went with Churchill's position as Minister of Munitions meant the pressure to find somewhere was becoming irresistible. However, although the war was over, the European political stage continued to be played and through that summer Churchill had been watching with growing anxiety the fluctuating fortunes of the anti-Bolshevik forces in Russia whose cause he had strongly espoused. It was a climate in which domestic mistakes could be made.

Around late July 1919, Churchill was introduced to two adjoining properties in Mayfair with leases owned by Lord Gerald Wellesley, the future 7th Duke of Wellington. No 2 Hyde Park Street is a truly huge early Victorian house on four floors in a superb position on the north side of Bayswater Road with remarkable views across Hyde Park. It is merely a few strides away and in a similar position to his father's old house and his childhood home at 2 Connaught Place where he had such fond memories of old Mrs Everest. Perhaps that was

No 2 Hyde Park Street which Winston bought in 1919; and immediately regretted.

the attraction. Tucked away at the back was Albion Mews West and the lease to No 1 was included. The asking price was ridiculously low and Churchill should immediately have been suspicious. But he wasn't and with his other distractions he clearly had not appreciated the importance of having surveys completed before any binding undertaken was given. He had got away with it at Bolton Street and although he had fairly comprehensive surveys carried out before purchasing Eccleston Square, this time he made a serious misjudgement. Through his solicitors Nicholl, Manisty & Co. he made an offer of £2,300 for the leases. He failed to make it clear moreover that it was the Trustees of his father's estate rather then him personally who were the intending purchasers. When the Trustees on their part arranged for a surveyor's report, it revealed the Hyde Park Street house and the Mews to be in a pretty parlous state. Churchill suddenly realised the properties involved far more expense than he could afford so early in August, his lawyers wrote again to Lord Gerald's solicitors, saying their client could not proceed and offering to reimburse any costs involved. It was not well received. Wellesley was surprised to discover that Churchill himself had not been the intended purchaser; and the offer to reimburse him 'did not commend itself'.[18] His solicitors wrote on 15 August to say he was not 'disposed to abandon the contract' and if Churchill did not complete the purchase in a reasonable time, he would take steps to enforce his rights. The following day, Churchill and Clementine left for a five day visit to the British Army on the Rhine but in a foretaste of other disputes involving his properties over the years, Churchill left instructions to obtain legal opinion. On his return he was informed that his Counsel Bryan Farrer of Lincoln's Inn thought that although the point was legally difficult, Churchill was probably correct in that there was no enforceable contract. But there was, as so often in the Law, no certainty.

Churchill drafted a letter to Lycett, Jepson & Co, Wellesley's solicitors expressing great regret that Lord Gerald should have thought he was trying to 'get out of a contract which although possibly not enforceable at law, Lord Gerald certainly considers binding in equity'. He believed the contract was open until signed and said it was the poor state of the property that compelled him to withdraw 'for financial reasons'. He regretted that 'owing to the stress of public affairs' he had not made this clear. The references to his finances and the pressure of public affairs were removed from the version sent but he did nonetheless confirm that legal opinion notwithstanding, he would remain true to his word and complete the contract.[19] The pressures on a man who only that week had been monitoring the movements of mighty armies clearly did not move the future Duke to any sort of compassion and a contract was drawn up for completion of the sale on Christmas Day. Lord Gerald did however obligingly agree to some work being undertaken at the property in the meantime, to Churchill re-advertising it before completion and indeed to deferring the execution of the Deed of Assignment until a new owner was found, thus potentially saving Churchill the £23 Stamp Duty.

Then, right in the middle of the wrangling about Hyde Park Street, with no certainty over the outcome and with Lullenden still not sold, Churchill alerted Sir Howard Frank to his interest in buying another farm. He was sent particulars of one in Buckinghamshire. Churchill looked at it but it did not appeal. He then told Frank that while he was motoring through Kent, he had been impressed with the beauty of the country around Maidstone and, no doubt thinking back to the glorious picture his old nurse Mrs

The estate agent Sir Howard Frank who introduced Churchill to Chartwell.

Everest had painted of a land flowing with strawberries, cherries, raspberries and plums ('I always wanted to live in Kent'), wondered if there were any fruit farms on the market. One of five or six hundred acres he said would interest him very much.[20] Whether Clementine ever knew anything of this is not clear but she would surely have been mightily relieved that nothing turned up. Although her husband seemed to have become wedded to the idea of living in Kent, the search for another country property would in practice take him two years and it would be longer still before they experimented again with serious farming.

There was some hope that Hyde Park Street might be off Churchill's hands before Christmas as serious interest was shown by Sir Lewis McIver the former MP for Edinburgh West but it came to nothing. Things were now becoming distinctly fraught moreover because in early October, Churchill had found and agreed to purchase a smaller town house a few minutes walk away: 2 Sussex Square, with two mews properties at the rear, Nos 7 and 11 Sussex Mews East. Fortunately, financial help was at hand from Churchill's old friend, the financier and philanthropist Sir Ernest Cassel who purchased the lease of Hyde Park Street from him for £2,300 in early January. This was evidently a temporary

Modern house on the site of No 2 Sussex Square, which Churchill bought in 1919.

arrangement to provide Churchill with some cash as he continued to search for a long-term buyer for the house.

The new property, 2 Sussex Square, a rather elegant early Victorian house, where Mary Churchill was born is the only one of the properties owned by Churchill to have vanished. But that was in the future and in 1919, a new London home had at last been found, although the Churchills were to be saddled with two town houses for rather longer than they hoped – and yet another legal dispute was only a year or so away. The lease on 2 Sussex Square was owned by an architect, Frederick Foster of Wyndham Place, not far away in Marylebone, and in retrospect somewhat unwisely, Churchill engaged him to supervise the necessary improvements. Foster was one of a number

Sussex Square (1930s). Shows part of No 1 (on left); no picture of No 2 survives.

of people with whom Churchill had to conduct business who felt obliged regularly to complain how hard done by he was; and how fortunate Churchill was to have his services. No sooner had the purchase price been agreed than Foster was telling him he had already received a much better offer.

The Trustees of Lord Randolph Churchill's estate purchased 2 Sussex Square on Churchill's behalf for £4,750 – the price to include an extension of the lease, some fixtures and fittings and five tons of coal – and agreed to increase their expenditure to £7,000 to cover the necessary works. They required improvements to be made to the kitchen and a new bathroom to be installed and although Churchill's tenancy began on 11 November and some furniture was stored there (thus to his regret committing him to House Duty charges), the transfer of the lease wasn't completed for another two months and the family could not move in until mid-February 1920.

By this time, another potential purchaser for Hyde Park Street had emerged in the shape of a Mr Davis who wanted to pull the house down and build 'superior flats such as are in extraordinary demand at the present time'. Churchill was most enthusiatic. The Church Commissioners who owned the freehold were not and to Churchill's enormous disappointment and frustration, they turned down the proposal on the 'most cursory examination'. He protested at length but it got him nowhere and it wasn't until early May 1920 that another old friend came to the rescue when the lease was finally sold to his neighbour at Lullenden, Lt.-Colonel Herbert 'Bertie' Spender-Clay who went on to live in Hyde Park Street until his death in 1937. He and Churchill were near contemporaries who had studied together at Sandhurst and, as young officer cadets, they had spent weekends at Lingfield races and at the Spender-Clay country seat of Ford Manor which abuts the Lullenden land.

Ford Manor, south front (c. 1910), the home of Churchill's friend Bertie Spender-Clay.

Both had also served in South Africa in 1899-1900 and it is quite possible it was Spender-Clay who initially drew Churchill's attention to Lullenden. It is difficult however to imagine a greater contrast between their two houses. Ford Manor is a monstrous mid-Victorian creation, sprouting turrets everywhere – 'Formidable,' said Pevsner, 'a rock-hard stone pile… making no concessions to the landscape or anything else…'[21] In 1904, Spender-Clay had married the Hon. Pauline Astor, Nancy Astor's sister-in-law; and the subject of the most striking of John Singer Sargent's full-length portraits. Later, their daughter Rachel married into the Bowes-Lyon family to become the Queen Mother's sister-in-law.

As the summer of 1919 eased into autumn, the sale of Lullenden seemed to be progressing satisfactorily and completion was set for 30 September. Then two weeks before the agreed date, Clementine dropped what Jean Hamilton called 'a bombshell'. Would the Hamiltons mind waiting until 1 November because the Churchills had nowhere else to go? They were of course maintaining their pattern of having either too many houses or none. They had sold 33 Eccleston Square, their tenancy on 1 Dean Trench Street was ending, 2 Hyde Park Street was uninhabitable and for sale, they had not at that stage found another town house (it was the month before Churchill chanced on 2 Sussex Square) and although Freddie Guest had offered them his house Templeton at Roehampton, it was let until the middle of October and it would be 'tiresome' if they had to take a furnished house for a month. Lady Hamilton was incandescent and even thought it was a delaying tactic on Clementine's part to withdraw from the deal. She lashed out, striking at all and sundry, armed only with a clutch of mixed metaphors – '…I really rather suspect that they will even now manage to keep it if Winston goes out, he is very unpopular at present, and as Lloyd George is in a very difficult position himself he will probably try to throw Winston over – Jonah out of the sinking ship – that old rat, Lord Fisher, is busy trying to scuttle the whole concern – 'Scrap the lot' is his cry – he has been lying in wait for years, and now yelling with senile ferocity, he is having a wild spring at the throats of the Cabinet'.[22] But it was to no avail. She had to wait until the Churchills could take up Freddie Guest's offer of Templeton.

Templeton, like all the Guests' residences is a big house for one family. It is a late eighteenth century mansion close to the north side of Richmond Park, but not the most attractive of Georgian houses and with a conveniently anonymous architect. When built, it stood in around 30 acres and its only neighbours were

Templeton, Roehampton, the home of Freddie Guest.

The interior of Templeton.

comparable properties, Clarence Lodge, The Priory, Mount Clare and Grove House, all discretely screened from each other by judicious landscaping. It came into the family when it was bought by Winston's Aunt, Lady Cornelia Spencer-Churchill in 1907 and then passed by descent to Freddie Guest. There is no shortage of bedrooms – probably around twenty – but its interior is out of proportion. The entrance hall, rooms and staircase are all too small. So, now, are the formal gardens but they appealed sufficiently to Churchill for him to make a few paintings there, one showing the two cedar trees that still survive on the lawn. The Churchills stayed at Templeton until 2 Sussex Square was ready in February 1920.

After the Hamiltons moved in to Lullenden, Churchill went back occasionally. He did a painting (now lost) of the barn during a weekend visit with Sarah and Diana while Clementine was unwell in mid-October 1920 and told his friends he approved of all they had done to the house. But the Hamiltons never really settled at Lullenden any more than the Churchills had done. It cost far them more than they had anticipated. 'I assure you I had no conception that a country place took it out of one's pocket so damnably...' Ian Hamilton wrote in 1921 to his friend Stella Speyer[23] (who was married to a nephew of the 'notorious' Sir Edgar), a sentiment Churchill would have echoed. Just like Percy Sharman's wife, Jean Hamilton suffered severely from asthma and Lullenden made it worse. She pleaded pitifully to her diary for some relief and a few years later, was saying the house would kill her in the end. 'We must give up Lullenden,' she wrote, 'in spite of its alluring beauty, it makes me too ill'.[24] Despite her every intention, she spent relatively little time there and lived mostly at their London house and at Deanston, the Hamiltons' Perthshire seat. When time allowed, she did however develop the garden with herbaceous borders, fruit trees, a hot house and the roses that Clementine so desperately wanted but never had. Like Clementine, she was a friend of the Horners and both she and Sir Ian often visited Mells – 'a jewelled garden' she called it, 'so restful and delicious'[25] and it is most tempting to believe Frances Horner had some influence on Lady Hamilton's gardening activities. The Hamiltons tried to sell Lullenden in 1924 for £20,000, believing it 'the sort of place and more especially the barn and its interior which the rich American wife of an Englishman goes into raptures over'.[26] In the event, they hung on until 1932, having let it in the meantime to several different tenants. Sir Ian Hamilton however ensured that Lullenden lived on in the names of his

Belted Galloway cattle ('belties') of which he built up a pedigree herd there, one of the foundation herds and still owned by the Hamilton family. A few of them were later to find a home at Chartwell, somewhere the Hamiltons themselves, quite extraordinarily, seem never to have visited although the two families continued occasionally to meet.

The eventual sale of Hyde Park Street in May 1920 realised £3,500 but Spender-Clay told Churchill that as Lord Gerald Wellesley had agreed to defer assignment of the lease, he would have to disclose the profit to him. Wellesley fortunately did not object. Foster however inevitably complained that his own hoped-for profits from the advisory work had evaporated and meanwhile he had engaged the firm of Bovis to carry out the building work and improvements at Churchill's new home in Sussex Square. In a pattern now becoming very familiar with Churchill houses, this was not to be as straightforward as he might have hoped.

Bovis, well-known in the twenty-first century as a massive global corporation, had been founded by a London builder, Charles William Bovis in the eighteen eighties but really saw its fortunes turn after it was bought by the émigré Prussian Jewish entrepreneur Sidney Gluckstein in 1908. Gluckstein soon recruited his

Sidney Gluckstein, owner of Churchill's builders Bovis with whom Churchill had disputes.

cousin, Samuel Joseph as his partner and together they formed a powerful and effective combination; although one that met its match in Churchill. During the War, they spun a coin to decide who would enlist and who would manage the company. Joseph lost and went to France but the company thrived, largely, like other building firms at the time, on Government contracts – digging defensive trenches, building the American Soldiers' Hospital in Kent, transforming the White City Stadium into temporary accommodation for Kitchener's army and, most intriguingly, undertaking a mysterious project involving a secret factory and thousands of tons of steel – probably to build Churchill's tanks.

Samuel Joseph survived to return at the end of hostilities and he it was who supervised the work at Sussex Square. After a few months of more or less satisfactory progress on the house however, and regular payments to Bovis by Churchill, the firm then imposed an increase of fifteen per cent to cover rises in wages and materials costs. Churchill thought it 'entirely unjustifiable'. It was 'to pile one injury on top of another as far as the unfortunate customer is concerned'.[27] The price hike meant going back to the Trustees for more funds and by early October Churchill had clearly had enough and put the property up for auction with a reserve of £5,000, based on Foster's valuation. He was in Dundee on 14 October 1920 attending the Annual Meeting of the Liberal Association when a telegram from Foster arrived telling him the move had failed and the house had only been bid to £4,400. Churchill did not try again and instead opted to dig in at Sussex Square and make further improvements.

First, however, he had to settle the existing building account of £7,500. The Trustees had only approved expenditure to £7,000 and had no more no cash in hand so brother Jack as Trustee approved the sale of £500 worth of Great Indian Peninsular Railway shares to meet the liability. It was then time for Churchill to contact the Trustees again. Their surveyor valued the house at £7,500 and although Lord Ednam (later the 3rd Earl of Dudley and Venetia Stanley's father), appeared on the scene and offered £8,500, Churchill was no longer interested in a sale and asked the Trustees for an additional £1,000 to enable him to install a studio and library at the rear in 7 Sussex Mews East. In the hope of resolving his disagreement with Bovis, he gave them the contract for this additional work shortly before Christmas, offering a thousand guineas to cover both the new business and the resolution of the outstanding disputed payments. Bovis however saw it rather differently and so with an impasse looming, Churchill summoned their 'representative' Samuel Joseph to see him at the War Office on the afternoon of 28 December. It is intriguing to speculate on the likelihood of this confrontation ever being discussed between the two men again – as for instance on the various occasions they met during World War II when Samuel Joseph, complete with knighthood, was by then Lord Mayor of London! It was indeed to be in a speech honouring him as the new Lord Mayor on 10 November 1942 that Churchill was to make the memorable comment that, 'I have not become the King's first minister in order to preside over the liquidation of the British Empire'.

The War Office meeting appeared to work and Churchill was able to write to Foster a few days later saying the matter had been resolved. Fred Foster himself hadn't finished however and when he asked for his fees and complained at the fact they had been eroded, Churchill told him bluntly that he too had '…suffered to a very serious extent by the great increase in the cost of the work' and felt he '…had a right to count upon your professional assistance…'[28] Foster thus joined the list of architects who worked for Churchill once but were never engaged again.

Churchill finally paid off Bovis in August and, perhaps in celebration, the same week spent £2,600 in ordering a new Rolls-Royce Cabriolet. Clementine was thrilled about the car but wrote promptly to Churchill with pragmatic advice 'Please get it insured before you ever get into it…'[29] Bovis too were never to be employed by him again but some months later, Sidney Gluckstein wrote a supplication to Churchill in the hope of gaining favourable recommendation for work on Lloyd George's new house at Churt in Surrey: '…If it is not unwarranted on our part, may we go so far as to intimate that a word from you, would be better than volumes from us.'[30] He might have chosen a better moment. In truth, he could not have chosen a worse moment. Not only had Churchill suffered frustrations with Bovis's work, his personal relations with the Prime Minister were ebbing ever lower. They were in disagreement over policy towards Ireland, Lloyd George had appointed Sir Robert Horne to the job Churchill wanted as Chancellor and only a few days earlier had infuriated him with some pointed remarks in Cabinet about Gallipoli. Gluckstein received short shrift from Eddie Marsh: 'Mr Churchill desires me to express his regret that he does not feel able to write to the Prime Minister as suggested by you.'[31]

It was to be some time before the new studio at Sussex Square was fully fitted however – Bovis had failed to put clear glass in the windows – and the final touch wasn't added until February when Clementine produced a 17th Century Persian Khorassan rug she had been thrilled to buy for £160 in the Brompton Road. She was concerned that Churchill might not like it but offered the reassurance that if even he did not, she was sure she knew somewhere she could re-sell it for £200. It was later during the furnishing of 2 Sussex Square that Churchill produced a dissertation on dining room chairs, showing immeasurably more interest in furniture than when his Aunt Leonie had been advising him on his Mount Street flat and he dismissed such matters as merely irritating. There should be twenty, he told Clementine, they should be comfortable, compact so the table wasn't crowded, and with arms. He suggested selling their existing dining room chairs, along with eight or ten others, and using the proceeds to buy chairs that conformed to his specification. Clementine promised to search for an appropriate model.

Churchill never used his professional position and status to cut through the bureaucracy that impinged on his domestic life. There is never a hint in his correspondence of 'Don't you know who I am?' He suffered the frustrations of absentee workmen and ridiculous regulations like everyone else but in June 1921 when his regular morning work at his desk in Sussex Square on official duties was impaired by the inefficiencies of the GPO (General Post Office), his exasperation was stretched to breaking point; and he gained an interesting first-hand demonstration of the closed shop at work. A telephone had been newly installed with a lead a yard too short. Despite almost daily letters and calls, 'Not the slightest result has followed, though the visits of the inspectors have been frequent,' he complained.[32] He had been told that private electricians were not allowed to undertake the work and when a workman in the house on other matters 'looked at the wire but regretted he had no authority to add the extra yard', his patience, like the telephone lead, came to an end. He wrote to Frederick Kellaway, the Postmaster-General telling him 'I imagine that five minutes and half a crown is all that is involved…'[33]

On New Year's Day 1921, Churchill was offered a new position by Lloyd George: to succeed Alfred Milner as Secretary of State for the Colonies, heading the department he had worked in under Lord Elgin for his first ministerial position in 1905. He was to take up his new appointment in mid-February and was also to have responsibility for the British mandated territories of Iraq and Palestine, a region for which he was to retain a life-long interest and concern. There was no ministerial house but with 2 Sussex Square, the Churchills now had a good London base. It was therefore the turn of the country again and a replacement for the ill-fated Lullenden experience. Churchill now moreover had a much sounder financial basis for house hunting as a result of poor working practices on Cambrian Railways. At mid-day on 26 January 1921, the 10.25 up express train from Aberystwyth was on a length of single track line between Welshpool and Newtown when it collided head-on near Abermule station with the 10.05 down slow train from Whitchurch which had carelessly been allowed on to the same track.[34] In one of the most serious of British railway accidents, seventeen passengers were killed and among them was Lord Herbert Vane-Tempest, a director of Cambrian Railways. He lived at the family seat Plas Machynlleth and was the unmarried brother of the 6th Marquess of Londonderry. More importantly, he was related to Churchill whose grandmother, Frances ('Duchess Fanny'), the wife of the 7th Duke of Marlborough had been born Lady Frances Vane-Tempest-Stewart. Through Lord Herbert's will, Churchill inherited some of the considerable wealth of the Garron Towers estate in Co. Antrim and although not as much as he had initially hoped, it did bring him an annual income of £4,000 and some fine silver.

The death of Lord Herbert Vane-Tempest in January 1921, however, was to presage a period of profound sadness and losses that affected the Churchills deeply. In April, Clementine's brother Bill Hozier shot himself, for reasons that remain unclear. At the end of May, Lady Randolph fell down the old staircase while visiting the Horners at Mells Manor, an accident from which she never recovered and she died the following month. Then in the summer came the greatest tragedy of all. Two-year old Marigold Churchill on holiday at Broadstairs in early August had been suffering from the usual children's complaints of colds and sore throats when her condition deteriorated. Her mother was summoned from Eaton Hall, the Duke of Westminster's Gothic extravagance in Cheshire where she was playing tennis. Churchill came down from London. But this was 1921, antibiotics were in the future and as her condition deteriorated into septicaemia, Marigold slowly faded and died with her parents at her side on the 23 August.

In July 1921, Churchill and Clementine were both looking for a country house, but largely independently of each other. Churchill went to look at Peelings, a modest house that looked seventeenth century although it was much older, at

Westham near Pevensey on the East Sussex coast. Together with its adjoining small estate, it was owned by the 9th Duke of Devonshire who at that time was serving as Governor-General of Canada but was the following year to succeed Churchill as Secretary of State for the Colonies. One of his daughters was later to become Lady Dorothy Macmillan.

Clementine was staying with the Horners at Menabilly, the historic Cornish house near Fowey with lush sub-tropical gardens that Frances Horner had rented from the Rashleigh family – it was later to be the home of Daphne du Maurier and the inspiration for Mandeley. She was entranced but thought it must be the place where Rip van Winkle fell asleep, so lethargic was the atmosphere. Clementine, ever the romantic, found it magic, tropical, airless, overgrown, neglected; and quite lovely and strange. Within the great kitchen garden with its buttressed walls she encountered the then novelty of vegetables and flowers growing wild together – when she picked the runner beans, she had to uncurl the tendrils of sweet peas which had grown onto them; and the artichokes formed a forest ten feet high.[35] She was, however, becoming worried lest the Vane-Tempest inheritance be spent unwisely. Churchill had enlightened her with his idea of owning a farm but she spotted a difference between owning it and living there. Why not endow it 'à la Chequers' she suggested, appreciating that there were no tax concessions available to two homes. 'Personally farming rather frightened me after our experiment at Lullenden which is now costing the poor Hamiltons dear, but I don't want to be bigoted about it...' she wrote.[36]

A day later she wrote again to Churchill, expressing interest that he had been to see Peelings. She too had seen it advertised in The Times and had written to the Duke of Devonshire's solicitor for photographs. It was however disappointing. There were only six bedrooms and she suggested that if they were to buy so important an estate, they would have to employ an extremely intelligent agent, a man who knew not only about farming, but about land development and building too. Clementine herself was no slouch when it came to spotting an opportunity. There was a stretch of 600 yards along the sea-shore at Peelings which she saw as valuable building land requiring capital to develop it. If this was available, they could make 'a delicious little garden village with good tennis courts, sailing boats etc'. But she asked Churchill not to risk their 'newly come fortune' in operations they did not understand and did have not the time to learn and to practise when learned. Politics she said were absolutely engrossing to him and he had his painting for leisure and his polo for excitement and danger. She longed for a country home, she said, but wanted it to be a rest and 'a joy Bunny' not a pre-occupation.[37] A crystal ball would undoubtedly have come in handy at that moment. Churchill had no intention of pursuing any interest in Peelings as it was probably the week in which he had first seen Chartwell and his heart already belonged elsewhere.

Although Sir Howard Frank had failed to find him a fruit farm, Churchill had taken old Mrs Everest's cue and fallen in love with Kent so Frank appointed one of his staff, a young man named Henry Norman Harding to act as a negotiator for him. Harding had originally joined Knight Frank & Rutley as an office boy and accompanied Churchill on journeys around the home counties looking at possible properties. There is no record of what Churchill saw and rejected but one day in early July 1921, Harding took Churchill to see Chartwell which the owner was just about to put up for auction. Churchill was entranced.

He showed it at the first opportunity to Clementine who initially shared his enthusiasm. She was staying for a tennis party with her friends the Cazalets at Fairlawne, near Tonbridge their rambling eighteenth century mansion that Pevsner called 'plain and rather puzzling'. The Cazalets were an old Kent Huguenot

Fairlawne, Tonbridge (early 20th century), home of the Cazalets where the Churchills stayed.

family and the Churchills knew the parents William and Maud as well as their two sons: Victor, soon to become Conservative MP for Chippenham, and Peter who later trained many successful racehorses at Fairlawne for the Queen Mother and was to train some of Churchill's horses too. The day before the Chartwell auction Clementine wrote of her first impression of the house that was soon to be the centre of her life. 'I can think of nothing but that heavenly tree-crowned Hill... I do hope we shall get it – If we do I feel we shall live there a great deal & be very happy...'[38] She wrote of the possibility of adding another wing – and sent Churchill a small explanatory sketch – to be paid for by some of the Garron Towers inheritance. She said they needed a minimum of twelve bedrooms and was already working out in detail who among the family would stay where.

There is tantalisingly no indication of what happened at the Chartwell auction but the property failed to sell and remained on the market. It seems, however, that soon afterwards Clementine went again to see it and it was then her enthusiasm waned and she became less than enamoured. Whilst appreciating the view, she saw through the veneer. The house faced the wrong way – West, across a public road to a steep bank covered with *Rhododendron ponticum* whose flowers were of a purple colour she especially disliked. And running from the Mapleton Road to the south of the house and right across the land down towards Chartwell Farm was a public right of way. Churchill, however, was 'blind to drawbacks, and deaf to reason'.[39] Clementine's concerns did serve nonetheless to delay things and for over a year nothing seemed to happen while Chartwell remained available. But she had only postponed the inevitable and appears to have been unaware that in the spring of the following year, 1922, Churchill's future architect was already being taken to see the house.

In the summer of 1922, Clementine was pregnant with her fifth and final child, Mary and indulged herself with two seaside holidays. In July she went with Goonie to the West Country and stayed in North Devon in a large, faintly arts and crafts property called Preston House set in an elevated position with breathtaking views across Saunton Sands. They visited Barnstaple which they liked, and Ilfracombe which they did not – 'We are both glad to have seen Ilfracombe as now we need never go there any more. It seemed to be composed of boarding houses and a great variety of "places of worship"...'[40] Then the following month, it was the turn of Essex. Frinton-on-Sea, on the Essex coast just north of Clacton was, like Cromer, another of the East Coast resorts that

Preston House, Saunton, Devon where Clementine and Goonie stayed in 1922.

Maryland, Frinton-on-Sea, which Clementine rented in 1922.

had become fashionable as holiday locations for London society. In contrast to Clacton, where the Churchill social circle was most unlikely to be seen, Frinton with its grassy Greensward sea front and firm golden sand was *the* place to take the children and to convalesce. Clementine rented a huge modern house called Maryland at the enormous sum of forty five guineas a week. It had a beautiful garden of over an acre which the children loved, and it was close to the sea and to the tennis club; and although her condition precluded her from indulging, she entered Randolph and Diana in the children's tournament, but being 'duffers' as Randolph described it, they won the booby prize. [41] Clementine loved Frinton and, still unaware that Churchill was now completely in love with Chartwell, had yet another attempt at persuading him to buy a country home. She found one in Frinton she thought was ideal. It could be used for the children's holidays or for convalescence she told him, and for her tennis weekends. If by chance they wanted to go to Deauville or Biarritz, then it could always be let; she was sure it would make thirty five guineas a week.[42] Churchill was unmoved. Clementine begged him, implored him to consider it. There was no response. She asked him to send a valuer to look at it and sought his permission to bid at the auction.[43] It was only small, she said. It had ten bedrooms and two bathrooms and she was sure it could be had for £4,000. She offered to sell her shares and some jewellery to meet half the cost.[44] Her husband remained silent. Clementine then tried another tack. She had seen some buildings owned by Trinity House standing in five acres on a lovely cliff which should felt would make an excellent speculative purchase.[45] Still Churchill was implacable. He had bigger fish to fry. He joined Clementine at Frinton for about ten days in mid-August although did not spend his time looking at houses and instead engaged in his favourite landscaping activities. He took his three detectives down to the sea shore in the guise of hired labour and then 'mobilised everybody on the beach and when the tide ran out dammed up the sunken pools left behind and then dug immensely complicated channels to release the stored up water'.[46] Then, at the end of this episode of family bliss, the children were moved out of Maryland to something smaller in the town and their parents returned home at the beginning of September to Sussex Square where Mary was born on the 15th.

Although in his mind he was probably now unswervingly committed to Chartwell, Churchill unexpectedly did explore one other option. He had been MP for Dundee since 1908 and had perhaps begun to believe the 'job for life'

The Old Mansion House, Auchterhouse (early 20th century), that Churchill considered buying in 1922.

tag that some people had attached to it. Or perhaps he felt he had not been as regular a presence in the constituency as he should and was laying down some ground bait for the voters at the next election. In any event, at the beginning of September 1922, a brochure fell into his hands detailing the impending sale of a property a few miles north of Dundee. The Mansion House with its surrounding estate in the tiny village of Auchterhouse is a typical, attractive (and of course, haunted) small Scottish castle, reputedly starting life in the 13th century and then converted into a baronial mansion in the 16th century by the Earl of Strathmore, who also owned Glamis. In 1922 it was part of the holdings of the 7th Earl of Airlie – to whom Clementine was related – but was to be sold at auction in Edinburgh on the 13th of the month. Churchill immediately sent a letter to James Allison the Liberal agent in Dundee, asking him to find a competent surveyor to make a general report on its condition and value so he could assess if it was worth sending a bid, but stressed that he did not want his name to be disclosed in any way.[47] There is no recorded response so it is not known if the report put him off or if he attempted to buy and his bid fell below the reserve. The property did not find a buyer and was not in fact sold until the following August when it was bought by the jute manufacturer William Harris Valentine. It was, however, the only time Churchill made anything approaching an attempt to buy a home in any parliamentary constituency he represented.

Had Churchill bought the Auchterhouse Estate on 13 September 1922, it would have proved a huge embarrassment only two months later. In October, Lloyd George's coalition government collapsed and he resigned as Prime Minister. The King sent for Andrew Bonar Law who agreed to become Prime Minister if the Conservative Party would elect him leader and immediately after the Party obliged on 23 October, Parliament was dissolved and a General Election called for mid-November. Churchill sent mixed and confusing messages to the voters of Dundee where he stood for re-election as a Liberal and a free-trader. Clementine told him she would be heartbroken if he lost but Dundee was unimpressed with his campaign and Churchill, who was incapacitated by an emergency appendix operation, came fourth, well behind the winning candidate, Edwin Scrymgeour who had been an anonymous prohibitionist when Churchill won in 1908 but now stood as a Labour-sympathetic Independent. So Churchill had no seat in Parliament – 'without an office, without a seat, without a party and without an appendix' he was later to write; but he was about to have the house of his dreams. The stage was set for the greatest property adventure of all for the day after the Edinburgh auction, Knight Frank & Rutley wrote to him regarding the impending re-auctioning of Chartwell and offering him first refusal on the house for ten days at £5,500.

Clementine seems to have been blissfully unaware of all these developments; Mary Soames was later to write that in the buying of Chartwell, her mother felt that Churchill, for the only time in their marriage, acted towards her with less than candour. The evidence bears this out. In the final stages of her pregnancy at Sussex Square; indeed on her wedding anniversary, just two days before Mary was born, she again wrote to Churchill about possible house purchases. Their friend the old rascal Wilfrid Scawen Blunt had died the previous Sunday at the age of eighty-two (in due course to be wrapped in one of his own Oriental carpets and buried beneath an atmospherically impressive stone tomb in the woods behind his home at Newbuildings Place) and she wrote of the possibility of Newbuildings coming on to the market. In the event, Newbuildings passed to Blunt's sometime lover Dorothy Carleton who bequeathed it back to the family but Clementine wanted, she said, to compare its merits with those of another property she had seen and which she was looking forward to showing again to Churchill. She added with touching naivety 'There is no hurry with regard to either property so meanwhile we can consider others as well…if only we could get a little Country House within our means & live there within our means it would add great happiness and peace to our lives'.[48] She had been married to Churchill for twelve years to the day. She loved him dearly but should by then have known him better.

Tomb of Wilfrid Scawen Blunt, Newbuildings Place.

Endnotes

1   WSB FM 9-1975. Diary 3 Oct 1909.
2   CHAR 1/125/4. CSC to WSC. 23 July 1918.
3   CHAR 1/125/6–10. CSC to WSC, 11 Aug 1918.
4   E. Adeane, personal communication, 10 Jan 2005.
5   CSCT 1/11/1–8. CSC to WSC, 9 Mar 1919.
6   Cassar, G. H. *Sir Ian Standish Monteith Hamilton*, Oxford DNB.
7   HP Lady Hamilton's Diary, 16 Mar 1919.
8   HP Lady Hamilton's Diary, 10 Aug 1919.
9   HP Lady Hamilton's Diary, 16 Mar 1919.
10   CHAR 1/133/7–10. WSC to Ian Hamilton, 24 Mar 1919.
11   HP Lady Hamilton's Diary, 12 Apr 1919.
12   HP Ian Hamilton to Wood & Walford, 15 Nov 1923.
13   HP Ian Hamilton to [?] Wood, 14 Dec 1923.
14   CSCT 1/11/10–13. CSC to WSC, 20 May 1919.
15   CHAR 1/133/19–20. Ian Hamilton to WSC, 21 May 1919.
16   HP Lady Hamilton's Diary, 20 Jul 1919.
17   CHAR 1/125/4. CSC to WSC, 23 Jul 1918.
18   CHAR 1/134/30–31. Lycett, Jepson & Co. to Nicholl, Manisty & Co., 15 Aug 1919.
19   CHAR 1/134/40–43. Nicholl, Manisty & Co. to WSC with draft letter to Farrer & Co. with revised draft letter by WSC, 19 Sep 1919.
20   CHAR 1/132/11. WSC to Sir Howard Frank, 30 Aug 1919.
21   Nairn, I. & Pevsner, N. *The Buildings of England – Surrey,* p. 210.
22   HP Lady Hamilton's Diary, 17 Sept. 1919.
23   HP Ian Hamilton to Stella Speyer, 10 Jun 1921.
24   HP Lady Hamilton's Diary, 3 May 1927.
25   HP Lady Hamilton's Diary, 11 Aug 1919.
26   HP Ian Hamilton to Wood & Walford, 5 Nov 1924.
27   CHAR 1/137/81. WSC to F. W. Foster, 28 Aug 1920.
28   CHAR 1/153/3. WSC to F. W. Foster, 28 Jan 1921.
29   CHAR 1/139/72. CSC to WSC, 18 Aug 1921.
30   CHAR 1/153/46. S. Gluckstein to WSC, 8 Dec 1921.
31   CHAR 1/153/47. Edward Marsh to S. Gluckstein, 13 Dec 1921.
32   CHAR 1/138/59–60. WSC to F. G. Kellaway, 23 June 1921.
33   CHAR 1/138/59–60. WSC to F. G. Kellaway, 23 June 1921.
34   UL Pringle, J. W. *Cambrian Railways accident at Abermule on 26 January 1921.* Ministry of Transport, 8 April 1921.
35   CHAR 1/139/54. CSC to WSC, 7 July 1921.
36   CHAR 1/139/58. CSC to WSC, 10 July 1921.
37   CHAR 1/139/62. CSC to WSC, 11 July 1921.
38   CHAR 1/139/85–92. CSC to WSC, 20 July 1921.

39 Soames, M. *Clementine Churchill. 2nd Ed.,* p. 247.
40 CHAR 1/158/32–35. CSC to WSC, 17 July 1922.
41 Churchill, R. S. *Twenty-one Years,* p. 24.
42 CHAR 1/158/40–41. CSC to WSC, 3 Aug 1922.
43 CHAR 1/158/42–43. CSC to WSC, 4 Aug 1922.
44 CHAR 1/158/44–48. CSC to WSC, 8 Aug 1922.
45 CHAR 1/158/51. CSC to WSC, 17 Aug 1922.
46 Churchill, R. S. *Twenty-one Years,* p. 35.
47 CHAR 1/157/68. WSC to James Allison, 5 Sep 1922.
48 CHAR 1/158/52–53. CSC to WSC, 12 Sep 1922.

CHAPTER 7
$\mathscr{C}$HARTWELL

The first time Churchill saw Chartwell he was captivated above all by the setting. The house is about two miles south of the small town of Westerham and only a little way to the north east of their old home Lullenden. At its highest point the property lies just over 200 metres above sea level on the east-facing slope of a narrow valley running through the North Downs. In 1921 the house itself was usually referred to informally as Chartwell Manor (and was still called 'The Manor' by employees until very recently) but even after its nineteenth century rebuilding, it had no great architectural merit – in truth it was still a dismal looking pile – but it offered a spectacular view across the Weald of Kent, and it

Chartwell from the south-east (*c.* 1870).

Chartwell from the west (*c.* 1870).

was a view that possessed Churchill. He said that for its size, the site was the most beautiful and charming he had ever seen.[1] On the opposite side of the valley was a magnificent bank of beech trees (Clementine's 'heavenly tree-crowned hill'), now largely gone and the view today gives an inadequate impression of what Churchill saw in 1921.

Just to the north of the house is a spring, the Chart Well which feeds a stream running down through the valley, now damned to create ponds and lakes. The name Chart in the Old English sense of rough ground or 'rough common overgrown with gorse, broom, bracken' occurs throughout the Weald and is commoner as a place name in Kent than in other counties. It appeared very early in the county in Great Chart, Little Chart and Chart Sutton although it was not used at Chartwell until later. In other counties, such names as Churt, Chard and Chartridge have the same root. As might be expected, the soils vary from the high ground above the house to the valley bottom and the underlying geology too varies. At the top, the Chart Well itself springs from the Lower Chalk layers. The house and most of the garden are on the Lower Greensand Hythe Beds within which are thick deposits of a coarse sandy limestone, the famous Kentish

Chartwell from the north-east (*c.* 1870).

Rag, a building stone that until recently was quarried locally and was used in the present garden for building walls and also for the loggia. Further down the valley, the Greensand appears as the Atherfield Clay, a deposit that occurs all over southern England from Dorset to Kent. Most of the gardened area at Chartwell has a shallow soil of little more than 15 cm depth, free-draining and quick to dry but like all light soils, also quick to warm up. Although chalky in places, the soils derived from the Greensand are slightly acidic and rhododendrons grow well locally. Further down the slope, over the Atherfield Clay, the soil is much heavier and temporary springs emerge at the geological junctions, most notably in the sloping area below the house.

The spring or 'well' was a feature and presumably an attraction of the site since the first occupation. A widely quoted description of the early history was given by Edward Hasted in his History of Kent published between 1778 and 1799. He examined some original documents and also relied heavily on an earlier account given by Thomas Philipott in his *Villare Cantianum* of 1659. A man named William At-Well is recorded as the owner of the land in 1362 and he then sold it, as 'Well-street' (the spring by the road), to the Potter family of Dartford in whose possession it remained for several generations. One of the family, a woman named Dorothy Potter, the daughter of a Thomas Potter, married Sir John Rivers (or Ryvers) from Chafford, also in Kent. He is sometimes said to have been the Sir John Rivers who was Lord Mayor of London in 1573 and grandfather of the poet Thomas Carew although Lord Mayor Rivers is recorded as having a wife named Elizabeth and there seem to have been several men with the same name.[2] Thomas Potter died in 1611 to be buried in Westerham Church and 'Well-street' passed down the Rivers family – an Act of Parliament of 1623 allowed the 'Alteration of tenure and custom of lands formerly of Thomas Potter and of Sir George and Sir John Rivers in Kent from gavelkind to the common law, and to settle them on Sir John Rivers and his heirs'. (A gavelkind was a type of land tenure common in Kent, a notable feature being the custom by which a tenant's land at his death was divided equally among his sons). The eldest son of John Rivers, also named John sold it to Thomas Smith, a scrivener or professional scribe from London and according to Hasted, he then sold it around 1661 to a Robert Whitby. His son Samuel Whitby sold it in turn in 1664 to a John Bridger. He had no sons but two daughters, one of whom died without issue while the other married a man named Francis Ellison and in turn the property passed to their son Thomas who married a Miss Eleanora Fowle in Westerham on 27 May 1757. According to Hasted, Thomas Ellison died sometime in the 1790s and the property was bequeathed to a un-named beneficiary.

On the 1742 map of Kent published by Andrew Dury and John Andrews, Well Street appears with three buildings and two walled gardens, a large wood to the east of the house but no ponds or lakes. On the Ordnance Survey 2 inches to 1 mile survey drawings of 1799, the house is named 'Foundling House' and a walled garden is present to the north with fields beyond, the three largest indicated as parkland and with woods further away. A foundling house, a home for foundlings or deserted children, is presumably what the property had become. Crockhamhill Common (the 'rough common') to the west of the house was shown with a few trees. The house appeared as Foundling House on two later maps: in 1801 on the privately printed first Ordnance Survey Map at a scale of 1 inch to 1 mile based on the earlier Ordnance Survey drawings by Captain William Mudge, and the map by John and Christopher Greenwood published in

1829 from surveys made in 1818 and 1819. The Ordnance Survey map of 1819 shows for the first time a large pond and also a winding road past Chartwell Farm which lies to the south-east of the house.

The property evidently changed hands again at least once because by 1836 it was offered for sale under the will of a Mr B. Fletcher, by when much development had taken place. The sale particulars survive and give a comprehensive picture of the property which then extended to over 200 acres of productive arable, meadow, pasture and woodland and included some areas of fine hop garden.[3] The estate was said be richly studded with timber and ornamented with thriving copse woods. The house, brick-built, with a slated and tiled roof, was approached through a planted fore-court enclosed by a wall and iron pallisades. It was described as once to have been of rather imposing appearance, but in consequence of neglect, had fallen into a partial state of decay and therefore required 'the out-lay of a few hundred pounds to render it a suitable abode for a genteel family'. It was nonetheless substantial and contained five servants' bedrooms on the upper floor, two large front bedrooms and two spacious back bedrooms on the first floor, and five rooms in the roof, approached by a back staircase. On the ground floor were an entrance hall and principal staircase, a spacious drawing room and dining room at the front, a breakfast room, dressing room, store closet, large nursery and housekeeper's room. In the basement was 'an excellent dairy and larder', kitchen, lumber room, a small parlour and two good cellars, a knife house, wood house, kitchen, pantry and a wash-house 'containing a remarkably fine spring of water, which is continually running'. Adjoining was a fuel house and piggery, enclosed by stone walls and a detached wood house and fowl house.

There were the usual agricultural buildings, good pleasure and kitchen gardens, productive orchards, several fish ponds, 'a large sheet of water, well stocked with fish which at a trifling expense might be converted into an Ornamental Lake' and eight cottages, four on the Estate (occupied by James Botley, Thomas Botley and Thomas Godfrey with one vacant), a cottage called Medhurst near Puddle Dock Wood occupied by John Woodham, and the other three in French Street occupied by Martha Geal, Joseph Selby, and Richard Chapman, at two shillings per week each. Puddle Dock – now often one word – is a hamlet about one mile to the south-east of Chartwell; Puddledock Lane leading to it runs from Well Street (now Mapleton Road) to the south of the estate. French Street – also now often one word – is a comparable hamlet about one mile to the north-east.

The farm buildings in 1836 were further to the south than the present Chartwell Farm. There was a 'Homestead' comprising 'a farm yard, containing Stone-built and tiled stabling for seven horses, with lofts over, Harness Room and Chaff Pitt at end; timber-built lean-to stable. Stone and Timber-built Wood barn, Cart lodge, Chaise-house, and Piggery, with lofts over, Barn, Cow-house and Calf pens. Stone and brick-built hop oasts with tiled roof, consisting of three lower rooms, (one fitted-up with four Furnaces and two Kilns,) and three spacious chambers over'. There were also timber built and thatched barns with a loose box, and two cattle sheds adjoining a cattle yard. In addition the property owner had rights to plant and cut timber from Westerham Common.

The sale took place at the Auction Mart in St Bartholomew's Lane, Cheapside in London on the 22 September 1836 under the direction of the auctioneer Mr W. W. Simpson. The price made is not known but the purchasers of the estate were a family called the Drinkwater Bethunes who then leased out extensive parts of it. The principal buyer was probably Colonel John Drinkwater Bethune

Chartwell stables and farm buildings (*c.* 1870).

(1762–1844). Like others of his family, he was a military man of some significance and he published a remarkable eye-witness description of Nelson's victory at Cape St Vincent in 1797 after discussing it personally with Nelson himself the day following the battle. His seat was Thorncroft House in Leatherhead and there is no obvious reason why he would want to buy property in Westerham. John Drinkwater Bethune's son, Captain John Elliot Drinkwater Bethune RN who was recorded as the owner of the estate in the Westerham Parish Tithe Survey of 1845, the year after his father's death, was a man of even greater distinction. Born in 1801, he was a lawyer, a graduate of Trinity College, Cambridge, and distinguished himself in India where he arrived in April 1848 as the Law Member of the Governor General's Council. A fluent Bengali speaker, he became passionate about the furtherance of women's education and the following year founded what became Bethune College in Calcutta, the first women's college in Bengal which still thrives. He was a mathematician of note and wrote an important early work on probability, published a biography of Galileo, made discoveries in the Fiji islands, wrote poetry and was also an artist of some repute contributing to a notable collection of landscape drawings of India. It seems likely however that he was so busy in foreign parts that he never lived at Chartwell himself as by 1841, Well Street had already been leased to a local farmer named Philip Green who was living there with his wife Elizabeth and five servants.[4] There were numerous agricultural workers and their families (including some of those mentioned as tenants in the 1836 sale particulars) nearby at Puddle Dock. John Elliot Drinkwater Bethune died on 12 August 1851 and had by then disposed of the estate. He had put it up for sale in 1848 with Green as a sitting tenant[5] although a Charles Ramsay Drinkwater Bethune still had an interest in the property in 1856 and there were Bethunes living in Westerham as late as 1861.[6]

The purchaser in 1848 was a man named John Campbell Colquhoun.[7] The Colquhouns were an old land owning family from Dunbartonshire and Stirlingshire in the West of Scotland. Their seats were Killermont on the banks of the River Kelvin in New Kilpatrick parish about four miles from Glasgow, and Garscadden nearby at Drumchapel. Killermont had been in the family since 1747 and Garscadden since it was bought by an Archibald Colquhoun in 1664. John Campbell Colquhoun's father, also named Archibald, was the son of an Agnes Colquhoun and a John Campbell and assumed the name Campbell Colquhoun on succeeding his mother to the Killermont estate in 1804.

Garscadden House, the Campbell Colquhouns' family seat at Drumchapel
(18th century engraving).

Killermont, the Campbell Colquhouns' family seat at New Kilpatrick (late 19th century).

Archibald Campbell Colquhoun, sometime Lord Advocate of Scotland, died on 8 December 1820, at the home of his son-in-law in Wiltshire. His son John Campbell Colquhoun, the purchaser of the Well Place Estate and the man who made the greatest mark on the property before Churchill himself, was born at

KENT.

VALUABLE

FREEHOLD ESTATE

EXONERATED FROM LAND TAX,

DELIGHTFULLY SITUATE

WITHIN ABOUT A MILE OF THE MARKET TOWN

OF

WESTERHAM,

IN A BEAUTIFUL AND RETIRED PART OF THE COUNTY.

PARTICULARS AND CONDITIONS OF SALE

OF THE

WELL PLACE ESTATE,

COMPRISING UPWARDS OF

200 ACRES

OF PRODUCTIVE

ARABLE, MEADOW, PASTURE, AND WOOD LAND,

(INCLUDING SOME FINE HOP GARDEN,)

BEAUTIFULLY UNDULATED,

RICHLY STUDDED WITH TIMBER,

AND

ORNAMENTED WITH THRIVING COPSE WOODS,

Which are pleasingly interspersed over the Estate:

A RESIDENCE,

Which in by-gone times was of rather imposing appearance, but which, in consequence of neglect, has fallen into a partial state of decay, and therefore requires the out-lay of a few Hundred Pounds to restore it. The

AGRICULTURAL BUILDINGS

On the Estate are of the usual description ; and there are

GOOD PLEASURE AND KITCHEN GARDENS,

PRODUCTIVE ORCHARDS, SEVERAL FISH PONDS, A

SHEET OF WATER, WELL STOCKED WITH FISH,

BESIDES

EIGHT COTTAGES & GARDENS

Well Place Estate sale particulars (1836).

Killermont on 23 January 1803. He was educated at Edinburgh High School and inherited Killermont at the age of seventeen on his father's death and then the following year, inherited Garscadden from his relative Jean Colquhoun. He went on to Oriel College, Oxford and later married Henrietta the daughter of Thomas Powys, the 2nd Baron Lilford. From 1832 to 1835 he was, like his father, MP for Dunbartonshire and then, in 1837, was elected Tory member for Kilmarnock. He lost his seat in 1841 but was elected for the English constituency of Newcastle under Lyme at a by-election in 1842 and then retired from politics in 1847 'suffering from failing health and political disappointment'.[8] He was strongly religious, a passionate supporter of the causes of evangelicalism and spent the rest of his life away from his Scottish roots pursuing protestant religious interests and as a writer, publishing historical works, pamphlets and biographies.

It is a puzzle why John Campbell Colquhoun bought Chartwell. Although it has been said it was convenient for his political interests and the Campbell Colquhoun family album contains a note by his grandson (who sold the house to Churchill) to the effect that he acquired it as a weekend retreat while Parliament was in session, he had left politics the previous year and in any event, could not occupy his new house for some time because Philip Green was still living there. However, following his purchase, Campbell Colquhoun did make one significant change. He renamed his new property Chartwell and the name appears for the first time in the 1851 census with Philip Green as occupier.[9] It is not known when Green's lease expired and Campbell Colquhoun moved in or indeed precisely who was living at Chartwell over the next twenty years. It may be that Campbell Colquhoun was there in or soon after 1852 as this is the approximate planting date of the famous Japanese cedar tree. It is possible however that he landscaped the grounds while the house was still tenanted because in 1861, the occupant, presumably another tenant, was a man named James Young who was farming '385 acres and employing fourteen men and seven boys'.[10]

Whether as landlord or occupier, Campbell Colquhoun clearly threw himself into working on his new acquisition and although no direct documentation survives, a good indication of the changes he made can be gleaned from the 1869 Ordnance Survey map. A new access was created along a short drive at the south leading to a forecourt on the west front. Well Street itself (the road) was re-aligned further to the west away from the house and the boundary with Crockhamhill Common planted to form a back drop. The old pollarded beech

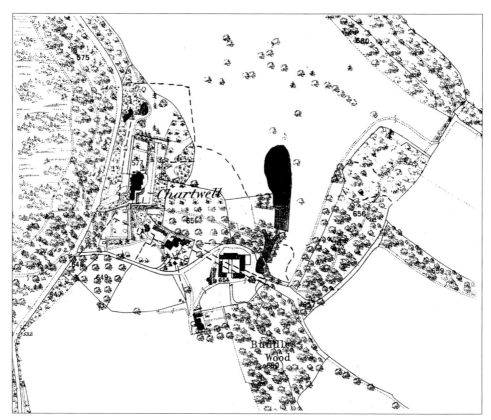

Chartwell from the 1869 1st Edition 25-inch OS map with old roads and field boundaries from the 1845 tithe sketched in as dotted lines.

were augmented with oak, Scots pine and exotic conifers including Monterey pine, Wellingtonia, European larch, Norway spruce and Japanese cedar. There may also have been some planting of the *Rhododendron ponticum* that Clementine abhorred as it was becoming increasingly popular at that time following its reintroduction to Britain from Spain around 1770. Photographs of the house, also dating from 1869, show rhododendrons in the grounds.

The walled garden to the north of the house was still there, with its semi-circular steps as now, leading to a new long terrace walk to the east. Shrubberies with specimen conifers had been planted around the Chart Well and also around a new pond below it (now called the Golden Orfe Pond). The most notable of the conifers was a Japanese cedar, *Cryptomeria japonica* which was planted by the Chart Well. Apart from its general appearance and size, the only real evidence for the date of its planting is an entry in the Campbell Colquhoun family photograph album which unequivocally gives the year 1852. It does not seem to have been subjected to growth ring analysis although other trees planted around the same time which have been ring-dated were a Scots Pine and a Himalayan Morinda spruce *Picea smithiana* and these suggest planting dates in the eighteen fifties. Other exotic conifers with similar ring dates were planted elsewhere in the park. The Chartwell Japanese cedar is now one of the finest in the country and the fact that Campbell Colquhoun was planting trees such as this suggests he was being guided

Japanese cedar at Chartwell, February 1957, aged 105.

by someone with significant horticultural knowledge. One possible influence may have been the Bateman family who were close friends. James and Maria Bateman were at that time developing their remarkable garden at Biddulph Grange in Staffordshire and had connections with the plant collector Sir Joseph Hooker, son of the then Director of Kew Gardens, Sir William Jackson Hooker (and whom he later succeeded), and also with the famous Veitch nursery. The Japanese cedar was first introduced into this country in 1842 when a small quantity of seed was obtained by Kew Gardens but it was not available in any numbers until the plant collector Robert Fortune sent a larger batch from Shanghai in 1844. All the old Japanese cedar trees in Britain are said to have been grown from Fortune's seed and it appears that the Chartwell tree is one of them. Significantly, Campbell Colquhoun was himself in contact with Sir William Jackson Hooker in 1851 and again in 1853. It is evident they were slightly acquainted and that Campbell Colquhoun himself visited Kew.[11] Although their correspondence does not mention seed, it seems highly probable that this was the route by which he obtained his tree.

All that remained in 1869 of the old Well Street Farm was the stables. The other buildings, including the oast houses, had gone and the site was a kitchen garden and orchard. A new farm, Chartwell Farm, with new oasts had been built where it is now, to the east of the estate and a new winding road led to it, as it does today. On 17 April 1870, the year after the map was published and following the death of his wife in January, which affected him deeply, John Campbell Colquhoun died at his London house 8 Chesham Street. He was buried with his wife close to Chartwell in the churchyard of All Saints, Crockham Hill and lies among a group of Campbell Colquhoun graves there with distinctive pink granite slabs. The inscription describes him as being 'of Killermont Garscadden and Chartwell'. He was succeeded as owner of all the estates by his elder son Archibald Campbell

Tea party at Chartwell, 28 August 1869. Far right are I. Campbell Colquhoun (?) and A. Campbell Colquhoun (probably the Archibald Campbell Colquhoun who owned Chartwell and died in 1872).

'The Honble Mrs Colquhoun. Chartwell August 28th 1869', as captioned in the Campbell Colquhoun family album and showing the enigmatic coats of arms on the old oriel window.

Colquhoun[12] although he barely lived long enough to enjoy his inheritance and died in 1872. The family estates then passed to his younger brother, John Erskine Campbell Colquhoun who followed his father's religious inclinations and took Holy Orders and in 1865 became Vicar of Crockham Hill. An indication of the way the property and estate had grown under the Campbell Colquhouns can be gained from the census of 1881[13] when the Reverend John Erskine Campbell Colquhoun and his wife Emily Agnes were living at Chartwell with their son

Chartwell from the east (*c.* 1870).

Chartwell showing the Campbell Colquhouns' late nineteenth century extension to the north (*c.* 1890).

and six daughters. They were employing a housekeeper, an Irish governess, two lady's maids, two housemaids, a kitchen maid, a scullery maid, a nursery maid, two laundry maids, a butler, footman, coachman, groom and page, a gardener/ domestic servant, an under gardener and garden labourer, a gamekeeper, and a farm bailiff responsible for ten labourers and two boys. There were seven or eight cottages, mainly at Puddledock, in addition to the main house and the families of the employees included around twenty-two children. Ten years later, the main change had been that the Campbell Colquhouns had yet another daughter (they eventually had seven daughters and two sons) and the servants had been augmented by a nurse and a cook. On the farm, there seems to have been a decline in the number of general labourers and an increase in horses as four men were employed specifically to look after them.

John Erskine Campbell Colquhoun also made major changes to the house. The 1896 Ordnance Survey map shows a northern extension (the family was undoubtedly running short of bedrooms) – this change is very evident from photographs of the period – a game larder to the south-east, a sundial in the

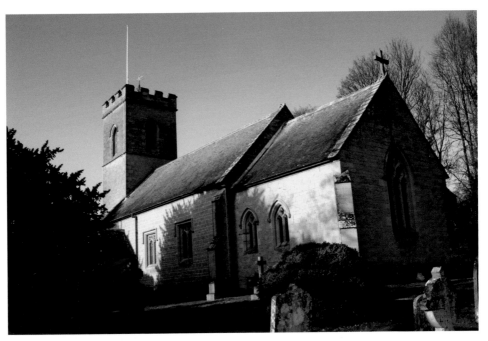

All Saints Church, Crockham Hill where the Campbell Colquhouns are buried.

Part of the group of Campbell Colquhoun tombs in Crockham Hill churchyard.

walled garden, a cottage, in truth almost a lodge, called Garden Cottage on Well Street (which had by then become Mapleton Road), another greenhouse, two sheds to the east of the shrubberies and a shed and two new stables behind the Stable Cottage, further evidence of the increasing importance of horses. The Reverend John Erskine Campbell Colquhoun died on 29 January 1917. He too is buried at Crockham Hill and his elder son, called predictably enough Archibald John Campbell Colquhoun, succeeded him to become the last owner before Churchill.

Remarkably, Archibald John Campbell Colquhoun and Churchill had known each other as schoolboys although they had not kept in touch. They were near-contemporaries at Harrow, arriving in the same term at Easter 1888 although Campbell Colquhoun left first in 1891. He went to Trinity College, Oxford, became a JP in Dumbarton and a Deputy Lieutenant for Dunbartonshire then saw distinguished service in the First World War when he was mentioned in despatches. He enlisted in the 6th Battalion Cameron Highlanders in February 1915 and took part in the tragic action at Loos in September that cost the British 50,000 casualties. During the action, in which he was wounded, he rescued the bell from the remains of the school in the village of Mazingarbe and brought it back to Garscadden.[14] Campbell Colquhoun rejoined his regiment in December 1915, was again transferred to hospital in March 1916, rejoined again in April and was once more transferred to hospital in May. The following year he inherited the family estates and although it is not clear if he ever lived at Chartwell, he let the shooting to a friend of Sir Ian Hamilton[15] and then to a Mr Turner who at the time of Churchill's purchase had the rights until February 1923. He certainly retained some of the staff as they were still employed by him in 1921 when through his own agent Crawford Scott, he offered the entire property for sale. It had by then grown to 816 acres and included several farms.

Knight Frank & Rutley held the initial auction of the Chartwell Estate in twenty-three lots at the Rose & Crown Hotel in Tonbridge on Tuesday 26 July 1921. The intention was to sell it as a whole except for a few very small parcels of land. If this intention was unrealised, it would be offered as two further options with various lots grouped together. If these were unrealised, as seems to have been the case, the Lots would be offered individually. Although the sale particulars survive, no results are recorded but it appears that the entire estate was sold off piecemeal over the succeeding twelve to eighteen months.[16]

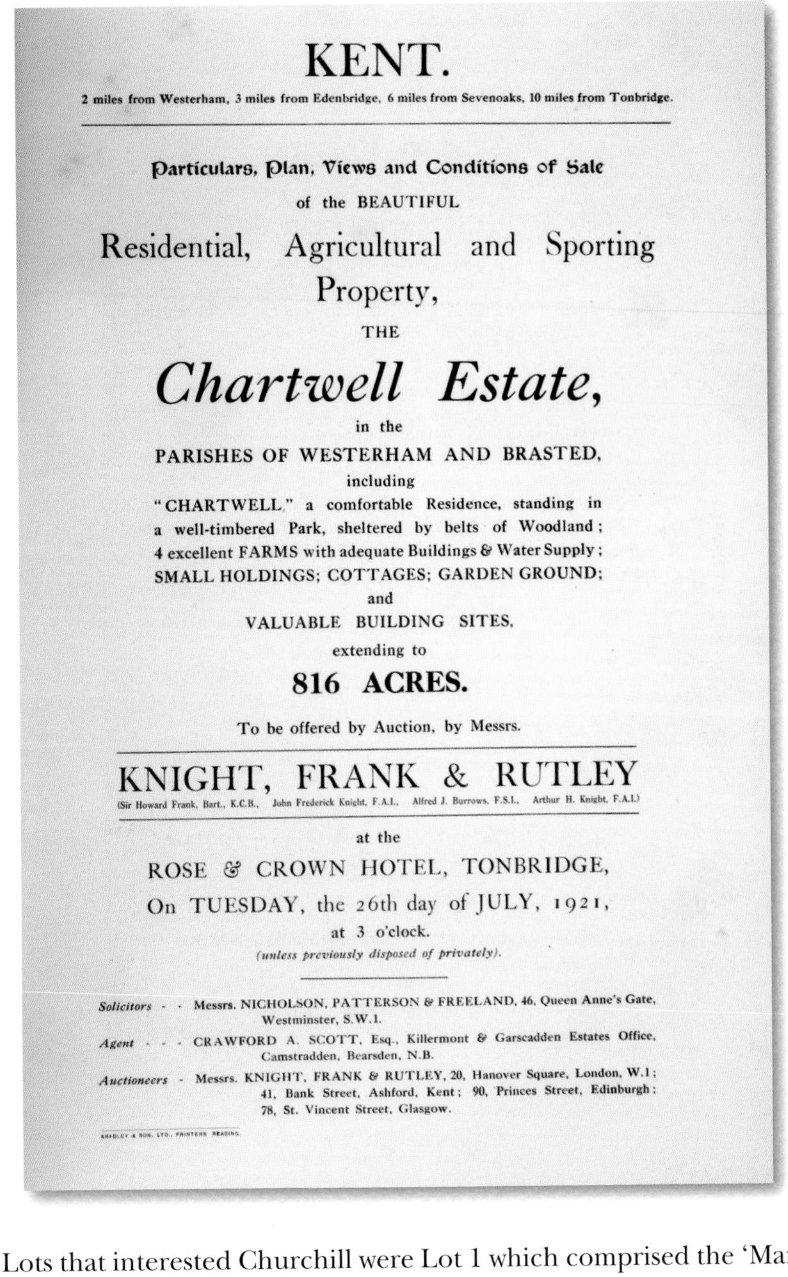

KENT.

2 miles from Westerham, 3 miles from Edenbridge, 6 miles from Sevenoaks, 10 miles from Tonbridge.

Particulars, Plan, Views and Conditions of Sale

of the BEAUTIFUL

Residential, Agricultural and Sporting Property,

THE

Chartwell Estate,

in the

PARISHES OF WESTERHAM AND BRASTED,

including

"CHARTWELL," a comfortable Residence, standing in a well-timbered Park, sheltered by belts of Woodland; 4 excellent FARMS with adequate Buildings & Water Supply; SMALL HOLDINGS; COTTAGES; GARDEN GROUND; and

VALUABLE BUILDING SITES,

extending to

816 ACRES.

To be offered by Auction, by Messrs.

KNIGHT, FRANK & RUTLEY

(Sir Howard Frank, Bart., K.C.B.,   John Frederick Knight, F.A.I.,   Alfred J. Burrows, F.S.I.,   Arthur H. Knight, F.A.I.)

at the

ROSE & CROWN HOTEL, TONBRIDGE,

On TUESDAY, the 26th day of JULY, 1921,

at 3 o'clock.

(unless previously disposed of privately).

Solicitors - - Messrs. NICHOLSON, PATTERSON & FREELAND, 46, Queen Anne's Gate, Westminster, S.W.1.

Agent - - - CRAWFORD A. SCOTT, Esq., Killermont & Garscadden Estates Office, Camstradden, Bearsden, N.B.

Auctioneers - Messrs. KNIGHT, FRANK & RUTLEY, 20, Hanover Square, London, W.1; 41, Bank Street, Ashford, Kent; 90, Princes Street, Edinburgh; 78, St. Vincent Street, Glasgow.

BRADLEY & SON, LTD., PRINTERS, READING.

The Lots that interested Churchill were Lot 1 which comprised the 'Mansion and Grounds' amounting to 79.435 acres and Lot 2 'Arable Field and Woodland' of 12.164 acres. All was available freehold except for 19 acres of Lot 1 which were tenanted on a yearly basis by a Mr W. S. Heaseman who was also the tenant of

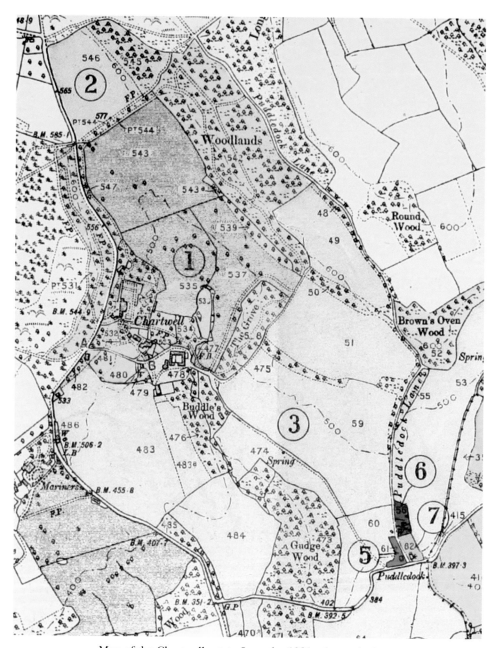

Map of the Chartwell estate from the 1921 sale particulars.

CHARTWELL FARM, LOT 3.

Chartwell Farm from the 1921 sale particulars.

Chartwell and Obriss Farms to the south and east which were included within the Campbell Colquhoun estate. In due course, Heaseman was given notice to quit and Churchill therefore retrieved this additional land in October 1926.

Churchill responded to Knight Frank & Rutley's price of £5,500 with an offer of £4,800 to exclude the butler's cottage, and subject to vacant possession of all the other cottages, a price he considered justified because the house would have to be very largely rebuilt; and there was dry rot in the north wing.[17] Five days later he increased his offer to £5,000 and this was accepted immediately.[18]

Clementine was still however in the dark. And she remained so a few days later when Randolph, Diana and Sarah were taken by their father on a mystery car ride in to the country. Churchill told them he was thinking of buying a country house and they were being taken to see it and give their impressions. It was magical. They adored it, finding it mysterious and overgrown. Churchill kept asking them if they liked it. The children were delirious. 'Do buy, do buy it,' they said.[19] Churchill said he was not sure and it was not until they had almost arrived home that he confessed. It was effectively his already.

Any hopes, however, that the children's delirium would be mirrored by their mother were soon to evaporate. Clementine was quite simply appalled. In the fourteen months since she had first seen Chartwell and had turned the matter over and over in her mind, its defects had almost totally supplanted any virtues. She could see the spiralling costs and the anguish, the Garron Towers inheritance evaporating, the commitments in staff, time and heartache ever growing. It would be Lullenden, magnified many times. And to a large degree, she was to be proved right. The purchase of Chartwell revealed Churchill at his most implacable, his most egoistic, his most deaf and blinkered to outside reason and influence. Chartwell possessed Churchill as he possessed Chartwell and as the years went by, and even when in due time Clementine was to soften her views (largely as their disposable income and means to pay increased), it remained a feature of their lives that served to unite and divide them in equal measure.

In his customary way, Churchill applied to the Trustees of his father's will to help finance the purchase. Through Nicholl, Manisty & Co., his solicitors, he asked for a mortgage of £3,500 and suggested this would represent the proceeds of the £200 of East Indian Railway shares they held. His cousin, Sunny, the Duke of Marlborough replied on the Trustees behalf and to Churchill's great disappointment, only offered £2,500. Churchill wrote to the Duke, arguing forcibly. He did not see why the stock could not be sold and pointed out that experts (un-named) he had employed thought he had done well to obtain Chartwell for £5,000. The timber alone was recently valued at £1,800, there were eighty acres worth £1,600 and two good cottages which could not be worth less than £300 each. He proposed spending £7,000 or £8,000 on the property and when the work was complete, he believed he would have a first class, medium sized house standing in its own park and grounds within twenty-five miles of London. He thought it would then be worth over £15,000 and questioned the Duke's discretionary powers in refusing to sell the railway shares. He felt the Duke would be taking an exceptional course, unsupported by legal advice.[20] [21]

The Duke held his ground, pointing out that he had not actually refused to sell the shares and reminding Churchill that whilst Trustees may lend money up to two thirds of the value of property, 'the word is may not shall'. The financial markets moreover were not favourable. 'Vast proportions of the land of England today are unsaleable,' he said, and he would only advance the further £1,000 when the improvements to Chartwell had been effected. In reality, Churchill's assessment of £15,000 as the likely worth of Chartwell proved an exaggeration and Marlborough's caution was justified.

Capitulating to his cousin's arguments, Churchill somehow found the remainder from his own funds and completed the purchase in November when he paid the balance of £4,500. He also took over the outside effects in the shape of the contents of the various garden buildings and outhouses, the wood house, tool house, carpenters shop (which included two hand snow ploughs, useful in the event of bad weather), hayloft, loose boxes and the boat house with a 10 foot dinghy; total value £102 18s 0d. There were also 92 trees, about £240 worth of standing timber.

He told Campbell Colquhoun that he planned a very large reconstruction of the house on modern lines as far as their finances allowed, preserving all the old walls and beams. But having decided that Chartwell was largely to be rebuilt, Churchill needed an architect. Of those with whom he had come into contact previously, Fred Foster, who presented him with so many problems over 2 Sussex Square was clearly out of contention. Walter Cave who worked at The Wharf for H. H. Asquith seems not to have been considered; and nor fortunately was Paul Phipps who had built the uninspiring Rest Harrow for the Astors. Another candidate might have been Detmar Blow although he was older and perhaps approaching the end of his career. Churchill was certainly familiar with his output as around the turn of the century, he had worked extensively at Breccles Hall, the house that subsequently became so well known to the Churchills when it was the home of their friends, Venetia and Edwin Montagu. In 1911 Blow also designed the remarkable neo-Dutch style hunting lodge, the Château de Woolsack for the Duke of Westminster at Mimizan in the south-west of France where Churchill stayed on several occasions – in a locality that was to feature in many of his paintings. This extraordinary half-timbered building has red brick walls with pierced gables to pediments with bull's eyes and is built square around a central courtyard with an open roof supported by stone columns. Ingeniously, the courtyard can be reached from all the rooms; but it was perhaps not quite appropriate for Westerham.

So why not Lutyens? Churchill had seen Lutyens' work at friends' homes

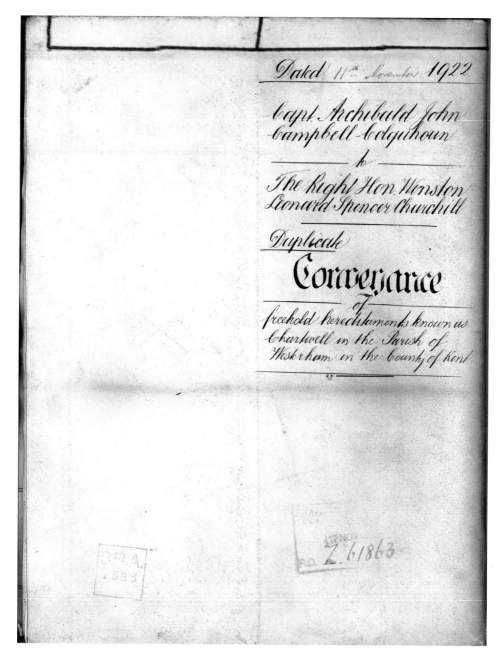

Dated 11th November 1922

Capt. Archibald John
Campbell-Colquhoun

to

The Right Hon. Winston
Leonard Spencer Churchill

Duplicate

Conveyance

of

freehold hereditaments known as
Chartwell in the Parish of
Westerham in the County of Kent

Above and opposite: Conveyance of Chartwell from Captain Archibald John Campbell Colquhoun to The Right Honourable Winston Leonard Spencer Churchill dated 11 November 1922.

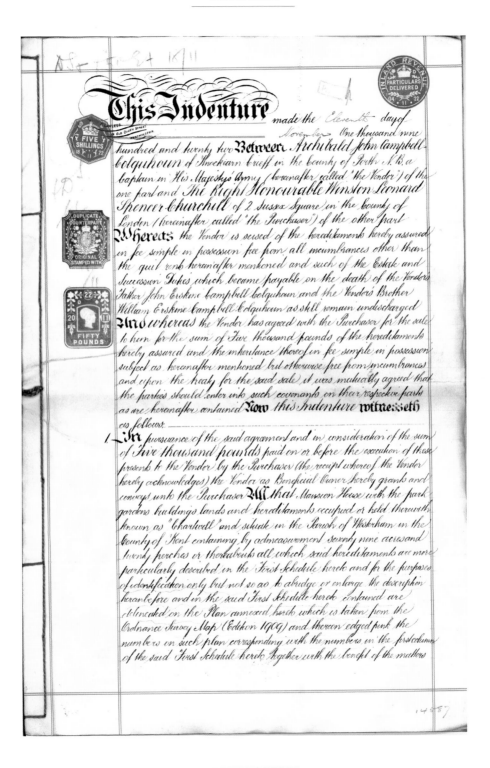

This Indenture made the Eleventh day of
November One thousand nine
hundred and twenty two **Between** Archibald John Campbell-
Colquhoun of Knocklearn Crieff in the county of Perth N.B. a
Captain in His Majesty's Army (hereinafter called "the Vendor") of the
one part and The Right Honourable Winston Leonard
Spencer Churchill of 2 Sussex Square in the County of
London (hereinafter called "the Purchaser") of the other part
Whereas the Vendor is seised of the hereditaments hereby assured
in fee simple in possession free from all incumbrances other than
the quit rents hereinafter mentioned and such of the Estate and
Succession Duties which became payable on the death of the Vendor's
Father John Erskine Campbell Colquhoun and the Vendor's Brother
William Erskine Campbell Colquhoun as still remain undischarged
And whereas the Vendor has agreed with the Purchaser for the sale
to him for the sum of Five thousand pounds of the hereditaments
hereby assured and the inheritance thereof in fee simple in possession
subject as hereinafter mentioned but otherwise free from incumbrances
and upon the treaty for the said sale it was mutually agreed that
the parties should enter into such covenants on their respective parts
as are hereinafter contained **Now** this Indenture **witnesseth**
as follows:—

1. **In** pursuance of the said agreement and in consideration of the sum
of Five thousand pounds paid on or before the execution of these
presents to the Vendor by the Purchaser (the receipt whereof the Vendor
hereby acknowledges) the Vendor as Beneficial Owner hereby grants and
conveys unto the Purchaser **All that** Mansion House with the park
gardens buildings lands and hereditaments occupied or held therewith
known as "Chartwell" and situate in the Parish of Westerham in the
County of Kent containing by admeasurement seventy nine acres and
twenty perches or thereabouts all which said hereditaments are more
particularly described in the First Schedule hereto and for the purposes
of identification only but not so as to abridge or enlarge the description
hereinbefore and in the said First Schedule hereto contained are
delineated on the Plan annexed hereto which is taken from the
Ordnance Survey Map (Edition 1909) and thereon edged pink the
numbers on such plan corresponding with the numbers in the first column
of the said First Schedule hereto Together with the benefit of the matters

Chartwell from the east (mid 20th century)

and, at Hoe Farm, had actually lived for a short while in a house Lutyens had modified. The two men were in time to become fairly well acquainted and some years later when Churchill was considering building a small cottage within the Chartwell grounds, he thought he should ask Lutyens to proffer his views on it. He felt he might do this for nothing because '...he has always begged to give advice'.[22] Moreover, in 1922, whilst Lutyens was admittedly still busy in New Delhi he was also, in a memorable expression 'working more for the dead than the living' in creating graves and war memorials and might have welcomed the interesting and distinctly lively challenge; both of Chartwell and Churchill. It remains one of architectural history's more tantalising thoughts: what kind of house would be at Chartwell today if Edwin Lutyens had been allowed to get his hands on it? Certainly not the galleon-like building ploughing its way through the Wealden sea that eventually emerged. However, Lutyens never did work for Churchill and the creation of the landlocked galleon was due to a man named Philip Tilden.

The first reference by Churchill to Tilden is in a letter dated 29 September 1922[23] by which time he had already been engaged and Churchill was asking

Campbell Colquhoun if he could start work on the house before completion of the purchase but it is not known for certain when or where they first met. Tilden in his almost unreadable, pretentious and inappropriately titled autobiography *True Remembrances* says his first meeting with Churchill was at Philip Sassoon's house Port Lympne in Kent and this does seem to be generally accepted. He colourfully conjures up a picture of a fireside conversation one evening when they were left alone to talk 'for long hours' on architecture, beginning with a discussion of Lutyens' designs for the cenotaph. He also says he first saw Chartwell 'at rhododendron time'[24] which would place the visit in April or May of 1922, when the property had already stolen Churchill's affections although well before his actual purchase.

Philip Armstrong Tilden was born in 1887, the son of a distinguished chemist Sir William Augustus Tilden FRS who was an authority on terpenes – the chemicals found in turpentine – and on the development of artificial rubber.

Philip Tilden (*c.* 1920) by Alexander Corbett.

No 3 Pelham Crescent, Philip Tilden's London home and studio.

Tilden junior began studying at the Architectural Association in London in 1905 but gradually became estranged from his father following the death of his mother and Sir William's remarriage to a much younger woman. Tilden then found himself moving in artistic and literary circles in London among such notables as Ford Maddox Ford, Joseph Conrad, Edward Thomas and Wyndham Lewis and also with the artistic set of Chipping Campden in Gloucestershire where he mixed with the likes of John Masefield and Ernest Gimson. He was lured to Campden by Charles Ashbee's Guild of Handicraft – and by Charles Ashbee himself who fell in love with him. In 1908, Tilden was articled to Thomas Collcutt, architect of the Wigmore Hall, and then notionally joined the partnership himself which traded for some years as Collcutt, Hamp and Tilden; although Tilden worked almost entirely on his own account. By 1912, he was based in Chipping Campden but working on domestic commissions in many parts of the country. In 1914, he married, itself an awkward event for a homosexual; but it was compounded by the woman being considerably older than him and of mysterious and exotic antecedents. She claimed, improbably, to be a member of the ancient Royal family of Sweden.

With the outbreak of war, and unlike most men of his generation, Tilden failed to enlist and instead went to live on Dartmoor where he took up the marginally less hazardous pursuits of chicken farming and designing ornamental bookplates. The mysterious wife left for a time and went home to Sweden while Tilden broadened his life experience by moving in temporarily with a Belgian painter; but his luck was turning. In April 1916, he was staying at Prussia Cove in Cornwall where four years earlier he had designed an extraordinarily durable property called Porth-en-alls House, right on the seashore. It was never finished because of the outbreak of war but the house has remained to this day, steadfastly resisting the worst that the Atlantic can throw at it. While at Prussia Cove, Tilden met a woman named Agnes Conway, the daughter of the art historian, explorer and mountaineer Sir Martin Conway. She was entranced by Tilden, he reciprocated by designing bookplates for her and in the Spring of the following year, her father commissioned Tilden to restore, rebuild and extend his ancient family seat, Allington Castle in Kent. Wartime restrictions meant the building work itself could not begin until the end of hostilities but the task was worth the wait and it has been said that nearly all Tilden's important commissions over the next ten or fifteen years can be traced back to his friendship with Conway.[25]

Thanks to Sir Martin Conway's introduction, Sir Louis Mallet commissioned plasterwork from him for his house at Otham – a property that Tilden said the Churchills thought of buying to be near to their friend Philip Sassoon but were put off because it contained so much antique furniture. He repaired Easton Lodge at Great Dunmow in Essex after a fire for Daisy, Countess of Warwick (but fortunately did not interfere with Harold Peto's gardens there), designed gardens for Sir Robert Hudson at Hill Hall in Essex and restored Long Crendon Manor in Buckinghamshire for Mrs Laline Hohler (to whom he was introduced by Vita Sackville-West, another friend of Mallet). And so the train continued, one client introducing another, along a route which took Tilden to Woodbury Hall in Bedfordshire, to Watlington Park in Oxfordshire, Garsington Manor where he built a terrace and loggia for Lady Ottoline Morrell and then, most importantly, to Lympne in Kent and Sir Philip Sassoon.

Churchill's friend Philip Sassoon has inspired some spectacular eulogies: 'one of the best known and most glamorous figures in Britain in the first forty years of the twentieth century' and 'the most eligible bachelor and the greatest host of his time' are fairly typical. He had no difficulty living up to them. Sassoon had haughty good looks, exotic ancestry (the family was descended from Baghdadi Jews who derived their fortune from numerous enterprises, not least the Indian opium trade), the right education (Eton and Christ Church), connections (in the First World War he was private secretary to Douglas Haig) and a successful career in politics (including many years as Under-Secretary of State for Air).

Sir Philip Sassoon.

In the late nineteenth century, the Sassoon family moved in the Prince of Wales' circle and knew Lord and Lady Randolph well so Churchill's friendship with the family was long standing and in time he became a frequent visitor to Philip Sassoon's homes, most notably to Trent Park at New Barnet which Sassoon's father had bought from the Crown in 1908 and to his remarkable Kent house, Port Lympne. Churchill also stayed at times in the early 1920s at Sassoon's extravagant London home 25 Park Lane, which was owned by a Sassoon family trust. This truly gigantic house on the corner of Stanhope Gate was built in 1895–6 by

No 25 (now No 45) Park Lane, the Sassoons' London house (1896).

Port Lympne, Sir Philip Sassoon's Kent house.

Smith & Sayer for Barney Barnato, an East End Jewish diamond merchant who made good in South Africa. The Duke of Westminster had considered him of insufficient standing to be allowed to build on the Grosvenor Estate so he chose this site further south but in the event, died before moving in. It was one of the few private London houses to have its own ballroom. It became No 45 with the Park Lane renumbering of 1934 and in more recent times housed the Playboy Club.

Sassoon, like his father before him, was Unionist Member of Parliament for Hythe and he bought 270 acres overlooking Romney Marsh and the Channel near the village of Lympne which lay in his constituency. In 1912, he built a house there in a spectacular but somewhat precipitous position (it is now showing signs of slowly beginning to slide down the slope) and although it was completed the following year, he was not able to take full advantage of it until after the war when it was properly fitted out. It was originally called Belcaire but later re-named Port Lympne by Sassoon in affected recognition of the old Roman name Portus Lemanis. The architect was Herbert Baker who had worked with his former colleague Lutyens in New Delhi as well as with Cecil Rhodes in South Africa – his Dutch Colonial style is very obvious in Port Lympne's massive curved gables. Despite his colonial experience, at Lympne Baker was actually working in his old home county (he was born at Cobham) and was an accomplished domestic architect so it's fair to assume his name must have cropped up in conversation between Sassoon and Churchill when Chartwell needed attention. However, although Baker never did work at Chartwell, the irony is that he may have been at least partially responsible for a Churchill home without either man ever knowing it. He was working for Ernest George and Peto in 1886 when they designed the Mount Street apartment block that included Churchill's first bachelor flat.

After World War I, and perhaps because Baker was by then too busy with India and with other commissions – he was about to begin the redevelopment of the Bank of England – Sassoon turned to Philip Tilden to complete Port Lympne. Much of the abiding impression that Port Lympne conveys today is Tilden rather than Baker but it is hard to see what there could possibly have commended him to Churchill. Port Lympne is all steps and terraces, outrageous neoclassical embellishments, exaggerated but not quite vulgar interiors, an impressive though truly incongruous Moorish Courtyard and massive wrought iron gates bedecked with trophies of war. Lady Honor Guinness said it was like a Spanish brothel; she did not say how she knew.[26] The place is everything Chartwell is not and although Port Lympne and Sassoon do seem to have brought the two men

Trent Park, Sir Philip Sassoon's house at New Barnet.

together, it is barely conceivable that Churchill did not look critically at other examples of Tilden's work before handing him Chartwell. Nonetheless, apart from Sassoon's other home, Trent Park (at which Churchill painted) and the Park Lane house, both of which received the Tilden touch but were also totally different from Chartwell, there's no firm evidence that he did so.

The gardens, both at Port Lympne and Trent Park are also distinctively different from Chartwell. Apart from the terraces (one supporting a miniature vineyard), the most celebrated horticultural feature of Port Lympne is its huge double herbaceous border; deceptively appearing flat in illustrations but in reality running up the entire length of the prodigious slope. Philip Tilden is often given credit for the Port Lympne gardens (especially by Philip Tilden) but whilst he dictated the overall shape, the horticulture almost certainly was not his and later, between 1927 and 1936 it was Norah Lindsay who planted the huge double border, the front entrance, loggia, and the East, West and South Terraces.[27]

Just as there is no reliable documentary evidence to confirm the widely accepted view that Churchill was directed towards Philip Tilden by Philip Sassoon, nor is there any evidence for another, but perhaps more plausible possibility, one that would have given him a better impression of Tilden's domestic architecture. In 1920, Tilden received a commission (itself through a Sassoon introduction) from Lloyd George who had bought land at Churt on the Surrey Downs. The site had some similarities to Chartwell, the position being elevated and looking down on to two lakes although the house, which in time was named Bron-y-De ('facing south'), was to be built from scratch. Unfortunately,

Bron-y-De, Lloyd George's new house at Churt, designed by Philip Tilden (1921).

within a year of its completion, the property proved to be too small and Lloyd George commissioned an extension – it was for this work that Sidney Gluckstein of Bovis wanted Churchill's recommendation. At that time, however, Churchill and Lloyd George were relatively estranged, and there seems no evidence of Churchill having visited Churt before 1921. But nor should it be overlooked that Tilden knew Churchill's aunt Leonie Leslie, a woman whose judgement Churchill respected. Tilden claimed to be close friends with her and described her as 'charmingly helpful, and a good dumping ground for confidences'.[28]

After the war, Philip Tilden initially set up his practice in a beautifully elegant post-Georgian house that Louis Mallet found for him: 3 Pelham Crescent which had been built by George Basevi just off the Fulham Road in South Kensington. He nonetheless retained a Devonshire home, swapping his little chicken farm for Rowden, a house with over 500 acres at Sampford Courtenay, on the edge of Dartmoor, and was rather often staying there, or on his way to Devon, when Churchill needed him at Chartwell. During the several years of their relationship, however, Tilden moved his practice three times; first, briefly to Hill Street in Knightsbridge, then to 59 Doughty Street in Holborn and finally, during 1926, to Morley House at 320 Regent Street.

The house Churchill bought was rambling and large; it had after all accommodated the Campbell Colquhoun legions. It had however grown up piecemeal and was not appropriate for the Churchills' needs. They required bedrooms of larger size and better quality, new kitchens and bathrooms, a large study/studio, a library and adequate space for dining and entertaining groups of twelve or more, some at least of whom could be accommodated in style. The house also needed effectively turning through one hundred and eighty degrees so the important rooms would benefit from the view across to the Weald and away from the dreaded rhododendrons. And not least, there were some fine old features buried beneath the Victorian superstructure and worthy of resurrection – and which Churchill had told Campbell Colquhoun he wanted to recover. Churchill also had a scheme to build a staff cottage in the grounds and asked Tilden to produce some plans.

There is no evidence of the nature or date of Churchill's original architectural commission but Tilden made his first visit to Chartwell in the spring of 1922 and by the end of September, the weather was deteriorating and he was anxious for essential work to start. He asked Churchill if Campbell Colquhoun would

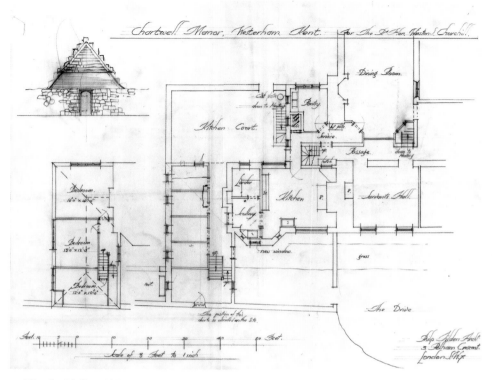

Plan by Philip Tilden of the ground floor of Chartwell before building work, with some alterations marked.

agree to this even though completion of the purchase would not take place until 11 November. Almost the entire house was clothed in ivy and he wanted this stripped off and the shrubs around the house cleared away so the brick work could begin to dry out before the winter. Churchill too was clearly impatient to start. No sooner had Campbell Colquhoun given permission for Tilden to begin his work than Churchill was pressing his architect for drawings. Tilden wanted to produce a model of his proposed reconstruction but Churchill vetoed this on grounds of costs. Architects like to produce models because they enable clients unfamiliar with interpreting two dimensional drawings to see exactly what is intended; but they are expensive. Tilden produced perspective drawings instead but nonetheless pleaded that such things could not be rushed although he promised to produce some sketches for the part of the house on which they were to begin and also 'a sketch for the cottage which we suggested making out of old materials'.[29] Sadly, practically all Tilden's drawings of Chartwell have disappeared but there clearly was no single master drawing, no proper master design. The work was largely planned and performed *ad hoc* and this played no small part in the problems that were to ensue. The intention was to create 'a habitable house' in the main part of the building, starting at the south end and proceeding to the centre. Work on the kitchen wing at the north end and a new eastern wing was to follow later.

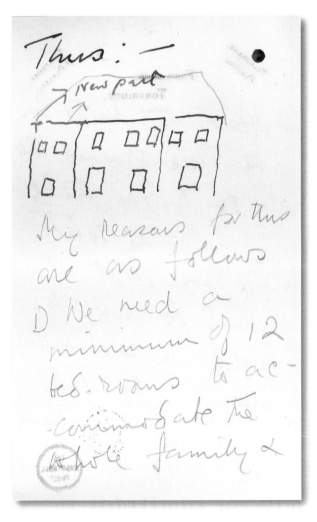

Clementine's sketch drawing of Chartwell sent to Churchill showing the need for a new extension.

Tilden's reason for working first on the south side where the nurseries were to be created – this became known as 'the children's wing' – was that the family could stay there before the rest of the house was complete; even, he thought, to stay there at Christmas in what he called 'a picnicy way'.[30] The agreement was that no more than £1,250 would be spent to create two or possibly three rooms in the basement, a schoolroom on the ground floor, and a bathroom, together with a big studio/study on the first. But even by the standards of Churchillian and architectural optimism, the time scale was unrealistic and in the event, it was an ambition that missed its mark by sixteen months and many thousands of pounds.

Although Tilden did produce plans for a cottage in the Chartwell grounds, as Churchill had asked, the design he offered was of a building with a pantiled roof and white weatherboarding. Tilden himself admitted it was really too good for a workman and thought it would make a good holiday house for letting, Churchill was enthusiastic at this possibility of reducing the general expense and as the discussions continued, the relationship between architect and client was warm. 'Do not … let me lead you into any course which your better judgement condemns,' said the client. [31] But as costs on the main house began to mount in the coming months, the Tilden cottage was quietly forgotten.

Chartwell from the south showing stepped gable (*c.* 1960).

By October, the main building contractors had been appointed. Tilden had chosen two brothers, Alec and Harold Brown of Brown & Sons, 'Builders, Practical Plumbers, House Builders' from Nettlebed, Henley on Thames although almost all the secondary work, fitting out and finishing was undertaken by a local firm, William Wallace of Prospect House, Westerham, a true Jack of all trades. He could turn his hand to everything from carpentry, painting and decorating to laying carpets, hanging pictures, wiring Clementine's electric hair drier, 'cutting a hole in the garden wall for flowers' and adjusting the maids' lavatories. He worked however not for Brown or Tilden but directly for Churchill and invoiced him for everything he did. Wallace in turn, sub-contracted some tasks, especially in the estate cottages, to other local firms. All Wallace's invoices were made out to Clementine and are sometimes annotated with comments in Churchill's hand; and sometimes, no doubt much to Wallace's relief, with the word 'Pay'. In practice, they were generally settled within a month. However, the fact that Tilden had no direct control over the firm undertaking a considerable proportion of the work at Chartwell can only have added to the problems that ensued.

Browns immediately started work on stripping away the ivy and it came off in great green blankets, as ivy does, tearing down many of the hanging tiles in the process. At the time, this did not matter because Tilden had taken the decision,

Philip Tilden signing off for payment of £1000 to Browns for building work at Chartwell.

First work at Chartwell, stripping off the ivy and hanging tiles (Autumn 1922).

without apparently consulting Churchill, to remove all the hanging tiles that so characteristically bedecked the southern end and part of the west front of the house. They certainly added to the aura of nineteenth century gloom but their removal was a portent of much trouble to come.

With the whole building bereft of ivy and wall tiles and its old brickwork freshly exposed, work began on the southern end. Externally, what Clementine called 'the tower arrangement' retained its dormer but the Campbell Colquhoun's oriel windows facing west and south disappeared – and took with them some intriguing armorial sculptures adorned with dates, the significance of which for the present remains obscure. In their place came two first floor west facing windows which poured light into the tiny bathroom adjoining Churchill's bedroom at the end of his studio, and a new three storey bay facing south. Above the bay was a small third floor window while towering over the entire southern end and helping create the house's galleon-like appearance, was a massive stepped gable which in an earlier age would surely have needed the Monarch's licence to castellate.

The construction of the windows, of which there are so many at Chartwell, was entrusted to the long established Birmingham firm of Henry Hope & Sons which had been founded in 1818 and had a distinguished manufacturing history.

Churchill felt strongly about windows and the amount of light they admitted, partly for his painting but also because of the quality of life in general. 'Light is life' he had said the previous year when they were having comparable discussions with Fred Foster about the alterations at 2 Sussex Square.[32] But Tilden too had strong views about windows, and especially strong views about mullions which he liked. He and Churchill discussed them face to face in some depth during a meeting at Sussex Square on the 6 November. On his original sketches, it had appeared that all the new windows were to have brick mullions to match those of the existing windows but on his drawing they appalled Churchill because they looked about 12 inches wide. Tilden explained that the actual thickness was only 5 inches and they were on the ground floor only, to give the appearance of greater stability. On the upper floors, they were to be of 3 inch oak. Churchill, however, wanted all new windows to be of oak throughout the entire building; and he got his way. He did give in to Tilden for the west front however where it

was agreed the old brick mullions would remain because they would be very expensive to alter and because hardly any was a living room window; the reduced light was acceptable for 'kitchen, servants' hall, pantry, lavatory, staircase, bathroom etc'.

By mid-November, Tilden was still going down to Chartwell for regular picnics with the Churchills (he seemed inordinately fond of picnics) but in early December, the decision was taken for the family to have a break. It had been

Work begins on the west front of Chartwell (early 1923).

a gruelling time. With the loss both of his parliamentary seat and his appendix and with the demands of the work at Chartwell looming ahead (although just how great these demands were to be was not then apparent), Churchill decided to let Sussex Square. He placed it with a London agent and they found a tenant in Lady Linlithgow, wife of the controversial future wartime Viceroy of India. Churchill meanwhile took a six month lease of a Villa called Rêve d'Or, high up in the wooded district of La Croix des Gardes in Cannes. It was and is an area of particular beauty, effectively an urban forest with its hillsides clothed in Mediterranean botanical delights – umbrella pines, strawberry trees, holm oaks and especially mimosas '…all in tight bud just now…' Clementine wrote a few days before Christmas.[33] It is not obvious how Churchill knew of the house but their friends Consuelo and Jacques Balsan with whom they sometimes stayed lived not far away at Eze in the hills between Nice and Monte Carlo. Consuelo, born Consuelo Vanderbilt, had previously been married, miserably, to Churchill's cousin, Sunny Marlborough and at her home Lou Sueil, she created one of the great gardens of the Mediterranean – a remarkable formal knot garden by the designer Achille Duchêne (whom Marlborough had employed at Blenheim) was surrounded by steep slopes, ingenious steps and clever seasonal plantings. Even Clementine, who never warmed to the South of France in the way her husband did, called Lou Sueil a 'marvellous scented nest … almost too beautiful and too comfortable'.[34]

At Rêve d'Or, Churchill really did relax and produced numerous paintings; as he was to do many times in the years to come when he re-visited this favourite coastline; although he never, it seems, painted the Villa itself. From Rêve d'Or he made regular visits to attend to matters in London and check on progress at Chartwell; sometimes staying at the Ritz and sometimes, in almost identical surroundings, with Philip Sassoon at 25 Park Lane.

Cannes, with its pregnant mimosa blossom and winter sunshine was a world away from cold, grey and exceedingly wet Kent. 'The weather is appalling and detrimental to us…' Tilden wrote early in the New Year, although in spite of his gloomy prognosis, work was proceeding well.[35] 'The builder has found his feet...' he said and he was glowing with pride at his achievements in the studio where he had removed the old ceiling to reveal the ancient oak roof timbers of the early house, dating back to long before the Campbell Colquhoun's occupation. This was the room that became the pulsating heart of the house, the room that was to be the centre of Churchill's life, his private sanctuary, the place to which he returned in days of triumph and failure, of joy and grief, the room where speeches were planned, books written; where a Nobel Prize for Literature was won. Here at least, his architect had done him proud.

In mid-December, Tilden had written at length to his absentee client, outlining his plans and his expectations for the next phase. He hoped the southern end of Chartwell would be ready for occupation in early March. He anticipated the new east wing which would include the dining room in the basement, drawing room on the ground floor and Clementine's bedroom on the second, being ready at the beginning of August and he proposed to erect 'a new tower or annex' in the corner of the new wing, incorporating the existing back stairs. This would in practice give Clementine her own private staircase.

By mid-January, Tilden thought the house was beginning to look charming, despite the weather being atrocious. Churchill reported back to Clementine on the progress; in person when he was at Rêve d'Or and by letter when he stayed in London. In late January he was discussing with Tilden the details of the biggest and most dramatic change – the new extension at the rear of the house, an addition that would afford such superb views for the occupants. It allowed some sensible reallocating of existing rooms, produced a good pantry between the kitchen and the dining room in the basement (Tilden thought it prudent to have them all on the same level), a cook's sitting room above it, Clementine's maid's room close to her bedroom above that and an additional servant's room or bedroom on top; and all for £400–600. The old oak ceiling of the library had been exposed and meant it could be used as an attractive additional reception room – and as it was in direct line with the drawing room and boudoir, the result was a vista of over 80 feet when the doors were all open. Tilden was also thrilled to have discovered in the library an old four-light window of the original house hidden under plaster, exactly where he had planned to place one. The new arrangements brought other benefits too – mundane but practical. There could be a lavatory in the old cook's sitting room while a 'dirty dark bedroom' on the top floor of the old house would become a box-room, linen room and housemaid's cupboard lit by a skylight … and so it continued, with the result, in Churchill's summary that 'every room becomes a good room, and every window a proper window giving full light and air'.[36]

Clementine, detached on the Boulevard du Soleil in Cannes, intervened as she felt appropriate. It was important she wrote to be sure that Mr Tilden understood the difference between the linen room and the sewing room in 'the tower arrangement' where she anticipated two or three maids would sit and sew every day. On a few occasions, she wrote personally to Tilden with notes of changes, as she had done just before Christmas 1922 when it was her insistence that ensured the pantry was re-sited in the basement. But by March 1923, alarms over the domestic arrangements were emerging. There was particular concern about the proposed height of the new kitchen at the north end

Construction work on the west front of Chartwell (early 1923).

of the house. Churchill conveyed the anxiety to Tilden: 'I am sure a nine-foot ceiling will never do for a kitchen. Some other arrangement will have to be made or the cook will be unable to carry on under such conditions. ... I have never seen a large house with a low kitchen, and its existence at Chartwell would be fatal to the whole organisation of the household...'[37] And Clementine was furious that Tilden had ordered the kitchen range from Benhams and fitted it without consulting her, to the extent that Churchill suggested a postponement of the completion of the work until they took up residence at the end of July 1923 (optimism was then still the watchword). At that stage, however, he was still courtesy itself. '... I am so sorry to worry you with these matters but after all the kitchen is the main spring of a comfortable house and it would be a thousand pities when everything else is going well if some serious defect or inconvenience occurs in connection therewith ...' he wrote.[38] But Clementine did like the idea of the proposed new reception room giving a vista of 80 feet; very grand she thought and appropriate for 'a State Festival'.[39]

Construction work at Chartwell; Tilden's 'fine high front door of stone' (1923).

By early spring, changes were pending at the front as Tilden proposed massive modernising alterations. The smaller dormer at the northern end – the most recent Campbell Colquhoun extension – was to be reduced, and the pseudo-Elizabethan chimneys rebuilt in a plainer arts and crafts style, not least because during the re-roofing, one of them was found to have a huge crack that had been letting in water for ages. Local builders told Tilden there had been work for them at Chartwell every year to patch the roof which 'leaked like a sieve'.[40] The plan was for the old heavy Campbell Colquhoun inheritance to be swept away in favour of the clean, fresh lines of the nineteen twenties and the massive dormer-capped porch and oriel window over the front door were to go. Churchill unfortunately was not convinced and wanted the monstrosity to stay. Tilden was distraught. '…the omission of this bay over the front door, and the terrible bourgeois porch below it would be the making of the house … is it not possible to reconsider… the … bay immediately over the front door which breaks up the entire dignity of the house…if you allow me to make the front of the house perfectly flush straight through, I know I can make a perfectly satisfactory exterior … I feel sure you would agree with me if you were with me on the spot…I propose we should have a really dignified and fine high front door of stone, with a very nice 4-light window above to light your studio, conforming with those other windows on that face…' And he sought an ally: '…may I not enlist the sympathy of Mrs Churchill …'.[41] Churchill capitulated. Another round to the architect; he got his 'fine high front door of stone' with a studio window above. The door surround came, together with a number of fine wooden interior doors, window frames tiles, fire backs and a weathervane from Crowthers, the well known London dealers in the North End Road but it was to be years before their accounts were settled and they were in the thick of what Churchill's lawyers later called 'the great tangle' in the winding up of the Chartwell expenses.[42]

The west front of Chartwell today is Tilden at his most successful. The sadness is that it belies the hotchpotch behind. For despite its ugly and forbidding protuberances, the west front of the house had always been relatively uncluttered, whereas the east side looking across the valley was a jumble. It was like a child's play house to which extra bits had been added when the mood struck, or new boxes of bricks arrived as birthday presents. It remains a jumble, Tilden merely having rearranged the pieces and added some big new ones of his own.

In early July 1923, Tilden took stock of the first phase of the work. Thus far, £8,122 had been spent of the original figure of £8,700 which had been suggested as 'adequate for making a habitable house'. A further £1,159 was now needed to complete it. Churchill had agreed extras at a cost of £310 which left a shortfall of £271. Tilden also told Churchill that although he had hoped the new wing could be completed for £1,500, this now seemed unlikely although both he and Brown had made 'most extraordinary efforts' to give full value for money to date.[43]

At the beginning of August 1923, Tilden obtained an estimate from Brown of £2,561 4s 5d for the next phase: the new eastern wing and the kitchen wing at the northern end and he urged Churchill not to delay in accepting. The problem, claimed Brown, was of obtaining suitable labour in the district because of government work at Lingfield where local conditions and agreements had been over-ridden. At Tilden's suggestion, no competitive quotations were

Construction work on the east face of Chartwell (late 1923).

obtained, a move they may both have lived to regret, and he told Churchill that if he did not make a swift decision, an alternative course was to build only the bare carcass and leave the fitting up until later. Churchill however took Tilden's advice and Browns were appointed to carry out the additional work on a reduced estimate, negotiated by Tilden, of £2,061 4s 5d on condition that work on the 'new drawing room wing' (the east wing) was to begin at once and that every effort was to be made for the builders to be out of the main part of the house by September. Later that month, Tilden again brought Churchill up to date on the costs, but expressed his disappointment that Churchill was now blaming him for the total being higher than his expectation and pointing out that this was due to the extra work Churchill had requested and to unforeseen problems, like the defective chimney stack. It was an exchange familiar to any architect.

Some time during the summer of 1923, as it became apparent that any sort of civilised living at Chartwell was still a considerable way off, Churchill took a lease on an Edwardian house called Hosey Rigge, situated on Hosey Hill at the edge of Hosey Common about 1 mile to the north of Chartwell and the family based themselves there until the following spring. The strange name originates in Old English and means a ridge on a hill but in Churchill fashion, it soon acquired an inevitable nickname – Cosy Pigge, Cozy Pigge or Rosy Pigge. The house is a modest but handsome brick property of four or five bedrooms with the main rooms facing south to benefit from the wonderful elevated views. It was built by the Streatfeild family who had long owned extensive lands in the area. The children's novelist Noel Streatfeild was related to them and it was another family member, the church architect Granville Edward Streatfeild who designed it in 1904. By the time Churchill rented the house, Hosey Rigge was owned by Alice Liddell (immortalised by Lewis Carroll as Alice in Wonderland) and it was handily placed to keep an eye on the work taking place down the road and near enough for the children to use the Chartwell grounds for games and exploration. The first letter with a Hosey Rigge heading is dated 24 August but they had been there for some while before then.[44]

Clementine was away in Cromer in August staying at the Newhaven Court Guest House while she took part in a tennis tournament and Churchill amused the children at Chartwell one weekend by building them a tree house in a the huge old lime tree by the front drive. It was an impressive affair, two storeys high, at least 20 feet up and reached by climbing a rope and then embarking

Hosey Rigge house (1940s) near Chartwell which the Churchills leased in summer 1923
during building work at Chartwell.

on carefully placed struts. There was a cross-bar halfway up the tree to prevent
bigger people from climbing any further.[45] Ten months after the work had begun,
Chartwell was just beginning to emerge from the dust and disruption and to be
seen by Winston and Clementine from their vantage point on Hosey Hill as a
real family home in the making. But they wanted to live there properly and
were both becoming weary of the work dragging on; and of Tilden in particular.
Clementine, writing from Hosey Rigge, felt that Tilden's services would be better
used elsewhere. Three days earlier, a devastating earthquake had struck Japan
and she suggested he 'hurries up with Chartwell & then emigrates to Tokyo...'

No 62 Onslow Gardens, Venetia
Montagu's London house.

where she thought he could spend his time putting up pagodas.[46] She was also evidently becoming concerned that exactly as she had anticipated, Chartwell was running away with their funds. Churchill wrote to her from where he was staying on the Duke of Westminster's beautiful four-masted yacht, *Flying Cloud* which was moored at Bayonne and begged her not to worry about money, reassuring her that Chartwell was to be their home for many years, to be handed on in due course to Randolph. It will have cost £20,000 he said (omitting to add that this was rather more than the combination of his purchase price of £5,000 and the £7-8,000 worth of work he had told his cousin Sunny Marlborough he planned to spend) and will be worth at least £15,000. They would soon be clear of 'Tilden, Browne Mott & Jeff & Co. for ever' and 'the spring of 1924 will cover with its verdure the stains and blemishes with wh they have disfigured our gardens...' He was also pondering their London accommodation and wrote that although there was no hurry he thought they should sell 2 Sussex Square and buy either a small flat or a smaller house.[47] They looked at several houses and contemplating renting one for six months if they could obtain a sale. Clementine was staying with Venetia Montagu at her elegant London home 62, Onslow Gardens and took the opportunity to look at two or three. She saw one in Park Street in Mayfair that she liked but was particularly taken with a house in Cowley Street in Westminster, just across the road from the Houses of Parliament although the rent proved too high; '... for millionaires & not for us,' said Clementine.[48] Sussex Square however was to remain their London home for well over another year – until the electorate and Stanley Baldwin combined to present them with another – and when Knight Frank & Rutley produced their valuation of Chartwell in support of Churchill's wish to increase the mortgage, they produced a relatively modest figure of approximately £12,000; and that on the assumption that all work would be completed by the end of 1923 and the house would have six reception rooms, twenty-two bedrooms, seven bathrooms, kitchen and domestic offices, a front drive, entrance gates and a wall or fence.

In November, Churchill came face to face with another of the quaint and archaic customs which at that time went with the ownership of ancient property in England. Just as he had been obliged to pay the tithes at Lullenden, so he was now required to attend the Court Baron and Customary Court of the Manor of Westerham on the 14th. Courts Baron were archaic Mediaeval survivals which persisted to deal with matters of customary tenure and were presided over by the Steward or Bailiff of the Manor. Although they became obsolete in practice when copyhold tenure was abolished by the Law of Property Act of 1922, they survived in several places, including Westerham, where the last session was held in March 1934. His lawyers had earlier explained to him that although he held the Chartwell Estate 'in fee simple', the greater part of it was still subject to the customs of the Manor of Westerham, and he had to pay a Quit Rent of 7s 1d to the Lord of the Manor. It was necessary that he should 'make an acknowledgement' that he held the property affected according to the customs of the Manor. Churchill could not however attend the Court at the George & Dragon Hotel so incurred a non-attendance penalty of 3/-.

The reason Churchill was otherwise engaged on 14 November was because the previous day, Prime Minister Stanley Baldwin had surprised his party by announcing a General Election, arguing that only by reintroducing protection could unemployment be properly contained. The very same week, Churchill had published a powerful letter in support of Free Trade and so Liberal Constituencies were suddenly forming a queue for his favours. After a ferociously anti-Baldwin, anti-Protection speech in Manchester, he accepted an invitation the following Monday to stand as Liberal Candidate for West Leicester. Despite a vigorous campaign, however, his attempt to re-enter Parliament with its promise of high office in a prospective Liberal Government failed. He was beaten into second place by the Labour candidate Frederick Pethick-Lawrence, and Baldwin was still Prime Minister although the Conservative majority was slashed.

Time passed; 1923 slipped into 1924. In January, Churchill and Clementine spent a week in Paris, staying with Edward Stanley, Lord Derby. He had been Ambassador in Paris from 1918 to 1920 and retained a flat there. Then Baldwin lost a crucial Commons vote, his Government fell – and Lord Derby was among a number of Tory nobles who retired from political life. Ramsay MacDonald, the man who had taken over Churchill's lease in Eccleston Square, formed Britain's first Labour administration. And still the work at Chartwell continued. Clementine wrote at considerable length to Churchill on the apportionment of the various rooms and her thoughts on the management of the house when it was finally complete. She did not want to introduce into Chartwell the inconveniences she had seen in many lovely old houses; the wrong balance of living and sleeping accommodation. She did not see the merit of Tilden's idea of creating another sitting room out of the old pantry and lavatory. They already had their own private sitting room and the relatively few guests would have the use of the drawing room and library. The most important guests stayed in a room that had long been known (and well before the Churchills' time) as the Henry VIII. (This seems to have been in perpetuation of some fanciful belief that Henry VIII had once stayed at Chartwell, perhaps on his way to Hever Castle, the home of Anne Boleyn; rather in the fashion of 'Queen Elizabeth slept here'). An extra sitting room Clementine said would mean more furniture, more fires, more flowers (for Clementine's rooms, flowers were essential) and more housemaids. She was insistent that she did not want more than two housemaids at Chartwell. What was in short supply was servants' bedrooms. It was a telling commentary on the priorities of the age and of the concern she and Churchill always showed towards their staff. She was not enthusiatic about two or three of the servants having to sleep out; she recognised that it was cold and uncomfortable in winter and it was difficult to persuade extra non-resident labour from outside to come in and do housework. It's evident however that throughout their time at Chartwell, the Churchills did have a huge turn-over of domestic servants while outside staff tended to stay. This may have been in part because they found Clementine difficult and demanding but there were more pragmatic reasons too. Clementine tried to persuade London staff to come to Chartwell which many did not like and while she was correct in that it was cold in winter, it was also true that the nearest Green Line bus stop was some distance away from the house and the walk was a long one. Moreover the servants' dining hall was uncomfortably close to the dining room so the staff, to their irritation, were constantly being told to be quiet as they interrupted the family and guests' dining.[49]

In February, Churchill was staying at the Duke of Westminster's lodge at Mimizan, hunting boar and wrote to Clementine who was with Consuelo and

Jacques Balsan at Eze. '…Chartwell… I am sure will need the eye of the master in the absence of the mistress in the next few weeks. So important to get it finished & get the grass & greenery growing. 'Finish' – that is the vital thing…'[50] But the lure of the House of Commons was suddenly there again. A by-election loomed in the Abbey Division of Westminster itself. He had a foot in both Liberal and Conservative camps and stood as an Independent Anti-Socialist but with considerable Conservative support, despite there being an official Conservative candidate. His friend Philip Sassoon told him he was bound to get in. Philip Sassoon was wrong. Churchill lost by just forty-three votes but he was edging back to the Conservative fold.

There is not a single date on which it can be said the Churchills took up residence at Chartwell. There was not one arrival with a furniture van in the modern fashion. They stayed there for odd days and weekends in what Tilden used to call 'a picnicy way' well before the house was finished and the first recorded guest in the visitors' book was Clementine's brother in law Bertram Romilly on 5 January 1924. By the summer, visitors were becoming more regular – Goonie Churchill stayed for the first time on 28 June, Nellie Romilly, Clementine's sister on 3 August. Hubert Cox, an old friend of Lady Randolph's on 12 August and then, over the 18 and 19 August, Churchill's cousin Freddie Guest, Lloyd George, the Deputy Chief of the Naval staff Sir Roger Keyes and Churchill's former private Secretary at the Colonial Office, the MP and ally of Lloyd George, Sir Archibald Sinclair were all there discussing the likelihood of a General Election being held in the autumn. Jack Churchill brought his son Peregrine for the first time a week later. The visitors' book is not infallible but does provide a valuable record of people who were at the house overnight – to dine and sleep as Clementine's diary put it. Day visitors are not recorded. It can probably be said fairly however that the family's real occupation dated from just before Easter 1924 when Churchill himself moved in; although Clementine was not there officially to cross the threshold with her husband. She was with her sister and brother-in-law visiting her mother in Dieppe who was by then 'getting very old and feeble'. So Churchill left Hosey Rigge and took possession of his house alone, perhaps appropriately. It was his discovery, his project, his house and it was to be some years before Clementine truly saw it as a shared venture with which she genuinely felt at ease. On Maundy Thursday 17 April 1924, Churchill wrote his first letter from Chartwell, the first of many thousands to come, letters that were to chart the course of English history over the next half century. Appropriately, correctly, it was to Clementine. 'This is the first letter I have ever written from this place, & it is right that it shd be to you....' he said.[51] Word spread locally as the possessions were moved in and a fortnight later, he had to write to the Secretary of the Cudham, Biggin Hill and District Horticultural and Fanciers Association declining their invitation to become a Vice-President on the grounds that he was not yet 'properly installed' at Chartwell.

By the late spring, however, Churchill made a significant decision. As there was still no end in sight to the building work, he realised he needed independent advice and guidance in respect of the work done and the fees charged by the various contractors, so he engaged John Leaning & Sons, Chartered Surveyors of John Street, London and they represented him until 1927. Leanings became the conduit by which Churchill questioned almost every bill although usually the contractors were able to justify their charges by pointing out that additional work and materials had been requested or specifications altered since the quotation. Ranged against Leanings were Fleetwood, Eversden & King, surveyors engaged by Tilden and who in due course also came to represent the major contractors with whom Churchill had disputes. Leanings began with Browns, the main contractors and reported to Churchill in July that up to May, the cost of their building work already amounted to £12,400. But they did have some quick success because Browns immediately offered to reduce their profit from 17½ to 12½ per cent. This may have been in anticipation of Churchill discovering that by early July, he was still paying a builders' wage bill of £60 a week when very few people were employed on site and little work was being done. He gave notice to Brown that he expected him to terminate his work by 11 July but pressed them over many weeks for their accounts, largely through the medium of his hard working secretary Clarice Fisher.

Clementine had her customary summer holiday with the children, this time staying with Jack and Goonie and their children at a large Victorian house called Tan-y-Graig which they had rented at Pentraeth overlooking the magnificent expanse of Red Wharf Bay just north of the Menai Bridge on Anglesey. The wide golden sands were just a few strides away. Work continued at Chartwell in her absence and then, at the beginning of October came a mishap of momentous significance. Clarice Fisher had to write to Tilden telling him that as a consequence either of the walls shrinking or the floor sinking, the bidet

Tan-y-Craig, Anglesey where Clementine stayed with Jack and Goonie in 1924.

in Clementine's bathroom had cracked right across. Were Bonhams the suppliers or Browns the builders responsible she wondered. Shanks, the manufacturers, said it certainly was not them, contributing to another dispute that rumbled on for years.[52]

Shortly before the bidet cracked from side to side, Churchill had made up his mind to accept an invitation from the Epping Conservatives to stand for them when the election was called although he actually stood as a Conservative-backed Constitutionalist. The election took place on 29 October and Churchill was back in Parliament with a majority of 9,763; and it was in

Churchill and Clementine in Epping (1924).

Parliament, representing the same constituency (later re-named Wanstead and Woodford) that he would remain for the next forty years. Although he was by then a Tory in all but name and had at last publicly returned to the Conservative ranks, he did not really expect to be invited to join Baldwin's government. As things turned out, he was quite extraordinarily wide of the mark and Baldwin appointed him Chancellor of the Exchequer.

At the end of November, Churchill paid off Browns with a final cheque for £1,000, thanking them for their services and expressing pleasure that the long and complicated accounts had been settled. In spite of the difficulties and expenses which had been involved, he thought that Chartwell would be looked on as a very graceful and pleasant country house and that they would always be glad to have been associated with its construction. All seemed to be finalised. The building was complete, Chartwell was done, the dream realised, the new home ready and a new life of domestic bliss stretched ahead. Sadly, it was all much too premature. Other bills still had to be paid; and the quality of the workmanship proved. The end of the year was nonetheless a time for happier matters and a moment to pause for genuine celebration. Churchill was back in

The west front of Chartwell; 'Tilden at his best' (early 1960s).

Parliament and back in office, the family were together for their first Christmas at Chartwell and there were sufficient bedrooms for Jack and Goonie and their children and for Nellie and Bertram Romilly with theirs. Brendan Bracken came too and then at the New Year, they were joined by Ethel Desborough, the Irish barrister and politician Sir Edward Carson and his wife Ruby, the former Prime Minister Arthur Balfour and Philip Sassoon, no doubt with a close personal interest in learning what Philip Tilden had achieved. Churchill no doubt told him. Chartwell was however fulfilling the role that Churchill had always intended for it and the headaches and heartaches of its reconstruction could at least temporarily be set aside.

With Churchill's appointment as Chancellor of the Exchequer came a house and for the first time his notepaper had a Downing Street address, No 11 which had been the official residence of Chancellors since 1828. Their own house at 2 Sussex Square and its associated mews had therefore become redundant and at the end of the year Churchill put them in the hands of his friend Sir Howard Frank of Knight, Frank & Rutley. Frank had found Chartwell for him and for once, the sale was relatively straightforward. Conveniently, the new owners were almost within the Churchill social circle and may have heard about the house by personal contact. The purchaser was Commander Harold Swithinbank, one of whose daughters, Isobel, was married to Sir Stafford Cripps. Swithinbank's wife Amy was the daughter of the man who invented Eno's Fruit Salts and Swithinbank himself was a man of whom Churchill would surely have approved. His country house was Denham Court in Buckinghamshire but he also owned a succession of fine steam yachts, most notably the beautiful *Venetia* on which Sir Stafford and Lady Cripps were often entertained. Ex-Royal Navy and a staunch Tory, he always had God Save The King played before a gramophone concert was commenced on the yacht and in best naval tradition he saluted the quarter deck when he came on board. He paid £10,750 for the

Commander Harold Swithinbank, purchaser of 2 Sussex Square.

Sussex Square leases in January 1925, of which £9,082 was payable to the Trustees of Lord Randolph's will, £818 to Clementine in respect of the interest she had in the lease and £850 to Churchill himself in respect of his personal interest in the lease of 7 Sussex Mews. Clementine was soon making lists of furniture to move to Downing Street, though leaving their old home with much regret.

With his new job and therefore less time to spend at Chartwell – though an ever increasing amount to spend on it – Churchill then contemplated something that eighteen months previously would have been unthinkable. He and Clementine investigated the possibility of letting their new dream home. There was interest from a Mr McCormick and Clementine suggested putting him in contact with the agent who had let Sussex Square to Lady Linlithgow and seeing how he reacted to 70 guineas a week for June and July. If however he wanted it until the end of September, then it would need to be at least 80 guineas because they would have to take a large house abroad or go to a hotel for the children's holidays. Churchill was enthusiastic but did wonder where they would go. 'It is like offering a snail a fine rent for his shell' he said.[53] As things turned out, the snail and his shell stayed put; probably because they all realised the costs of becoming nomads for the summer would have outweighed the benefits. Then a few days later, there was a sad distraction when Clementine's mother Lady Blanche Hozier died at her Dieppe home with her daughters at her side.

But there was still no final escape from the Chartwell builders and their bills and it was now the turn of Henry Hope and Sons, makers of doors and windows. Through Tilden's office, they were chasing Churchill for settlement of bills throughout the spring of 1925 but he was resisting. Hopes' bills did not tally with their estimates, the windows were not watertight and, a real bone of contention, despite numerous attempts they had been unable to produce a door from the dining room to the garden that satisfied Churchill. He wanted a glass panelled door that could be locked from both sides, something they seemed incapable of manufacturing. They had tried but the result had been a complete travesty. He told Hopes '...you cannot rest content with the extraordinary blemish which is constituted by the unsightly alteration to the door...'[54] Henry Hope, suitably chastened, offered to go to Downing Street personally to see Churchill to try and resolve the matter and they met at No 11. Seldom can the Chancellor's office have witnessed such momentous discussions as those on the afternoon of Tuesday 26 May when Churchill and H. Donald Hope, the Smethwick window manufacturer, thrashed out the design of a door bolt. Even so, it still took until the beginning of July for Hopes to have completed the work to Churchill's satisfaction and for Churchill to settle the bill.

Then there was the electrical work. The electrical contractors appointed by Tilden were H. A. Lamb & Sons of the Fulham Road but predictably Churchill was not happy with their efforts. Matters came to a head in August 1925 when the lights would not work and he called in a local electrician to check the system. What the man discovered caused considerable concern – he found the work to be 'of a most inferior description' with poor quality cables. A piece of wire he removed for examination had actually perished so the following month, on Churchill's behalf, Leanings engaged a Mr Chadwick from Waring, Withers & Chadwick of Soho Square to make an independent expert inspection. The principal players, Churchill, Leaning and Chadwick met at the Treasury one evening in October to plan their action and Chadwick was asked to produce a detailed report. Churchill was by then becoming both angry and uncomfortable. 'Lamb's man has been down this week but not working on any plan... where is Chadwick's report... I have been driven out of my bedroom by the cold...', and, in passing, while he was in the mood to strike out at any workmanship, electrical or not, he was 'sure the use of unseasoned oak was a breach of contract...'[55] Five days later, Chadwick's report materialised. It was damning; although Chadwick's were still chasing payment for their work eight years later by which time Churchill had forgotten who they were.[56]

Chadwick found switches and sockets were fitted in the wrong places, some were of unsuitable type, moisture was collecting around the wiring, wires had been left bare... Tilden laid into Lamb. 'It has been … a source of very great anxiety to me that the electric lighting has given so much difficulty at Chartwell. … I must point out that I consider that you should have had more respect for the quality of work applied to this particular class of building.'[57] (Syntax was never Tilden's strong point). Lamb hit back. 'I have not the slightest doubt that the trouble is due to dampness, which will break down any cable under certain conditions. … The point I cannot understand is that we were not called in when a trouble developed, we find it not unusual to have to return to buildings to put right faults that develop during the drying period especially after such a wet summer we had in 1924. …'[58]

The problems with Lambs and their workmanship rumbled on for another year with both parties regularly sniping at each other. Lambs complained at having to take out the wiring put in by Payne, the local electrician. Although at that precise moment, the country had just been plunged into a General Strike and Churchill was personally plunged into producing the Government's newspaper *The British Gazette*, he nonetheless still found time for truly important matters and through his secretary Clarice Fisher, told Lambs that the wiring would not have been put there in the first place had their work not been defective. Then, in September 1926, came a serious disaster. An expensive glass chandelier in the drawing room crashed to the floor, 'Fortunately not killing anyone...' said Churchill.[59] He claimed the fixing was utterly inadequate to sustain the weight. Mr Lamb's response from his office in the Fulham road was a classic 'not me guv...' He said the chandelier was fixed by another firm, not known to him and the work was done when his men were away from the job. And he seemed to be right. Churchill had to concede that the mystery chandelier installer had been seen by several witnesses. Clementine, however, thought Lamb had been culpable by taking down the original fittings and installing heavier ones. Lamb stuck to his guns and said he would swear an affidavit... Eventually, peace broke out, agreement was finally reached through Fleetwood, Eversden & King and Lamb was paid off at the end of 1926.

The 'moisture' that seemed to play a part in the electrical difficulties was perhaps the biggest problem with which Churchill and his builders had to contend. There were times when it was less a case of moisture and more one of indoor rainfall. Dampness had been recognised as a factor at Chartwell from the beginning but it gradually worsened and in November 1924, inevitably, Churchill blamed Tilden for it; and while he was in the mood, also blamed him for the fact that the roof leaked and the chimneys smoked. John Leaning tried to pour oil on the waters. '...I must say that unless there is actual negligence on the part of the Architect he cannot be held liable for defects in a building or their consequences. The damp wall was an old one and could only be made dry by tiling vertically. The leaky roof was the old roof and the rough cast bay would have been waterproof if done in cement unless in a very exposed position. Smoky chimneys may occur in any house and have sometimes to be experimented with to get them to draw...I have of my own knowledge [seen] how much he [Tilden] had this work at heart (117 visits) and the result is in my opinion a triumph in its design and character...'[60]

Their defence of Tilden notwithstanding, two months later, Leanings produced a report on the possible origin of the dampness. It did not make for enjoyable reading. They discovered it had different causes in different parts of the house; although in one sense, it all had the same cause: poor workmanship. There were for example defective flashings, incorrectly installed gutters, walls built solid instead of hollow and incorrectly fitted tiles. Churchill thought the blame was to be shared between Brown the builder, Wallace the local Westerham carpenter and of course Tilden the architect and he told Leaning 'I cannot help noticing you do not seem to assign very much responsibility to the architect in the matter. He, it seems, is immune from all unpleasant consequences'.[61] And he told Tilden as much personally. He wrote to him on 2 February observing that according to his [Tilden's] view, the architect was responsible for nothing. If that was his doctrine, Churchill thought it very extraordinary, so extraordinary that it ought to be tested. He did not intend to let the matter lapse or drag on indefinitely. Tilden meanwhile, clearly becoming exasperated with his client's attitude had written the previous week to Leaning. '… It is really time that this extremely unsatisfactory state of affairs should be settled and I have written a strong letter to Mr Churchill…Please take the matter up strongly with him so that we can settle the whole affair satisfactorily from everybody's point of view. It is, of course, impossible to blame either the builder or the architect for a building that neither of them had anything to do with…'[62] Leaning replied, after seeing both Tilden's and Churchill's letters: 'I have received your two letters which do not seem to me to help matters very much. Mr. Churchill is thoroughly convinced that no solution would be any use and the mere fact of the present failure after all the precautions you refer to seems to prove that he is right….'[63]

The walls at the gable end had been treated on Tilden's recommendation with a patent protective liquid produced by a firm called the Szerelmy Company, based in Rotherhithe New Road, SE16. The patent brew however was patently useless and in the light of what was happening, Tilden wrote to the company on 11 February: '… We feel that some explanation is due from you as to the total failure of your material to do what it is supposed to do….'[64] Leaning then hauled in the Szerelmy Company's manager, a Mr Blockson, and told Tilden 'In the presence of Brown …I have brought him to book very much'.[65]

But it was in fact far worse than any of them had imagined and it was not the failure of the liquid but the poorly cut and fitted flashings at the nursery end and the original decision by Tilden to remove the hanging tiles without taking account of the consequences that had the most dramatic effect by admitting water to the inside. When Tilden's quantity surveyor, Thomas visited with Brown and Wallace, appropriately on Friday 13 February, they were 'astounded and shocked' at what they saw. It was raining heavily and water was streaming through the walls and ceiling at the gable end. Something had to be done, and done quickly. Tilden immediately wrote to Churchill to apologise for the 'displeasure and discomfort'. Extraordinarily however, instead of treating the cause, Tilden continued to treat the symptoms and turned to another firm with another proprietary protective treatment, George Lillington & Co. 'metallic liquid suppliers' of 69 High Holborn. They were invited to inspect the walls and asked Tilden if he would like to buy their 'Metallic Liquid'.[66] There is no recorded reply but it seems he did not and instead walked further down High Holborn, which was clearly replete with waterproofing firms, until he came to No 104 and the picturesquely named Waterex company. They were given the work and lined and sprayed the walls of the nursery wing inside and out and coated the inside with waterproof cement.

To general relief, the Waterex cement seemed at first to work and Churchill reported to Tilden in May that it was holding its own. What had not been agreed was the responsibility for paying the Waterex company. Churchill maintained that Tilden was as culpable as anyone and believed he had admitted as much. Tilden was not persuaded: 'I consider that Mr Churchill's idea that I have ever felt responsible for the condition of the gable … absolutely ridiculous. I repudiate the fact that he says that I have ever expressed my sense of responsibility in the matter....'[67]

The problem of the damp however was compounded many times by the presence of dry rot. The existence of dry rot at Chartwell had been known since the very beginning. Tilden on his first visit spoke of the house being 'weary of its own ugliness so that the walls ran with moisture, and creeping fungus tracked down the cracks and crevices';[68] Churchill indeed had used the fact that it was present in the 'northern wing' (the extension put up by John Erskine Campbell Colquhoun) as part of the justification for his offer of below the asking price. But it was in the southern part of the house too and Tilden clearly understood very little about it. 'I have been making all enquiries with regard to the particular growths that were discovered in the gable end' he wrote in January 1925.[69] His enquiries revealed that although it generally fed on wood, it could feed on mortar too but that a spray of izal oil into the interstices of the brickwork would destroy its roots [*sic*]. A combination of izal oil and tar would he believed cure it but not for the only time, he protested his personal innocence and said he felt very deeply the insinuations that defective work in the old building was in any way due to him. This was, he considered, 'quite impossible'. He maintained he had been particularly insistent on getting rid of all softwood in the house and having the damaged timber cut out. Nonetheless, when in August 1925 Payne the local electrician was called in to investigate the electrical defects, he found the dry rot still there; clearly it had not all been cut out by Brown the builder.

Dry Rot is an insidious problem in buildings. Its cause is a species of wood rotting fungus, probably originating in the Himalayas and brought to Europe in imported timber. It has the extraordinary ability to spread considerable distances across brickwork and plaster from one piece of timber to another and by its action, the timber is degraded and loses structural strength. In extreme cases, buildings have fallen down because of its effects. It is also extremely difficult to eradicate, and this was certainly so in the nineteen twenties when fungicide technology was crude and the products extremely toxic.

By the end of the year, Churchill was opening his heart to Leaning and summarised his dissatisfaction with Tilden, holding him responsible for pretty well everything that had gone wrong – not just the dry rot which had not been cut out but also the leaking gable wall, the white plaster used around the bay window which produced an unsightly white blister, the removal of the weather tiling so exposing the old bricks to the weather, the 'foolish staircases' which ran all through the bedrooms, the two separate redecorations of the interior which were again all ruined, and the damaged linoleum in the nursery wing. He thought the advice he had received and its results deeply discreditable. Nothing had been achieved, one ineffective remedy had succeeded another, the rooms were uninhabitable and the damage continued to spread.

Christmas nonetheless passed peacefully and the family were together. Then, as soon as the New Year turned in 1926, things started to come back and haunt them; chickens began to come home to roost. The weather was foul, rain was driving in again through the gable end wall and the children had to leave the nursery wing. Back came John Morgan from the Waterex company. This time they covered the wall with rebated wall tiles which looked like bricks and bedded

Construction work on the south-east face of Chartwell with the
'unsightly white blister' around the bay window (late 1923).

them in with their impervious cement. Then cracks began to appear in the new
east wing. One went straight across the drawing room ceiling. Others were at
the junction of the new and old walls. Churchill thought they indicated further
subsidence. As it was more than two years after the work had been finished, he
considered it particularly serious and it looked to him as if the whole of that
end of the building, 'all brand new', was not properly constructed. Mr Wheater
(the plastering sub-contractor) admitted the drawing room ceiling was loose and
dangerous. Tilden wrote again to his surveyors '... Mrs Churchill who has very
great influence over Mr Churchill has given it as her opinion that the house

is falling down... I want you professionally and independently to make an examination of this concrete, as I will not be played about with over the house, which has been excellently built....'[70] Tilden naturally also wrote to Browns: '... A matter has arisen which is also exercising Mr Churchill very much, and which also necessarily reflects upon yourselves. Mr Churchill has written very fully to Mr Leaning with regard to the question of certain cracks appearing in the Drawing room wing, and he opens up the whole question as to the foundations of this extension of the building....'[71]

Wallace, the local builder/carpenter was instructed to open up two inspection pits and look at the foundations; and chose that moment to reveal that he thought Brown's workmen had been negligent when putting them in. He had watched them do it in a loose and careless manner with rough stone and a slurry of cement and concrete. With commendable restraint, considering the foundations were holding up a wall over 50 feet high, Churchill, confessed himself 'disquieted'. His view of course was that Mr Brown and Mr Tilden were responsible for ensuring that the end of the building did not give way and he would insist on the necessary measures being taken at their expense. He was reminded of some relatively minor foundations to a garden wall that were also put in by Browns and which were similarly investigated earlier. That wall they discovered was standing on 'mere rubbish'. There were also concerns with the kitchen wing which was 'built by Brown as an after thought, mostly to Mr Churchill's instructions' according to Tilden.[72] That too was unduly wet, the drip courses were not correct and the walls were hollow.

Tilden sent his own surveyors Messers Cyril B. Tubbs & A. A. Messer to inspect the foundations. They wrote a report, then Leaning wrote a report and it was mutually agreed that there was indeed no danger although the foundations were not laid in accordance with the best principles. Churchill was thus reassured that his house would not fall down and it seems probable that the cracks were simply the result of the plaster drying out at the junctions between different types of brick and around reinforcing steel girders. In any event, shortly afterwards, he reported 'everything seems to be working smoothly'[73] although over a year later, the various parties were still arguing over who should pay and Churchill's lawyers were warning him that if the matter came to litigation, it would be very expensive to fight.

Moreover, the cost of the entire venture was beginning to hurt and once again the possibility of letting Chartwell was discussed. Churchill contacted Knight Frank & Rutley about having a tenant for May, June and July 1926. They felt they had a likely candidate although since the previous spring, Churchill had lowered his expectations of the likely income and from 70 or 80 guineas last time, concluded that at 40 guineas a week, this could still make a major contribution to the cost of the kitchen wing, 'or at least to pay bills' but there's no evidence that the scheme came to anything. Although there were no recorded guests in May, the Churchills were certainly there and entertaining in late June and throughout July. In any event, it seems improbable that anyone would have wanted to live in a building still beset with so many imperfections. And indeed, in May, Churchill was still having to issue pleas to Leanings. 'We never get to the end of our troubles' he said, 'that bad plasterer' employed by Browns, or Brown himself, he did not know which, had done his work so badly that there was another fall of plaster in one of the servants' rooms. As it was an attic room with no traffic overhead, it was clearly faulty workmanship and he wanted to know what could be done about it.[74] History does not tell us.

By late summer, the costs of running two houses were having a serious impact on Churchill's finances and for the third time in eighteen months, he contemplated letting and decided the house was to be put in agent's hands from the New Year with every effort made to obtain a let from May to September. This time, however, he contemplated more, much more, and drew up for Clementine a list of proposed economies. It comprehensively impinged on almost every aspect of their lives. There were to be draconian savings on estate activities and their livestock, the chicken-houses and cow-houses would be pulled down and not re-erected, the tiles being stored, the tool-house would be pulled down and re-erected, and the clearance of trees and bushes between the house and the lake and the replanting of certain apple trees would be all the estate work attempted. The Christmas holidays would be spent in London with Chartwell only visited with hampers for picnics and not re-opened until the Easter holidays at the end of March, domestic staff would be reduced, no bill was to be paid without Churchill personally approving it, there would be no more champagne, no port was to be opened without special instruction, cigars would be reduced to four per day, no fruit would be bought other than on special occasions, there would be no cream, two courses and a sweet only for dinner and one for luncheon, visitors would be invited only rarely (apart from Jack and Goonie). It was all frankly ludicrous;

and for a man whose bills for vintage Pol Roger champagne, port and cigars alone regularly exceeded all other household expenditure, wholly impractical. So apart from a reduction in the livestock activities, almost nothing changed, Christmas was spent at Chartwell, and the house, yet again, was not let.[75]

Throughout Churchill's disputes with his builders and their sub-contractors, there was an under-current of his belief that Tilden himself was equally culpable for the problems and as early as the spring of 1923, Churchill was expressing the view that he could have done more to keep the building costs down. And for almost as long, Churchill believed that Tilden was himself over-charging and that the basis on which his fees were calculated was unfair and unreasonable. It had been agreed at the beginning of the commission in 1922 that he would charge on the general basis set out by the Royal Institute of British Architects (RIBA), at the rate of 7½ per cent on alteration work, and 6 per cent on new work. Tilden pointed out that at Chartwell, where they would be re-using a great deal of old material, this would benefit the client, not the builder or architect. In reality, however, where the distinction between what was old and what was new was blurred, it was inevitable that Churchill would be given scope to question the accounts. And so it proved, with the disagreement eventually bubbling to the surface in the early summer of 1924. Tilden submitted an account at 7½ per cent, a rate Churchill had either forgotten or conveniently overlooked. He claimed this figure had never been mentioned to him, adding that he had a verbal agreement that fees should in any event only be levied on a maximum of £10,000. Tilden's secretary Bray leapt to his master's defence, boldly pointing out to Churchill that Tilden had in effect acted as clerk of works to the job and had only charged out of pocket expenses, when he was entitled to a fee of £5 5s 0d per day. It was this turn of events, coinciding with his disputes with the builders, that prompted Churchill to engage Leanings to act on his behalf and once they had weighed into Browns, Churchill let them loose on Tilden himself and asked them to negotiate with him over his fees.

Although they were working for Churchill, Leanings were to reveal themselves as skilled and diplomatic arbitrators and were more responsible than anyone for ensuring that Chartwell was eventually completed to Churchill's satisfaction. They did not on balance feel Tilden had charged too much: '...some architects would have charged 10 per cent on the cost. Domestic work involves far more detailed direction than commercial work and is charged by the leading men such as Ernest Newton, Sir E. Lutyens and others on a higher scale. For originality and ability, Mr Tilden is entitled to rank with the best of them and deserves as good fees…'[76] With spectacular understatement, they said it was not a new problem, the matter of the accountability of an architect for estimates. They did not however think Tilden was entirely to blame [for the building problems] and hoped that before long he would be remembered for the quality of his work. They had tried to be fair and were sorry if Churchill thought their judgement one-sided. But if either party thought the matter would be resolved swiftly, they were grossly mistaken and it was to be a running sore for the next two or three years.

Churchill was never slow at involving lawyers in any of his personal disputes. He had used them already at Chartwell in his disagreement with Browns and during 1925 Nicholl Manisty & Co entered the fray against Tilden who was both surprised and distressed. 'I have felt it very much this last week that the inclusion of solicitors in this matter, except purely in an advisory capacity, is an insinuation that we are not all working for you'.[77] The involvement of the solicitors, however, tended to slow down rather than hasten the resolution of the dispute and, as happens with lawyers, brief bursts of activity and weekly, if not daily letters were followed by long spells when nothing happened.

Meanwhile plaster continued to cascade down at regular intervals. In December 1926, there was a fall in Churchill's bathroom, another on the stairs, one in the servants' bedroom and two in the drawing room exactly where, for several days beforehand, three servants had been sitting sewing. Chartwell was 'as usual a picture of shade as well as light…' wrote Churchill a month later as men hammering down a carpet caused yet another heavy fall in the drawing room.[78]

Adjoining the loggia at the northern end of the terrace to the east of Chartwell is a rather elegant, pillared building, initially called the garden house. It is a Tilden creation but the idea for it came originally from Clementine and it was in her mind from the beginning. Churchill was less than enthusiastic. They already had the game larder close to the south-west corner of the house that he had asked Tilden to convert to a summer house by removing the east-facing wall, and they had the loggia which Tilden built outside the dining room. 'For my part', he told Tilden, 'I should have thought that one garden house, ten feet square, would accommodate all the sun that is our portion in English summers. I consider too that there is too much made of the romance and usefulness of garden houses, for not only, as you sit there, do spiders, suspended by their invisible threads, alight upon your head, but your feet are not immune from the constant attack of those little woodlice, that career, like so many tanks, across the floor…'[79] Clementine had her way, however, but perhaps even then becoming conscious of the cost of operating through Tilden, Churchill originally planned to take it upon himself to organise the work, simply paying his architect for the design and specifications and the first mention of the building is on an undated invoice from Tilden for some working drawings, probably written in the winter of 1922–23. At the same time, Churchill also purchased a Tilden design for a fountain but this was never executed. Not surprisingly, the garden house/ loggia does not seem to have been a priority but by autumn 1924, materials were finally being ordered and work was well under way in early 1925 when The Trussed Concrete Steel Co. was commissioned to supply a vaulted ceiling. Wallace the Westerham carpenter fitted the windows and did the joinery but Tilden was eventually brought on board presumably because Churchill's time became increasingly scarce after the election of 1924. During Tilden's love affair with the Waterex company, he obtained an estimate from them for roofing the building with Waterex cement in order to make it into a terrace on which people could walk.

In late 1933, Churchill asked his nephew, Jack's elder son Johnny Spencer Churchill, a professional artist, to decorate the loggia. It was his first major work and Churchill said he could choose any subject he liked. He created a complex *trompe l'oeil* showing the four major characters in the life of the Duke of Marlborough the account of which Churchill was then writing. Marlborough himself, Prince Eugene of Savoy, Queen Anne and Sarah, the Duchess occupied the four niches. At the corners of the vaulted ceiling were four plaques of figures representing the four rivers on which Marlborough's battles were fought – Danube, Moselle, Meuse and Rhine

Johnny Spencer Churchill, Churchill's nephew.

with, in between, lunettes of the battles of Blenheim, Ramillies, Oudenarde and Malplaquet. Above it all was a balustrade with Diana and Sarah looking down on the scene. Johnny spent two cold months in January and February 1934 working in the loggia with almost daily interjections and advice from Churchill whose criticisms of the fact that the representations of the battles were inaccurate were counterbalanced by encouraging artistic advice from Sir William Nicholson who was staying at Chartwell while working on a commissioned picture of Churchill and Clementine taking breakfast in the dining room. Eventually the work was done and received official approval and from thence the garden room/loggia became known as the Marlborough Pavilion.

Vines being pruned in the loggia adjoining the Marlborough Pavilion (February 1957).

When Tilden submitted to Leanings his accounts for work on the garden house in the spring of 1927, it served only to compound the existing financial dispute. This time Tilden charged 8 per cent; Leaning thought 6 per cent was more appropriate as Tilden had let his client in 'for considerable inconvenience and extra expenditure'. Tilden appeared genuinely hurt at Churchill's overall

The loggia and Marlborough Pavilion.

Johnny Spencer Churchill's frieze in the Marlborough Pavilion.

attitude to the Chartwell work. 'I am most sorry for Mr Churchill that Chartwell has proved so unlucky to him for I hoped and wished it to be a really beautiful & well-built house & I tried my best during its construction to make more visits and pay more attention than any other architect perhaps…'[80]

Churchill and Mary at Chartwell (*c.* 1927).

By early May 1927, however, matters did seem to be coming to a head. Tilden's surveyors, Fleetwood, Eversden & King wrote to Tilden '… We consider that the time has now come to definitely take action and let Mr Churchill do his worst. In our opinion no settlement is intended on their side and they are only temporizing to avoid paying.' And they felt their tough stance had paid off.[81] We agree there could be no case of legal proceedings, but there was one of firmness, and not being bullied as you will see by the copy enclosed of a letter received this morning from Messrs. Nicholl, Manisty & Co. We venture to think our firmness has brought the matter to a satisfactory settlement. …'[82] And a month later, Tilden too seemed triumphant and thought the matter had been resolved. 'To my mind this satisfactory result to what might have been an extremely difficult and distressing affair, has been due to your level-headedness and straight dealing.…'[83] But he was also now prematurely counting his chickens because the dispute rumbled on through the summer of 1927 and then at the end of October, came another of those bombshells with which the Chartwell story is so liberally littered. Churchill's secretary Clarice Fisher rang Tilden's office to tell them that dry rot had reappeared; and was rather unfortunately present in one of the beams that held up the whole of the nursery wing. It could probably be put right by cutting away a large number of flooring joists and part of the new staircase and the insertion of a steel girder; but who was to be held responsible and who was to pay?

The matter was immediately passed to the lawyers. Tilden later said the recurrence was 'a misfortune to us all – and a very real unhappiness to myself'.[84] But he was in no doubt who was at fault; and it certainly was not him. He placed the blame squarely on the Westerham carpenter Wallace whom he said he had warned about the risks attendant on placing linoleum on a wet floor. It would he said, set up dry rot. Tilden clearly knew no more about dry rot than anyone else involved and whilst enclosing a wet floor with linoleum in this way might have predisposed the timber to attack, this would only be relevant if all the existing dry rot had not been removed and the fungus was therefore still present. Nonetheless, commented Tilden, if Churchill wanted professional advice, he would arrange for his man Thomas to visit the property.[85] And with that pompous flourish, Tilden said that apart from not having received any fees in respect of the garden house, the matter of Chartwell was now closed.

Churchill took a different view and instructed his lawyers to write to Tilden, criticising his account, questioning his remark that the matter of Chartwell was closed, stating that no indemnity had been given to him, and telling him that legal action was being considered. Tilden clearly did not relish confronting Churchill in Court and saw an escape route. He suggested reducing his charges for the garden house on condition that Churchill wrote agreeing that all points of difference between them had been finally and definitely settled. Churchill's lawyers pointed out this would mean Churchill could have no further claims against him either in respect of the dry rot or any other matter connected with the work at Chartwell. Churchill was having none of it and summarily rejected the proposition.[86]

Tantalisingly, there is no record of any further communication between Tilden, Churchill, his lawyers or Leanings and it must be assumed than a mutually acceptable settlement was reached. Nor is there any evidence that Churchill and Tilden ever met again. Tilden continued building and altering houses but the work available to him declined markedly after the late nineteen twenties and he and his Swedish wife gradually withdrew to their Devonshire home. He joined the Home Guard in World War II and devoted more and more time to writing a series of novels, unbearable to read and with one exception, providentially unpublished. He undertook the alteration of Sir John Carew

Pole's Cornish house, Antony and under his patronage, met a number of other clients for whom he undertook alterations. He was even asked by King George VI and Queen Elizabeth to advise on a suitable country house for Princess Elizabeth following her marriage in 1947 but nothing came of it. Philip Tilden died at Shute Barton in Devon in 1956 at the age of sixty-eight. The fate of Browns the builders and Lambs the electricians is not known. They disappeared from the record along with the Waterex company. The two firms of surveyors, John Leaning & Sons and Fleetwood, Eversden & King also vanished. The firm of Henry Hope & Sons continued making windows for many years and became major producers of metal frames. The firm surfaced in a complex legal dispute in the United States in 2002 involving claims made by its America subsidiary. Wallace the local carpenter went bankrupt in autumn 1929, 'shaking Westerham to its foundations' and left to make a fresh start elsewhere.[87]

Could all the heartache and delays have been avoided? Was Tilden the most appropriate architect? Tilden's biographer says Churchill was virtually alone among his clients with whom he did not retain a close friendship. It is almost axiomatic that architects and their clients fall out and Churchill's track record with his previous architects certainly was not good. Churchill was an impatient perfectionist. He was also intolerant of fools and incompetents and took an interest in every craft and trade in the builders' profession and thought he knew a fair bit about many of them. The trauma that accompanied the rebuilding of Chartwell was perhaps the inevitable consequence of a well-meaning but relatively feeble and technically flawed architect working with a man who for much of the time simply had bigger things to command his attention, to whom money had never come easily and from which he was not readily parted. Churchill was not Freddie Guest or Philip Sassoon or Sunny Marlborough. He was neither landed gentry nor nouveau riche although he spent his life moving in the circles of those who were. He needed real budgetary control, a more imaginative, more competent architect to whom he could delegate properly and to whom all the workforce was answerable through a proper contract. Looking back at what it took to achieve the architectural jumble that is Chartwell today, it is inescapable that Churchill needed Lutyens.

But Chartwell is what it is and the Churchills lived there, mostly happily, for forty years. Despite everything that went wrong and was wrong with the building, Clementine created in its interior a gracious and comfortable home.

Tilden himself commented that she always took great personal interest in the decoration and it was she who decided the general colouring throughout the house.[88] She had good and discerning taste and what her daughter later called a 'straightforward sense of practicality', believing that to employ a professional decorator would have been a great extravagance.[89] The twenties was a time of clean colours and fresh, plain walls and Chartwell was no exception. There were 'acres of palest cream paint (which went very well with the old beams), a pale blue for Clementine's bedroom, and an ethereal cerulean blue for her barrel-domed bedroom, where the curtains and her four-poster bed covered in tomato-coloured moiré silk were sensational'.[90] The rooms were adorned with bold floral patterned chintzes and with furniture they had inherited from the family or bought second hand 'for a song'. The extravagant exception was the new dining room with its specially woven rush mats, vivid green glazed cotton curtains and beautiful unstained oak tables and chairs, designed by Tilden and made by Heal's.

So Chartwell, the former foundling house, the one time country retreat of a fairly modest Scottish family, became the hub of the rest of Churchill's life, the place where he worked, played and where he entertained. The Chartwell visitors' book reveals much – a list of over five hundred names, each with a story to tell. There were many occasions when this relatively insignificant property on the outskirts of a relatively insignificant little English town did become host to the powerful, the power brokers, the rich, the famous and the glamorous of the world: Harry Truman and Harold Macmillan, Charlie Chaplin and Bernard Montgomery, Friedrich Prince of Prussia and Elizabeth the Queen Mother, Laurence Olivier, Diana Cooper and Ethel Barrymore. Lawrence of Arabia came and entranced the Churchill children with his Arab robes. There were Mitfords, Clarks, Grimmonds, Astors, Grosvenors, Guests and Guinnesses, Randolph Hearst and Edward Heath. But many of these names appear just once. On one occasion they came, to be wined and dined, to listen and to sleep; if they were lucky before one in the morning. It is the repeated signatures that tell more because they tell a story of family and of close friends. For the Churchills' social circle was not large; it seemed large because collectively, Winston's and Clementine's extended families were so big but the visitors' book betrays how, in a literal sense, they were most at home, most at ease, with the selected group of people to whom they were related or whom they knew extremely well.

Endnotes

1   CHAR 1/159/28-31. WSC to A. J. Campbell-Colquhoun. 25 Sep 1922.

2   Nixon, S. *Thomas Carew*. Oxford DNB.

3   SLH. D237. Well Place Estate.

4   1841 Census.

5   WCHL 8/92. Conveyance, Chartwell.

6   1861 Census.

7   1851 Census.

8   Wolfe, J. *John Campbell Colquhoun*. Oxford DNB.

9   1851 Census.

10   1861 Census.

11   K John Campbell Colquhoun to Sir William Jackson Hooker. 3 Jul 1851; 14 Apr 1853; n.d.

12   1871 Census.

13   1881 Census.

14   GU. MS Gen 1376/12/10. Robieson, W. Notes on the Mazingarbe Bell. March 1973.

15   HP A. H. Hastie to Ian Hamilton. 9 Oct 1921.

16   KS U2396E10. Chartwell.

17   CHAR 1/159/21–22. WSC to Knight, Frank & Rutley. 15 Sep 1922.

18   CHAR 1/159/25. WSC to Knight, Frank & Rutley. 20 Sep 1922.

19   Churchill, S. *A Thread in the Tapestry*. p. 22.

20   CHAR 1/161/75–79. WSC to The Duke of Marlborough. 13 Oct 1922.

21   CHAR 1/161/83–87. The Duke of Marlborough to WSC. 17 Oct 1922.

22   CHAR 1/344/14–17. WSC to CSC. 18 Jan 1939.

23   CHAR 1/159/43. WSC to A. J. Campbell-Colquhoun. 29 Sep 1922.

24   Tilden, P. *True Remembrances – the memoirs of an architect*. p. 116.

25   Bettley, J. *Lush and luxurious. The Life and Work of Philip Tilden 1887-1956*. p. 10.

26   James, R. R. [Ed.] *Chips: The Diaries of Sir Henry Channon*. 29 Jan 1935.

27   Allyson Hayward, personal Communication, 1 Mar 2006.

28   Tilden, P. *True Remembrances – the memoirs of an architect*. p. 49.

29   CHAR 1/159/48. P. Tilden to WSC. 3 Oct 1922.

30   CHAR 1/159/39. P. Tilden to WSC. 28 Sept 1922.

31   CHAR 1/159/56–57. WSC to P. Tilden. 14 Oct 1922.

32   CSCT 2/14/6–7. WSC to CSC. 6 Feb 1921.

33   TP CSC to P. Tilden. 22 Dec 1922.

34   CHAR 1/179/5–7. CSC to WSC. [? 8 March 1925].

35   TP P. Tilden to WSC. 5 Jan 1923.

36   CSCT 2/16/3–6. WSC to CSC. 27 Jan 1923.

37   TP WSC to P. Tilden. 11 Mar 1923.

38   TP WSC to P. Tilden. 24 Mar 1923.

39   CSCT 1/12/1–3. CSC to WSC. 29 Jan 1923.

40 TP P. Tilden to WSC. 3 Mar 1923.

41 TP P. Tilden to WSC. 3 Mar 1923.

42 CHAR 1/215/3–4. WSC to Nicholl, Manisty & Co. 15 Jan 1930.

43 CHAR 1/395/3–4. P. Tilden to WSC. 10 Jul 1923.

44 TP CSC to P. Tilden. 24 Aug 1923.

45 Churchill, S. *A Thread in the Tapestry.* p. 30.

46 CSCT 1/12/19–21. CSC to WSC. 4 Sep 1923.

47 CSCT 2/16/16–18. WSC to CSC. 2 Sep 1923.

48 CSCT 1/15/30–31. CST to WSC. [n.d.]

49 Mary Soames, conversation with the author. 2 Aug 2006.

50 CSCT 2/17/1–2. WSC to CSC. 17 Feb 1924.

51 CSCT 2/17/11–12. WSC to CSC. 17 Apr 1924.

52 CHAR 1/189/50. Shanks & Co. Ltd to John Leaning & Sons Ltd. 22 Oct 1926.

53 WSC to CSC 25 Mar 1925. [Cited in Soames, M. *Speaking for Themselves. The Personal letters of Winston and Clementine Churchill.* p. 293. Original not traced]

54 CHAR 1/182/38. Clarice Fisher to Henry Hope & Sons. 11 May 1925.

55 CHAR 1/182/84–85. WSC to John Leaning & Sons Ltd. 6 Dec 1925.

56 CHAR 1/245/37. Violet Pearman to WSC. 3 May 1933.

57 TP P. Tilden to Lamb & Sons, 10 Nov 1925.

58 TP Lamb & Sons to P. Tilden, 14 Nov 1925.

59 CHAR 1/189/43. WSC to John Leaning & Sons Ltd. 4 Sept 1926.

60 TP J. Leaning to WSC. 27 Nov 1924.

61 CHAR 1/182/7–9. WSC to John Leaning & Sons Ltd. 26 Jan 1925.

62 TP P. Tilden to J. Leaning. 28 Jan 1925.

63 TP J. Leaning to P. Tilden. 16 Feb 1925.

64 TP P. Tilden to Szerelmy Co. 11 Feb 1925.

65 TP J. Leaning to P. Tilden. 16 Feb 1925.

66 TP George Lillington & Co. to P. Tilden. March/May 1925.

67 TP P. Tilden to John Leaning & Sons Ltd. 10 Nov 1925].

68 Tilden, P. *True Remembrances – the memoirs of an architect.* p. 116.

69 CHAR 1/395/68-69. P. Tilden to WSC. 27 Jan 1925.

70 TP P. Tilden to Fleetwood, Eversden & King. 29 Jan 1926.

71 TP P. Tilden to Brown & Co. 25 Jan 1926.

72 TP P.Tilden to Fleetwood, Eversden & King. 29 Jan 1926.

73 CSCT 2/19/4. WSC to CSC. 7 Feb 1926.

74 CHAR 1/189/34. WSC to John Leaning & Sons Ltd. 16 May 1926.

75 CSCT 3/24/1-5. Typescript by WSC. [?] Sep 1926.

76 TP J. Leaning to WSC. 27 Nov 1924.

77 TP P.Tilden to WSC. 10 Feb 1926.

78 CSCT 2/20/8. WSC to CSC. 30 Jan 1927.

79 Tilden, P. *True Remembrances – the memoirs of an architect.* p. 119.

80 CHAR 1/395/107. P. Tilden to Clarice Fisher. 17 Mar 1927.

81   TP Fleetwood, Eversden & King to P. Tilden, 12 May 1927.

82   TP Fleetwood, Eversden & King to P. Tilden, 25 May 1927.

83   TP P. Tilden to Fleetwood, Eversden & King. 23 June 1927.

84   Tilden, P. *True Remembrances – the memoirs of an architect.* p. 117.

85   CHAR 1/395/132. P. Tilden to WSC. 29 Oct 1927.

86   CHAR 1/395/130–131. Draft letter from Nicholl, Manisty & Co., to Tilden [annotated 'approved' by WSC, 7 Nov 1927]. [05] Nov 1927.

87   CSCT 1/17/32-26. CSC to WSC. 30 Sep [1929]

88   CHAR 1/173/12. P. Tilden to WSC. 25 Apr 1924.

89   Soames, M. *Clementine Churchill. 2nd Ed.* p. 254.

90   Soames, M. *Clementine Churchill. 2nd Ed.* p. 254

CHAPTER 8
THE CHARTWELL ESTATE

Although Churchill bought Chartwell for the view and for what he could do with the house, the fact that it came with substantial land was a massive further attraction. As a reinstated land-owner he could pick up again the farming and other rural activities that had ground so inauspiciously to a halt at Lullenden; and Clementine could perhaps finally have her rose garden. Although the estate extended to 816 acres, of which Churchill bought around 92 – not so different from his holding at Lullenden – there is no clear indication of how extensive the gardens were when Churchill completed his purchase in 1922 or where the various features were disposed. The sale particulars referred to a productive kitchen garden surrounded by a well-clipped yew hedge, a range of hot houses and vinery, a 70 feet range of frames, a fruit room and potting shed, a tennis court and orchard; but with almost no other detail. A considerable quantity of gardening equipment was also included in the purchase price

The gardens were therefore being run effectively even if Campbell Colquhoun was not living on the premises, and he asked Churchill if he would take on two in particular of the Chartwell staff. Fred Best the coachman who lived at the stables must have been almost part of the furniture. He was fifty-eight and had worked at Chartwell for over forty years, had taught the family to ride and hunt and was excellent with horses. Unfortunately he had 'only a small experience of motors and motor driving' and in any event, Churchill did not want a coachman and would probably require early possession of the stables where Fred Best lived as they could serve as a temporary headquarters from where he would supervise the building operations.[1] Nonetheless, Fred Best did stay for well over ten years, mainly occupied with taking care of Churchill's ponies and, in due course, he taught Mary Churchill to ride.

Then there was Edmund Waterhouse, the gardener. He was born at Burwash in Sussex although his wife Kate was a local girl from Brasted. They and their numerous children lived in one of the Puddledock cottages. Waterhouse was already 60 and although he had not been at Chartwell for as long as Best, Campbell Colquhoun commended him not only for his ability to supervise two or three men and for his expertise with vegetables but because, most helpfully and crucially 'he understands the water system'. Nonetheless, Churchill told Campbell Colquhoun the story of his experience with Robert Leigh at Lullenden, and was understandably cautious.[2] He was still paying half Leigh's pension and did not feel he ought to incur any 'fresh obligations of that kind' but agreed to take on Waterhouse for a year on the understanding that he would vacate his cottage at the end of that time unless they proved to be suited to each other. Campbell Colquhoun would be responsible for his pension. He explained that he intended to have no more than one gardener and one single man to assist him; an ambition that proved to be a serious under-estimate. Although the garden would be upset by the building operations, he did want to take advantage of the current season's fruit and vegetables; although that wish was thwarted because it emerged that Waterhouse was not being paid a wage by Campbell Colquhoun, merely an allowance for looking after the house and was permitted to sell the kitchen garden produce by way of income.[3]

The Butterfly Walk, Chartwell.

The sloping site at Chartwell dictated much of what had to – or could – be done with the garden. Terraces with solid supporting walls were essential, as were steps to give access. Philip Tilden undertook some redesigning of the garden before his departure from the scene at the end of 1927 but there is little documentary evidence of what was done although it is possible to glean some detail from builders' and suppliers' invoices. In addition to designing the pergola, the garden house (later called the Marlborough Pavilion) and re-modelling the old game larder to create a summer house, Tilden seems also to have been responsible for the paved walk, wall and border (now called the butterfly walk) beyond the summer house and alongside the tennis court. The removal of the old tennis court and creation of the new hard court on what had been the kitchen garden with its surrounding yew hedges was also probably his doing. He formed a 'small postern' arched doorway, now bricked up, into the rose garden, added a stone staircase south of the garden house, and extended the terrace wall ending in the grass bank by the southern end of the house. The creation of the upper and lower terraces, the concreting of the kitchen courtyard and then walling it using stone from an old wall near the tennis court, and the building of the steps from the upper terrace to the lower garden were also undertaken in 1923 and 1924 while he was supervising the overall works. Nonetheless although Philip Tilden would have the world believe he could design a garden as well as he could design a house, it is hard to place much credence in his abilities. How could the Churchills have any confidence in a man who, when he lived in Pelham Crescent, confessed he had never even gone into its own little garden, other than to look for his lost cat?[4]

Neither Churchill nor Clementine had a great knowledge of gardens and gardening and Clementine at first found the sheer size of Chartwell daunting. Throughout her life, however, she loved flowers and knew what she liked when she saw it, as her many accounts of visits to friends' gardens give ample testimony. Her taste in colours was 'exquisite' although her view of trees uncompromising: 'no trees were better than trees she did not like'.[5] Most of her Chartwell plantings have gone without trace – the great glade of the giant lily, *Cardiocrinum giganteum*, the drifts of Himalayan poppies, destined to fail on thin dry soil, the vines covering the pergola, the azaleas close to the water garden; although many others, like the blue anchusas and white foxgloves above the golden orfe pool have been recreated.

Churchill too loved flowers – after all, it was his rose garden in Bangalore that had so captivated him as a young man – but he was no practising gardener. He was more a mover of the scenery. In the garden, as in the house, it was Clementine's inspired practical good taste that prevailed over her husband's bull-headed impetuousness and impatience but in many ways, the Churchills were in exactly the same position as many another garden owner and garden lover before and since. They knew roughly the effect they wanted but had no funds to spare for a proper garden designer so what the Chartwell garden did not have was an overall blueprint, a plan for the future, a scheme to create a coherent whole.

As time, energy and finances allowed, it was destined to develop piecemeal over the coming years. But as it had no presiding horticulturist, there was no-one knowledgeable who could judge what would and would not succeed, what would appear as good, or better, in ten years time as it did when planted, what would grow best on the Chartwell soil and what would give year round interest and appeal. So, again like others in the same position, they turned on the one hand for advice to more experienced friends and on the other, for putting the advice into practice, to a good head gardener.

The knowledgeable friends were many but it was Mary Soames' view that the most significant and influential was her mother's cousin Venetia Montagu.[6] Although nothing remains of Venetia's own garden at Breccles Hall and no illustrations of it date from before 1922, later descriptions and photographs of the property reveal features that in time appeared at Chartwell and that may have been her creations: a walled garden with rectangular beds, a magnolia against the house, drifts of naturalised bulbs and an angularly geometric rose garden and it is widely thought that Clementine's beloved rose garden (the walled garden to the north of the house) in particular was created under Venetia Montagu's influence.[7] There is no record of Venetia Montagu staying at Chartwell until she came for the weekend of 11 to 13 July 1925 (although she may of course have been a day visitor) but a rose garden of some sort did exist before then. In November 1924, Sarah Churchill wrote to her father from Chartwell telling him one of the sheep had to be chased from the rose garden 'with much vigour' by her cousin Moppet (Maryott Whyte, Clementine's first cousin who looked after the children and the nursery); fortunately it did no damage.[8] It does seem probable however that the present rose garden was a Venetia Montagu creation for it was about eighteen months after her visit that its construction was under way: Churchill wrote to Clementine from Italy in the January: 'As soon as yr garden is done two of the men shd be got rid of (Townsend and the tall man) & the others can stay till I come back'.[9] She created a traditional, formal English rose garden of conventional design with an architectural heart and edges softened by a jumble of perennials and shrubs in gentle colours, including penstemons, catmint, cherry-pie, ceanothus, peonies, fuchsias and *Lilium regale*. It seems likely that the fountain designed by Tilden but cancelled by Churchill was intended for the centre of the rose garden. Roses and clematis bedecked the walls and the pergola leading from the rose garden to the stone loggia was covered with vines.

The Walled Garden, Chartwell.

Lady Churchill's Rose Garden, Chartwell.

Some information about progress in planting the garden in the early nineteen twenties can be gleaned from a few plant orders and receipts that survive. The first recorded purchases were in 1923 when the orchard was comprehensively replanted with a good range of apples, pears, plums, damsons, quinces, filberts and Kentish cobs; although strangely for a Kentish garden, then at the heart of English cherry growing, there were only two un-named fan-trained cherries. The fruits were mainly predictable and reliable varieties popular at the time but included a few interesting apples such as 'Braddick Nonpareil' and the Irish 'Kerry Pippin'. The trees were obtained from the long established and famous Bunyards nursery at Maidstone and two hundred strawberry plants and three hundred asparagus crowns (sufficient for an enormous asparagus bed) were also purchased.[10] Then, three years later, Bunyards Nursery delivered one hundred apple trees for which Churchill had negotiated a discounted price of 5/- each instead of 7/-.

In April 1924, at Tilden's suggestion, Norman Luff from the long-established firm of landscape gardeners and nurserymen A. Luff & Sons of Wimbledon Park visited Chartwell and gave a quotation for landscaping and planting. It was an extensive proposal and encompassed resurfacing the drive, building various walls, steps and paving around the house, making a wall and border alongside the tennis court, constructing beds with numerous loads of peat for rhododendrons and supplying the rhododendron plants themselves along with yews for hedging, box trees in six oak planting boxes and a range of other shrubs and climbers such as clematis, ceanothus, pyracantha and jasmine including some for the 'six new tubs' (these appear to have been large green planting boxes designed by Tilden for the Lower Terrace). The quotation amounted to over £560.[11] Churchill was not enthusiastic and said so to Tilden who had to write to Luffs telling them that Mr Churchill was 'not at all anxious' to indulge in architectural work in the garden beyond that which had already been arranged. He was only interested in purchasing some of the rhododendrons but he thought they should not be supplied until the autumn. Apart from the post-war rock garden, this seems to have been the only occasion when an outside landscaping contractor was invited to quote for work at Chartwell and although much of the construction was ultimately undertaken, it was done instead by Churchill's own employees, by Browns and by the local builder Wallace.

The only other significant planting information to survive from the nineteen twenties relates to the arrival of the first gunneras. These huge and impressive South American bog plants, often likened to giant rhubarb, have long been, and remain, a notable Chartwell feature. Their origin can be traced to Clementine's aunt Mary Hozier. Churchill saw them in 1927 at her garden in Haslemere and was given two roots which 'thrived enormously'. The following year he asked if he could have some more. Mary Hozier was more than happy to oblige – they grew like weeds in her garden she said – and she sent them in the autumn.[12]

Churchill himself was more than happy to lend his hand to practical gardening. Work on the house was still not finished and he had barely taken up residence in 1924 when he first turned his attention to serious garden work with the assistance of old Waterhouse, his chauffeur Aley, his detective Sergeant Walter Thompson and six hired hands. They formed 'a powerful labour force', turfing and levelling the main lawn. He was sure Clementine would be pleased with the effect.[13] However, the professional gardening knowledge, the means to turn Venetia Montagu's and Clementine's visions into reality, was initially in the hands of old Edmund Waterhouse. In telling Campbell Colquhoun that he would try Waterhouse for a year, Churchill added that he did recognise the value of old servants and that 'their modern successors are not always of the same quality'.[14] He said Clementine had ideas about getting a younger gardener from Scotland although with no indication of who he was or from whence he might come. Churchill had promised he would retain Waterhouse beyond the first year if they proved to be suited to each other and evidently they did because he stayed for almost five years. It appears to have been a happy and efficient arrangement; from time to time, when Churchill was away, Waterhouse would write to him describing progress ('I shall not be able to finish turfing before Friday morning...')[15] and Churchill in return would send notes that betray a close attention to what was being done: in May 1926 for instance he wrote several pages of instructions to Waterhouse, including such detail as 'Collect the weeds and mud around the side of the upper lake...'[16] It appears that Waterhouse was seen as the senior man on the estate for the same note included instructions to be passed on to the stockman Joseph Martin, to Fred Best and other employees. And then, in May 1927 Churchill was telling Waterhouse to finish turfing the water garden, and to tidy by the loose boxes and the saw bench; 'Do not however, move the rubble you have dumped there. I will see about that when I am on the spot...'[17]

In 1925, the aging Waterhouse was seriously ill and had an emergency prostatectomy in Edenbridge Hospital. Churchill was greatly concerned about his condition and although Waterhouse did return to Chartwell, it was evident that his abilities to undertake heavy and taxing work were limited. By the spring of 1927, Churchill had decided he would have to go and broke the news to him on the morning of Tuesday 10 May, explaining that he really needed a younger man with specialist knowledge to take care of his proposed new developments in the garden. He reassured him that Campbell Colquhoun had agreed to look after his retirement needs and said his son Bob was welcome to stay on working on the estate; which he did. Waterhouse moved to Betsoms Bank Cottage in Westerham and with the help of a warm testimonial from Churchill, undertook some jobbing gardening and then, using a loan of £375 together with a £75 subsidy from Sevenoaks Rural District Council, was able to build a bungalow on a site given free of charge at The Paddocks. Churchill was greatly pleased to see this example of the provisions of the 1923 Housing Act in action and his own builder William Wallace undertook the work; two years before his bankruptcy.

The younger man who replaced Waterhouse was to cement even closer the link between Chartwell and Breccles Hall and further enhance the influence on Clementine of Venetia Montagu. He was Albert Edwin Hill, a farmer's son, born at Wymondham in Norfolk in 1895 and the deputy gardener at Breccles. Venetia Montagu's head gardener was a man named Jack Fitt who came to her from nearby Earlham Hall in 1924. He had been appointed there in 1913 to supervise the landscaping for its owner Sidney Morris but was made head gardener in 1916, taking over the breeding of the popular border flowers called monbretias (now usually known as crocosmias) of which Morris had an important collection of magnificently large flowered varieties known as the Earlham hybrids. When Sidney Morris died in 1924, he bequeathed his collection to Fitt who took the plants and his expertise to Breccles where he continued to breed new varieties although they were still called Earlham hybrids. Fitt had a team of six or seven gardeners, including Norman Pearce, Jimmy Mann who looked after the kitchen garden, Billy Dove who made the machinery work, and his number one assistant, Albert Hill who lodged with Fitt and his wife.[18]

In November 1924, soon after Fitt's arrival at Breccles, Edwin Montagu died, to be buried in the woods behind his house, the funeral attended by numerous exotically attired Indian dignitaries in recognition of his time at the India Office, to the astonishment of the nearby village of Attleborough. Venetia lived on

Albert Hill with Atco Mower at Chartwell (1929).

at Breccles until her own death in 1948 when her ashes were interred in her husband's tomb. But through the nineteen twenties and thirties, there was still a stream of regular and important visitors and Breccles was an exciting place for the workers. Expensive and glamorous cars with comparably glamorous occupants were constantly coming and going along the entrance drive; and from time to time, the dreamy peace of rural Norfolk would be interrupted by Venetia's personal De Havilland Gypsy Moth. Winston and Clementine were regular visitors and Churchill made a number of paintings in and around the grounds. His visits were particularly appreciated by the gardeners and domestic staff who would discreetly collect his discarded cigar stubs which were of exactly the right size to fit in their clay pipes.[19] There is a story that Churchill built the kitchen garden wall at Breccles and although this seems improbable, it is likely that he at least titivated it with a little personal brick laying. In honour of the Churchills' visits and friendship with the Montagus, Fitt named one of his monbretia hybrids 'Lady Churchill', perhaps to commemorate Lady Randolph or more likely in the mistaken belief that Clementine was titled. Among the thirty five or so other monbretia hybrids that are known to have been raised at Breccles were the appropriately named 'Albert Hill' and 'The Honourable Mrs Edwin Montagu'.

Albert Hill with his wife May and children moved into Garden Cottage at Chartwell on the day Edmund Waterhouse moved out. His family grew up there and his daughter Doris became a great friend of the young Mary Churchill, the two girls playing together and getting up to much mischief. On the celebrated occasion in 1931 when Charlie Chaplin came to stay, they played on the tennis court that had been meticulously prepared before his arrival. Doris, as an employee's daughter, came off worst in the retribution that followed.

The boundary wall and Garden Cottage, Chartwell.

Hill took some of the monbretias with him to Chartwell although whether he continued breeding them there is not known and there is no record of where they might have been planted. It is reasonable to suppose however that Chartwell in those early years contained many of the typical flowers of a English garden. In some of Churchill's paintings are vases of daffodils, tulips, mallows and chrysanthemums as well as roses and there are references to snowdrops and crocuses in his letters to Clementine. The large and magnificent evergreen *Magnolia grandiflora* on the south east corner of the house was probably planted around nineteen twenty four – Philip Tilden may have been responsible for the massive and over-dominant pattern of wooden trellis on the south wall which partly supports it. Churchill painted its flowers too and could reach out from his study window to pick the blooms. Almost certainly flowers for cutting were also plentiful as Clementine invariably had them in the house and later, in the nineteen thirties, there were orders for freesias, hyacinths, irises (border irises were an especial favourite), daffodils, tulips, St Brigid and De Caen anemones, alliums, eremurus, snakes head fritillaries, watsonias, cyclamen, heleniums, monardas, alstroemerias, camassias, scillas, helianthus, pyrethrums and muscaris from well-known nurseries such as Barr and Sons of Covent Garden and Bedford, W. A. Constable of Tunbridge Wells, John Forbes of Hawick, Moyses Stevens of Berkeley Square, Waterers of Twyford and John Vanderschoot in Holland along with roses from Murrells of Hemel Hempstead. There were clematis from Jackmans, trees and shrubs from Hilliers, fruit plants from Laxtons and Bunyards, gentians from Clarence Elliott, and seeds and vegetable plants from the leading firms like Suttons and Carters with sweet peas from the specialists Robert Bolton. Chartwell was humming with activity, vibrant with colour and redolent with fragrance. Clementine at last had her English country garden.

Working at Chartwell under Albert Hill in the late twenties were two under-gardeners: Bill Knight who was appointed in 1925, and Victor Trowbridge who came in 1927. Churchill was realising, as many another land owner has realised, that a full and productive garden simply cannot be run properly, as he had initially hoped, on a shoestring with 'a man and a boy'. Throughout the early years, his own male staff at Chartwell generally comprised three gardeners, a chauffeur, butler, odd job man and carpenter – in addition of course to estate workers, secretaries and Clementine's domestic staff – a lady's maid, two housemaids, a cook and a parlour maid. And whilst personally he enjoyed lending a hand with laying lawns and planting, Churchillian 'gardening' was really on a much larger scale. Within weeks of moving in, he was seriously re-arranging the landscape. What interested him above all was creating water works – lakes, streams, ponds, swimming pools. It is not hard to see where he acquired this fascination with controlling nature through manipulating the flow of water – he can only have been recalling 'Capability' Brown's great works at Blenheim – but it was a fascination that was to become almost an obsession and to drive his family and all others associated with it to distraction.

When Churchill bought Chartwell, the spring rising in the old Chart Well itself alongside the Mapleton Road, flowed east down the side of the valley to turn south and into a lake. Although it actually extended to around two and a quarter acres, it was silted up and overgrown with weeds to the extent that Churchill's nephew Johnny considered lake much too grand a title. He thought it looked more like the pond in Kensington Gardens. The stream emerged at the southern end and continued on down the valley to where it formed another lake in Chartwell Farm. It was obvious that the Chartwell pond/lake needed draining and clearing. It was equipped with a ram pump to provide a domestic water supply although Churchill recognised that mains water might be needed to supplement this for the garden. A second lake would be useful therefore and on 1 July 1924, and using only his own employees and hired casual labour – nine men at the height of operations – Churchill began to build a dam above his existing lake in order to create a second of just under an acre in extent up-stream. The dam was constructed with a sluice or penstock supplied by Adams-Hydraulics Ltd of York. It took two months to complete, Churchill himself being 'at it all day and every day' in dreadful weather and by 19 August, 'owing to the fact that the months have got mixed and apparently we are having April instead of August', the upper lake was already seven feet deep. The lower lake was practically empty and Churchill and his happy band of brothers set about removing the residue from it. 'Thompson and I have been wallowing in the most filthy black mud you ever saw, with the vilest odour, getting the beastly stuff to drain away' he wrote to Clementine who was staying at Pentraeth on Anglesey. Three days later he wrote again, triumphantly reporting that the water level in his new lake had reached seven feet six inches and was rising steadily at the rate of two or three inches every twenty four hours. But in a portent of something that was to beleaguer him for year after year, Churchill was obliged to add 'However, I regret to say that two or three leaks have made their appearance' and, with naïve optimism 'They do not amount to much'.[20] Some additional concrete rectified matters.

In order to transport the malodorous black mud to its resting place, Churchill, never a man to shun mechanical assistance, built a little railway with 18 inch gauge track, the first of three occasions when he resorted to iron rails to help his landscaping activities although little information survives about this first adventure. Then early in November 1925 just as he was about to stock his new lake with trout at a cost of £40, serious trouble struck. The sluicing arrangements may have been inspired by 'Capability' Brown's Blenheim but the mechanics were not as durable and Churchill's penstock jammed. Representatives of Adams-Hydraulics were summoned, as they were to be summoned at regular intervals over the next few years because the sluice repeatedly gave problems. The difficulty was compounded because the penstock itself lay at the bottom of the dam in about nine feet of water and short of 'fishing' for it from the surface (or sending down a diver which seems not to have been considered), the lake had to be drained each time to attend to it.

Work on the lake continued for some time and in December 1925, the railway was back. Churchill this time hired a considerable length of 2 feet gauge track, including a turntable and two windlass driven side-tipping 1 cubic yard Jubilee wagons from a firm in London. The equipment was transported by road to Chartwell for about two weeks at a total cost of £62 17s 11d. In 1926, they were still at it; he wrote to Clementine of sparing two or three of his 'lake men' for other tasks. By early September when she was staying with Consuelo and Jacques Balsan at Grantully Castle, Aberfeldy which they were renting, it was still a live issue as she enquired how the lake was proceeding.[21]

During 1927, more work was undertaken and the new upper lake was lined with a proprietary bitumen sheet called Callendrite, invented at Millwall in 1878 by a Mr W. O. Callender at who based it on the bizarre notion that the Ancient Egyptians used bitumen for the preservation of 'their illustrious dead'.[22] Churchill was fascinated and took great personal interest in the way the Callendrite was laid and later covered with clay. His next water works, however, were on a smaller scale as he increased the number of ornamental pools below the Chart Well, and when construction of the series was complete, he made an interesting calculation. He discovered that the lower pool was at least ten feet higher than the high water level of his new top lake, about two hundred yards away. He put a hypothesis to his long-time friend and fount of all scientific knowledge, the physicist Professor Frederick Lindemann (later to become Lord Cherwell, always addressed as 'Prof' and with whom Churchill was to become especially close during World War II). If a watertight pipe was led down from the higher level, he asked, would the water flow down one side of the valley and up

Churchill alongside one of his ponds.

the other (rising to its own level) and so deliver itself by siphoning into the top lake by gravity.[23] Churchill had thought this would triple the flow of water into the lakes and over-ride the impact of the continuing leaks but Lindemann was not enthusiatic and escaping water became a constant family topic. Mary Soames told me her childhood was beset with leaking lakes and when young Randolph wrote to Churchill after a visit to Chartwell in 1930, it was the all consuming subject. He was sorry to have to say that he found the soil behind the central part of the dam rather moist. He promised however to ring his father in the evening to let him know if had increased and hoped he would not feel worried – as it might not get any worse.[24]

There was another reason for Churchill wanting to enhance the flow of water into and out of the lakes. His knowledge of water movement may have given him a clue that before long, there would be consequences of his constructional work for his neighbour downstream. And so it proved. When Churchill bought Chartwell, he had to covenant not to disconnect the water supply from his lake to the owner of Chartwell Farm. At the auction in 1922, a man named Percy Janson who lived at Mariners to the west of Chartwell, had bought the 170 acre farm to the south of Churchill's land. He only retained it however until March 1929 when he and his family sold it for £6,000 to a Major Harold Pilbrow who lived in a house called Mapleton to the south of Chartwell on the road to Four Elms, a house the Churchills always thought utterly hideous.[25]

In the summer of 1930, the water supply down the valley practically stopped, Pilbrow's much smaller lake was almost empty and he was having to rely on mains water (coming through a meter and therefore expensive) for his farm buildings. 'Can you let me know when you are likely to let the water down as it used to flow in the olden times?' he asked his neighbour.[26] Churchill said he felt no guilt about the matter, claiming that all the water that flowed into his lakes flowed out again and it was only in winter when the lakes were emptied for cleaning that the flow was interrupted for about a month.[27] 'What can have happened to it?' mused the mystified Major.[28] They exchanged letters on the matter regularly over the following months but in a conclusion with familiar resonances for twenty-first century water supply, Churchill was of the view that Pilbrow's problems arose because his pipes were leaking.[29]

Despite their differences over the disappearance of Pilbrow's water, Churchill generally had a good if pragmatic relationship with his neighbour and was fortunately on fairly amicable terms with the Major when some potentially awkward matters had to be negotiated during 1929 and 1930.

Churchill catching ornamental fish by one of his ponds.

In the extreme south-westerly corner of the Chartwell estate and to the south of the right of way track from the Mapleton Road to Chartwell Farm, a small tongue of land ran alongside the road for some 150 yards. At the northern end of this narrow strip, is a two-storey, red brick, part tile-hung cottage called Garden Cottage, built by the Campbell Colquhouns sometime in the last quarter of the nineteenth century. It was still owned by Archibald Campbell Colquhoun's sister Lilian who was born at Chartwell in 1872 and in 1899 had married a Captain Henry Bosanquet. He retired as a Naval Captain in 1918 and took up a post as Secretary of the King George's Fund for Sailors, but seems to have been content to take a back seat and leave his wife to negotiate on behalf of her inheritance against Churchill's overtures.

In the late summer of 1928, Churchill had built a substantial and rather handsome new cottage just to the south of Garden Cottage at the northern extremity of the strip of land, alongside the road. Its official name was Well Cottage or Wellstreet Cottage but unofficially it was referred to as the Butler's Cottage and was intended to provide accommodation for a married butler although it was also viewed as an investment, one that would be greatly enhanced

Wellstreet Cottage, Chartwell.

if it had a decent garden. So in the summer of 1929, Churchill bought a small parcel of land from Pilbrow in order to extend his holding southwards alongside the existing strip. They agreed terms for the sale of just over 2 acres at £100 an acre and then, with the agreement of his brother Jack, as a trustee of his father's will with whom Chartwell was mortgaged, Churchill withdraw his new cottage from the mortgage to give him more flexibility in its use and disposition.[30] He later set up a Trust for the ownership of Wellstreet Cottage with Clementine, Brendan Bracken, Frederick Lindemann and Jock Colville among others serving at various times as Trustees from whom he rented it.

Churchill's friends at Knight Frank & Rutley advised him that it might be worth adding a garage to the cottage and that if he took 2 roods 23 perches of his newly acquired two acres and added it to the new cottage it would afford him the scope to create a small kitchen garden, plant fruit trees and possibly build a tennis court. The property would then be worth £1,250, not a bad return on his investment. If the right of way could be moved, this would obviously be even more advantageous and would possibly add to the value of Chartwell as a whole. There then followed prolonged discussion regarding the right of way which had always concerned Clementine who had seen it as an inconvenience from the beginning.

Local consultations indicated that the right of way was probably ancient but an added problem was that it not only provided public access across Churchill's property, something that caused him considerable irritation, but also provided Pilbrow with vehicular access to his farm. There was another route into Chartwell Farm from the Puddledock end but this was rarely used and Pilbrow was content to see the old track moved if Churchill built him a new road instead. Nonetheless, altering rights of way is a protracted and complicated procedure at the best of times, with its roots deeply embedded in the best and worst practices of ancient English Law. '… may I warn you that you are undertaking one of the most irritating and wearisome tasks that even you have had to meet…'[31] [32] was the comforting observation offered by Brigadier General Arthur Currie and it was well over a year later after much consultation and head-scratching that the local authority eventually agreed to the diversion of the right of way. Churchill then paid for a new road to be made for Pilbrow along the re-positioned right of way adjoining his new southern boundary. In due course, the parcel of new land did become an orchard.

At about the same time, Churchill built an enormous wood store in the stable yard, not least because filling it with timber gave him the excuse to fell and dismember large numbers of old trees. At the end of the twenties too, the boundary wall along the Mapleton Road was completed, its design based on one just down the road, at what is now another National Trust property, Quebec House in Westerham, the birthplace of General Wolfe. Churchill reputedly spotted the wall while driving past one evening and remarked that this was what he wanted. He took an active role in the construction of this seventy-five metre long 3.5 metre high boundary which now has its own listed building status. During the summer of 1928, Churchill embarked on another building scheme, but this time one with a difference. It was the first structure to be built in large measure by his own hands. Variously called Marycot (the family's preferred name), Mary's Cottage, Mary's House or even, later and somewhat disparagingly, a doll's house or Wendy house, it was a tiny one-bedroomed cottage for his daughters Mary and Sarah constructed on the lower, eastern boundary of the kitchen garden. 'Mary has taken the greatest interest in the work…' he wrote to Clementine 'and laid the foundation stone

Marycot, Chartwell.

with great ceremony...'[33] It is not clear exactly why or when during the nineteen twenties the passion for bricklaying took hold but Churchill's tutors were two of his own employees, the general hands Whitbread and Kurn and a professional bricklayer named Benny Barnes who often found himself picking up where Churchill had left off when other duties took him away from his wall building.[34]

Churchill bricklaying; date unknown.

The quality of Churchill's bricklaying has been debated over the years and exactly how much was built by him and how much by Barnes will never be known but it has passed into Churchillian folklore that as a result of his brick-laying activities, he became a member of the bricklayers' union. The truth is slightly more complex however. The fact that Churchill laid bricks as a hobby was well known and at the beginning of September 1928 a photograph was published in the national press of him at work on Marycot. The picture unfortunately showed

THE GREATER PART OF THIS WALL WAS BUILT BETWEEN THE YEARS 1925 & 193- BY WINSTON WITH HIS OWN HANDS

Wall plaque at Chartwell commemorating Churchill's bricklaying.

one corner brick perched extremely precariously while Churchill, trowel in hand, beamed contently from above. The response by the public was mixed. He received one indignant letter from a professional bricklayer pointing out the poor quality of his work and expressing concern about the critical brick – 'Now Sir, this is not on a par with your State work, and I would urge you to attend to its alignment and correct placing...'[35] He was also written to by a man named James Lane who was Mayor of Battersea but also Organiser of his local Division of the Amalgamated Union of Building Trade Workers. He suggested that 'All good workmen become members of an organisation with a view to keeping up the traditions of an honourable occupation...'[36] Churchill responded that he did not think he was sufficiently qualified but asked to see the Rules. The Divisional Secretary nonetheless urged him on, adding that through the Union he would improve his craftsmanship and pointing out that when William McKinley was President of the United States, he had to become a member of the appropriate craft organisation before he could lay a foundation stone. After more extensive enquiries, Churchill duly filled in an application form and sent a cheque for the 5/- admission fee.

On 10 October he was issued with a membership card signed by George Hicks the General Secretary and the Press were inevitably onto the story. 'Mr Churchill joins Bricklayers in Union', 'New Role for Versatile Winston' ran the headlines. Sir Abe Bailey wrote to congratulate him as did a handful of union members, one even offering to work as his hod carrier but most members were not as happy. 'You damned old hypocrite!' wrote one, signing himself A British Subject sodden with Taxation. 'It would do you & the country good if you were forced to earn your daily bread by laying bricks instead of playing at it, & making yourself look a fool'.[37] This was all hardly surprising as the A.U.B.T.W. was a seriously left wing organisation and only a few weeks earlier, its Conference had passed a resolution that '…this Conference…calls upon the Labour Party Executive and the Parliamentary Labour Party to expose the danger of war to the workers and to mobilise them for organised action against the war preparations of the Baldwin Government…'[38] Several outraged messages were then sent to the Executive Council regarding the 'alleged admission of Winston S. Churchill as a member of the union' and the matter was debated at length at its meeting on 26 October. Agenda item 3 was simply 'Winston S. Churchill'. It emerged that the admission form had not been completed properly, the proposal had not been seconded, the cheque had not been cashed and, most importantly, Churchill had not given any details of the length of time he had worked at the bricklaying trade. Although it was clear that the whole matter had not been intended to be taken too seriously, and had been 'viewed generally in a wrong light', it was felt appropriate to make an official pronouncement and it was resolved unanimously 'That this Council declares that Mr Winston Churchill is not eligible for membership of this union, and that Bro. Lane, No 2 Divisional Organiser, be advised to this effect accordingly.'[39] Brother Lane was exonerated from having wilfully violated the rules and the following week, a formal statement outlining the matter with a copy of the resolution was circulated to all divisional councils, branches and committees. The circular was copied '… exclusively to the *Daily Herald* being the official organ of the Labour Movement, and not to any other newspaper'.[40] Churchill himself issued a statement saying that he had never intended to join the Union but had been pressed to do so and that now he had been issued with a card he did not understand how the matter could be 'gone back upon'.[41]

Churchill famously built a large part of the wall of the kitchen garden itself. It is a notable construction, stretcher bonded and with a double pitched tile coping. A plaque now attached to the wall states 'The greater part of this wall was built between the years 1925 & 1932 by Winston with his own hands'. Apart from the relative contributions of Churchill himself and Benny Barnes however, there seems some uncertainty about the timing of the construction. The brick-making firm of W. T. Lamb & Sons (not to be confused with H. A. Lamb & Sons, electricians) state that 'around 1928' Churchill approached his friend George Mowlem-Burt, the Chairman of John Mowlem Construction Ltd for advice on buying bricks that would blend with those used on the main house at Chartwell. These may have been for use on Marycot and he was referred by Mowlem-Burt to Bertrand Cardain Lamb of W. T. Lamb & Sons and in due course arranged to visit their brick works at Godstone. Following this visit, Lamb's son Richard went to Chartwell with samples but unfortunately the match was not good enough so four bricks were removed from a wall and taken away in order that a better fit could be obtained; on condition that if Lamb's could not achieve an acceptable match, they would pay for them to be replaced. Richard Lamb returned with the new samples and the match being satisfactory, Churchill placed an order for 4,000. In truth, it is said that Churchill ordered 4,004 bricks to allow for those removed but only 4,000 were to be paid for! Richard Lamb later said that on his second visit he gave Churchill some instruction in the correct way of laying bricks. There appear however to be no relevant invoices dating from this period although in 1934 and 1935, Churchill did purchase from Lambs two batches of 2,000 and 4,000 bricks, particularly liking the 'plum coloured tinted ones' and stated that he would probably need 8,000 in total although with no indication of their intended purpose.[42]

Towards the end of 1928, much thought was being given both in Cabinet and in the nation at large to the possible date of the General Election which was due the following year. Churchill's value to the Government as Chancellor of the Exchequer was enormous and Prime Minister Stanley Baldwin had shown considerable interest in Churchill's lake building and landscaping activities – not for their intrinsic appeal but because it helped keep his mind clear for affairs of state. 'Do remember what I have said about resting from current problems. Paint, write, play with your dams. But a big year will soon begin and much depends on your keeping fit' he had written in August before going on holiday.[43] But fit as Churchill kept, and no matter how many dams he built, it was to be of no avail. The General Election took place on 30 May 1929. Churchill retained his seat at Epping although on a minority vote but the aftermath of the General Strike and high unemployment were to tell against the Conservatives and Baldwin's Government fell. Ramsay MacDonald was back in power to form his second administration. The Chancellor was out of Office and out of 11 Downing Street. The Churchills once again had no London home although in the short term, that was to be no great problem. Drawing to the end of work on The World Crisis, his vast account of the First World War which in time was to yield him significant income, Churchill dived into another literary project and began his massive study of the life of his hero and ancestor, John 1st Duke of Marlborough. In the late summer he undertook a three month visit to the United States and Canada, accompanied by Randolph, Jack and Jack's son Johnny although Clementine was unable to join them because her health was not good. Churchill's intention was to enjoy some sightseeing and also attend to business matters, not least with plans for the sale of his literary works in America. He stayed in New York with his long-time friend the Democrat politician Bernard Baruch but his return there on 24 October after visiting Civil War battlefields coincided with the Wall Street Crash. Over the years, Churchill had used his visits to North America to enable him to speculate on the New York stock market and the disaster cost him over £10,000 and made a significant hole in the estimated earnings of nearly £22,000 (including an enormous £6,000 advance on the Life of Marlborough) he had proudly accrued since leaving office. He sailed home the following week and broke the appalling news to Clementine on his arrival.[44] The loss had consequences for their domestic arrangements.

After losing office, they had already made provision for London accommodation in November and December by renting Venetia Montagu's London home, 62 Onslow Gardens in South Kensington, a gracious white painted early Victorian house in the grid of uniformly gracious white painted houses in the streets between the Brompton and Fulham Roads and they adhered to this plan. Buying anywhere in London however was put on hold and for once, family invitations seem to have been in short supply so the Churchills became Metropolitan nomads for the next two years. A favoured residence was the Goring Hotel in Grosvenor Gardens and according to Mary Soames they also took a number of furnished houses on short term lets although there is no evidence of where these were as Churchill tended to use Chartwell headed notepaper for his correspondence. It seems likely however that they returned to Venetia Montagu's house in the second winter.[45]

And at Chartwell itself, it was economy time again. During the winter of 1929–1930, the house was effectively moth-balled and only Churchill's study stayed open as a functioning facility. Fortunately, Wellstreet Cottage, the butler's putative new house, did not yet have its butler and so the family were able to take advantage. Mary with her nurse and cousin Maryott Whyte moved in and Winston and Clementine came and stayed at weekends. Mary Soames remembered it all

Churchill's study with the old beams uncovered by Tilden; 'the pulsating heart of the house'.

being 'very cosy'[46] although by later evidence, it must have offered pretty Spartan accommodation.

After Churchill had built Wellstreet Cottage and bought the 2 acre plot from Pilbrow, there remained one extremely narrow strip of woodland that did not belong to him. It amounted to a little over a tenth of an acre and ran alongside the road. It was still owned by Lilian Bosanquet and during 1930, when his finances were beginning to recover, Churchill attempted to buy it from her or see if she would exchange it for an equivalent strip of his newly acquired field.[47] Her agents, Savills, said she was willing to consider an exchange on a reasonable basis but as many people who conducted business with Churchill discovered, their reasonable was his impossible and the negotiations foundered. Churchill took the pragmatic view that the woodland was worth nothing to anyone except him and that Mrs Bosanquet was asking for far too large an area in exchange.[48] The boundary therefore was fixed by independent assessor and properly marked although five years later, the matter was raised again when Churchill, seeking once more to extend both his holdings and his investments, wanted to build yet another cottage.

'Mary's First Speech', oil painting by Winston Churchill (*c.* 1929).

Endnotes

1   CHAR 1/159/28–31. WSC to A. J. Campbell-Colquhoun. 25 Sept 1922.

2   CHAR 1/159/28–31. WSC to A. J. Campbell-Colquhoun. 25 Sept 1922.

3   CHAR 1/159/41–42. A. J. Campbell-Colquhoun to WSC. 29 Sept 1922.

4   Tilden, P. *True Remembrances – the memoirs of an architect.* p. 84.

5   Soames, M. *Clementine Churchill. 2nd Ed.* p. 254.

6   Mary Soames, conversation with the author, 15 Jan 2004.

7   Soames, M. *Clementine Churchill. 2nd Ed.* p. 254.

8   CHAR 1/172/80. Sarah Churchill to WSC. 29 Nov [1924]

9   CSCT 2/20/2. WSC to CSC. 7 Jan 1927.

10   CHAR 1/167/27–28. List of trees supplied by George Bunyard & Co. Ltd. [1923?]

11   CHAR 1/173/4-6. A. Luff & Sons to WSC. 11 Apr 1924.

12   CHAR 1/199/105. Mary Hozier to WSC. 6 July 1928.

13   CSCT 2/17/11–12. WSC to CSC. 17 Apr 1924.

14   CHAR 1/159/28–31. WSC to A. J. Campbell-Colquhoun. 25 Sept 1922.

15   CHAR 1/195/17. E. Waterhouse to WSC. 27 Apr 1927.

16   CHAR 1/189/75–78. [WSC] to E. Waterhouse. [May 1926].

17   CHAR 1/195/18. WSC to E. Waterhouse. 2 May 1927.

18   Peter Fitt, conversation with the author 24 May 2006.

19   Peter Fitt, conversation with the author 24 May 2006.

20   CSCT 2/17/16–17. WSC to CSC. 22 Aug 1924.

21   CSCT 1/14/5–6. CSC to WSC. 5 and 6 Sep 1926.

22   CHAR 1/195/45–47. George M. Callender & Co. to C. M. Fisher. 22 Sept 1927.

23   CHAR 1/199/98–9. WSC to F. A. Lindemann. 25 May 1928.

24   CHAR 1/214/9–10. Randolph Churchill to WSC. [1930]].

25   KS U1673T9. Conveyance.

26   CHAR 1/393B/218. H. J. Pilbrow to WSC. 19 Aug 1930.

27   CHAR 1/393B/217. WSC to H. J. Pilbrow. 23 Aug 1930.

28   CHAR 1/393B/216. H. J. Pilbrow to WSC. 2 Sep 1930.

29   CHAR 1/393B/202–203. WSC to H. J. Pilbrow. 10 Oct 1931.

30   CHAR 1/393B/224. Nicholl, Manisty & Co to WSC. 6 Mar 1930.

31   CHAR 1/393C/310–311. Arthur Currie to WSC. 23 Apr 1929.

32   Soames, M. *Clementine Churchill.* 2*nd*. *Ed.* p. 256.

33   CSCT 2/21/17–21. WSC to CSC. 10 Aug 1928.

34   Doris Edelston, conversation with the author, 17 Jan 2007.

35   CHAR 1/201/3-5. P. T. Norrie to WSC. 6 Sept 1928.

36   CHAR 1/201/53. J. F. Lane to WSC. 4 Sep 1928.

37   CHAR 1/201/27-28.'A British Subject sodden with Taxation' to WSC. 18 Oct 1928.

38   WU MSS 78/AU/1/1/10. Minutes of the Executive Council 18 July 1927 to 29 January 1929.

39   WU MSS 78/AU/1/1/10. Minutes of the Executive Council 18 July 1927 to 29 January 1929.

40   WU MSS 78/AU/3/1/2. Circulars to Branches 1928–1930. Circular 20/26. 31 October 1928.

41   CHAR 1/201/35-39. Press statement issued on behalf of WSC. 1 Nov 1928.

42   CHAR 1/393C/361. Violet Pearman to W. T. Lamb & Sons. 2 Feb 1934

43   CHAR 1/200/7. S. Baldwin to WSC. 11 Aug 1928.

44   CSCT 2/22/40–42. WSC to CSC. 19 Sept 1929.

45   Mary Soames, conversation with the author, 2 Aug 2006.

46   Soames, M. *Speaking for Themselves. The Personal letters of Winston and Clementine Churchill.* p. 349.

47   CHAR 1/393A/101. WSC to Lilian Bosanquet. 3 Nov 1930.

48   CHAR 1/393A/101. WSC to Lilian Bosanquet. 3 Nov 1930.

CHAPTER 9
A LOOSE CANNON

Out of office for the best part of the coming decade, Churchill had time for many things. Politically, the period has become known as his Wilderness Years. By late 1931, he and Clementine had been living on and off at The Goring Hotel and sundry short-term furnished lets for nearly two years and their finances were by then stable enough for them to consider buying a London home again. It needed to be close to Westminster, convenient for Parliament and spacious enough for private and business use; although the bulk of their possessions would remain at Chartwell. Using a different agent, Hampton & Sons, Churchill found what he wanted just a brisk walk from the Houses of Parliament and almost next door to the imposing structure of the Roman Catholic Westminster Cathedral. The large red brick blocks of apartments in Morpeth Terrace were built shortly before John Francis Bentley's vast and highly individual brick cathedral itself reared up alongside to be completed in 1903. The central block called Morpeth Mansions must have been familiar to Churchill as a number of eminent individuals lived or had lived there. At the beginning of November, a large apartment, No 11, which spread across the top two of the six floors became available. The lease was held from City & West End properties by Frances Stevenson, Lloyd George's secretary and long-term mistress who later became his second wife. She had taken the lease initially in 1915 and then renewed it for fourteen years from June 1924 so it was due to expire at midsummer 1938. She lived there with her daughter Jennifer (probably fathered by Lloyd George) and shared it with her youngest sister Muriel but was moving to a new home in Worplesdon, to be closer to Lloyd George's home at Churt. Churchill agreed to take over the remaining years of the lease at £380 per annum. He was offered the tenant's fixtures and fittings, and the carpets and curtains at valuation but stalled an answer until Clementine returned from Paris where she had been staying – to tell him she already had sufficient soft furnishings in store.[1] Frances Stevenson was not particularly fond of Churchill – and in later years perhaps understandably felt that Lloyd George was the greater war-time Prime Minister. She also took a singularly dim view of Churchill and Clementine arriving at the flat unannounced one Saturday morning shortly before completing the purchase while she and her sister Muriel (known to her family as Moo) were in the midst of having their hair done. After checking some details, the Churchills left, evidently without any apology for the disruption their visit had caused. Frances also took a dim view of Clementine wanting to buy two Venetian lamps that she told her emphatically were not for sale and later claimed that at the last moment before signing the lease papers Clementine said they would withdraw unless the lamps were included. Muriel also disliked Churchill and told of him bringing his own men from Chartwell to knock down a stone parapet outside the main sitting room window; and then being told by the leaseholders to replace it for safety reasons.[2]

No 11 Morpeth Mansions is a large and handsome apartment, set apart from others in the block by dint of its two floors and its roof terrace which although rather spartan and tucked between the chimney pots, is nonetheless spacious

View from the roof terrace of 11 Morpeth Mansions across Westminster Cathedral towards the Houses of Parliament.

and affords views across the adjoining cathedral to the Palace of Westminster and the Thames. When Churchill bought it, the property comprised a dining room, drawing room and small sitting room together with two bedrooms, a bathroom, kitchen and large pantry on the fifth floor. Upstairs were Churchill's and Clementine's bedrooms with a shared bathroom between, a further bedroom and Churchill's 22 feet long south-facing study and adjoining secretary's room. A door close to the secretary's room gave access to the roof terrace; although it was little used by the family because access to it meant disturbing Churchill's working areas.[3]

The terms of the agreement were relatively straightforward and normal. Churchill had the use of the common entrance hall and the quaint if rather cramped lift and was responsible for routine internal maintenance while the landlord took care of the exterior. The floor must be covered to ensure it was not noisy for the tenants below and no birds, dogs or other animals could be kept without consent. No alterations were to be made without the specific permission of both the landlord and the superior landlord, a condition that was immediately invoked as Churchill did wish to introduce a number of changes. He wanted to enlarge the day room/study into the adjoining passage and improve the bathrooms. But he needed an architect. Philip Tilden, like all his predecessors, was of course now beyond the pale, and the new man to step into the unenviable position of architectural advisor to Churchill was Charles Goodwin from Edenbridge, the first and possibly only architect with whom Churchill had anything approaching a continuing warm relationship. He drew up the plans and supervised the work. Approval was not obtained until the end of April when the works were undertaken by a builder named Parsons based in Waterloo Road.[4] Churchill spent most of the time at Chartwell working on his life of Marlborough while the changes were in progress at Morpeth Mansions although coincidentally the Churchills' domestic arrangements in Westminster were in due course to be affected by happenings taking place at just the same time on a rather grander scale a few thousand miles away. Just as Westminster City Council was approving alterations to Churchill's bathrooms, lavatories and drains, Adolf Hitler's National Socialist Party was gaining forty per cent of the vote – thirteen and a half million – in the German Presidential Election.

But the purchase of the Morpeth Mansions lease had all been far too routine and problem-free for a Churchill home. There must be a snag, a dispute and

Morpeth Mansions, Morpeth Terrace; Churchill leased
apartment No 11 from 1931 until 1940.

a legal tangle lurking out there somewhere; and so it proved. The catalyst was
an innocent suggestion by Churchill's lawyers, Nicholl, Manisty & Co. that he
should have the electrical wiring checked by a surveyor as there was a rumour it
might be defective.[5] Churchill agreed to do this and assumed the owners would,
if necessary, put it right. The Landlords asked their electricians, a firm called
Jackson & Boyce to look into the matter. It set in train a sequence of events
that was to end in Court before a Judge with Churchill represented by a future

Solicitor-General; and ironically, revealed a side to Churchill's relationships with architects that would hitherto have seemed the stuff of fiction.

The electricians' report stated that the lighting was good and the general condition of the electrical installation, although old, was no worse than thousands of other installations in London and Jackson & Boyce did not consider it in any way dangerous or constituting an undue risk of fire. The following year Charles Goodwin therefore perfectly reasonably engaged the same firm to undertake some work for Churchill; or more specifically for Clementine as it entailed the provision and installation of new electric lights. It was a decision he was to come to regret.

After Jackson & Boyce had completed their work, they sent their bills to Goodwin. The main account amounted to £116 9s 11d and with a smaller subsidiary account, the total was £122 14s 5d. Goodwin demanded a trade discount of twenty per cent and believed he had been over-charged. He offered £100. Jackson & Boyce would not give a discount as they claimed they were retailers not wholesalers and demanded the total. They tried to negotiate with Churchill personally, appealing to his sense of fair play but he would have none of it. He said he would support his architect's opinion (a most novel position) or alternatively go to arbitration. As the weeks passed, the impasse grew ever greater. Meetings between Goodwin and the electricians got nowhere and inevitably, the lawyers were soon involved, Nicholl, Manisty & Co for Churchill and McKenna & Co for Jackson & Boyce. The cheque for £100 was returned, letters flew to and fro, offer and counter offer was made, everyone protesting that they wanted an out of court settlement but not really advancing towards it. Churchill and Goodwin then agreed to accept responsibility for £22 8s 0d and this together with their offer of £100 narrowed the disputed sum to £22 15s 5d. Churchill's lawyers advised him to offer £10 or £12 and he agreed to this. Jackson & Boyce wanted £16, narrowing the disputed sum to £4, but as the sum grew smaller, Churchill's position grew more entrenched. '...we have been treated with great asperity by this firm...' he said, and then bizarrely in view of his recent history of building disputes, added '...It is a very serious thing for any firm to dispute the architect's judgement...'[6]

In mid-March McKenna & Co issued a summons on behalf of their clients in the Westminster County Court and much to Churchill's surprise and consternation, it was in the newspapers within days. He had expected the judge simply to consider the matter and send it to a technical referee. He also wished to make it clear that he was only contesting the issue because he felt bound to support his architect. In due course, His Honour Judge Dumas did consider the matter but opted to try it himself. Churchill was not happy and was even less happy with his solicitors. He felt they should have handled the case themselves and not engaged County Court Agents, a firm called Lucas & Bailey. He was gradually sinking into a legal mire. Although the case was a small one, anything that touched him acquired publicity he said and told Nicholl, Manisty & Co bluntly: 'It is now important to win this case and I am relying upon you in the matter'.[7]

Churchill then took it upon himself to send the papers to an old friend the barrister and MP Terence O'Connor KC (later to be knighted and become Solicitor-General) who alarmingly gave him an opinion that his defence started 'with formidable difficulties'.[8] But Churchill nonetheless knew best and asked his solicitors to engage O'Connor as leading counsel and when O'Connor did finally appear in Court, the judge changed his mind and decided not to try the case himself but agreed it should be refereed by a barrister with appropriate knowledge and agreed also that it should be done 'without any further publicity'. Throughout the summer, letters and legal opinions continued to fly between Churchill, Jackson & Boyce and their respective lawyers as they tried to reach an out of court settlement. Churchill, now fully backed by O'Connor, was adamant that he would not budge but by early December his experts, Tomlinson Lee and Marsh said they wanted payment of their fees which amounted to £42. The conclusion was finally reached on the afternoon of 3 January 1934 before the arbitrator Paul Sandlands KC in Essex Court, his Temple chambers. Judgment went against Churchill. He was instructed to pay Jackson & Boyce £20 13s 11d plus costs of £22 10s 0d. It was he told his lawyers 'a very unsatisfactory business' and two days later sent off his cheque, having been assured there would be no publicity.[9] After a further fortnight, it all became more unsatisfactory when the bills for his own costs arrived. His experts Tomlinson Lee and Marsh wanted another £47 5s 0d, the fees for his junior counsel Pitt and the County Court Agents Lucas & Bailey amounted to £127 4s 0d and although Terence O'Connor made no charge, there was even seven guineas to pay Parsons the builder who had also been required to attend. A dispute that he could have been settled for £4 finished costing him almost £257; entirely because for the only time in his life he totally and unreservedly chose to side with his architect and back the man's judgement.

No 11 Morpeth Mansions became Churchill's 'alternative Cabinet' rooms throughout much of the nineteen thirties. Although many allies, friends and colleagues came to stay at Chartwell for longer meetings and discussions of strategy, it was in the red brick block within sight of Parliament itself that Churchill gathered his facts and formulated his ideas, planned his questions for the Government and wrote the speeches, articles and books in which he thundered his convictions. His allies, official and unofficial, inside and outside Parliament gathered for long hours in the study, talking, confiding, planning and preparing over glasses of fortifying liquid in the pall of the smoke from many a hundred Havanas.

Churchill came in a little way from the political cold in the summer of 1935 when Baldwin invited him to become a member of the Air Defence Research Sub-Committee of the Committee of Imperial Defence, a stepping stone perhaps to a return to the Government. The General Election in November might provide that opportunity. But it was not to be. Churchill's electorate in Epping returned him with an increased majority; as the country returned the Government. But with so powerful a mandate, Baldwin had no need of Churchill and his hoped for call to return as First Lord of the Admiralty did not materialise. It was to be another Prime Minister, a few years later, who did not have the luxury of choice when he sent the invitation.

The early months of 1937 brought sadness and further frustration for Churchill. In April he was deeply into writing the final parts of his account of the life of Marlborough when news reached him of the death from cancer of his cousin Freddie Guest. Churchill had no greater champion in his political ambitions than this long-time friend and confidant and he wrote to Eddie Marsh, who was finally at the end of his long Civil Service career, telling him Guest's death was a great blow. Then, immediately after the Coronation of King George VI on 12 May, Stanley Baldwin retired as Prime Minister, paving the way for a smooth transition to Neville Chamberlain. A new government was assembled. Churchill remained outside it.

A year before the lease on the Morpeth Mansions flat expired, Churchill negotiated with City & West End properties for a five year extension at an annual rent of £420, a period that would take him through to the summer of 1943.[10] He had further electrical improvements made (not by Jackson & Boyce) together with redecoration, plumbing and then, a few months later, he installed a limited central heating supply. All seemed settled. The Churchills had their country house at Chartwell and now a good base in London was assured for the next six years. But the notions of a settled domestic arrangement and Winston Churchill do not sit easily in the same sentence and at precisely the time he was negotiating the new Morpeth Mansions contract, another London property came over the horizon. This time, it seems to have been Clementine who took the initiative with the agents Mullet, Booker & Co who had on offer a forty-two year lease on a substantial house not far from his father's old home at Connaught Place. Porchester Terrace runs north from the Bayswater Road opposite Kensington Gardens and No 58 was one of a group of three-storied early Victorian houses at the northern end. It was an imposing eight bedroomed property, set well back from the road with a wide arching carriage drive and two exits to the road. The rear garden gave direct access to the mews. The previous owner, the suffragist and educationalist Annie Leigh Browne had died in 1936 and the property was in the hands of her executor, sister and fellow feminist, Lady Lockyer. The owners, the Paddington Estate were willing to grant a new lease at £350 conditional on the tenant putting it in good repair. Churchill went to see it and found it in a lamentable state. There were other considerations too: there was some doubt if the garage was large enough for a Daimler and if Churchill took it on, he needed to know if the owners would agree to him building a library and two other rooms at the rear – he had in mind a chauffeur's flat above the extended garage and a new small 'cottage'.[11] He was particularly anxious that there should be no liability to put the house in order when the lease terminated – he would do so at the beginning but not at the end. The owners had prepared a massive list of works they considered essential and the cost amounted to £1,570. It needed complete rewiring, re-plumbing, re-pointing, decorating and sundry other repairs. Churchill had a fairly complete survey undertaken and Charles Goodwin estimated the cost of the additional building work and alterations Churchill would want and this brought the total to just over £4,000.

Through November 1937, Churchill and Clementine pondered the issues carefully. The possibility of selling Chartwell was still under consideration but there was no certainty they would find a buyer. They would also have to dispose of Morpeth Mansions on which they had only just renewed the lease. Even

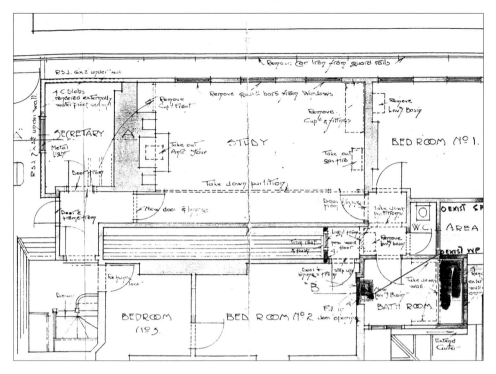

Part of Charles Goodwin's planning application for Churchill's proposed changes to
11 Morpeth Mansions (1932).

Churchill was this time cautious about owning too much at once. 'Whatever
happens, we must not have Chartwell, the flat and No 58 on our hands at the
same time' he wrote to Clementine.[12] After further lengthy talks, Churchill set
out his considered proposal. It was a good thing he said to have a plan on paper.
They would ask £550 per year for the Morpeth Mansions lease but would settle
for £500 with the fixtures and fittings to be agreed later. They should instruct
their lawyers to proceed with the lease for Porchester Terrace and Goodwin
should complete his plans for altering the garage to produce a self-contained
flat. Reconstruction of the main house would begin in the following spring,
proceed through the summer and be completed by the autumn; ready for their
return from any holidays They would live at Chartwell using only limited facilities
until the following spring then reopen it fully for the summer which would
give the best chance of a favourable sale. They would gradually move furniture
from Chartwell to Porchester Terrace and if Chartwell itself was not sold by the

following autumn, it would be closed entirely. Leaving it unfurnished would save them about £130 in rates. The Chartwell grazing would be let, the garden staff would be reduced to Albert Hill plus one man and a boy. The estate man Jackson would be given notice in the spring. But there were still nagging doubts and only a few weeks later Churchill was writing that it would be imprudent to commit themselves to large expenditure while they still owned two other properties and while the world was in such an uncertain state. He stressed he had still decided nothing but had merely assembled all the elements necessary for a decision.[13]

Porchester Terrace remained under consideration through Christmas and into the New Year while Churchill was at Blenheim and Clementine was skiing in Switzerland with Mary, Diana and Diana's husband Duncan Sandys. A most serious matter then struck Churchill and he wrote to Goodwin saying he had suddenly realised he had made no provision for anywhere to keep their considerable quantity of silver.[14] But his prevarication was becoming all too revealing and by early April Churchill's lawyers wrote to ask if he was still interested in the purchase. Fortuitously, however, the situation had now changed significantly. An old friend, the Austrian born financier Sir Henry Strakosch had offered to cover all Churchill's share losses and to purchase his American stocks at the £18,000 price he had paid for them (an extraordinarily generous gesture as the stocks had lost almost 70 per cent of their value).[15] Knight Franks' letter and Strakosch's offer were the impetus he needed. Chartwell need not be sold and he wrote to his agents telling them of his decision not to go ahead with Porchester Terrace.[16] He and Clementine stayed put at Morpeth Mansions and once again, the idea of selling Chartwell evaporated. Had he decided to buy 58 Porchester Terrace, his ownership would moreover have been fairly short-lived, for reasons that even he would have been unlikely to foresee. The area suffered from a number of air raids in 1940 and 1941 and then on 14 March 1944, the northern part of Porchester Terrace was hit by a V-1 flying bomb and No 58 and several other houses were damaged beyond repair.[17]

In June 1939, as the likelihood of war grew ever greater, Churchill decided to ask Colonel Bill, the representative of his landlords, City & West End Properties, what he was doing to comply with government regulations and make provision for an air raid shelter in the basement of Morpeth Mansions.[18] He replied that his surveyors were working on it but he was sure that in the passageway in the basement part of Flat 2A, residents would be safe from all but the biggest bombs.[19] Churchill, knowing better just how close the danger was, suggested that the necessary work should be done before the end of July.[20]

Endnotes

[1]   CHAR 1/228/61. V. Pearman to Hampton & Sons. 12 Nov 1931.

[2]   Ruth Longford, personal communication, 31 July 2006.

[3]   Mary Soames, conversation with the author, 2 Aug 2006.

[4]   CHAR 1/233/11. Violet Pearman to Nicholl, Manisty & Co. 26 Apr 1932.

[5]   CHAR 1/223/70–71. WSC to Nicholl, Manisty & Co. 14 Nov 1931.

[6]   CHAR 1/403/42. WSC to Nicholl, Manisty & Co. 5 Mar 1933.

[7]   CHAR 1/403/62–64. WSC to Nicholl, Manisty & Co. 7 Apr 1933.

[8]   CHAR 1/403/70–75. T. O'Connor to WSC. [15] [Apr] [1933].

[9]   CHAR 1/403/133. WSC to Nicholl, Manisty & Co. 28 Jan 1934.

[10]   CHAR 1/309/25. WSC to J. G. Bill. 31 July 1937.

[11]   CHAR 1/408/3–4. PS to WSC to The Ecclesiastical Commission. 1 Nov 1937.

[12]   CHAR 1/408/7–8. WSC to CSC [Nov] [1937].

[13]   CHAR 1/408/32–33. WSC to CSC. [Dec] [1937].

[14]   CHAR 1/408/74. WSC to C. Goodwin. 7 Feb 1938.

[15]   CHAR 1/328/4. WSC to B. Bracken. 19 Mar 1938.

[16]   CHAR 1/408/79. Nicholl, Manisty & Co. to WSC. 6 Apr 1938.

[17]   WCA Paddington Bomb Damage Records.

[18]   CHAR 1/351/27. WSC to J. G. Bill. 20 June 1939.

[19]   CHAR 1/351/26. J. G. Bill to WSC. 21 June 1939.

[20]   CHAR 1/351/25. WSC to J. G. Bill. 22 June 1939.

CHAPTER 10

$\mathscr{E}$MULATING 'CAPABILITY' BROWN

At Chartwell, as well as in Society at large, Churchill in the nineteen thirties was a loose cannon and it became an exciting as well as a maddening time for the people who lived and worked with him. At the beginning of 1931, he had a casual and none too serious exchange with Sir Howard Frank about the possibility of selling the house. He said that although he hoped to live out his days there, nonetheless, if someone would offer him £30,000 (a 'fancy price') he might consider uprooting himself.[1] Frank thought no-one would ever give him that sort of money[2] and so within a short while, Churchill was embarking on his next big project: a Chartwell swimming pool. The family enjoyed swimming but the lakes were too dangerous so the first swimming pool which later became known as the reservoir was built above the upper lake (an 'upper-upper' lake) during 1931 using yet more railway lines and more workmen. In the middle

Chartwell swimming pool.

Chartwell lakes.

of this however, Churchill decided to build yet another lake, 'an upper-upper-upper, or fourth lake on the far side of the valley'.[3] This was to be fed by the Churchill cross-valley siphon arrangement and everyone, Chartwell resident, casual labourer and unsuspecting guest was equipped with shovels and pressed into action. The earthworks had to be exceptionally strong because the position was so high up the valley wall. But it was all impracticably far from the house and '...something went wrong again. The pool tended to leak or seep, even at one point threatening to slide down the hill'.[4] So the upper-upper-upper lake too was abandoned, this project being replaced by the construction of another swimming pool, which survives still, an altogether grander enterprise at the lower end of the series of pools that punctuated the valley slope below the old Chart Well. Although the first swimming pool which was little more than a pond and indeed the other upper lakes had been built on an *ad hoc* basis using his own, somewhat fragile expertise, even Churchill had to concede that he now needed professional advice and turned to Charles Goodwin.

Although he had first been engaged to work on the London flat, Goodwin appears on the Chartwell scene in January 1934 by which time the swimming pool had been dug and he was advising Churchill on heating it. Goodwin engaged a man named Fretwell from Leatherhead to give specialist help. He proposed installing hot water boilers at a cost of £342 18s 0d, a sum that appalled Churchill who wanted to buy a second hand steam boiler and use that instead. Fretwell pointed out that this would be even worse, as there would have to be a man in constant attention and it would need lighting every morning.[5] Churchill capitulated in the face of even more expense but produced a bizarre scheme for a 15 feet high removable chimney that could be taken down or even screened by a tent during the part of the year that the pool was not being heated. The actual solution was no less outlandish as the boiler house chimney was eventually concealed in the trunk of an old oak tree and the filtration equipment was hidden by *Gunnera* leaves.[6]

Work went ahead on the construction of the boiler house during early 1934 and the swimming pool was filled during April. The pool covered an area of 3,900 square feet and had a maximum depth of 7 feet 4 inches. It held 20,000 gallons and Churchill used mains water to fill it at a cost of 1/6 per 100 gallons. Early 1934 was however an inauspicious moment to choose for doing this because rainfall had been low, a serious national water shortage was pending and within two months, the situation was being described as an 'unprecedented drought'. Although he was told he could still make moderate use of garden sprinklers, Churchill's swimming pool filling brought a swift rebuke from the East Surrey Water Company following complaints from their customers that they were unable to obtain a proper supply because Churchill was taking the water during prohibited hours. He was told only to fill it between ten at night and six in the morning.[7] By the end of May however, all was well, the pool was full and Churchill was delighted that, on a low coke consumption, a water temperature of over 75 degrees Fahrenheit could be easily maintained. He constructed a sand and gravel filter system for the pool although his efforts, like those of many another DIY enthusiast seeking to save money, were to prove inadequate and a few months later the Paterson Engineering company was installing a proper one at a cost of £207. Churchill also bought and personally experimented with different coloured Cementone paints (in delicate shades) for the bottom of the pool and found it all 'quite amusing'.[8] A shade called No 7 and described as 'Water Green Tint' seemed the best although there appears to have grown up a belief that Churchill preferred Wedgwood Blue, an assertive colour that persists in the pool today and has caused successive gardeners and garden advisors much anguish.[9]

Finances however were still stretched and the Westerham Men's Club was to suffer in consequence. Just at the moment his home-made filtration bed was failing and he was having to find £200 for a proper replacement, Churchill received a polite letter from the club secretary that advised him of his re-election as an Honorary Member, but also delicately pointed out that the club was badly in need of funds. Churchill's own secretary helpfully wrote '£1 1s 0d Cheque?' on the letter before showing it to him. Churchill in turn annotated it 'No, only 10/-'.[10]

In the August of 1934, Churchill and Clementine went separate ways for their holidays, Clementine going to Scotland, Churchill spending time at another of the Riviera houses he loved so much. Their old friend the American actress Maxine Elliott had commissioned the architect Barry Dierks to build her a magnificent home called Château de l'Horizon at Golfe-Juan near to Cannes and Churchill stayed there, painting and working on his life of Marlborough. It was a house he was to stay at on a number of occasions in the years before Maxine Elliott's death there in 1940.

Churchill continued to enjoy gracious living in 1934 when he and Clementine were together again for an autumn cruise in the Mediterranean on Lord Moyne's 1200 ton yacht *Rosaura*, a superbly opulent vessel that had lost one of its old twin funnels when it was converted for his use from its earlier more prosaic manifestation as the cross-channel steamer *Dieppe*. The ship was requisitioned by the Navy in World War II and sunk off Tobruk in 1941. It was a relaxing holiday for the Churchills although it presaged their longest period of separation and one that caused Churchill much heartache. As Walter Guinness (the third son of the brewing magnate Lord Iveagh), Lord Moyne had been financial secretary to the Treasury under Churchill's Chancellorship in 1924-5 and then entered the Cabinet as Minister of Agriculture. After the fall of Baldwin's government however, he retired from politics and indulged his wealth and time in more exciting things. He was an inveterate traveller and sometime big game hunter although the latter activity gradually gave way to an interest in wild life for its own sake and he used his beautiful yacht to travel to far-flung places in search of specimens. It was this passion that prompted him to invite Churchill and Clementine to join him on a four-month cruise to the

East Indies with the intention of studying the local fauna and more specifically of capturing a giant Komodo dragon lizard for the London Zoo. Churchill had neither time nor real inclination for a such a voyage but Clementine did and in December they parted although keeping in touch by regular letters, among which is the series of missives Churchill called the Chartwell Bulletins which chronicle, not only news of his writing and his adventures at Chartwell but also trenchant political commentary.

By the end of 1934, Charles Goodwin was well ingratiated at Chartwell and found himself advising not only on the design of changing rooms for the new swimming pool but also on a system for sewage disposal via a septic tank. Waste drainage water from all the roofs and yards at Chartwell was collected, as it had been for over a hundred years, in an open cesspool in Buddles Wood, just across the boundary of Major Pilbrow's land on Chartwell Farm from where an overflow discharged into the wood itself. It was all highly unsavoury and Pilbrow seems to have been uncommonly indulgent in raising no objection but some while later, Churchill, his conscience pricked, thought that for health reasons, he should at least install a small filter and put a wooden cover on the pit.[11]

In 1934, Wellstreet Cottage at Chartwell had a new tenant in the shape of Clementine's life-long bachelor friend Horatia Seymour. Her father had been Gladstone's Private Secretary and she had first visited Chartwell in May 1931, taking a liking to it before moving in a few years later as a paying tenant. Churchill made a number of alterations and improvements to the cottage for her although he found her 'a little exacting'[12] and at Charles Goodwin's suggestion, a redundant lavatory basin was even brought from Morpeth Mansions for her benefit. Nonetheless she had to pester Churchill (she was 'miaowing a good deal' he told Clementine[13]) over delays in the work the following spring when she asked if she could install electricity in the kitchen at her own expense, buy a small electric cooker and generally make it habitable for her cook. Ostensibly providing accommodation for servants, Churchill had built the cottage without such amenities and during their sojourn there, his own family had had to manage, a contrast with his and Clementine's unremitting demands on Tilden for the best possible equipment when the Chartwell kitchen was being built. Horatia Seymour remained at Wellstreet Cottage until the summer of 1946.

The same year that Horatia Seymour came to live at Wellstreet, Churchill found himself involved with the life and home of another itinerant woman but one from the opposite end of the social spectrum. It offers a telling commentary on Churchill's attitude to the working classes and began a year earlier with the death of 'Donkey' Jack Smith. He and his wife Mary were gypsies, well-known local Westerham characters who had lived for some fourteen years in a crude hovel on the common land of Windmill Hill above Chartwell, together with their donkey. On hearing of Donkey Jack's death in 1933, Churchill paid for his funeral expenses in order to spare him burial in a pauper's grave.[14] Then in January of the following year because of his evident concern with the Smith family, Churchill was sent notification by the magnificently named Herbert Knocker, Deputy Steward of the Manor of Westerham that the Parish Council had suddenly received formal complaint about what was termed 'a serious encroachment' on the Common; to wit, the erection of a hut and kitchen used as a dwelling house.[15] The splendid man Knocker then suggested that to circumvent the difficulty, he, Churchill, might be interested in purchasing the Manorial Rights of Windmill Hill, together with Mrs Smith's hut, from the then owner Captain John Warde at Squerryes Court. As Lord of the Manor, he would acquire rights not only in relation to gypsies but also to timber and gravel extraction.[16] Churchill was becoming interested. He moved to asking Knight Frank & Rutley to produce a valuation which they assessed at £250 and added that they did not think Mrs Smith's hut was really objectionable. They told him 'In our opinion, there is a certain 'pride of ownership' to an owner of 'Chartwell' with such a beautiful house, and the acquisition of the control of the Manorial Rights must be an attraction. Possibly if you purchased, a 'Manor of Chartwell' might be created...'[17]

It was the perfect way to gain Churchill's attention: simultaneously massage both his ego and his wallet. Nonetheless, he discovered to his disappointment that there was no worthwhile timber on the Common and the sand, gravel and stone rights were not worth having so he was only disposed to offer £150. Captain Warde was not interested and he then began to have second thoughts about a sale. He too was a shrewd businessman and it struck him that if he sold his own estate, which was in sight of the Common, its value would be enhanced if the Common itself had not passed out of his control. Perhaps Churchill would like to buy just the small area that included Mrs 'Donkey Jack's' hut.[18] Churchill would not, the negotiations ended and he never did become Lord of the Manor.

Within a few weeks of the chance of a sale evaporating, Knocker struck, issuing Mrs Smith with an eviction notice which he just happened to copy to Churchill. It ordered her to demolish and remove the illegal building on Windmill Hill.[19] The claim itself would be heard at the next Court Baron on 7 April at the George & Dragon; in practice the last ever held in Westerham. Churchill was unable to attend but the eviction notice was ratified and the matter dragged on through the summer and was only finally brought to a conclusion in October when Churchill wrote to the Parish Council saying he was prepared to offer Mrs Smith accommodation on his own land. She immediately availed herself of his generosity and moved into a hut in Chartwell Wood. Major Pilbrow at Chartwell Farm was not happy, pointing out to Churchill some months later that '... the hut which you have had erected for the old lady from the Common is erected in such a position overlooking my land from whence there is no public right of way that all her comings and goings have to be over my private land and she even obtains her drinking water from my spring'.[20] Churchill immediately made alternative arrangements for Mrs Smith's water and despite a serious leg injury occasioned when she was knocked down by a push bike on Hosey Hill, she lived on at Chartwell until her death. Churchill bemoaned the fact that no compensation of any kind was available to her for her injury and had she deteriorated further, he said would try to get her into a decent home at some small cost.[21]

There were other additions to the list of Chartwell residents during 1934. Churchill and Clementine had become interested in bee keeping. Clementine had been a member of the Kent Bee Keepers' Association 'without making use of the privileges' for several years and she now plunged in with enthusiasm. She was referred for advice from one person to another and eventually it fell to a Mr Sewell from Theydon Bois in Essex who wrote copiously to her with notes, guidance and drawings by way of instruction.[22] She told him she had read the instructions aloud to her gardener ' who seemed quite intelligent about it...'[23] Skeps and hives were bought and Albert Hill was put in charge.

By the extreme south-western boundary of the Chartwell estate, the Mapleton Road turns southwards and on the corner, close to the junction with the new road to Chartwell Farm, lies Chartwell Cottage a two-storey tile hung property built by the Campbell Colquhouns around the end of the nineteenth century and in 1935 occupied on a life tenancy by Mrs Couchman, widow of the Campbell

Chartwell Cottage.

Colquhoun's butler. She was born Dessie Maria Heritage and was one of Mrs Campbell Colquhoun's ladies' maids when she met and in 1896 married Herbert Couchman. Throughout his life, Churchill was firm but fair with his servants and employees and could display considerable kindness, admittedly not always altruistic but nonetheless genuine and thoughtful. One of the Chartwell under-gardeners Victor Trowbridge was to marry his sweetheart Lucy Barnett later that year. Churchill had a plan to build a cottage for him, a gesture that would at least have helped retain his services although under-gardeners were not exactly scarce and Trowbridge could not have been difficult to replace. Trowbridge could afford to pay 6/- per week (the interest on £300 at 5 per cent) and Churchill thought he could get at least £100 housing subsidy.[24] His preferred option was to build adjacent to the garden on the north side of Wellstreet Cottage if he could more effectively persuade Mrs Bosanquet to part with her strip of woodland than he had done five years earlier. This would give him a new access to the road for Wellstreet Cottage and so release the land to the north. The alternative was to build to the south of Chartwell Cottage if this proved impossible. Churchill retained Charles Goodwin as his architect while Lilian Bosanquet this time brought her husband on board and he roughly sketched out some measurements of the potential exchange plots and then arranged for a local man from Westerham, Timothy Weller, ominously described as 'builder and undertaker' to put marker stakes in the ground.[25] Churchill wanted to discuss the layout with Weller who was not particularly happy as he had been engaged by Captain Bosanquet and did not really want to become involved without his permission. Dessie Couchman was not happy either; in truth, she was extremely distressed as she felt the view from her house would be obstructed if he built to the south. Knight Frank & Rutley suggested to Churchill that he might covenant not to build for fifteen or twenty years on the land adjoining Chartwell Cottage at the side where it would cause the most obstruction and also that in the event of Mrs Couchman's death, he should have the opportunity to purchase Chartwell Cottage at a price to be fixed by valuation.

Churchill did get what he wanted – and Dessie Couchman did not after all lose her view – when Lilian Bosanquet and her sister in law Eveline Bosanquet agreed to an exchange of 633 square yards of land on the north east side of Chartwell Cottage with 728 square yards of Churchill's land to the south east of Chartwell Cottage. The deed of exchange was effected on 14 May 1936 and the new cottage was built just to the north of Wellstreet Cottage. It was known as Garden Cottage, Gardener's Cottage or sometimes simply by the name of the gardener who happened to be living there at the time – although built originally for the under-gardener Victor Trowbridge, it later became the head gardener's house.

In the spring of 1935, further modification took place on the Chartwell lakes and although ostensibly fairly straightforward, it was to entail earthworks, earth moving, machinery and mud on a scale that even Churchill could not have imagined. Fortunately for Clementine, far away in the Tropics on Lord Moyne's yacht searching for monster lizards, she never saw what happened and her husband's accounts of his adventures with his own monster, a geriatric excavator with a mind of its own, only reached her in his Chartwell Bulletins.

Other Churchill letters at other times were called Bulletins – and the expression Chartwell Bulletin was first used in September 1927 – but the numbered series written to Clementine on her cruise form a neat and unified group. There are twelve in all, written between 1 January and 13 April 1935. Some were accompanied by annotated photographs of happenings at Chartwell as the lovelorn Churchill, separated from the woman he adored at this time of domestic upheaval – admittedly domestic upheaval entirely of his own making – poured out his heart on to his writing paper.

All began promisingly as the New Year turned.[26] The swimming pool was being filled for the new season using water from the spring. It was looking clear and limpid. Churchill could therefore turn his attention to two major projects: a new island in his lower lake and, first, a ha-ha. It had been Clementine's idea, to use a ha-ha ditch with a two feet high mound of earth (which was predictably christened the he-he) on the house side to screen the swimming pool from above; much more attractive and more practical than the existing temporary fence. Churchill decided the ditch itself would be four feet deep and concealed in the bottom, six feet below the top of the slope, would be the fox-proof fence which was needed to protect the swans on the lake. He told Clementine her eye would plunge, as she desired, across a valley of unbroken green and in due course he moved a lower bed of rhododendrons as she had wished to enhance the impression of rolling green slopes. A mechanical excavator was being used on a construction site nearby and Churchill saw an opportunity to obtain its

The swan fence at Chartwell.

services relatively cheaply. While his 'Kat' was away, he would play with his toys.

Churchill spoke to the site manager for Mears Brothers, the civil engineering firm operating the equipment, pointing out the machine he wanted, a Ruston No 4 excavator, and they agreed to hire it to him for £25 per week. Delivery was £10 extra. It came complete with a back-acting trench digging attachment and the price included the fuel, driver's wages and the loan of a one cubic yard capacity side tip wagon which he would run on his old rails. This would carry the spoil to a big hole behind the oasthouses on Chartwell Farm which Major Pilbrow was gradually filling and to which he welcomed Churchill's muddy contribution. Churchill accepted the quotation, having first expressed the hope that one week meant seven days, and having also queried the size of the wagons which he suspected only held half a yard.[27] Mears clarified the matter – they assumed he had 24 inch rails but on checking that they were only 18 inch gauge, then indeed, smaller, half yard wagons would be supplied. They also advised employing a horse rather than the windlass he had used previously to haul them.

Earth-moving at Chartwell with railway tracks and the Ruston excavator before it 'ground to a halt in a large glutinous abyss' (1935).

And they had to disappoint him by saying that a week was not seven days but a normal working period of five days, each of eight hours.[28]

The following week, Churchill thought again and realised the operation would be too much for his miniature railway, even with the addition of horse-power and he ordered the larger gauge system with a proper power source – a 2 ton German Montania locomotive at £6 per week, including fuel and driver. Mears most obligingly offered the loan of 200 yards of 24 inch track including curved rails and two crossings, provided Churchill paid for their transport from Brasted; about 4 miles away. What Mears Brothers did not point out to him was that the Ruston No 4 Universal Excavator was a model that had been introduced as long ago as 1926. In its time it was an effective if quaint contraption with an engine that was started with petrol and then ran on paraffin but by 1935, the technology, and self-evidently this particular machine, after a hard working life, had had its day. It was quite frankly clapped out. And the Montania locomotive was unreliable. But Mears could not be held responsible for the weather. It was to be a wet and muddy three months.

The excavator arrived on Saturday 12 January and the railway the following Monday. At first Churchill was entranced, as he always was with things mechanical. Because of the wet weather, the excavator did not start digging the ha-ha until the Friday but then completed it within twenty four hours. Churchill likened it to a huge animal, referring to it as 'he'. It lifted nearly a ton with one 'mouthful', pushed heaps of earth like an elephant and pulled rocks out of the ground 'as if they were walnuts'.[29] The day after he wrote this account to Clementine, work was due to begin on the already drained lower lake and Churchill estimated it would take just two days to cut through the isthmus and he would thus achieve his objective, like Poseidon, of creating an island, after which the machine could be used for other tasks.

The island project too began well although the loaded wagons were constantly falling off the rails causing 'delay and vexation', Churchill wrote in the next Chartwell Bulletin.[30] Then having got his priorities – the mechanical digger and news of Randolph's campaign for the forthcoming Wavertree by-election – out of the way, Churchill, almost as an aside and buried insignificantly in the middle of the same letter, reassuring told his far-away wife 'The house was nearly burned down yesterday'. Bizarrely, the maids, packing away Clementine's bed clothes had wrapped two hot light bulbs inside. Arnold the estate manager and Inches the butler had fortunately intervened in time to save Chartwell from being reduced to ashes.

Two days later, the digger was still digging, the railway was carrying the spoil to Pilbrow's pit and Churchill with his usual optimism predicted that the island would be completed and everything tidied up in a fortnight. In reality, he was deluding himself and sparing Clementine the truth. Conscious that Clementine had always believed Chartwell would prove something of an anxiety, and because it had been impossible to shield from her the difficulties with Tilden and the house, Churchill seldom bothered to burden her with the problems on the estate. In his letters over the years, not just the Chartwell Bulletins, he chose to tell her positive things – which flowers were opening, how the gardeners were progressing. But this time it was harder to conceal the reality. Before long both digger and railway locomotive had broken down, and both continued to break down. By 17 February, Churchill was becoming utterly exasperated. The digger had only worked for one morning in an entire week. 'I did not expect you were going to give me such an old and obsolete machine for the £25 a week,' he complained; and he wanted his hire period extended.[31] It was also still raining. Albert Hill the gardener had almost finished turfing the garden paths (reinforced at Churchill's suggestion with wire netting) but the weather was holding up its completion.

A week later, progress was even slower. The trucks were still falling off the rails and island building was proving a bigger and longer business than Churchill had expected. Musing in one of his letters over the declining health of Prime Minister MacDonald, whose eyesight was failing and who was by then being described as 'rambling and incoherent in Cabinet',[32] Churchill told his wife 'Ramsay sinks lower and lower in the mud, and I do not think the poor devil can last much longer'.[33] He could have been looking out of his window at his mechanical digger as he penned these lines because almost immediately afterwards the monster ground to a halt in a large glutinous abyss and could do no more work for three weeks. It took four hydraulic jacks, railway sleepers and much effort to extricate it. Despite his ever increasing adversity, Churchill was nonetheless unstinting in his praise for the exertions and tenacity of the British workman as Mears Brothers' employees spent forty hours without rest or sleep to recover the brute. Although people talked of the slackness of British labour, Churchill wrote, he had never seen or heard anything like it, 'where no necessity existed except pride in the job'.[34] The contractors themselves gained shorter shrift, especially when Churchill discovered they had themselves rented the machine from another contractor who had in turn rented it from a third; and none was taking responsibility. He told Clementine it had been sub-let twice and he did not think he would get out of it for under £150 although eventually he settled for £109; but not before the lawyers had been consulted. More importantly, Churchill now had his island which he thought would look delightful once it was green again and the lake was refilled.[35] Sitting at the dining room table he considered the view truly pleasing as the new channel of water took the eye between the tall trees on the island and the 'mainland'.[36]

No sooner had the aquatic landscape been remodelled and the ha-ha re-turfed than Churchill turned his attention to the old orchard, setting the entire garden staff to work tearing out the old trees and grass although waiting for dry weather 'to shake the mould from the coarse grass roots' [? sic] before relaying.[37] Half way through the work however, Churchill realised what many another person laying grass over a large area has discovered – that seed is significantly cheaper than turf. And ever anxious to ensure everything was ship-shape before Clementine's return from the East Indies, he then attacked the many seedling sycamores and elders that were springing up on the rhododendron bank and spoiling the whole effect from his bedroom window. They were swiftly truned into scaffold poles and faggots.[38]

Water works and turfing were not the only activities during the nineteen thirties. Considerable building was undertaken in the garage/stable yard – what is in effect a tiny hamlet of tenanted cottages and buildings at the eastern side of the estate, below the kitchen garden. The buildings include two fine brick-built Campbell Colquhoun late nineteenth century stables with green painted weatherboard walls and a hipped tiled roof. The various cottages in the stable yard have confusingly been named and renamed over the years, sometimes simply being referred to by the person who happened to be the current incumbent. Churchill wrote in some detail to Clementine on her cruise about the progress in the renovation of a small eighteenth century building, often known as the Chauffeur's Cottage but later as Howes' Cottage and is today called Lake Cottage. This building had once been a stable but had been suffering for some years from severe damp caused by a faulty overflow pipe and Churchill had feared that it would require complete rebuilding. Sam Howes had succeeded Aley as

Orchard Cottage (left), Studio Cottage (centre), Lake Cottage (right).

Herdsman's Cottage, Chartwell.

Churchill's chauffeur and was an invaluable and much liked if unexpected member of staff. He was a Londoner, an engineer by trade and had never previously been in service but came to Chartwell from industry during the slump at the end of the 1920s. He courted and then in 1932 married Olive Ward, one of Clementine's parlour maids, a woman whom Mary Churchill found a terrifying character. Howes also worked for Churchill at 11 Downing Street while he was Chancellor but could nonetheless be a liability. In 1935, Churchill received a warning from the Metropolitan Police for 'allowing Samuel Musgrove Howes to drive a motor vehicle when he was not licensed to do so'.[39] Howes eventually left Chartwell to return to industry in Coventry and had an extraordinary meeting with Churchill during the war when the Prime Minister was surveying bomb damage in the city. Churchill's bodyguard, Inspector Thompson spotted Howes in the crowd and stopped the car. A visit to the city's Mayor was cancelled while Churchill and his former chauffeur stood and talked at length. Howes later emigrated to the United States and achieved much success in an engineering firm there. In early 1935, Churchill employed Benny Barnes 'who charges 1/6d

Orchard Cottage Chartwell.

an hour and saves about five times as much' to renovate Howes' cottage under the guidance of his architect Charles Goodwin; and as he proved so efficient and economical, he then sent him up to the hill to undertake the essential work for Horatia Seymour at Wellstreet Cottage and stop her 'miaowing'.

In the summer of 1938, another old building in the garage/stable yard was altered in order to house Churchill's ever-increasing archive and then later that year, Churchill built yet another cottage, one that was to prove unexpectedly invaluable in the succeeding decade when the main house was closed. Usually called Orchard Cottage as it lies at the foot of the orchard, it is a pretty two-storied, three-bedroomed house designed by Charles Goodwin[40] and constructed while Clementine was away on another of Lord Moyne's travels on the *Rosaura*, this time to the West Indies. At the beginning of December a letter reached her in Barbados reporting on progress.[41]

Endnotes

[1] CHAR 1/393A/93. WSC to Sir Howard Frank. 14 Jan 1931.
[2] CHAR 1/393A/94–95. Sir Howard Frank to WSC. 12 Jan 1931.
[3] Churchill, J. S. *Crowded Canvas*. p. 58.
[4] Churchill, S. *A Thread in the Tapestry*. p. 25.
[5] CHAR 1/257/8. W. E. Fretwell to WSC. 19 Feb 1934.
[6] Churchill, J. S. *Crowded Canvas*. p. 58.
[7] CHAR 1/393A/121. East Surrey Water Co. to WSC. 25 Apr 1935.
[8] CHAR 1/257/22–23. WSC to E. F. Parry. 29 May 1934.
[9] CHAR 1/257/49. Violet Pearman to Freeman Sons & Co. 28 June 1934.
[10] CHAR 1/257/54–55. A. R. Walter to WSC. 2 July 1934.
[11] CHAR 1/393A/106. WSC to H. J. Pilbrow. 13 Jul 1939.
[12] CHAR 1/273/139–145. WSC to CSC. 13 Apr 1935.
[13] CHAR 1/273/116–122. WSC to CSC. 5 Apr 1935.
[14] Soames, M. *Speaking for Themselves. The Personal letters of Winston and Clementine Churchill.* p. 371.
[15] CHAR 1/393C/376. H. Knocker to WSC. 28 Dec 1933.
[16] CHAR 1/393C/371-373. H. Knocker to WSC. 29 Jan 1934.
[17] CHAR 1/393C/377. Papers accompanying Note from Violet Pearman to CSC. 10 Feb 1934.
[18] CHAR 1/393C/353. Knight, Frank & Rutley to WSC. 5 Mar 1934.
[19] CHAR 1/393C/346. H. Knocker to WSC. 31 Mar 1934.
[20] CHUR 1/30/124. H. J. Pilbrow to WSC. 3 June 1935.
[21] Reid, P. G. *Churchill. Townsman of Westerham.* p. 27.

[22]   CHAR 1/393A/44–46. G Sewell to CSC. 22 Jul 1934.

[23]   CHAR 1/393A/43. CSC to G Sewell. 24 Jul 1934.

[24]   CSCT 2/25/56–62. WSC to CSC. 8 Mar 1935.

[25]   CHAR 1/393A/55. T. O. Weller, to WSC. Nov 1935.

[26]   CSCT 2/25/1–7. WSC to CSC. 1 Jan 1935.

[27]   CSCT 2/25/1–7. WSC to CSC. 1 Jan 1935.

[28]   CHAR 1/275/46. Mears Bros. to WSC. 7 Jan 1935.

[29]   CSCT 2/25/8–14. WSC to CSC. 18 Jan 1935.

[30]   CSCT 2/25/15–19. WSC to CSC. 21 Jan 1935.

[31]   CHAR 1/275/51. WSC to Mears Bros. 17 Feb 1935.

[32]   Marquand, D. James Ramsay MacDonald. Oxford DNB.

[33]   CSCT 2/25/31–37. WSC to CSC. 31 Jan 1935.

[34]   CSCT 2/25/42–46. WSC to CSC. 23 Feb 1935.

[35]   CSCT 2/25/56–62. WSC to CSC. 8 Mar 1935.

[36]   CSCT 2/23/47–55. WSC to CSC. 2 Mar 1935.

[37]   CSCT 2/23/47–55. WSC to CSC. 2 Mar 1935.

[38]   CHAR 1/273/139–45. WSC to CSC. 13 Apr 1935.

[39]   CHAR 1/275/26. Metropolitan Police to WSC. 19 Feb 1935.

[40]   CHAR 1/342/3. Sketch plan by Charles Goodwin. 16 June 1939.

[41]   CHAR 1/344/14–17 WSC to CSC. 18 Jan 1939.

CHAPTER 11
ℒIVESTOCK

Churchill's life was always shared with animals – domestic pets, horses and farm livestock – and Chartwell with its estate and its water gave him ample opportunity to indulge himself. When he bought the property in 1922, no livestock was included at the auction but he did agree to take over the crops and stock at valuation. This was a curious arrangement since Campbell Colquhoun also owned several farms and the more logical course would appear to have been to include all livestock in the farm lots rather than leave some in the Chartwell house Lot 3 where the 'farming' was at best a small-holding operation. Exactly what animals Churchill bought is not recorded but there are regular references in the correspondence to farming matters, to cows, pigs, sheep, chickens, geese, turkeys, swans, all the sundry two and four footed creatures that might be expected in a hobby-sized small holding – it was never a working farm because Churchill took the view that no animal should be slaughtered once he had said 'Good morning' to it.[1] The operation was however serious enough for him to take on the services of Joseph Martin in January 1925 as farm manager/ stockman to look after the cattle. It was nonetheless all part of the worthy but slightly dotty idea that they should be 'living off the land'[2] and in the spring of that year, milk was even being sold from the Chartwell dairy. The pigs were kept in sties close to the lower lake and near the boundary with Chartwell Farm although throughout the 'farming' era, the sheep seem to have been animals that were actually owned by Chartwell Farm but allowed to graze on Churchill's land. The children loved bottle-feeding the lambs.

But within a few months, Churchill was anticipating the economies he felt were on the horizon and decided to relinquish any pretence at cattle farming. Martin was given notice although as usual when staff were told they had to go, Churchill later agreed he could stay on, initially until October and he did not finally leave Chartwell until May the following year. Red Poll cattle in fact were still there in the late summer of 1926 when along with the chickens and all except one of the ponies (called Energy, the last of Churchill's polo ponies – he had finally given up playing the previous summer) they were disposed of; almost the only economies on Churchill's infamous list that really were enacted.[3] Churchill could not however bear to be without his pigs and several remained, bringing him considerable success at the local Edenbridge Show. The hiatus moreover did not last long and practically every known form of farm livestock was back again two years later;[4] while Mary Churchill still kept her bantams[5] which wandered into the dining room to feed on fallen crumbs.[6] When Arnold left Chartwell in 1933, however, it did finally seem time to be realistic and Churchill instructed him to make arrangements before he left to sell all the animals except one sow and the black mare. Even then, Churchill still could not resist any sort of bargain and by the time he was writing the Chartwell Bulletins to Clementine in early 1935, he was succumbing to his daughters' urgings and buying goats. Mary and Sarah had seen two goats at a gypsy encampment and persuaded their father to pay £1 each for them. They nibbled around the pool he told Clementine. There was a white nanny named Mary and a brown nanny named Sarah who unfortunately died by eating some fertiliser that Albert Hill had spread on the grass. Goat Mary however not only survived but was pregnant and produced kids which in turn bred and before long there was a small herd of the animals munching their way around Chartwell although officially they were kept in the old stables.[7]

The most notable among the livestock that have been almost ever-present at Chartwell however are the birds; and above all the black swans with which Churchill and Chartwell have become inextricably linked. The black swan is a remarkable bird, not a black form of the familiar white mute swan but a distinct species that occurs naturally only in West and South-West Australia. To maintain the tradition, the Western Australian Government re-stocked Chartwell with a gift of black swans in 1975. It is not just black swans in reality but the idea of swans being black that people find so compelling and long before Captain Cook landed in Australia in 1770, public houses in England were being named The Black Swan. Real black swans were first seen in England at the old Royal menagerie in Windsor Great Park around 1810. The first time Churchill seems to have truly noticed them came just as the First World War was about to be unleashed. On the evening of 28 July 1914 he crossed the road from the Admiralty and went for a walk in St James's Park as a relief from the 'planning and preparing' and spent some time watching the pair of swans on the lake with their 'darling cygnet – grey, fluffy, precious & unique'.[8] He had however presumably seen the specimens that his friend Sir Philip Sassoon kept at Trent Park and it was Sassoon who first

'Black Swans', oil painting by Winston Churchill (1948).

supplied him with a pair for his own lakes. They arrived at the beginning of June 1927 but received a hostile reception from the highly territorial Jupiter, one of the resident pair of mute swans (its mate was called Juno) and a fence had to put around the upper lake to give them protection; and it is a fence that in one form or another stayed until recently, latterly to keep marauding foxes at bay. Churchill was entranced. He observed that the swans sang to each other (unlike the more or less silent mute swans, black swans have a rather musical call) and danced minuets with their necks. He bombarded Sassoon with questions – had they already mated or was their crated journey their first introduction, was there any chance of them breeding, should they have a house to live in, what would happen to them in the winter..?[9]

In due course the black swans did breed and by 1935, there was a small and highly promiscuous herd. Churchill wrote to Clementine on her tropical cruise to say that all the birds had mated, not only the parents but both brothers and both sisters had paired off too. He did not think it his duty to interfere however and observed that the Ptolemys always did it – and Cleopatra was the result.[10] Churchill referred in one of his Chartwell Bulletins to Carolina ducks too and to a pair of Mandarin ducks sent in 1935 by Philip Sassoon.[11] The following spring, Phillip Sassoon added further to the Chartwell waterfowl by arranging for James Wilson his head gardener at Trent Park to send Churchill a consignment of hand-reared tufted ducks and beautiful South American rosybills. Then, two years later, in July1938, there was a celebrated avian burst for freedom. Three of the swans took it upon themselves to depart, the local and national press pounced on the story and accounts ensued of 'Chartwell black swans' being spotted on the Thames, at Dartford, at Sheerness, heading for the Isle of Wight and across much of southern England.[12]

The peaceful life of the Chartwell swans was however rudely interrupted one day in the summer of 1939 by the arrival of three Embden or Bremen geese, a species long thought to have German origins, which descended on the lake and began to provoke the resident birds and their cygnets. Churchill who was having lunch at the time, grabbed a large stick and ran towards the lake shouting 'Horrible Nazis' and commanded Hill the gardener to build a prison camp for them.[13]

On Clementine's return from her cruise in the spring of 1935, she also added to the Chartwell menagerie with two more black swans she had bought in Sydney. She also suggested that she was bringing a pair of wallabies and an opossum but fortunately these never materialised. The most endearing of her acquisitions however was the Bali dove, 'a dear little pinky-beige bird with coral beak and feet, who lived in a wicker cage resembling a lobster pot'. From the description it may perhaps have been a spotted dove which is a common species on Bali and is often kept in cages. Rather remarkably, it survived for two or three years at Chartwell and on its ultimate demise, Clementine arranged for it to be buried by Albert Hill beneath the sundial which had been moved to the centre of the vegetable garden. The writer and traveller Freya Stark suggested its epitaph in some obscure and enigmatic lines by her close friend the Scottish writer William Paton Ker which are engraved on the sundial's base:

The Bali Dove Sundial, Chartwell.

Here lies the Bali dove

It does not do to wander
Too far from sober men,
But there's an island yonder,
I think of it again.

Another bird that fascinated Churchill and also had a brief sojourn at Chartwell was the Stanley crane, a beautiful and elegant grey-blue creature that he must have remembered from his time in South Africa. His source of Stanley cranes for Chartwell was Sir Abe Bailey, a flamboyant South African of English and Scottish descent, friend of Cecil Rhodes and owner of some of the major mines in the Transvaal. He was also a successful racehorse breeder, gambler and newspaper proprietor and had been a friend of Lord Randolph. He had known Churchill for many years and his son, John, married Diana Churchill in 1932 although it was an unsuccessful relationship and they soon separated, to divorce in 1935. Bailey's horses, including his only classic success Lovely Rosa which won him the

1936 Oaks, were trained by Harry Cottrill at Seven Barrows in Lambourn and in August 1935, two cranes that had just arrived at the Berkshire stables from South Africa were dispatched by train to Westerham. Churchill was instructed to clip a wing before letting them loose and to keep them indoors at night. He built them a little house and bought them special crane food. Cranes however are really not birds for an English garden, requiring care and attention considerably beyond anything the average groundsman and estate worker could be expected to provide although they did survive until the spring of 1937 when the female died. Churchill contacted the London animal dealers, G. B. Chapman about a replacement but thought their quotation of £37 10s 0d too expensive for a hen bird from Europe – they were impossible to obtain they said from South Africa – so he asked Bailey if he could find him another. A year later, two birds arrived on the S S *Windsor Castle* at Southampton for onward transit to Chartwell and one was still there, though bedraggled, the following January but its future is unknown and it seems to represent the end of tropical bird keeping at Chartwell, at least outdoors.

Cage birds, however, were another matter and Churchill kept budgerigars at Chartwell at various times and also a parrot, an African Grey named Mr Parrot that he obtained in the mid-1930s from the socialite and heiress Daisy Fellowes who was married to his cousin Reginald. It lived in a large cage in the Chartwell dining room. Like many parrots, it was a disagreeable creature, pecking anyone who came within striking distance including Churchill himself and seems to have been found a better home when the family returned to London in 1939.[14] The 'Churchillian parrot' surfaced however in a bizarre media story in January 2004 when claims were widely published that a 104 year old macaw owned by Churchill in the war and taught to say unpleasant things about Hitler was still alive. The matter was totally debunked by Mary Soames.[15]

Throughout the nineteen thirties, planting at Chartwell continued apace and many invoices survive detailing the purchases. There were bulbous plants in quantity – crocus, muscaris, anemones, iris, cyclamen, colchicums, galtonias, hyacinths, daffodils, tulips in great numbers (over one thousand in November 1936 alone), *Lilium giganteum*, camassias, snowdrops, scillas and lilies. A few years later, when he was ill, the Duchess of Kent sent Churchill some bulbs of red amaryllis (although he called them red lilies) and Churchill was much taken with them. He included them in some of his paintings and said they must always be at Chartwell so they were added to the collection to form the foundation of a large stock that survives still.[16] There were small perennials including primroses, polyanthus and other kinds of primula, gentians, violas and pinks along with larger herbaceous perennials including dahlias, verbascums, eremurus, heleniums for late summer, monardas, more gunneras, alstroemerias, pyrethrums, a considerable range of border irises, a flower that was always one of Clementine's favourites, lupins, anchusas and daisies. Freesias and prepared hyacinths were bought for flowering in the house, ornamental trees and shrubs came for the garden: rhododendrons (though not in the dreaded purple), formal bays and Portugal laurels, roses and camellias. The fruit garden and orchard was for ever expanding with peaches, figs, a fan-trained Morello cherry with the old cherry varieties 'Emperor Francis' and 'Guigne d'Annonay' as free standing trees. The raspberry varieties included 'Norfolk Giant' (no doubt the influence of Albert Hill), and room was even found for 'Lloyd George'. There were white and blackcurrants and a profusion of strawberries. Clematis and climbing roses bedecked the walls, sweet peas were there for cutting, the kitchen garden was productive (in 1937 over 300 lbs of seed potato tubers were planted) with Jerusalem artichokes, onions, and the rest. There was even an attempt at mushroom growing.

Clementine at last could be in her element and she took a close interest in the garden, the gardeners, what they did and how they did it. Perhaps she did not always trust their efficiency or memory as her own engagement diary contains occasional prompts. Across two pages of 1 and 2 August 1933 for instance, she wrote 'Prune Wisteria'.[17] Her diary also betrays her regular attendance at horticultural shows. The Agricultural Show at Epping was perhaps a constituency obligation but the Westerham Flower Shows in July and September, and the flower shows at Canterbury and elsewhere were pure pleasure. As a member of the Royal Horticultural Society, she or her secretary appear to have entered all the dates of the Society's shows in the diary at the beginning of the year, for her to attend whenever possible. The Chelsea Flower Show in May was almost invariably highlighted and Clementine seems generally to have visited in the afternoon, following a lunch engagement, although in 1930, she went in the morning and her diary reveals that Albert Hill the gardener went separately the following day. In 1939, she had a conflict between her garden and her dress designer; the diary entry 'Chelsea Flower Show' for the afternoon of 16 May is overwritten '3.45 Hartnell'.[18]

'The Kitchen Garden at Chartwell', oil painting by Winston Churchill (1948).

A tradition was established of Chartwell being opened to the public either for local good causes including the churches and the Kent County Nursing Association, the YWCA or under the National Gardens Scheme (the 'Yellow Book' openings) where it was described as 'a charming garden'. The first recorded date under the National Gardens Scheme (although it was not in the Yellow Book) was on 2 July 1933 when the event raised £25 1s 1d and Mary, selling buttonholes, made an additional £2 10s 0d.[19] [20] Thereafter it was opened several times each year although it was made clear that it was impossible for the garden to be open on any Saturday. There was a crisis in 1935 when a Saturday date was printed in error and then an abnormally late frost laid everything low. Clementine agreed to a second opening on 7 July.[21]

Churchill meanwhile continued to take a close interest in the mechanics of it all. He went to great lengths for instance in the summer of 1937 over choosing a grass cutter and personally examined a 30 inch Atco Lawn Mower, an Albion, an Allen Self-Propelled Motor Scythe and a Pattison's Long Grass Cutter all of which were delivered to Chartwell for demonstration. He eventually opted for the Allen scythe which cost him £40 10s 0d and it may have been to help pay for it that shortly afterwards he sent his man Jackson round the estate collecting scrap iron to sell.

The last years of the nineteen thirties saw a resurgence of Churchill's practical interest in butterflies of which little had been heard since East Africa in 1908. It was a resurgence that could be laid at the pen of a man named Walter Murray. He was a naturalist and writer who had escaped from the misery of a third floor

Good Gardening magazine (March 1938) where Churchill read about butterfly farming. Front cover: roses in a pewter jug by Winifred Walker.

flat in London to live in a run-down country cottage in a Kentish village, a story he later told in his much reprinted book 'Copsford'. Early in 1938, Murray wrote an article entitled 'Stocking the garden with Butterflies' in the magazine *Good Gardening*.[22] In his article, Murray wrote of being able to purchase butterfly pupae relatively inexpensively for hatching out to liberate the adults in the garden. A copy of the magazine fell into Churchill's hands a year later, early in 1939. Self-evidently, he had not bought a year-old copy of *Good Gardening* although the event does offer the only documentary record of him ever reading a gardening magazine. Perhaps he simply picked it up at the dentists. Although during that last peacetime spring, he was spending every available moment at Chartwell working on his History of the English Speaking Peoples, Churchill was nonetheless sufficiently enthused by what Murray wrote to telephone personally the Kent butterfly farm owned by the Newman family.

Newman senior, Leonard Woods (known as L. W.) was born in Singleton in Sussex in 1873 and had worked initially for a firm of tobacco brokers. By inclination however he was always an entomologist and then enterprisingly become one by profession through establishing his so-called butterfly farm at Old Bexley and earned a living by breeding them and sending butterfly and moth eggs, larvae and pupae to schools and to like minded people around the world. An Edwardian collector could buy a dozen eggs of the dark green fritillary for 4d although it cost 1/6 for a comparable number of swallowtails. Newman was also able to satisfy the needs of those who preferred their specimens dead by supplying them pinned and mounted. Collecting equipment was available too. He and his son, L. Hugh Newman, who was born on the farm in 1909, surrounded by butterflies, were an unusual couple in bridging the gap between the Victorian naturalist collector who wanted anything and everything, preferably stuffed, and the twentieth century conservationist who realised that the survival of the creatures in the wild was rather more important than having them hanging gloriously mortified on your drawing room wall.

When Churchill rang in 1939, it was L. Hugh Newman who answered the phone but Churchill was soon passed to the father with whom he had a lengthy conversation and indicated his interest in enriching the butterfly fauna at Chartwell. A visit to Bexley was arranged for early May and despite the Press that week being full of headlines clamouring for Chamberlain to appoint Churchill to the Cabinet, he nonetheless found time to motor down the Kentish country

Frank Jenner, the Westerham taxi owner and part-time Churchill chauffeur.

Old wooden garages, Chartwell.

lanes to inspect the butterfly farm – where Frank Jenner the Westerham taxi owner who doubled as an occasional Chartwell chauffeur and was much used for picking up guests at the station – lost his way. Churchill was fascinated by the farm and left promising to invite the Newmans to lunch at Chartwell the following week to plan their involvement. World events really were now crowding in however and the French Socialist leader Léon Blum came to England a few days later and went to visit Churchill at Chartwell. The Newmans' lunch invitation never arrived and butterflies took a back seat for the next six years. The impending world turmoil saw off *Good Gardening* magazine too. Its Editor H. H. Thomas wrote in his October editorial that as a luxury magazine *Good Gardening* '…was bound to suffer in times like these, for pleasure gardening must now give way in large degree to the cultivation of food crops…'[23]

Butterflies were not the only small creatures that held a fascination for Churchill and it might have been his love of water that stimulated his passion for fish; not so much fish on the end of a rod and line (although he did enjoy salmon fishing, generally when staying with such friends as the Duke of Westminster); it was ornamental fish that really interested him and brought him into contact with a most persistent character from Harringay: Stanley Plater FZS 'Naturalist, Tropical Fish Expert, Wholesale and Retail'. It was in the mid nineteen thirties, after constructing the series of ornamental ponds below the Chart Well that Churchill first turned his attention to an ornamental species of fish that was to entrance him for the rest of his life, the golden orfe. He wrote to potential suppliers – Harrods, the Army & Navy Stores and Associated Purchasers asking about golden orfe and also silver tench.[24] All quoted for golden orfe, Harrods said silver tench were not in season while Associated Purchasers told him no such creature existed. Churchill pursued matters with Harrods livestock department which was operated not by Harrods staff but under an agreement by Stanley Plater. Harrods advised Churchill to buy golden orfe in the proportion of two or three males (at 37/- each) to sixty females and the first fish were delivered – some from Harrods with a selection of plants and some from elsewhere, in the autumn of 1937 but within a short while some of the Harrods fish and most of the plants had died and Churchill demanded replacements. Most failed to materialise. Churchill was not happy and he was even less happy when he took it upon himself to contact London Zoo to obtain a second opinion about golden orfe. Their golden orfe expert visited Chartwell and said the correct ratio was not 2 or 3 to 60, but 40 to 60. Churchill summoned Stanley Plater and his Harrods manager to Chartwell. They came immediately; and presumably gave him satisfactory answers as the following year he asked them to send him samples of some new stock they had received. He was not however going to commit himself to paying £1 each for 4 inch long fish without having seen them first.[25] There is no evidence that Churchill ever bought any more golden orfe and it is possible that at least some of the Chartwell fish today are the descendants of the original stock. He did however write to Clementine in April 1945, following one of his rare wartime visits to Chartwell, saying 'One big goldfish was retrieved from the bottom of the pool at Chartwell. All the rest have been stolen or else eaten by an otter. I have put Scotland Yard on the work of finding the thief. I fear we shall never see our poor fish any more, and nothing is left but unfruitful vengeance, and that about 1,000–1 against a thief & 20,000–1 against an otter'.[26] Nonetheless, it is not clear if this referred to all the gold coloured fish in all the ponds, including the orfe, or simply to the goldfish.

Stanley Plater clung to Churchill like a limpet and in September 1939 when Harrods closed its livestock department for the war, he gave all his fish to him to place in the Chartwell ponds. On 9 September, when Britain had been at war for less than a week, he wrote to Churchill and in the hope that he might have 'an hour or so to spare' to gaze into the water and try to identify them, he sent a list of the varieties – lionheads, orandas, celestials, shubunkins, calicoes, fantails, veiltails, fringetails, common carp, higoi carp, Chinese carp, golden carp, mirror carp, bronze carp, speckled carp, golden orfe, golden tench, golden rudd, golden comets, goldfish, catfish, blackmoors 'and a few others'.[27] He also offered to come and see Churchill any day or weekend with pockets full of various worms to give the fish a treat. Churchill's secretary Kathleen Hill had to reply that unfortunately the First Lord's official duties did not permit him to spend much time at Chartwell.[28]

One of the great enigmas about Churchill's relationship with Chartwell is that it was on the one hand (and after Clementine) the second great love of his life. He poured money, time, affection and heartache into the property, said he wanted to spend the rest of his life there and yet periodically seemed totally at ease with the notion of selling it. Although the practical, pragmatic explanation was simply that it was costing more than he could afford, his comments and actions betray almost a detached and unemotional lack of interest in the place.

So it was, yet again, early in 1937 although it is not obvious if the idea came from him or from Knight Frank & Rutley but by June he had decided he would be willing to accept £25,000 and buy a London house and then perhaps later, find a smaller place in the country.[29] Decisions did need to be made because the lease on Morpeth Mansions would expire in the following year but there was certainly no necessity for a complete clear-out. Knight Frank & Rutley were keen to produce an illustrated brochure but Churchill simply wanted the details to be circulated to a few suitable buyers; and he agreed to a reduced asking price of £20,000.[30] The first potential purchaser who saw the house in November 1937 was Lady St Just, wife of the banker Edward Grenfell, but her interest came to nothing.

In spite of Churchill's wishes, a pamphlet with five photographs was then produced – 200 copies at a cost of about ten guineas – but Clementine insisted that a photograph showing the empty swimming pool should not only be absent from the brochure but the original plate and any surviving copies must also be totally destroyed.[31] When Clementine disliked a picture, she really disliked it and wanted it expunged from history; as Graham Sutherland was in due time to discover. She also wanted a second agent, Ralph Pay & Taylor to handle the sale in addition to Knight Frank & Rutley and, like Churchill, wanted the sale to be private and for there to be no particulars in the Press. The only other recorded interest in purchasing Chartwell came from a Lady McAlpine (it is not clear which one) who viewed the house in March 1938 but that too led nowhere and Churchill then made the considered decision to stay put and renew the Morpeth Mansions lease. Knight Frank & Rutley had one more attempt at persuading him about Chartwell and in January 1939 asked if he would consider putting the house up for auction. The answer was no.[32]

Endnotes

1   Churchill, S. *A Thread in the Tapestry.* p. 25.

2   Mary Soames, conversation with the author, 2 Aug 2006.

3   Soames, M. *Speaking for Themselves. The Personal letters of Winston and Clementine Churchill.*
     p. 302.

4   CSCT 2/21/15–16. WSC to CSC. 7 Aug 1928.

5   CHAR 1/214/32. Mary Churchill to WSC. 12 Sep [1930]

6   Mary Soames, conversation with the author, 2 Aug 2006.

7   Mary Soames, conversation with the author, 2 Aug 2006.

8   CSCT 2/7/18. WSC to CSC. 28 Jul 1914.

9   CHAR 1/194/45. WSC to Sir Philip Sassoon. 9 Jun 1927.

10   CSCT 2/25/15–19. WSC to CSC. 21 Jan 1935.

11   CSCT 2/23/47–55. WSC to CSC. 2 Mar 1935.

12   CHAR 1/332/17–25. Letters and newspaper cuttings. Jul 1938.

13   Churchill, J. S. *Crowded Canvas.* p. 151.

14   Churchill, J. S. *Crowded Canvas.* p. 144.

15   *Finest Hour* 117, p. 4, 2003-4.

16   CHUR 2/197. WSC to Duchess of Kent. 20 Apr 1942.

17   CSCT 4/4. Diary of Clementine Churchill for 1933. 1-2 Aug.

18   CSCT 4/7. Diary of Clementine Churchill for 1939. 16 May.

19   CHAR 1/393B/162. Margaret Babington to Maryott Whyte. 7 Jul 1933.

20   Elizabeth Milner, personal communication, 20 Jul 2006.

21   CHAR 1/393B/140-146. Margaret Babington to Violet Pearman. 6 Jan 1936.

22   Murray, W, J. C. *Stocking the garden with butterflies.* (Good Gardening, March, 1938).

23   Thomas, H. H. *Editorial.* (Good Gardening, October, 1939).

24   CHAR 1/289/6–7. Note by Violet Pearman. 18 Aug 1936.

25   CHAR 1/332/32. Harrods Ltd. to WSC. 1 Sep 1938.

26   CSCT 2/34/42–53. WSC to CSC. 6 Apr 1945.

27   CHAR 1/350/7. S. Plater to WSC. 9 Sep 1939.

28   CHAR 1/350/11. Kathleen Hill to S. Plater. 17 Nov 1939.

29   CHAR 1/393B/178. Violet Pearman to Knight, Frank & Rutley. 5 Jun 1937.

30   CHAR 1/393B/175. Violet Pearman to Knight, Frank & Rutley. 19 Nov 1937.

31   CHAR 1/393B/173. Knight, Frank & Rutley to CSC. 17 Feb 1938.

32   CHAR 1/393B/165. Violet Pearman to Knight, Frank & Rutley. 16 Jan 1939.

CHAPTER 12
WARTIME ACCOMMODATION

In August 1939, as the apparently inevitable conflict with Germany approached, Churchill and Clementine were together with Mary, relaxing in the company of their friends Jacques and Consuelo Balsan in France; although not at the magnificence of Lou Sueil, their home in the South but at their other house, a château in the village of St Georges-Motel near Dreux in Normandy. Tennis was played, swimming was enjoyed and pictures were painted; the Anglo-French artist Paul Maze had a studio in the Moulin de Montreuil attached to the château and he and Churchill painted together. There were fine meals and sparkling conversation; and then, at the other end of Europe, Hitler signed a non-aggression pact with Russia.

Poland was suddenly vulnerable and it became obvious that holidays and peace were over for a considerable time. The family returned to England and

The Cabinet War Rooms.

on 1 September Churchill was at Chartwell when news came that Poland had been attacked. He returned to London where Neville Chamberlain bowed to the inevitable and asked him to join a War Cabinet. Shortly afterwards the Morpeth Mansions flat was host to one of the most tense of political gatherings when late on the evening of Saturday 2 September Bob Boothby, Anthony Eden, Duncan Sandys, Brendan Bracken and Duff Cooper met with Churchill following Chamberlain's conciliatory speech to the House of Commons. They 'argued long into the night' and then the next morning the Prime Minister sent Berlin the historic and fateful ultimatum. Shortly before noon, England was at war with Germany, an air raid warning sounded over London and Churchill went onto his roof terrace to see the first barrage balloons of the conflict. By the end of the day, Chamberlain had invited him to take over as First Lord of the Admiralty, the post he held on the outbreak of the last great conflict and which he had left in 1915 under the cloud of the Dardanelles.

Although the coming six years were for Churchill to be politically all consuming, domestic life had to continue. The family still had to live, bills to be paid, houses to be run. Clementine's support for her husband would never be in greater need. And now, for the first time in their lives, the Churchills returned to a home they had known previously. Admiralty House had always been too big for one family and during their first tenure, it was Clementine who decided to restrict their accommodation to the upper part of the building. This time, it was the Office of Works and war-time economies that limited them to the top two floors[1] although the state rooms were made available for the wedding party after Randolph's ill-fated marriage to Pamela Digby on 4 October. As the early weeks of the war unfolded, Churchill arranged for a bedroom to be created for him above the Upper War Room in the Admiralty itself which served as the operational headquarters for the Navy. The Morpeth Mansions flat immediately became surplus to requirements and the newly extended lease was sold although there is no record of when this happened or at what price.

But what was to be done about Chartwell? Churchill had told his agents at the beginning of the year that he had decided not to sell but the situation was now very different and it was evident that he would not be living there for the foreseeable future; and also that as a large country house, it could have some use as official war-time accommodation. At the beginning of the war Clementine did offer at least part of the main house at Chartwell for evacuation purposes and the authorities sent down two mothers and seven children, who nonetheless stayed for only one week, 'finding the country too dull after the amenities of the Old Kent Road'.[2] Later there were a number of suggestions to use Chartwell as a maternity home or hospital, but they were all turned down by medical officers on the grounds that the place would be too difficult to run. In the autumn of 1943 the Ministry of Labour and National Service approached the local Tunbridge Wells office of the Ministry of Health to ascertain if the offer of Chartwell for official use still stood as they had been asked to investigate if it might be suitable for use as a war time nursery for the children of mothers in Westerham.[3] Churchill was not consulted but after contacting Clementine, Churchill's Principal Private Secretary John Martin said he understood Chartwell had been inspected and found unsuitable; and in any event, it needed to be kept as an alternative country residence for the Prime Minister.[4]

There were both practical and economic considerations about keeping Chartwell open. In January 1940, a reminder arrived from the company responsible for servicing the boilers. As with most domestic matters thereon, it fell to Clementine to say that Chartwell had been unoccupied since September, would probably remain unoccupied for the duration of the war and that the boilers were only lit occasionally. It was decided that they would be kept running in cold weather only and inspections would be reduced to once a year. The decision was indeed taken that the main house would be shut down. Chartwell would not be totally neglected however, for the new Orchard Cottage was available and that is where the family would stay when on visits.

The Churchills had only been back at Admiralty House for some seven months when fate dealt its historic decree that they were to move again. Two days after Chamberlain's rough passage in the House of Commons on 8 May and his failure to form a coalition, the German forces turned their attention to France, Belgium and the Netherlands. The King sent for Churchill and on 13 May he addressed the House for his first historic speech as Prime Minister at the head of a National Coalition government.

The British Minister, in peace and war, has the use of two official residences, No 10 Downing Street and Chequers. The appearance of 10 Downing Street, one of the most famous houses in the world, is too well known to bear detailed repetition. It is in reality two houses, the front being part of a terrace of low cost housing built by the property developer Sir George Downing in 1682 and the back a much finer and slightly earlier building of around 1677 overlooking Horse Guards Parade. The rear house was then the home of the Countess of Lichfield who took a poor view of the cheap housing being built so close by. Later, both houses were presented by King George II to the then Prime Minster Sir Robert Walpole who had them joined together and elegantly refurbished by William Kent before he moved in during 1735. The adjoining house, No 11, became the official residence of the Chancellor of the Exchequer in 1828 and the two are linked within and more or less share a common half acre L-shaped rear garden that can at the most charitable be described as horticulturally modest. It has never had a serious professional designer and is essentially an outdoor meeting place for receptions and photo-calls.

Whilst in the early years some Prime Ministers lived in Downing Street, others used it only as offices and remained in their own town houses. By the time Churchill moved into the house in 1940, it had benefited from the addition of such modern amenities as central heating and had become accepted as both the residence and workplace of the Prime Minister with an additional flat in the former attic area previously occupied by servants. In any event, with no other London home, the Churchills had little choice but to accept what was on offer although it is not clear exactly when they moved in. Churchill certainly did not immediately push out his predecessor and continued to sleep in his old room for at least a month. Ronald Tree wrote of still visiting Churchill at Admiralty House in the summer of 1940.

Churchill worked both in the second floor flat and in the basement offices – known as the garden rooms – at the rear. A small bedroom and dining room was fitted out there too. Steel reinforcement and window shutters had been installed to protect this area of the house and on the evening of 14 October 1940 while Churchill was dining there during a heavy air raid with Sir Archibald Sinclair, Oliver Lyttleton and John Moore-Brabazon, a high explosive bomb fell nearby on Horse Guards Parade. Churchill later recalled thinking impulsively of the huge plate glass window in the No 10 kitchen and immediately told the butler to put the dinner on the hot plate in the dining room and take himself and the other servants to the shelter. About three minutes later, another large bomb fell close by on Treasury Green, seriously damaging the No10 kitchen and pantry and demolishing the hut used by the soldiers who guarded the street. Three civil servants who were on Home Guard duty were killed and windows were smashed, doors torn from their hinges and furniture and furnishings throughout the house covered in grime although fortunately neither the house itself nor the adjoining Treasury caught fire.[5] It was the closest Churchill came to suffering personal injury as a result of enemy action during World War II and as a result of the raid, he was short of a bed for the night. For a brief period therefore – perhaps only a few nights – he slept in what became known as 'The Barn', the disused Down Street underground station just off Piccadilly which the London Transport Executive made available to him. The station between Green Park and Hyde Park Gate on the Piccadilly line was particularly deep but had always been relatively little used and was closed in 1932; the main occupants during the war were the Emergency Railway Committee.

The former Down Street Underground station where Churchill
slept after bomb damage to 10 Downing Street..

There were other close shaves for No 10 and some rather more secure accommodation was clearly required. As early as October 1939 the War Cabinet had moved from No 10 and into secret underground war rooms built in the basement of the Office of Works opposite the Foreign Office and St James's Park. A flat, which became known as the No 10 Annexe, was therefore fitted out above these rooms for Churchill and Clementine and some furniture, valuables and personal possessions were moved there from No 10 with only the garden rooms, cabinet room and private secretaries' office remaining in use in Downing Street. Nonetheless, despite its forlorn appearance, Churchill continued to use No 10 itself for working and dining throughout the war, returning to the Annexe to sleep. A better reinforced air-raid shelter was constructed in the basement of No 10, capable of accommodating up to six people who were working or dining with the Prime Minister.

Whilst 10 Downing Street was never hit directly, another Churchill home fared less well during the bombing. Several houses in Sussex Square suffered damage in the autumn of 1940 although the Churchills' old home at No 2 had escaped. Then, although the worst of the Blitz was over by the spring of 1941, London was hit by ninety-four German bombers on the night of 9 March[6] and the Sussex Square house was irreparably damaged together with 11 Sussex Mews West which Churchill had incorporated as his studio and library.[7] Fortunately the house was empty at the time.

The Prime Minister's alternative official home, his country residence Chequers, customarily used at weekends, lies near the town of Great Missenden among rolling Buckinghamshire countryside, some forty miles from London. The house, at once one of the best but least known of English country houses is a pleasing if unspectacular brick building with characteristically stone-mullioned windows and slender, angular Elizabethan chimneys. It was extensively rebuilt from an earlier house by the then owner William Hawtrey between 1520 and 1597 and in a long and distinguished history, it had served as the prison for Lady Mary Grey, younger sister of the nine-days Queen Jane Grey, and been owned by the grandson of Oliver Cromwell. By the early twentieth century, the house, then called Chequers Court, had been most effectively disguised beneath a veneer of Gothic revival and a photograph of it taken in 1910 displays a remarkable similarity to the appearance of Chartwell at the same date. Its lease was then taken on by Arthur Lee, Conservative Member of Parliament for Fareham and

Chequers, the east front during the War.

his wife Ruth and they immediately engaged Reginald Blomfield to restore it externally and internally as closely as possible to its original Tudor appearance. In 1917 the Lees bought it outright and immediately outlined to the Prime Minister Lloyd George a scheme by which ownership would be transferred to a trust, the house to serve as a place of rest and relaxation for Prime Ministers in perpetuity. The extraordinary gift was accepted, the necessary legislation passed and an inscription on a stained glass window of the Lees' arms in the house recalls the event: 'This house of peace and ancient memories was given to England as a thank-offering for her deliverance in the Great War 1914–18 and as a place of rest and recreation for her Prime Ministers for ever.' Lloyd George thus became the first beneficiary and it was in February 1921, only a month after he took up residence that Churchill made his own first visit. He wrote to Clementine 'Here I am. You wd like to see this place – Perhaps you will some day! It is just the kind of house you admire – a panelled museum full of history, full of treasures – but insufficiently warmed – Anyhow a wonderful possession…'[8]

The garden at Chequers was largely the inspiration of Arthur Lee who unfortunately commissioned an able but not truly distinguished designer-architect, the former Member of Parliament Henry Avray Tipping, to undertake the work. Essentially, Chequers is a house with a wooded park rather attractively lapping at its feet, the only notable garden feature being the parterre which Tipping created below the long broad paved terrace that runs the full width of the south front of the house and from which it is separated by a lavender hedge. The parterre is planted with low box hedges enclosing eight beds planted with roses. Attractive enough when properly tended, it gives the impression of being an opportunity lost but no doubt Clementine found her love of roses and rose gardens amply satisfied by the arrangement although in wartime it barely received the attention it needed.

Throughout the war, Churchill and the family moved to Chequers for most of the weekends when he was in England – it should not be overlooked however that he did travel many thousands of miles during the course of the war and was sometimes out of the country for long periods. Norma Major has recounted Churchill's time at Chequers in considerable detail and it is evident that he took his routine and his idiosyncrasies with him wherever he lived or stayed. Predictably, there were brandy and cigars after dinner followed by a film in the Long Gallery which was turned into a Churchillian cinema. The house absorbed the Prime Minister's entire office along with his chauffeur and valet, secretaries and switchboard operators; and never far from animal companions, Churchill had his cat Nelson, acquired at Admiralty House and taken to Chequers via Downing Street as a constant companion. There was 'an endless stream of special advisors, politicians, diplomats, chiefs of staff and foreign guests' with as many as three shifts of guests in a single weekend.[9] 'Nobody came to Chequers expecting a long night's sleep' Norma Major wrote and noted that being unable to cope with Churchill's nocturnal behaviour, Anthony Eden avoided the place if at all possible. Not only were many of the great decisions of the war made after discussions at Chequers but the public too was admitted within its walls by proxy as some of Churchill's most memorable speeches, the words that etched themselves into the conscience of the nation, were broadcast from the house.

By the summer of 1940, it was considered prudent to ascertain if there was sufficient air-raid shelter at Chartwell. It was felt that overall there was adequate provision for the staff living in the cottages and that the cellar leading out of the day nursery was ideal for anyone sleeping in the main house.[10] Churchill thought however that additional provision would be needed for Clementine when she was staying at Orchard Cottage and he enquired if an Anderson shelter was available. This remarkably crude and inexpensive device had been designed in 1938 by two engineers, William Paterson and Oscar Kerrison in response to a request from the Home Secretary, John Anderson for an uncomplicated domestic shelter that could be installed in gardens. They produced a simple structure made from fourteen sheets of corrugated iron which made a unit 2 metres long, 1.4 metres wide and 1.8 metres high (although some larger models were also built) which was buried to a depth of 1.2 metres. Provided there was sufficient garden space to install it, an Anderson shelter was provided free of charge to anyone with an income of less than £250 per year. Others paid £7. The first were installed in London at the end of February 1939 and by the end of the war, two and a quarter million had been made. They were extremely effective, if rather liable to flooding.

By the time Churchill first enquired about a shelter for Chartwell at the end of August 1940, construction had ceased although he was told there were still a few available – a six seater for £10 and a 10 seater for £15.[11] He asked his secretary to buy the larger version and it was despatched at the beginning of September at a total cost of only £11 15s 0d. A second shelter was sent in December at a cost of £8 12s 0d.

There was, however, another problem about Chartwell. Thanks to Churchill's rearrangement of the landscape its pattern of lakes was uniquely valuable for identifying the property from the air. It was a most useful navigational aid and of course a sitting target itself for the Luftwaffe; the propaganda value of bombing it would be enormous. It had to be camouflaged and the tell-tale lakes obscured. The troops of the Canadian 7th Corps were instructed to undertake the work. Churchill, preoccupied as he was in the late summer of 1940, nonetheless kept in touch with what was happening and passed on instructions regarding what could and could not be done. The swimming pool should be camouflaged, the reservoir drained and the middle lake emptied by siphoning – but on no account should the penstock be opened and care must be taken to ensure the fish did not escape.[12] The lake camouflage was largely achieved by driving stakes into the mud and attaching brushwood to them to disguise the overall shape and size. Memos flew between senior commanders on the need to safeguard the Prime Minister's goldfish and just before Christmas 1940, the mission was accomplished and Brigadier Hertzberg, Chief Engineer to the 7th Corps could confirm that the ponds were now useless for the guidance of aircraft by night.[13]

But just as Chartwell was conspicuous from the air, so there were occasional and comparable problems with Chequers. It too was in a distinctive location as it lay close to two areas of high ground to the north – Coombe Hill with the distinctive Boer War Memorial on the top, and Beacon Hill. Moreover the Victory Drive was said to point at the house like an arrow and following an attempt to disguise it with tennis court stain, it was later turfed over.[14] Early in the war, the house and surrounding area had been photographed by German reconnaissance planes and during 1940 bombs fell close by suggesting that both its location and significance might be known to the Luftwaffe. Sensible precautions had already been taken in the summer of that year and anti-aircraft guns were positioned on Beacon Hill, a company of Coldstream Guards was billeted in a series of Nissen Huts along the Lime Walk and a 'Jim Crow' spotter was positioned in a roof-top hut close to Churchill's bedroom. (This was the expression Churchill himself had conjured up for highly trained look-out men who were generally stationed on the roof of buildings to spot danger from enemy aircraft.) Only if the house was being attacked directly however were the guns to open fire as this would have underlined the significance and importance of the target. Churchill himself was unhappy about Bofors guns being diverted from their fighting positions and suggested 'What about a few rockets, which are at present only in an experimental stage'. The military however were unimpressed and the anti-aircraft guns stayed, Churchill later agreeing that Bofors guns could be sent to any house where he was staying for the weekend. Although several bombs did fall nearby on Great Missenden, Chequers was never targeted leading to a mischievous belief that this was deliberate and that an unspoken agreement existed that Berchtesgaden would similarly be spared. Churchill scotched the rumour, commenting that there was absolutely no reciprocity and as far as Hitler as a target was concerned he 'would bomb the bastard' wherever he could find him.[15]

The danger from the air was particularly acute at Chequers on bright moonlit nights and it was decided that an alternative weekend retreat for Churchill and his party was required. For once, it was not a distant relative who provided the solution to Churchill's housing needs but a political colleague. Ronald Tree was the Member of Parliament for Market Harborough, an Anglo-American Conservative who had been recruited to the Ministry of Information as Private Parliamentary Secretary to the then Minister Sir John Reith in January 1940 and remained at the Ministry for the best part of three years. His wife was the interior designer Nancy Lancaster, the niece of Nancy Astor. Her first marriage to the American Henry Field, a grandson of Marshall Field who founded the Chicago department store that bears his name, ended tragically with his death after only five months. The short-lived union nonetheless left her enormously wealthy and three years later she married Tree who was Field's cousin. In 1933, their combined inheritances enabled them to buy Ditchley Park in North Oxfordshire, some three miles to the west of Blenheim.

Ditchley Park (1930s) where Churchill stayed on moonlit nights.

The estate had come onto the market following the death of the seventeenth Viscount Dillon, a descendant of Charles II and whose family had owned it for three hundred years. The house 'one of the most influential buildings of the 1720s'[16] had been built principally by James Gibbs in 1722 and decorated by William Kent and others but by the time the Trees first saw it in June 1933, the property gave the impression of a 'sleeping beauty', filled with 'an unforgettable picture of magnificence and accumulated junk'. They set about bringing it into the twentieth century. Architectural advice came from Nancy's uncle by marriage, Paul Phipps, who had worked for them at their previous home, Kelmarsh Hall, an early Georgian house in Northamptonshire and had also built the seaside pile of Rest Harrow for Nancy Astor. Then, while Ronald Tree bought the grand furniture and the pictures, the disposition of the rooms and the decoration in all its opulence fell to Nancy.[17]

Although Churchill had only visited the house once as the Trees' guest in June 1937 (probably to attend their magnificent Coronation Ball), it clearly created a favourable impression. It was extremely comfortable, beautifully appointed, of practical size (twenty-nine bedrooms) and discreetly located down a long single track road. Although only a few miles north of Oxford, it is invisible in its seclusion and no other buildings can be seen from the house itself. So while visiting the House of Commons on the dark Tuesday afternoon of Guy Fawkes' Day, November 5 1940, Tree was summoned to the Prime Minster's room. He later recalled Churchill's exact words to him. 'Would it be possible for you to offer me accommodation at Ditchley for certain weekends – when the moon is high?' he asked.[18] Although the 'me' of the request embraced a full staff of secretaries and assistants, Tree could hardly have said no and confirmed that there would be adequate accommodation for the party – more space in truth than at Chequers. The first visit was arranged for the forthcoming weekend. Over the intervening three days, scrambler telephones were installed at Ditchley and a company of the Oxford and Bucks Light Infantry stationed around the house with machine guns. Although surprisingly the Press would be informed, the arrangements were to be treated as top secret. Tree made only one request of the Prime Minister – he was even bold enough to call it a stipulation – Churchill would be responsible for inviting any guests and he and Nancy would have no control over the list. As much as anything, he was anxious that there should be no jealousies among their friends if word got out that the Prime Minister was

Group at Ditchley Park, probably 15 December 1940. Left to right: Brendan Bracken, Lord Cranborne, Richard Law, Churchill, Clementine, Lady Cranborne, Ronald Tree, Nancy Tree.

staying there and they were choosing the visitors.

There was only one slight problem about Churchill using Ditchley: it had already been allocated for another purpose. At the outset of the war, plans were laid for the dispersal of the Government to various parts of the country should the need arise. Under the 'yellow move' the senior levels of the administration would stay in London while many civil servants would be transferred elsewhere, especially to seaside towns with empty hotels. Should matters reach the stage where London was invaded, the 'black move' would come into play and Central Government would move to the West Midlands – the War Cabinet for example would go to Hindlip Hall in Worcestershire and Churchill, his family, private office and servants would go to Spetchley Park near Worcester which was equipped for his arrival with air raid shelter and emergency rations. After Churchill's second visit to Ditchley, Edith Watson, the Prime Minister's Private Secretary received a tactful note from a Mr Wilkinson of the Swinton Committee (the Home Defence

(Security) Executive under the chairmanship of Lord Swinton and at one time responsible for MI5) saying that under the 'black move', Ditchley had been allocated to them. She wrote to Eric Seal, Churchill's Principal Private Secretary 'They have heard that the PM has his eye on D —— [*sic*] & would be very grateful to know if this is so in order that they may look for alternative accommodation'.[19] They did.

The Ditchley visitors' book contains entries for twelve weekends when Churchill stayed – 9–11 November, 16–18 November and 14–16 December 1940; 11–13 January, 15–17 February, 19-21 April, 9–11 May, 6–8 June, 6–8 September and 1–3 November 1941; and 28 February – 2 March and 26–28 September 1942.[20] These weekends did not however always coincide with a full moon (although it may have been 'high') and certainly in 1942, when the danger from air-raids overall had declined, there is no obvious reason why he should have continued to use the house. On several of the Ditchley weekends, momentous events took place, starting with the first when news of the death of Neville Chamberlain was received. The following weekend and its full moon coincided with the most massive of the air raids on Coventry while in January 1941 the visit coincided

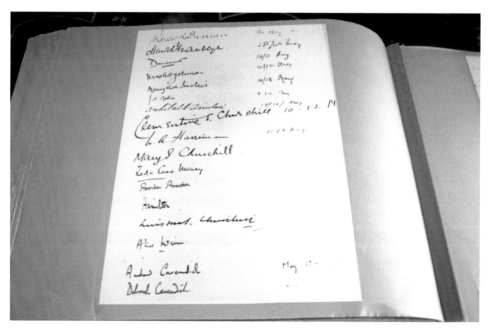

Ditchley Park Visitors' Book, 9–11 May 1941.

with the publication of the Lend-Lease Bill in the United States, and then, on 11 May it was at Ditchley that news reached Churchill of the flight of Rudolf Hess.

It is said that three convoys left Downing Street for Oxfordshire on a Friday afternoon, two as decoys, Churchill's party arriving at the house around five, to leave before lunch on Monday morning. Clementine's signature appears in the visitors' book on all the dates except 1–3 November 1941 but her own diary entries do not always exactly coincide with the book and she, and sometimes Mary, visited on other occasions. Her last entry for 'Dytchley' is 8–9 May 1943.[21] (Clementine always used the alternative spelling with a 'y'; Ronald Tree had this spelling as his printed letter heading but used the more modern version with an 'i' when writing). She found the house was 'mostly shut up' but 'as pleasant & agreeable as before…'[22]

Churchill was provided with a private study and the principal guest bedroom, the yellow bedroom at the top of the grand staircase, where he slept in a large four-poster bed hung with yellow silk moiré which the Trees brought with them from Kelmarsh. Clementine had the adjoining room and they shared the intervening bathroom. Although the furniture was more sumptuous, Churchill's view from his windows must have made Ditchley seem a home from home as he looked down on the lake, a panorama remarkably like that from his own rooms at Chartwell. He was however clearly preoccupied during his weekends there and Tree remarked that throughout the whole of his time at the house, he could remember him going out of doors on only one or two occasions, and then merely to walk around the Italian garden, deep in conversation with one of the guests. Clementine however would have appreciated the gardens which Ronald Tree had also begun to bring up to date. In the past, 'Capability' Brown and J. C. Loudon had worked at Ditchley and now Tree, encouraged by Edward Hudson, who owned the magazine Country Life, had engaged the eminent landscape architect Geoffrey Jellicoe and the gardener Russell Page who designed much of the new planting. Jellicoe brought an Italian influence to Ditchley and worked in a style and on a scale that fortunately, Churchill never attempted to emulate at Chartwell and there are no indications that either he or Clementine absorbed anything from Ditchley for their own garden.

After the first visit, Tree wrote to Churchill saying that he hoped he would come 'as often as it may suit your convenience'.[23] Ditchley was entirely at his disposal and he even said that if the Prime Minister wanted a complete rest, they, the Trees, would go away for the weekend. In the event, Churchill did not take complete rests but kept himself busy and there were usually ten, twelve or more guests – in addition to the more expected like Brendan Bracken, 'Prof' Lindemann, American diplomats and close family members, David and Prim Niven and Venetia Montagu were among the others while the Marlboroughs often drove over from Blenheim. Late Saturday evening relaxation, as at Chequers and as became the custom at Chartwell, often involved the party watching a recent film, arranged by the Ministry of Information film unit. The strain on the Ditchley organisation was nonetheless considerable and after only two weekends of entertaining the Churchill party, Churchill's secretary Kathleen Hill was enquiring if it would be in order to supply extra food coupons to Nancy Tree's chef.

At the beginning of 1941, Churchill still had not ruled out using Chartwell from time to time and so the matter of a proper air raid shelter, something more substantial than an Anderson, was discussed. In the best Civil Service fashion, the Office of Works produced a proposal for a massive structure that would be proof against anything except a direct hit from the largest of German bombs. Their only alternative was a shelter more like that at Chequers which would be blast proof and would support the possible collapse of the house on top of it. They were concerned however about the consequences of a near-miss as they

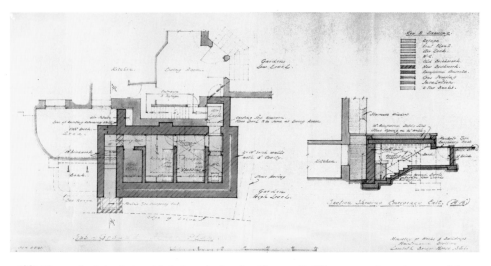

177 Plans of original air raid shelter design for Chartwell; 'These people make everything impossible'. (1941)

explained that the (unspecified) nature of the soil at Chartwell meant a bomb might bury itself deeply before exploding and then blow the shelter in through the floor. Churchill was utterly frustrated by their procrastinations and annotated the proposal with a note that 'These people make everything impossible. I think it will be better just to do without'.[24] It then emerged that the scheme would cost £2,500 to £3,000 and would take at least ten to twelve weeks to execute because of the need to underpin part of the house and it was this that sounded its death knell.[25] Churchill demanded a revised and cheaper proposal and one was then produced that could be done for about £600 in four to five weeks. Churchill's Principal Private Secretary Eric Seal obtained Treasury approval for the revised scheme but Churchill almost immediately rejected this too saying he would rather not go to Chartwell than sanction so much expense.[26] They would make do with another Anderson Shelter.

But if the Prime Minister was to work from Chartwell (which now became known in official secret papers as The Grove Camp), there were other considerations. There would need to be adequate staff accommodation (although it was agreed that Chartwell would only be used during the summer and tents and other equipment would be stored for the winter[27]), a guard, telephones and provision for a 'Jim Crow Party'.[28] Sir Alan Brooke, the C in C Home Forces, was anxious to know if the guard would be withdrawn from Chartwell and from Chequers during or immediately preceding active operations (an invasion) in this country. Churchill responded 'In the period contemplated I should be at my post in the Central War Room. There would therefore be no objection to the Guards being withdrawn as proposed from Chequers and from Chartwell. I should however expect to receive definite prior notice of such withdrawals'.[29]

Little of this ever took place however because it was eventually judged that using Chartwell on more than the odd occasion was too risky and too impractical and Churchill appears to have visited on only about ten occasions during the war, sometimes just calling in, occasionally staying overnight in the cottage with limited use of one or two rooms in the main house; although there was no water supply or proper heating. He was there on the afternoon of Sunday 19 May 1940, he called for lunch on 6 July 1940, was there again on the evening of 2 June 1941, 17 and 20 June 1941, during September 1941, in late April 1942, on 22 April 1943 to stay for Easter, on 14 June 1943, 30 June 1944 and in early April 1945.[30] Churchill's security staff were concerned at how quickly word spread around Westerham when he was due to make a visit (and sometimes even if he was not) and the resident Military were instructed not to discuss any proposed visits in the local pubs and canteens.[31]

On or about 15 April 1941, Chartwell was occupied by the military. Men of the Canadian 1st Division were stationed there and half an acre of pasture land was requisitioned for use under Regulation 51 of the Defence Regulations, 1939.[32] It was later reported that the soldiery had done no harm and had only occupied an area in the woods on the far side of the lakes. Churchill declined any of the regular compensation payments to which he was entitled in respect of this.[33]

On the agricultural front, history was however beginning to repeat itself although on this occasion and unlike Lullenden, it was Clementine and the staff rather than Churchill himself who had to deal with official edicts to turn over as much land as possible to arable production. Just as in the First World War, county agricultural committees were established and in late 1940, Churchill received a leaflet from the Kent committee entitled 'Making More of Less Grass Land'. He immediately passed it to Clementine with a note asking what could be done about the land at Chartwell.[34] In fact, parts of the Chartwell estate had already been ploughed under during 1940 and good crops of oats, wheat, swedes and potatoes produced – although it had been an exceptionally favourable summer. Plans were laid to use even more land the following year and a grant of £12 was made to Churchill to plough a further 6 acres of grassland under the Cultivation of Lands Order, 1939,[35] all much to the consternation of gardener Albert Hill who 'sucked his teeth with more than usual vigour and said 'I've been expecting this'.[36] Hill did his best to direct the farming operations further up the valley and away from the house and the gardens and at least avoided turning the place into a cereal field because the general feeling was that potatoes, swedes or mangels would be easier to harvest than grain crops. The work was largely done under contract by Harold Pilbrow's workforce from Chartwell Farm and it was he who applied for the ploughing grants but overall it was not a success, mainly because the area was surrounded by woods and there was a huge rabbit population against which the cost of fencing would have been prohibitive. By the summer of 1942, Chartwell no longer had any pretence at being an arable farm and there was no land remaining under cultivation. It was sown to permanent pasture and let for grazing, principally to Major Reginald Marnham who bought Chartwell Farm from Pilbrow in late 1941.[37] Churchill agreed Marnham could have any grazing not required for the few Chartwell heifers, the horses or the pony; on payment.[38]

It fell to Clementine to make more frequent visits to Chartwell, ensure that nothing was falling down, that not too much damage was being done either by the resident soldiery or the weather and to report back to her husband on the state of his fish. Her diary records around fifty visits between the outbreak of war and VE day on 8 May 1945, sometimes apparently alone, sometimes with Mary, Horatia Seymour, her cousin Moppett Whyte or friends. One important Chartwell matter that required war-time attention and that was left to the Prime Minister himself however was the Churchill bees and the sugar ration. In April 1943, Churchill heard a rumour that the ration to domestic bee owners was being discontinued and immediately sent a minute to Robert Hudson, the Minister of Agriculture and to Lord Woolton, the Minister of Food, demanding to know how much sugar was still issued to professional bee keepers and the nature of the saving brought about by 'starving the bees of private owners'.[39] His mind was soon put at rest. The ration had not been discontinued or even cut. Owners had been entitled to receive 10lb of sugar per colony, either all 10 lb in the autumn or 5lbs in the spring plus 5 lbs in the summer. As not many had applied in the autumn, a special concession had been granted and the spring allowance increased to 10 lb.

Although the house was little used and the heating system had been completely drained down, Clementine realised that routine maintenance would still be needed and a considerable amount of carpentry, painting and other essential work was undertaken on the main house and the cottages by the local Edenbridge builders A. W. Southon – who have continued to work at Chartwell to the present time. Southons made routine checks on the buildings and recommended remedial action where necessary although nothing was easy because a special Building Licence was needed for work costing more than £10. They told Clementine in 1941 for instance that Albert Hill's cottage was smitten by dry rot, something that must have brought back for her particularly painful memories of her husband and Philip Tilden twenty years earlier.[40] From the spring of 1943 when it was apparent that the threat of invasion had passed and that the war would be eventually be won, Clementine began to take a more serious interest in the improvements that would be needed. In May 1943 she was already planning a revision of the heating arrangements though recognising that '… it may not be possible to carry out these until after the war…'[41] and in the autumn of 1943 she obtained an estimate for installing tubular heating. The cost, £30 8s 7d did not deter her but on discovering that she would need a Government licence for the 157 lbs of steel involved, she decided this could not be justified and so did not proceed.[42] In the summer of 1944, Clementine even invited architects (Stanley Hall and Easton and Robertson) to sketch out some structural changes and improvements to the house, using Charles Goodwin's plans.[43]

It was the lack of heating in particular that caused problems and the situation was becoming truly serious by the autumn of 1944 when Benhams in their routine inspection of the dormant central heating system reported that the house had become so damp that it was imperative that it be turned on. Clementine applied for – and obtained – a special licence for 5 tons of coke in order that the boilers could be fired and coke continued to be obtained thereafter – sometimes considerably in excess of the permitted quota.[44]

Although Chartwell was never hit by enemy fire, bombs did fall nearby and it lay in the centre of what towards the end of the war became known as 'doodle-bug alley', the route followed across southern England by V-1 flying bombs. One fell without causing damage at the back of the British Legion in Westerham in 1944[45] and later one hit a country house a mile away where five adults and twenty two homeless children under the care of the London County Council were killed. On 1 March 1945, one of the last V-2 rockets to fall in England landed on the Madan Road Estate in Westerham, demolishing Council houses and killing one man. Clementine visited the site a week later.[46]

It is not clear exactly when at the end of the war Churchill and Clementine moved back to No 10 Downing Street. At the beginning of April 1945, Churchill told Clementine that he had moved the cabinets back and had one or two meals there. He said he had given orders for the rehabilitation of the house as otherwise they would have been unable to use it that year and he asked her to write to him if she had any strong views about this so he could have them carried out.[47] It was from the No 10 Cabinet Room that he made his VE Day broadcast at 3 p.m. on 8 May 1945 although he was still using the Annexe right up to the announcement of the election results on 26 July and he dined there with the family that evening.[48]

By 1945 plans were being laid for the main house at Chartwell to be reoccupied and the debt the nation by then owed to Churchill was even being recognised by some civil servants. In a gesture that would have been unthinkable a few years earlier, the local office of the Ministry of Works said in May 1945, a fortnight after VE Day, that they would do everything in their power to ensure Churchill's comfort at Chartwell and would even 'brush all formalities aside' to expedite the transfer of the local Chartwell switchboard (number Westerham 93) from Orchard Cottage back to the main house.[49] Gestures of gratitude came from other quarters too but only the most modest were accepted. The Permutit Company, manufacturers of water softening equipment, for instance offered a water softener for Chartwell as a token of the esteem in which Churchill and Clementine were held by the company.[50] They replied that they were unable to accept so costly a gift but would be interested in purchasing one; which they did, at a cost of £243 2s 0d. Rather less charity came from the War Department who wrote to ask if Churchill would like to keep the two old Nissen huts left behind by the anti-aircraft unit which had been stationed at Chartwell in the early part of the war. The huts would undoubtedly have been useful as stores on the estate and interest was expressed in the offer but the official from the War Department then told his war-time leader and saviour that he would have to pay £20 each for them.[51] Churchill declined the munificent gesture and the Nissen huts were disposed of elsewhere.

Gardener Albert Hill who had been ill for some while died from cancer on D-day. Some three weeks later on 30 June 1944 Clementine spent the day at Chartwell, and seems to have met his immediate replacement, a man named Harris as her diary records 'Gardener – Chartwell 6.30'[52] although he may not have begun work immediately as it was following a later visit on the gloriously hot 11 August that she wrote 'new gardener at work'.[53] Harris managed to the best of his abilities on his own and although it was all hands to the deck – even Max Beaverbrook helped the Chartwell cause at the end of the war by donating a cock and some pullets to provide a supply of eggs.[54]

Churchill's first visit to Chartwell after VE Day was on 18 May, the Whitsun holiday weekend and word spread rapidly through Westerham that he would be returning. After a delay to visit Jack who was ill, Churchill and Clementine finally arrived in the town in the early evening to be greeted by 'the biggest crowd Westerham had ever seen'.[55] Churchill made a short speech and was mobbed before they continued their journey to Chartwell.

A start was also made on bringing the estate and the gardens back to a civilised condition and for the second time in his life, Churchill benefited from the labours of his country's defeated enemy. Major Marnham had German prisoners clearing away barbed wire on his land and Clementine arranged for a contingent of ten prisoners to be billeted in the estate cottages and undertake similar work at Chartwell although they were only available when not required for essential agricultural tasks and in the autumn of 1945, their involvement at Chartwell could not begin until after the harvest.[56] In due course they undertook work in the gardens too, clearing footpaths and overgrown vegetation. They also helped re-face the walls in the rose garden; a carved stone in the south-west corner is inscribed 'POW work. German. 1946'. The prisoners worked under the supervision of a much-liked Chartwell stalwart who no doubt warmed to the task: ex-CSM Henry Whitbread. Always known for no obvious reason as Tighe (pronounced Tiggy), Whitbread was a teetotal, non-smoking highly outspoken socialist who improbably worked for Churchill for fifteen years before and three years after the war at Chartwell as a general outdoor help and had been one of his two bricklaying tutors. Churchill wrote a long and detailed instruction of how the lakes and swimming pool were to be cleared. Wire netting should be placed over the penstock to ensure the large fish in the upper lake did not escape and Harris the gardener and Whitbread would supervise matters and also keep a sharp eye open to drive away any herons. Churchill felt a drag net would help but he was equally certain that he was not going to pay for it and wondered if one could be borrowed locally; or perhaps Plater from Harrods might be persuaded to oblige.[57] Plater had kept in touch and visited Chartwell at least once during the war to check and report on the condition of the fish.

Estate agents have memories like elephants and Knight Frank certainly did not forget that on several occasions Churchill had considered the possibility of selling Chartwell. In the autumn of 1944 therefore, as the end of the war appeared to be approaching but without telling him, they talked again to possible clients. Although it was five years since Churchill had last said no to their overtures, they had interested a 'Mr Mourayieff' [sic but probably Mouravieff] in a possible purchase of Chartwell for about £20,000 for use as a private hotel and wrote to ask if he would again consider a sale.[58] By return post, Churchill's secretary Kathleen Hill confirmed that the house was no longer on the market.[59]

The General Election of 1945 was called for Thursday 5 July but the results were not known until three weeks later because of the need to collect votes from the many service personal who were still overseas. The day after polling

Churchill went with Clementine for a short holiday in France and he relaxed with his paints for the first time since the beginning of the war. He then flew on to Germany for the Big Three meeting with Stalin and Truman at Potsdam but returned home in time for the announcement of the election result on 26 July; in time to receive the most devastating news of his political life. In dramatic contrast to the ringing endorsement Lloyd George and his Coalition received at the end of the First World war in 1918, the Conservatives at the end of the Second were trounced. The landslide rejection of Churchill and his party by the electorate in the summer of 1945 was remarkable for its unexpectedness, most of all to Churchill himself and his family. Although he retained his own seat at Woodford with a handsome majority (only one Independent stood against him), he and his party were out of office and out of power and it was the Labour leader Clement Attlee who was summoned to the Palace after Churchill tendered his resignation to the King.

At the weekend, Churchill went to Chequers with the family, close friends and advisors and on the Sunday evening, 29 July, his was the last signature in the visitors' book; after his name, he wrote 'Finis'. Churchill had had no reason to imagine other than that 10, Downing Street and Chequers would continue to provide them with hearth and home and there is no evidence that they were looking for any other London accommodation before the fateful result was announced. But when it was, they had to move quickly and soon found a house at 28 Hyde Park Gate which they agreed to purchase from the stockbroker Claude Pearce Serocold. They paid an additional £425 for fixtures and fittings and £20 for the kitchen table. Hyde Park Gate, a short street running south from Kensington Gore close to the Royal Albert Hall was already a distinguished address, and today it is replete with consulates and blue plaques including the official English Heritage plaque for Churchill himself. Robert Baden-Powell was one of several notable former residents of the street and it may be that Churchill's own address, No 28, had resonances for him from long ago because it was from the neighbouring house No 29 that Lord Elgin wrote to him in December 1905 confirming his first ministerial appointment as Under Secretary for the Colonies.[60]

Although probably all of similar age, almost every house in Hyde Park Gate is distinctly different from its neighbour and whilst all look large and imposing from the front, many of them are not in reality big houses. While No 28 had

No 28 Hyde Park Gate with the official, although
inaccurate, English Heritage blue plaque.

dining room and sitting room space of ample and gracious proportions, there
were only around five functional bedrooms. Inside it does not feel like a large
house and it also presented an unfortunate feature for an elderly and slightly
infirm couple in that the change in level from front to back meant there were
several small and inconvenient flights of stairs. In due course, provision would
have to be made inside for a wheelchair lift. The garden is small, walled and wide
but relatively private for a central London house and only slightly overlooked.

While the purchase of the Hyde Park Gate house progressed, however,
Churchill and Clementine had nowhere to go. Chartwell was not yet properly

refurbished and there was, once again, no London home. Churchill stayed for a short while in early August at Claridges[61] and from there attended and spoke in the newly assembled House of Commons. Then, for the final time in their lives they were given shelter by the family as their daughter Diana and her husband Duncan Sandys lent them their flat, No 67 Westminster Gardens in a monstrous 1930s block among a group of monstrous blocks on Marsham Street in SW1. They were living there on 15 August when the Japanese surrender was announced after Hiroshima and Nagasaki and a small crowd gathered outside.

Westminster Gardens apartments where Diana and Duncan Sandys lived and where Churchill and Clementine were staying when the Japanese surrender was announced.

Following the end of the war that came with the surrender, Churchill went to Italy as the guest of Field Marshall Alexander to stay at a villa by Lake Como '…a small palace almost entirely constructed of marble inside…it…must have been finished by one of Mussolini's rich commerçants who has fled…[62] He left Clementine and his staff to take care of the arrangements for Hyde Park Gate where completion of the purchase was agreed for 28 September. It was a novelty among Churchillian house purchases in that the property was in good order and apart from some redecoration, little work needed to be done.[63]

Enjoying himself, and the weather being so good, Churchill decided to delay his return and travelled from Italy to France and to his beloved Riviera, staying this time at the Villa Sous le Vent at Antibes, made available to him by Eisenhower. Like the vast Château de l'Horizon, the home of his friend Maxine Elliott at Golfe-Juan, the house had been built before the war by the American architect Barry Dierks but was never occupied by the Germans, probably because it did not have a particularly good view of the sea. Churchill did not return to England until the beginning of October by which time 28 Hyde Park Gate was his and Chartwell too was almost ready for civilised living again.

Endnotes

[1]   *Speaking for Themselves. The Personal letters of Winston and Clementine Churchill.* p. 316.
[2]   CHAR 20/149/29. Kathleen Hill to F. Brown. 20 Sep 1943.
[3]   CHAR 20/149/31. S. Charlton to J. Martin. 20 Sep 1943.
[4]   CHAR 20/149/27. J. Martin to A. Charlton. 27 Sep 1943.
[5]   Churchill, R. S. and Gilbert. M. *Winston S. Churchill.* Vol. 6. p. 843.
[6]   Fitzgibbon, C. *The Blitz.* p. 220.
[7]   WCA Paddington Bomb Damage Records.
[8]   CSCT 2/14/6–7. WSC to CSC. 6 Feb 1921.
[9]   Major, Norma. *Chequers.* p. 189.
[10] CHAR 1/394/13. Mary Shearburn to WSC. 28 Aug 1940.
[11] CHAR 1/394/9. P. Allen to Kathleen Hill. 4 Sep 1940.
[12] CHAR 1/394/82. WSC to Maryott Whyte. 28 Oct 1940.
[13] CHAR 1/394/75. C. Hertzberg to Maryott Whyte. 20 Dec 1940.
[14] Major, Norma. *Chequers.* p. 194.
[15] Major, Norma. *Chequers.* p. 195.
[16] Sherwood, Jennifer & Pevsner, N. *The Buildings of England. Oxfordshire.* p. 573.
[17] Wood, M. *Nancy Lancaster – English Country House Style.* p. 61.

18 Tree, R. *When the Moon was High – Memoirs of Peace and War 1897–1942*. p. 130.

19 CHAR 20/32/76. Edith Watson to E. Seal. 20 Nov [1940].

20 Tree, R. *When the Moon was High – Memoirs of Peace and War 1897–1942*. pp. 193-197.

21 CSCT 4/13. Diary of Clementine Churchill for 1943. 8-9 May.

22 CSCT 1/27/4. CSC to WSC. 9 May 1943.

23 CHAR 20/32/77. R. Tree to WSC. [11] [Nov] [1940].

24 CHAR 20/32/7–8. WSC to [C.] Thompson. Jan 1941.

25 CHAR 20/32/1–2. [F.] Root to E. Seal. 9 Jan 1941.

26 CHAR 20/32/18–19. C. Thompson to E. Seal. 8 Mar 1941 – 11 Mar 1941.

27 CHAR 20/32/60–61. S. Lamplugh to C. Thompson. 23 Oct 1941 – 25 Oct 1941.

28 CHAR 20/32/43–46. [C. Thompson] to WSC. 25 Feb 1941.

29 CHAR 20/32/47-50. Correspondence between C. Thompson and E. Speed. 5 Mar 1941 – 12 Mar 1941.

30 See Churchill, R. S. and Gilbert. M. *Winston S. Churchill*. Vols. 6-7 & Churchill, W. S. *The Second World War*.

31 CHAR 1/394/73. CSC to C. Thompson. 27 May 1941.

32 CHAR 1/394/66. Army Form A 2016 . 16 Jul 1941.

33 CHAR 1/394/49. J. Pluck to Kathleen Hill. 10 Feb 1943.

34 CHAR 1/394/116. Circular letter from Kent War Agricultural Committee. 31 Dec 1940.

35 CHAR 1/394/108–111. Kent War Agricultural Executive Committee to WSC. 17 Jul 1941.

36 CHAR 1/394/114. Maryott Whyte to CSC. 7 Jan 1941.

37 CHAR 1/394/99. A. E. Hill to Elizabeth Layton. [Jun 1942].

38 CHAR 1/394/103. Note by WSC. 13 Dec 1941.

39 CHAR 1/394/22. WSC to Minister of Agriculture and Minister of Food. 19 Apr 1943.

40 CHAR 1/394/190–191. A. W. Southon & Sons to CSC. 8 Oct 1941.

41 CHAR 1/394/177–180. Grace Hamblin to A. W. Southon & Sons. 19 May 1943.

42 CHAR 1/394/144. Grace Hamblin to Sevenoaks and District Electricity Company Limited. 6 Oct 1943.

43 CHAR 1/394/134. CSC to H. Robertson. 27 Jul 1944.

44 CHAR 1/394/46. Grace Hamblin to Benham & Sons. 18 Oct 1944.

45 Reid, P. G. *Churchill. Townsman of Westerham*. p. 31.

46 CSCT 4/13. Diary of Clementine Churchill for 1943. 11 Mar.

47 CSCT 2/34/42–53. WSC to CSC. 6 Apr 1945.

48 Churchill, R. S. and Gilbert. M. *Winston S. Churchill*. Vol. 8. p. 109.

49 CHAR 1/394/161. Kathleen Hill to CSC. 23 May 1945.

50 CHAR 1/394/125. Permutit Co. Ltd. to A. W. Southon & Sons. 1 Jun 1945.

51 CHUR 1/30/174. War Department Land Agent and Valuer to WSC. 26 Nov 1945.

52 CSCT 4/12. Diary of Clementine Churchill for 1944. 30 Jun.

53 CSCT 4/12. Diary of Clementine Churchill for 1944. 11 Aug.

54 *Speaking for Themselves. The Personal letters of Winston and Clementine Churchill*. p. 536.

55 Reid, P. G. *Churchill. Townsman of Westerham*. p. 34.

56   CHUR 1/41/31. CSC to WSC. 11 Sept 1945.

57   CHUR 1/30/92. The Fish Pool at Chartwell. 10 Nov. 1945.

58   CHAR 1/394/85. Knight, Frank and Rutley to WSC. 1 Sep 1944.

59   CHAR 1/394/84. Kathleen Hill to Knight, Frank and Rutley. 2 Sep 1944.

60   CHAR 2/24/50. Lord Elgin to WSC. 13 Dec 1905.

61   Eden Diary, 1 Aug 1945. Avon Papers. Cited in Churchill, R. S. and Gilbert. M. *Winston S. Churchill*. Vol. 8. p. 118; original not seen]

62   CSCT 2/34/66-67. WSC to CSC. 3 Sep 1945.

63   Soames, M. *Clementine Churchill. 2nd Ed.* p. 434.

CHAPTER 13
*F*ARMING

Although Churchill's attempt at farming when he owned Lullenden had been fairly futile, the experience did not put him off trying again. But Chartwell really was not the place to do it. There were only 90 acres, a large part of it was garden and although a procession of two and four-footed livestock had been accommodated there over the years, it was hobby smallholding rather than farming. Now, out of office and with time available, there was every incentive to try once again, with the official Government encouragement of a drive for ever more home food production that was to see its outcome in the 1947 Agriculture Act. In August 1945 he made enquiries through local agents about farms for sale in the Ashford-Westerham area but was told there were few available.[1] He then turned for advice to his neighbour Major Reginald Marnham the new owner of Chartwell Farm.

Chartwell Farmhouse.

Harold Pilbrow had first considered selling Chartwell Farm at the beginning of 1932 and offered it to Churchill but he was not interested.[2] He did not then have the money and was in any event still recovering from the effects of a serious accident when he was knocked down by a car in New York. Pilbrow did not find a buyer and stayed put but eventually received £14,000 when he sold it to Marnham in 1941. Since April the following year, Marnham had been renting part of Churchill's land to graze some of his dairy shorthorn herd, an arrangement that made a significant contribution to his overall milk production. The agreement was that he would hand the land back to Churchill twelve months after the end of the war but would be willing to do so sooner if necessary. Churchill told Marnham that he would like to establish his own small dairy herd and various ways of achieving this were discussed. The simplest, that Marnham would keep two of Churchill's cows with his own herd and supply him with the milk was dismissed as it would have been illegal. The second option, that Churchill have his own milk shed and dairy but that Marnham would supply him with winter fodder was also ruled out as Chartwell Farm could barely sustain Marnham's own cattle. The third option was for Churchill to establish his own herd and set aside around 5 acres of his land for winter food production, buying in hay and straw. But this too had its drawbacks – not least that the outlay in capital and labour would be out of all proportion to the milk produced – and he would be short of protein as his feeding stuffs ration would be negligible. It was his boyhood adventures in smallholding at Banstead Manor under Mrs Everest's guidance all over again.[3] He pressed ahead nonetheless and in August 1946, Winston S. Churchill was officially registered as a wholesale trader and producer of milk.[4] Two months later, Chartwell Estate was home to 3 cows, 3 heifers, 4 calves and 1 horse. Its livestock operation had lost £194 13s 5d over the previous year. In 1946, the loses increased to £282, the accountants' explanation being that the 'farm' was in a state of transition.[5]

Churchill was still keeping an eye open for other possible properties and at the end of 1945 feelers were put out on his behalf for a farm called Obriss a few miles to the south west of Chartwell. A splendid and ancient property, it had been owned by the Campbell Colquhouns as part of their enormous Chartwell Estate and was sold as a separate lot in the 1922 auction. No sale was however imminent in 1945 so Churchill never had a chance to buy what is perhaps the most beautiful farm in the area.[6] It was later purchased by the Landmark Trust.

Oast Houses at Chartwell Farm.

Then a golden and unexpected opportunity arose. In autumn 1946, Marnham decided to sell Chartwell Farm. Churchill engaged Knight Frank & Rutley to assess the property both as a whole and as land and house separately. The farm house was a substantial six-bedroomed property and the holding comprised 88 acres of permanent pasture and ley, 45 acres under cultivation, 24 acres of woodland, 6 acres of garden and five cottages. A particularly attractive feature of Chartwell Farm has long been the five mid-nineteenth century Campbell Colquhoun oast houses, two of which had been converted to create a tiled dairy and a sterilising room. There were excellent barns and cowsheds, garaging for four cars and a chauffeur's flat. It was all in all a most attractive farm in a beautiful setting; and literally on Churchill's doorstep. The advice was that the property was much better considered as a whole than as two parts and that £20,000 was the right price. Churchill did not waste any time and the day after receiving this valuation he wrote to Marnham offering just that.[7] After some negotiation and the examination of various options, he then agreed to purchase everything: farm, farm house and the entire dairy shorthorn herd for a total price of £25,000[8] of which Lloyds Bank agreed to make available up to £21,500.[9] In due course, Churchill joined the Shorthorn Society of the United Kingdom and registered 'Chartwell' as the herd name although he baulked at joining the Shorthorn Breeders Club because of his many other commitments.

When the newspapers learned he was buying more land around Chartwell, Churchill was inundated with letters from people wanting employment. Many of them were extremely long, many included references, almost equally long, many were from old soldiers, several were from people who knew (or whose father knew) Lloyd George and at least one was signed Your Most Humble Servant.[10] Others too jumped on the bandwagon. The Massey-Harris company immediately shipped a binding machine from Canada specially for him as none were available in Britain although Churchill had to put a stop to an attempt by the Fowler company to promote their tractors under his name in New Zealand.

A significant difference from Churchill's earlier farming foray was that this time, someone was on hand to give serious advice: his new son-in-law. Clementine, like other mothers, had spent some years hoping Mary would marry one of several eligible young men who came along – in 1943 she had met Wing Commander Guy Gibson of Dam Busters fame and thought he would be perfect for her daughter; only to discover 'Alas!' he already had a wife.[11] Clementine's wish however was fulfilled when Mary met Old Etonian Christopher Soames. Commissioned into the Coldstream Guards in 1939, Soames had a distinguished war record and was awarded the Croix de Guerre while attached to the Free French forces in the western desert. He was invalided out of the army after a mine shattered his leg and was appointed Assistant Military Attaché at the British Embassy in Paris in 1946. On 11 February the following year, he and Mary were married at St Margaret's, Westminster, where Clementine and Churchill themselves had married nearly forty years earlier. Although Clementine took time to come to know and warm to him, Soames and Churchill soon struck up a close and mutually beneficial relationship. Having Churchill as his father-in-law launched Soames on a successful political career while Churchill had found a man who could manage his rural affairs. In many ways, Christopher Soames was the son Churchill never had, offering much that Randolph never did or could and his marriage to Mary stands out like a triumphal beacon among the wreckage of so many other Churchillian partnerships.

At Clementine's suggestion, Soames and Mary moved into Chartwell farm house as Soames took on the farm management. Although he had no formal training in agriculture, he clearly knew much more about it than Churchill and his notes to his father-in-law on work in progress at the farm betray a need sometimes to explain as well as report.

Churchill (second right) observing farming operations with Christopher Soames (standing) and Anthony Eden (far right), probably at Bardogs.

Having acquired Chartwell Farm, the agricultural bug then took a serious hold and Churchill, urged on by Soames, began collecting farms like postage stamps. Agents formed a queue for his favours and the sale of Chartwell Farm had not even been completed when, in early December 1946, the auctioneers Fox and Mainwaring from Edenbridge were in touch about Parkside Farm, a holding of around 116 acres at Frenchstreet between Crockham Hill and

Brasted Chart to the north-east of Chartwell. There was a small, three-bedroom farm house, (with electricity to be laid on 'imminently'), a cottage, the usual farm buildings and 50 acres of arable, 27 of woodlands and around 35 of grass. What particularly attracted Churchill however was the kitchen garden of nearly two acres with soft and top fruit and four span-roofed heated greenhouses and a lean-to cold house. This had potential as a separate enterprise. The owner of Parkside Farm, Mr Gregory, was asking £12,500 for the freehold.[12] Churchill immediately went to see the farm and realised that Parkside and Chartwell Farms would work well together and could physically be linked. Knight Frank & Rutley as his agents made an offer of £10,000 to include any existing tenants' rights. The same day his offer was conveyed to Gregory's agents, Churchill sent his gardener Harris to look at the farm and he reported back that he was most impressed with the greenhouses which were being used principally for raising pot plants – there was a fine collection of cyclamen, tuberous begonias, pelargoniums, ferns, carnations and amaryllis as well as some hardy shrubs. He discovered however that unfortunately these were not included in the sale price on which Churchill had based his offer. It mattered little because Churchill's first offer was rejected and he eventually had to pay £10,250, although still without the plants.[13] Contracts were exchanged on 18 March 1947 and Churchill took possession of the farm early in July, immediately making the decision to use the historic name of Frenchstreet Farm for the market gardening enterprise and it was in this name that he applied to have the fuel permit transferred to him.[14] Later the name Frenchstreet Farm was sometimes used for the whole of the Parkside holdings.

The market garden enterprise initially seemed to be paying dividends and by the summer Churchill could enthusiastically report to Clementine that they had made £150 profit on lettuces and that he believed the garden would not only pay its expenses but could be a net contributor to the farm. The hot-houses he said were 'dripping with cucumbers, the grapes were turning black and a continuous stream of peaches and nectarines go to London…'[15]

No sooner had the purchase of Chartwell and Parkside Farms been completed in early 1947 than Fox and Mainwaring were in business again, this time offering Churchill Bardogs Farm, a mixed and dairy farm on Puddledock Lane at Toys Hill just to the south-east of Chartwell. Like Chartwell Farm, Bardogs had been bought at the 1922 auction by Percy Janson when he paid £3,500 for it. There was a good four-bedroomed farm house, two cottages and around 94 acres of temporary and permanent pasture, arable and woodland with a further rented 25 acres. It may have been that owners as well as agents were by now on the scent of Churchill's money and at Bardogs, the then owner, Mrs Livingstone was asking £8,700 – of which £8,500 was for the freehold and £200 for various tenants' right over newly seeded crops and temporary leys. She would also give notice to quit to the two tenants who lived in Puddledock Lane and give vacant possession on completion. Once again, Churchill took the bait and succumbed to add to his collection.[16] Almost by return post he sent a cheque for £870 as deposit and in early October, Bardogs Farm too was his. With the Bardogs Farm purchase came three fields which Churchill found himself renting, one of them held on a verbal agreement that obliged him to pay the owner, a Mr Quartermaine, five loads of manure a year.

The business was now growing ever more complex. The Chartwell Farm enterprise comprised arable, dairy, pigs, poultry (which lived in a large brick hen-house called 'Chickenham Place' that Churchill himself had built[17]), and the Frenchstreet market garden. The number of staff was increasing and employees were coming and going with great frequency. There were land girls, cowmen, assistant cowmen, gardeners, labourers, glasshouse workers, German prisoners and others, all to be accommodated in cottages, or lodging in other employees' cottages. Some were married with families – at Christmas 1947, all the children on the estate were invited with their mothers to tea and a conjuror;[18] there were 23 of them – and to complicate matters further, the Chartwell employees who were single seemed highly disposed to becoming engaged and married to each other even though some of the cottages in which they were expected to live, especially those on Bardogs Farm, were in a 'shocking state', little more than 'miserable slums'.[19] Clementine was as ever concerned with the staff domestic issues – she felt for example that all three gardeners should live on the estate to facilitate out of hours working and was particularly upset when Doris, the daughter of her late gardener Albert Hill indicated she was becoming somewhat disaffected as more and more duties were piled on to her at a time when she had a young baby of her own to tend. Doris, by then Doris Edleston, had married in 1938 and during the war while her husband was away in the army, she looked after domestic matters at Chartwell, cleaning the rooms that Churchill used on his occasional visits and catering for the secretaries in Orchard Cottage. She also looked after Clementine's friend Horatia Seymour at Wellstreet Cottage. At the end of the war, her husband Bert came to Chartwell too and began work as an assistant to gardener Harris while Doris looked after the four land girls at Bardogs Farm where Clementine fitted out the farmhouse as far as circumstances allowed.[20]

Much of the work at Chartwell fell to Christopher Soames to organise (although he did defer to Clementine on domestic matters) and by the end of 1947, he wanted a pay rise. Relying ever more on his son-in-law, the last thing Churchill needed was discontent in the family and he suggested to his accountant that Soames' salary be raised to £600 per annum.[21]

Later the same year, the agent Guy Hanscomb who had handled the sale of Parkside Farm on behalf of Gregory had another go and offered Churchill Couldens Farm at Edenbridge, a house and 52 acres for £8,000.[22] This time Churchill was not keen but there must have some expectation among local agents and owners that he was interested ultimately in owning and farming most of west Kent because in 1949, Knight Frank & Rutley were trying to sell him Dunsdale Farm on the Valence Estate just north of Frenchstreet. That also however led nowhere. He had decided his farm collection was complete and the three farms together were run under the business name Chartwell Farm with a 60 year mortgage on all three from the Agricultural Mortgage Corporation for £25,000, later raised to £30,000.

Soames and Churchill made a swift start in putting the new purchases to work. No sooner had the purchase of Frenchstreet Farm been completed and the decision made to run the kitchen area as a commercial market garden than an advertisement was placed in The Fruit Grower magazine requiring a 'Working Manager for Commercial Glasshouses'. They appointed a well qualified tomato and lettuce man, Charles Smith from Shropshire, whose son also joined the workforce and in May 1947, the family moved into one of the cottages.

Having the dairy shorthorns at Chartwell Farm, Churchill and Soames began to build up a pedigree Jersey herd at Bardogs and by late 1948, they had 74 pedigree and non-pedigree dairy shorthorns and 19 Jerseys, worth in total £7,470. The Chartwell-bred cattle generally had flowery names like Chartwell Poppy, Chartwell Daisy, Chartwell Wallflower, Chartwell Thistle, Chartwell Strawberry and Chartwell Primrose. In addition there were two horses, 20 sheep and 8 pigs. Churchill had also become very fond of the Belted Galloway cattle ('belties') of which Sir Ian Hamilton had built up a notable herd at Lullenden and he had eight of the distinctive black and white animals. The Belted Galloway is an old beef breed, especially noted for its ability to produce good meat from poor grass, of which Lullenden had plenty. Churchill's interest had begun in 1935 when Hamilton gave him four females from his own herd although he kept them on Churchill's behalf with his own animals at Lullenden. In 1939, Churchill joined the Belted Galloway Society and in the early part of the war, Hamilton felt some fresh blood was needed for Churchill's stock so he sold two of the old animals and approached the Secretary of the Society, John Kincaid, bailiff to Mr W. Emmott who owned a famous herd on his Moss End Farm at Warfield in Berkshire. Hamilton went to Warfield to choose two heifers from the Moss End herd and Emmott kept them until Autumn 1947 when the original animals together with their offspring were delivered to Chartwell. One heifer had been born on Churchill's birthday in November 1945 and was inevitably named Winnie by the farm staff.[23] As all arrived at Chartwell, they were greeted by a huge shout from Churchill who insisted on a toast (uncharacteristically in sherry) being drunk to the future welfare of the animals.[24] Later, the herd was further strengthened when in 1956, Sir Ian Hamilton's nephew, also Ian Hamilton, presented Churchill with a two-year old bull, Lullenden Anzac.

Lullenden Anzac, the two-year old Belted Galloway bull presented by Ian Hamilton to Churchill in 1956.

At Chartwell, there were also eggs and poultry and the field crops – wheat, barley, potatoes, hay and vegetables – together with the market garden produce, but unfortunately, the lettuce harvest had little impact and Churchill farming was not producing anything like a profit. On the contrary, an operating loss of £6,365 in 1947 had risen to one of £8,607 in 1948 and then became £8,707 in 1949. Their enthusiasm had run away with them and the lack of experience was beginning to tell. The County Farm Advisor told them they would do well to carry 80 head of cattle on the available land. They had 135. The decision was therefore taken to dispose of all the non-pedigree shorthorns (the residue of the Marnham cattle), leaving 60 pedigree shorthorns, the Jerseys and the belties.[25] But the loses continued: £8,751 in 1950; £8,414 in 1951. All the accountants could offer by reassurance was that the rate of loss had stabilised. Something more needed to be done but the situation had changed in that Soames was no longer able to give much time to the farms. He had stood successfully as a Conservative candidate at the 1950 General Election, winning Bedford with a slender majority and he later acted as Churchill's Parliamentary Private Secretary during his second premiership. The decision was therefore made to employ a full-time farm manager and a local man named Cox was appointed in April 1953, taking up his post at the end of September when he moved into Wellstreet Cottage, free of rent and rates, and on the £600 salary that Soames relinquished. Churchill hoped however that Soames would continue to manage the horses – what had in effect become a small Chartwell stud of yearlings, brood mares and their six foals – from Chartwell farm house. This would have the advantage of lightening the burden on the farm and transfer the expense to a taxable stud account.[26]

Cox did his best and Churchill was pleased with him. On a walk around the farms with Soames in the spring of 1950, Churchill was able to report that they were both much impressed by the tidiness and the improvements made. Cox had a good cultivation plan, overhanging branches had been cut back, and a large part of Bardogs and Chartwell Farms had been ditched and hedged although there was still a great deal more to be done. It already had been decided that there was little profit in milk and Churchill contemplated disposing of his beloved belties – he would be sorry he said to let them go as they were most ornamental and characteristic, but 'there is no doubt that six or seven milch cows of good quality would save three or four hundred pounds a year of loss'.[27]

The belties however were spared but during 1952, all the shorthorns were sold and the proceedings dispersed and invested in new stock. Nonetheless, although they bought some Devons for beef, and some cross-breeds, curiously they also bought more dairy cattle – Jerseys and Ayrshires. They also bought a substantial herd of pigs. Important as cows were, it was pigs that really attracted Churchill the farmer. He had always displayed a fondness for them even though as a young subaltern in India, he had no compunction about pinning the wild variety at the end of a stick. The remark that 'Dogs look up to us. Cats look down on us. Pigs treat us as equals' is widely attributed to him and is said to have been made at Chartwell[28] while a cartoon sketch of a pig was a frequent alternative to a pug-dog as an embellishment to his signature in his letters to Clementine – who reciprocated with little drawings of cats.

At Lullenden in the summer of 1918, he had paid Henry Ridley, the Lingfield builder, £28-10-0 for building two pig houses at the back of the cowshed but with Churchill then still in Government, it was left to Clementine to deal with the pig finances and when six of the Lullenden animals were sold (including two to the local vicar), she resisted the temptation to use the proceeds of £21 7s 9d to pay her household bills – 'See how scrupulous and God fearing I am!' she wrote.[29] Jeffrey, the 'tyrant' Lullenden farm hand, certainly knew his pigs and greatly impressed Sir Ian Hamilton who took him on after buying the farm.[30] Improbably, Sir Ernest Cassel also knew a great deal about pigs; at least that was the impression he gave Lady Hamilton when they lunched together with the Churchills at Lullenden on the pouring wet Sunday in July 1919, shortly before the Hamiltons bought the farm.[31]

Pigs were kept at Chartwell almost from the beginning and when five little porkers were sent to the butchers in March 1925, Churchill wrote to Clementine in confident expectation of them making £30 and expressed amazement at the fertility of the species as their old sow was due for yet another litter.[32] The pigs even survived the economic purge of 1926 and in late 1931, Churchillian pig farming was passing through one of its occasional sunnier times so pigs were inevitably on the agenda when Churchill's secretary Violet Pearman wrote to him while he was making a prolonged lecture tour of the United States. Churchill had only the previous week been seriously injured when he was knocked down by a car while crossing Fifth Avenue in New York so he was undoubtedly much cheered to read that one of the Chartwell sows had won the championship at the Edenbridge Fat Stock Show. Early the following year, Churchill, still away lecturing in the United States, received yet more encouraging information from Miss Pearman when she wrote again, initially expressing the view that although Ramsay Macdonald would make an admirable Presbyterian Prime Minister, he lacked the strength and power to lead the country back to prosperity and glory, but was then able to add, even more importantly, the news that Churchill had made a total profit of £26 12s 6d (excluding the cost of food) on two pigs and their offspring recently sold. But the proceeds were never huge – six years later, in 1938, the sale of 11 pigs from Chartwell to Mr Dove, the Westerham butcher, made only £11 5s 0d and moreover, this had to be offset against the bills from Arnold Spicer the Oxted vet who was charging 12/6 for every attendance. Even war did not stand in the way of Churchill and his pigs and in 1941, the local soldiery were helping the cause. Churchill's secretary Kathleen Hill negotiated a contract with the 1st Canadian Division who were camped at Chartwell, for the collection of swill at the rate of £2 10s 0d per 100 men per month.[33] It fell to gardener Albert Hill to implement the scheme.

After the war, Christopher Soames had waded into the pig cause with enthusiasm and once there was real agricultural land available after the purchase of Chartwell and Bardogs Farms, there was no stopping them. At New Year 1947, Soames wrote to his new father-in-law ('My dear Mr Churchill') who was confined to bed in the Mamounia Hotel in Marrakech with an infection telling him that a Chartwell pig had been massacred and sent to be cured so Churchill could look forward to delicious peach and milk fed bacon and ham for his breakfasts when he returned.[34]

Clementine, however, was as always cautious and shared neither her husband's nor her son-in-law's enthusiasm – at least not for pigs as a commercial undertaking, and she argued strongly to Churchill in 1948 against Soames' plan to establish a pig farm of around fifty animals on what was described as the 'piece of waste land' below the house. Although no born farmer, she had not been slow to pick up the rudiments of farm finance. If it was true that no more men would be needed, as Soames had claimed, her view was that clearly they must be under-employed at present. Nor did she believe a pig farm would provide an outlet for surplus potatoes as she thought, rightly, that the Government was obliged in any event to buy them. Her philosophy was disarmingly straightforward: 'I cannot believe that farming is so simple that when you have bought one item and sold it successfully, all you have to do is to multiply that one item indefinitely'.[35]

The intrepid farmers however carried on although far from improving the finances, the herd of pigs they bought in 1952 merely played a significant part in contributing to the farm's soaring loss which reached nearly £11,000 that year.[36] But still nothing stopped the heroic agricultural pair. The loss was again nearly £11,000 in 1953 although as Churchill's accountant later wrote to Cox, '…I can quite understand you sometimes find the result depressing. On the other hand I believe Sir Winston, like many others, finds it more pleasant to pay for the pleasure of farming than he would to pay the Inland Revenue'.[37] An attempt was nonetheless then finally made to stem the tide of loss and the decision was taken to sell Bardogs and Parkside but retain Chartwell Farm. Agreement was reached in November 1953 for the sale of Bardogs for £10,250 to Sir Arthur Jarratt, the business partner of Churchill's friend Sir Alexander Korda and chairman of the film distributing company, British Lion who lived nearby at Toys House.[38] And the same month, agreement was also achieved for the sale of Parkside Farm to the banker Rowland Baring, Lord Cromer (although the purchase was in his wife's name). Parkside was certainly a mixed holding. The fields contained or had contained wheat, barley, turnips, beans, silage and green manure. There were fruit plantations of 'Seabrook', 'Cotswold Cross' and 'Wellington XXX' blackcurrants, 'Cox' and 'Ellison's Orange' apple trees, large numbers of chrysanthemums, 1000 'Royal Sovereign' strawberries in pots, strawberries in the kitchen garden and field; and seeded lettuce in cold frames. There were also 41 head of pedigree Jersey cattle valued at £3,400 and 9 pigs at £1,185.[39] But although it was a long time since Churchill had sold any property the blight that generally accompanied his transactions clearly had not deserted him. He first had a dispute with Lord Cromer about the rabbit fence worth £115 that surrounded Parkside. Churchill felt it should be an extra cost. Cromer thought this most unusual and eventually Churchill had to instruct his lawyers to 'split or give way'.[40]

At Bardogs plans were laid for the sale to be finalised in March 1954. Cropping and planting programmes were adjusted accordingly and notice was given to several employees in anticipation. It all seemed to be progressing well when in January 1954, Cox had a meeting with Jarratt to discuss the details and Churchill was dismayed only two days later to receive a letter from Jarratt saying he could not proceed, offering the extraordinary explanation that he had no knowledge of farming and had no time to devote to it.[41] Churchill was not pleased. Cox seemed to think that Korda had a hand in the matter, suggesting to Jarratt that Churchill would never sell a property that was financially viable; something Korda himself vehemently denied.[42]

Undaunted by this disappointment, and despite another major farm loss in 1954, Cox, Churchill and Soames ploughed on and Churchillian pig owning was about to reach its zenith when in the summer, he and Soames set about building up a herd of Swedish Landrace pigs – out of which, according to Churchill, Soames at least expected to make a fortune.[43] At the time, the Landrace pig was something of a revelation. It had been bred originally in Denmark by crossing native pigs with large whites. Churchill told Clementine there were only about 1,500 in the country out of a national pig population of 5 million, sending her a small drawing by way of illustration of these porcine marvels. He and Soames had been told the Landrace hams were much admired and were led to believe that a single boar was worth five or six hundred pounds. They initially spent almost £1,000 (of Churchill's money) on eight of them which they kept at Bardogs, although only a week later, Churchill bought yet another for £300. In July 1955, the greatest living authority on Landrace pigs, Professor Clausen visited Chartwell from Denmark to advise on the herd but it was ultimately to no avail. The Landrace pig venture and the farms as a whole were still losing money at an alarming rate – £6,088 in 1955 – and serious common sense was called for.

Matters were finally brought to a head in 1956. Christopher and Mary Soames and their family – by then they had four children, Nicholas, Emma, Jeremy and Charlotte – had outgrown the accommodation at Chartwell and the following year they moved to a new home at Hamsell Manor, near Tunbridge Wells. This raised the question of what to do with Chartwell farm house. Clementine, ever the level-headed pragmatist, had foreseen this problem as long ago as 1948, when neither she nor anyone else could have known how much longer Churchill would live. She floated the idea to him of leaving Chartwell Farm to young Winston (Randolph's son, then aged eight) for him to come into possession when he was twenty-five – she thought twenty-one was a little too young for a farm and its intricate management. The Chartwell Literary Trust, which Churchill had set up for his children to receive the income from his literary works, could manage it with Christopher and Mary Soames still in possession, and with the Trust paying Soames' salary. If the Soames family decided to leave Chartwell Farm (there was some expectation then that Soames might come into possession of his parents' home Sheffield Park), the Trust would have authority to let it to a gentleman farmer. Revealingly, Clementine was uncertain what land had been left to the National Trust; she imagined only the pleasure grounds and vegetable garden close to the house and she therefore thought that Churchill should put a clause in his will that no part of the land near the house which would interfere with its amenities and views as a show place should ever be used or sold for building. As an after-thought, she suggested that to make up for Randolph having no income from the farm or use of the farm house, he might be paid £20-30,000.[44]

Churchill saw it rather differently and was minded to leave Randolph the farm house but not the farm, something Clementine thought impractical. She thought it was of vital importance that Randolph was not hurt in any way but said 'that his propinquity to Chartwell itself might make it extremely difficult for the National Trust to manage it without embarrassment'. She pointed out to Churchill that Randolph had never really taken any interest in Chartwell, had never stayed there for more than few days at a time and that even in his holidays as a child, he always wanted to get away from it. Clementine believed that a member of the family who dearly loved Chartwell and the neighbourhood and had lived there continuously should be in the farm house and take an active day to day interest in the management. She believed passionately that that person was Mary. She was born, she said, on the very day that Churchill bought Chartwell and she alone of their children loved country living and knew what it meant. Why not have the Chartwell Farm (in its entirety) valued, then bought by the Literary Trust and arrange for it eventually to become Mary's property, entailed on her son Nicholas? If Churchill did insist on leaving the farm house to Randolph, at least she said, let him have the farm too.[45] In the event Sheffield Park was broken up and sold on Soames' father's death in 1954 and by the time the Soames moved to Hamsell eight years later (with financial help from Churchill), it was apparent that hanging on to loss-making farms simply to keep the farm house in the family was unrealistic.

Cox wrote to Churchill in October 1956 raising the issue.[46] He had never expected to stay long at Chartwell and clearly had no great emotional attachment to it. He said he did not think it sensible to let the Chartwell farm house apart from the farm and as farming was no longer as lucrative and farm values were likely to fall, his view was that the remaining two farms should be sold with vacant

Mary and Christopher Soames at a cattle auction.

possession in the summer of 1957. It was advice that Churchill was to take. The farm loss in 1956 had been £7,438 and in the final year, 1957, it rose again to £9,285. Bardogs and Chartwell Farms were placed in the hands of Knight Frank & Rutley, the Jersey cattle livestock were sold at auction by Harry Hobson & Co on 18 June, the dead stock a few days later and the auctioneers E. B. Watson & Sons sold the farms at the Rose & Crown Hotel, Tunbridge on 16 July. Christopher Mann Ltd paid £35,000 for the 277 acres. With the cattle at auction went the much vaunted Landrace pigs (the 126 animals realising £4168 12s 6d), although the aging Churchill was not too infirm three years later to overlook pursuing his son-in-law for an outstanding payment on the enterprise of £764 3s 2d.[47]

Cox stayed on Chartwell to look after the animals on the estate – among sundry other creatures, Churchill had retained the Belted Galloways and having let his membership lapse, he rejoined the Beltie Society in 1959. The farm, even in its limited manifestation at Chartwell, nonetheless continued to lose money although the numbers soon dropped to the hundreds rather than the thousands of pounds. The farm sale moreover was far from the end of Churchill's and Soames' involvement with land and livestock and seemed merely to renew their energies and steer them in a different direction.

For most of Churchill's life, he was inseparable from horses. 'No hour of life is lost that is spent in the saddle' he wrote famously in *My Early Life*.[48] He was born into hunting society – and continued to hunt for many years, famously riding out at the age of seventy-four with the Old Surrey and Barstow Hunt when they met at Chartwell in 1948 – he served in a cavalry regiment (against his father's wishes) and for around thirty years he played polo, first in India, winning the Inter-Regimental Cup with his 4th Hussars team in 1899 and then maintained a string of polo ponies in England, at barely affordable cost. He had to pay over £100 per pony plus over £60 per month stabling for the four, quite apart from equipment, subscriptions, transportation, farrier's and veterinary fees. In 1922 he had a serious accident, and by 1925, Churchill realised this was one rich man's pursuit he really was not rich enough to pursue and wrote to Lord Kimberley asking him to help find a buyer for the ponies.[49]

But although Clementine did not realise it, racing too was in his blood. His father had won the 1889 Oaks with a filly called L'Abbesse De Jouarre carrying the pink silks with chocolate sleeves that Churchill himself was later to make even more famous and as a young officer cadet at Sandhurst he and his friend Herbert Spender-Clay had enjoyed weekends at Lingfield Racecourse. 'Young men have often been ruined through owning horses' Churchill wrote in 1930.[50] But clearly he believed older ones were immune because in 1949 at the age of 75 he bought Colonist II, a grey colt by Rienzo out of Cybele, the first of more than fifty thoroughbreds he was to own over the next 16 years. Some horses made him money. A few, like Colonist II made him a great deal, winning 13 races and netting £11,937 in prize money before he sold him in 1951 to Captain P. G. A. Harvey for £7,350. Other horses however lost it.

Colonist II aged sixteen at Newchapel Stud in 1962.

Churchill's racehorses were mostly kept at Epsom with only a few brood mares and foals at Chartwell but by 1955, the waning of the Churchill farms created the gap the new equestrian ventures were conveniently to fill. Having been given responsibility for the horses, Soames, like the animals, now had the bit between his teeth. The first thought was to run a Churchill stud from Hamsell Manor but this was put aside in favour of something much more exciting. Soames and Churchill decided to purchase a stud farm and embark on a breeding programme. They found what they were seeking only a few minutes drive away. Newchapel Stud lay south of Chartwell and about two and a half miles to the west of Lingfield on the fertile Surrey downland that had long been famed for the quality of its grazing. It offered stabling for 26 horses with around 80 acres of grass and woodland. Its paddocks were laid out within the oval railings that once contained the old 1895 Lingfield racecourse – the modern course closer to the town that Churchill and Herbert Spender-Clay visited on leave from Sandhurst was opened in 1900. Some adjoining fields were also rented for stud use, including one known as 'the Mormon field' which was owned by the adjoining vast London England Temple of the Mormon church.

Newchapel had supported some impressive bloodstock. The stud was started in 1920 by a Mr and Mrs W. H. Rudd, one of whose horses, Marvex, was involved in a famous triple dead-heat at Windsor in 1923. They then sold the stud to the whisky magnate Lord Dewar who used Newchapel to house the young animals brought over after weaning from his large stud at Homestall near East Grinstead. His 1931 Derby and 2000 Guineas winner Cameronian was lodged there as a yearling, and Fair Trial on which Gordon Richards won the Queen Anne Stakes at Royal Ascot in 1935 was also a Newchapel weanling. Following Lord Dewar's death in 1930, the bloodstock passed to his nephew John. He died in 1955 and his executors put the stud up for sale. During the Second World War, the Dewar horses had been sent to Ireland and greyhounds were kept at Newchapel so by the time Churchill bought it on 15 June 1955, the land had the advantage of only having been harrowed and grazed by cattle, although its buildings were somewhat run down.[51]

Soames and Churchill were fortunate in having a ready-made stud manager in the person of Major Arnold Carey Foster, an Epsom veterinary surgeon who looked after the horses Churchill had in training there with Walter Nightingall and who had originally bought Colonist II. Churchill wrote to Carey Foster in

Some of Churchill's brood mares at Newchapel Stud.

Arnold Carey Foster at Newchapel Stud with Novitiate, a
Newchapel bred filly by Fair Trial out of The Veil (1962).

May 1955 offering him the post as stud manager and vet at £1,000 a year for three years. 'At present', he said 'I view it as a stud farm providing accommodation for my thoroughbred stock'.[52] Carey Foster accepted with alacrity and Nightingall continued as Churchill's trainer although later he also had some horses with Peter Cazelet at Fairlawne.

Carey Foster and Soames bought four good mares for Churchill as foundation stock: Cedilla, Salka, Madonna and Turkish Blood. They had a fine collective eye. Madonna, bought as an eleven year old for 5,800 guineas, was probably the pick of the bunch and, mated to Hyperion, produced one of Churchill's finest horses in High Hat who had a glorious season in 1961, came fourth in the Prix de L'Arc de Triomphe and eventually won £15,000. Turkish Blood produced Vienna by Aureole who won nearly £19,000 and subsequent successful purchases included Sister Sarah, a bargain at 1,200 guineas as she produced The Veil, herself a successful brood mare, by Nimbus, and a fine sprinter Welsh Abbot by Abernant, who had five wins in thirteen starts, although to Churchill's great sadness, Sister Sarah died giving birth.

In the first year, 1956, the stud lost £4,146. The next year was better with a loss of only £2,873 but this was a temporary improvement and the losses in 1957 and 1958 were up again to £5,984 and £6,864. It was the farm accounts all over again. Soames produced a memorandum on the state of the business in 1959 and thought the tide might be turning. In 1955, they had bred Welsh Abbot and felt they may finally have a horse of sufficient quality to stand as a stallion. This was not however what Churchill had envisaged for his stud and would have involved expenditure of £5,000 for new buildings. It would also, as Soames recognised, completely alter the character and purpose of the enterprise but he offered to purchase a half share in the horse and in effect set up a partnership around Welsh Abbot as a stallion.[53] It came to nothing. The racing activities had meanwhile been running at a profit, a conspicuous novelty in Churchill livestock ventures, and apart from his winnings, the sale of horses plus the value of those he owned exceeded by £5,600 the cost of the animals bred and purchased in the first three years. Even after deduction of training and other expenses, there was still a small racing profit of £2,300.

But at the stud, the losses continued – they amounted to £3,496 in 1959. Yet the following year, Soames was urging Churchill to purchase more land. Carey-Foster had been approached by a local firm called Oakover Forest Services which owned the 63 acres of Goldhard Wood adjoining the Newchapel Stud. Any neighbour to Churchill assumed he had both a bottomless wallet and an incurable addiction to land owning and so they asked if he was interested.[54] Soames was all for it, believing the wood might otherwise be turned into a housing estate and he asked Churchill to give authority to offer £1,250 and be prepared to go to £2,000. Churchill agreed in principle but did wonder what they would do with it. In the event the sale never happened, Churchill did not buy the wood and although in subsequent years, it was largely cleared, Soames' fears proved groundless and there is still no housing estate there.

At the end of 1961, Soames wrote to Churchill, again reviewing the situation.[55] He pointed out that as racehorse owners, they had been lucky. With eight horses in training, they could expect to do well to win £8,000 per year. In reality, they had won £18,000 in 1960 and £27,000 in 1961 against outgoings of around £18,000. Churchill's total prize money up to 1961 was £70,000 and he had sold horses to the value of further £40,000. A valuation indicated the 14 horses were worth £168,000 of which High Hat was valued at £80,000 and Vienna at £20,000.[56] This had been High Hat's great season and Churchill decided to cash in and the horse was sold to his former aide-de-camp Captain Tim Rogers at valuation although as is common practice when a horse is sold as a stallion, he would continue to race in Churchill's colours.

But the racing was very different from the stud where Soames felt they needed eight good mares to keep it as a worthwhile enterprise. They had nine, of which only four or five were likely to produce anything of note and Soames' view was that they should sell the five worst mares at Newmarket in December 1962 and then sell the stud in the summer of 1963. He thought they should get £10,000 for the mares and £15,000 for the stud but was clearly anxious to maintain his own involvement, suggesting that the four good mares could be moved to his home at Hamsell Manor. Churchill however was obtaining conflicting advice from elsewhere. His secretary Anthony Montague-Browne and his solicitor Anthony Moir of Fladgates counselled against a sale, saying he did not really need the money and it would reduce the stud to a shadow of its former self. They also agreed with Carey Foster's view that Hamsell Manor was not an ideal place to try and breed high quality bloodstock – the grazing, soil and other facilities were just not good enough. 'I have not forgotten the limited attempt to do this on unsuitable land at Chartwell' wrote Carey Foster.[57] Soames then offered to buy some horses at current valuation but Browne and Moir were again opposed. They said there was uncertainty over the valuation the Inland Revenue would place on them and in any event they felt the Revenue would probably find the whole idea unacceptable. They also pointed out the tax advantages of not selling the stud until after Churchill's death and reluctantly Soames agreed: '…perhaps it is best that we should continue as we are' he wrote.

In April 1963, more land became available although this time, all parties were effectively giving Churchill the same advice – to buy. The property was Laylands Farm, a small farm with a bungalow and 38 acres lying to the south-west of the stud and it had a number of attractions. It would increase the overall value of the holding and it added a small dwelling house – which was important because Carey Foster had his own house at Quarry Farm on the opposite side of the road and this would not be available to Churchill after he retired. Churchill was paying £400 a year rent to Carey-Foster's wife who owned the house. Soames, ever enthusiatic about spending money thought it was a pity Churchill had not bought both house and farm when they were offered to him in 1956 although at the time, Churchill had thought the price too high.[58] Most importantly, however, the only access to the farm was along a winding track through the stud itself. Carey Foster felt it important that the farm did not fall into 'undesirable hands' and believed that if they bought it outright from Mr Gillett, the owner, they could probably have it for £17,000.

Churchill was now a spectator as property and assets were bought and sold on his behalf although he was clearly not going to be dragooned into doing anything unwise. Clementine was with him on the evening of Monday 20 May when Moir and Wood, together with Anthony Montague-Browne met at Hyde Park Gate to discuss the Laylands Farm proposition. Soames was not present. The atmosphere can hardly have been cheerful; it was only a few days after the long-awaited public announcement that Churchill was not to stand for Parliament at the next General Election.

It had emerged that other neighbours also had rights of way over the farm track so buying the farm would not stop everything but Churchill's advisors nonetheless unanimously recommended that he should go ahead and then recoup the money by selling some horses in the autumn – four fillies were in due course entered into the October Newmarket sales and two were retained to go into training. Churchill agreed to a bid of £15,000 for Laylands Farm with the authority to go to £17,500 if necessary. On 27 May Carey Foster bought it for £16,000 and contracts were exchanged two days later for completion at the beginning of September. Soames was not entirely happy and he wrote to Anthony Montague Brown saying he thought the price was too high.[59] The land needed fencing, there were only 30 acres and the buildings were poor. It would end up costing Churchill about £20,000 although he conceded on balance it was probably worthwhile. He was not however optimistic about the future. They were not going to have a very good year on the racecourse as they had no banker like Vienna or High Hat so he expected they would have to sell all the yearling colts and probably some mares to meet the racing and stud accounts. 'As you know', he wrote, 'I am hoping in the long term to keep the stud going so would like to have the opportunity to buy them privately…'[60] Churchill had in fact already expressed a wish to leave Christopher Soames part of the stud in his will. Anthony Montague Brown pointed out that this would ensure Soames a large financial advantage although it would diminish the estate Churchill was leaving to Clementine and the children. He advised that Soames should be left up to three mares of total value not more than £7,500 and should be given the option of purchasing some or all of the rest of the stud at probate value.[61]

Still the stud continued its acquisitions and on 6 January 1964, just a year before his death, and on the advice of Anthony Moir, Churchill paid £900 to a Mrs Lewis for a four and half acre paddock adjoining the stud. It was a field he had leased from her late husband for 1/- per year and Moir told him he really could not let anyone else have it.[62] Then, finally, in March 1964, the lifetime of property purchases which began with buying the lease of 105, Mount Street in 1902 finally came to a close and perhaps the most modest of all Churchill's housing investments was completed when – probably without knowing it – he bought a small semi-detached house at 23 Baker's Lane, Lingfield as staff accommodation.[63]

It was now left to Clementine and Churchill's advisors to consider and take decisions though even then, surrounded by financial security, Clementine was raising queries. What was the cost of running the herd of Belted Galloways, she asked in September 1964.[64] There was no simple answer but the average loss of the farming operations at Chartwell was down to £400-500 per annum, reduced by tax relief to £200-300 and even if it was stopped entirely, some expenses like grass cutting and the tractors would remain.

No 25 Baker's Lane, Lingfield, Churchill's last property purchase.

Churchill was now so out of touch and ailing however that there seemed no point in continuing with any pretence at racing. Montague Brown said that if the Press asked about the sale of the horses, they should say that at the end of the current flat racing season, Churchill would have no further horses in training. They would either be sold or leased but the stud would however continue breeding.[65] The concerns Soames had expressed were nonetheless justified and the stud lost £6,652 in 1963 and then, in the final year before Churchill's death in January 1965, the losses soared to £17,500. At the time of his death, he owned nine mares worth £16, 650 and a few other horses, the total value being £19,720.

Churchill revelled in his adventures in farming and bloodstock ownership; and he was generous in giving extra payments to jockeys, trainers and stable lads when his horses did well. Like his painting, these country pursuits provided an escape and a diversion from the pressures that came with high office and with simply being who he was. But unlike painting, the farming experiences did cost a huge amount of money – and although his accountants generally managed to keep him on the right side of the Inland Revenue, it was not always easy. 'One has to be particularly careful in handling Sir Winston's tax affairs' wrote one to Christopher Soames in relation to the worth of a colt by Colonist out of Moll Flanders '… I think that the valuation of the animal … should be made by an independent Valuer and not by yourself or Sir Winston'.[66] And there was an even closer shave some years later when the tax inspector suggested that the stud farm was a hobby and fell into Section 20 of the 1960 Act in which event Churchill would not have been entitled to recover the loss. As a result of serendipity or persuasion however, the inspector did finally agree that the stud was a genuine commercial enterprise.[67]

Colonist II, his first and most famous thoroughbred, remained Churchill's favourite and when he sold him in 1951, he commissioned the equestrian artist Raoul Millais (grandson of Sir John Everett Millais) to paint his portrait in a style that would be a companion to his father's painting of L'Abbesse De Jouarre. Millais offered to undertake the commission for nothing but Churchill – who was generous enough to give away his own paintings to friends – would have none of it. 'I hope ... you will not insist on this' he said, 'Virtue is its own reward, but not art...'[68] When the work was complete, Churchill declared it a masterpiece and it now hangs in the drawing room at Chartwell.[69]

Endnotes

[1] CHUR 1/32/161–162. Correspondence with A. J. Burrows, Clements Winch & Sons. August 1945.

[2] CHAR 1/400A/15–18. Violet Pearman to WSC. 15 Feb 1932.

[3] CHUR 1/32/163. R. Marnham to WSC. 23 Aug 1945.

[4] CHUR 1/32/211. Certificate. 2 Aug 1946.

[5] CHUR 1/15/235–6. Wood Willey & Co to WSC. n.d.

[6] CHUR 1/45/244. C. Soames to WSC. 22 Dec [1945]

[7] CHUR 1/32/308. WSC to R. Marnham. 15 Oct 1946.

[8] CHUR 1/32/284. R. Marnham to WSC. n.d.

[9] CHUR 1/32/294. Anon. Note re. land purchase. n.d

[10] See CHUR 1/32.

[11] CSCT 1/27/18. CSC to WSC. 30 May 1943.

[12] CHUR 1/35/6. Sale Particulars, Fox & Mainwaring. n.d.

[13] CHUR 1/35/18. G. Hanscomb to WSC. 16 Dec 1946.

[14] CHUR 1/35/12. Grace Hamblin to Local Fuel Overseer, Sevenoaks. 16 Apr 1947.

[15] CSCT 2/35/5–8. WSC to CSC. 13 Aug 1947.

[16] CHUR 1/34/13. Fox and Mainwaring to WSC. 24 May 1947.

[17] Beaverbrook Papers. A. Sinclair to Beaverbrook. 19 Dec 1949. Original not seen.

[18] CHUR 1/44/26. CSC to WSC. 16 Dec 1947.

[19] CHUR 1/34/25. CSC to WSC. 5 June 1947.

[20] Doris Edleston, conversation with the author, 17 Jan 2007.

[21] CHUR 1/32/411. WSC to [?] Wood. 9 Dec 1947.

[22] CHUR 1/35/23. G. Hanscomb to WSC. n.d.

23   Kincaid, J. *Belted Galloway News*, Jan 1964.

24   WCHL 8/1 [Closed file]. Mrs George Shield to WSC. 29 Dec 1945.

25   CHUR 1/46/312. C. Soames to WSC. 15 Aug 1949.

26   CHUR 1/37/47. WSC to CSC. 19 Apr 1953.

27   CSCT 2/38/5–11. WSC to CSC. [?] Apr 1950.

28   C. Soames: Reform Club Political Dinner, 28 Apr 1981. Cited in Churchill, R. S. and
     Gilbert, M. Winston S. Churchill. Vol. 8. p.304.

29   CHAR 1/131/69-71. CSC to E. Marsh. [?] June1918.

30   HP I. Hamilton to Stella Speyer. 15 Dec 1920.

31   HP Lady Hamilton's Diary, 20 Jul 1919.

32   CSCT 2/18/11–13. WSC to CSC 15 Mar 1925.

33   CHAR 1/394/67. Kathleen Hill to J. C. Dawson. 16 Jul 1941.

34   CHUR 1/45 C. Soames to WSC. 31 Dec 1947.

35   CHUR 1/32/406. CSC to WSC. 11 Nov 1948.

36   WCHL 8/11 [Closed file]. WSC's Farm Accounts Working papers 1949-52. Year ended
     30 September 1952.

37   WCHL 8/20 [Closed file]. [?] Wood to [?] Cox. 18 Mar 1956.

38   CHUR 1/28/31. Fladgate & Co. to WSC. 18 Nov 1953.

39   WCHL 8/88 [Closed file]. Working papers 1952-3.

40   CHUR 1/28/32. Fladgate & Co. to WSC. 18 Nov 1953.

41   CHUR 1/28/39. Sir Arthur Jarratt to WSC. 13 Jan 1954.

42   CHUR 1/28/42. Sir Alexander Korda to WSC. 14 Jan 1954.

43   CSCT 2/42/26-29. WSC to CSC. 10 Aug 1954.

44   CHUR 1/44/45. CSC to WSC. 1 Sep 1948.

45   CHUR 1/44/49. CSC to WSC. 1 Sept 1948.

46   CHUR 1/37/64 [?] Cox to WSC. 12 Oct 1956.

47   CHUR 1/133/2. WSC to C. Soames. 6 Mar 1960.

48   Churchill, W. S. *My Early Life; A Roving Commission*. p. 59.

49   CHAR 1/178/38. WSC to Lord Kimberley. 10 Aug 1925.

50   Churchill, W. S. *My Early Life; A Roving Commission*. p. 59.

51   WCHL 8/20 [Closed file]. [?] Wood to Middleton & Co. 8 Feb 1956.

52   CHUR 1/93/40. WSC to A. Carey Foster. 12 May 1955.

53   WCHL 8/87 [Closed file]. Memorandum on the future of Newchapel Stud. Apr 1959.

54   CHUR 1/159/101. A. Carey-Foster to C. Soames. 13 May 1960.

55   CHUR 1/133/47. C. Soames to WSC. 4 Dec 1961.

56   CHUR 1/133/31. A. Montague Brown to A. Moir. 14 Jul 1961.

57   CHUR 1/133/47. Carey Foster to A. Moir. n.d. [1961]

58   CHUR 1/37/86. Various Correspondence. 16 Nov 1956.

59   CHUR 1/133/158. C. Soames to A. Montague Brown. 31 May 1963.

60   CHUR 1/133/158. C. Soames to Montague Brown. 31 May 1963.

61   CHUR 1/133/25. A. Montague Brown to WSC. 4 July 1961.

62   CHUR 1/133/182. A. Moir to WSC. n.d.

63   CHUR 1/133/182. A. Moir to A. Montague Browne. Contract. 24 Mar 1964.

64   CHUR 1/133/197. A. Montague Brown to [?] Wood. 24 Sep 1964.

65   CHUR 1/133/206. Note by A. Montague Brown. 21 Oct 1964.

66   WCHL/20 [Closed file]. [?] Wood to C. Soames. 26 Jan 1956.

67   CHUR 1/114/57. [?] Wood to WSC. 4 Mar 1964.

68   CHUR 1/93/76. WSC to R. Millais. 3 July 1951.

69   CHUR 1/93/70. WSC to R. Millais. [?] Nov 1951.

CHAPTER 14
BUTTERFLIES AND GOLDEN ROSES

Although still very active politically after 1945 as Leader of His Majesty's Opposition, Churchill had his first chance since the late thirties to devote some time to work at Chartwell. He found however that it was in a sad state and Harris the gardener told him the garden could 'never be got back'.[1] Churchill also knew that Harris's main role was to work under Clementine's direction in the 'pleasure garden' and that 'borrowing' garden staff to undertake estate work had never gone down well. He therefore assembled a small work force of three, including Kurn who had once taught him brick laying, to continue to clear the estate. Together with two German prisoners, they made excellent progress and spurred on by Max Beaverbrook's gift of chickens, a smallholding gradually developed. The old beehives were dusted down and brought back into production, and the fanciful idea of living off the land, last seen at Lullenden in 1919, was gradually showing signs of reappearing.

Largely under Clementine's direction, the house was reorganised[2] and the disposition of a number of the rooms altered.[3] Some changes had already been made when it was intended that a caretaker couple would live there at the end of the war.[4] But the alterations were now on a more major scale. The large kitchen and associated rooms in the north basement went and a new, much smaller kitchen was inserted in what had been a staff bedroom on the top floor. The dining room moved to the floor below it and took the place of the principal visitors' room from where a small service lift linked it to the new kitchen. Clementine moved to the top floor and the old Tower Room became her bedroom, her former bedroom changing to a new sitting room. The ground floor office area remained and the two resident secretaries lived in Orchard Cottage. The large ground floor drawing room was turned into a studio although Churchill's study/bedroom with its beautiful beamed double height ceiling that Tilden had uncovered with so much satisfaction in 1923 remained unaltered. Churchill's passion for films led to a major change to the old dining room. Having had his own cinema at Chequers and, temporarily at Ditchley, he now had one at Chartwell furnished by a splendid projector and screen donated by his old friend Sir Alexander Korda.

The first post-war Christmas was spent at the new London home in Hyde Park Gate although Churchill went down to Chartwell for the New Year. Unfortunately, however neither he nor Clementine would see much of either home during the first three months of 1946 as they undertook a long visit to the United States – the visit on which Churchill made his Iron Curtain speech at Fulton, Missouri. Before departing, he wrote to Robert Southon, his builder, detailing work that should be done at Chartwell in his absence – this included making good the cellar after, appropriately, a gang of German prisoners had removed the escape hatch from the air raid shelter in front of the house.[5] But wherever Clementine found herself, the garden was not far from her thoughts; and she also knew Harris needed a guiding hand, so as she travelled west on the *Queen Elizabeth*, she sent a telegraph to her gardener telling him she had been thinking about flower seeds and could not remember if they had ordered any stocks. '…is not there a sweet scented variety called Midlothian' [*sic,* the East Lothian stock, a hardy biennial type] she asked, saying she thought they would look nice if planted in the bare patches in the rose garden; and she would like some for the London garden too. Scents were very much on her mind – she also asked Harris to obtain mignonette and heliotrope for the rose garden, and verbena from Hilliers for the rose garden South wall. Sweet scented geraniums would be welcome too.[6]

Even when she was at home, Clementine regularly wrote notes of instruction to Harris and supplied lists of plants she wanted him to purchase. In 1946, she ordered a large collection of camellias for the rose garden, her choices apparently based on an article she had read in The Times. In the same year, she ordered three Morello cherries, also for the rose garden, a 'Mermaid' rose for the kitchen garden and tree peonies from Hilliers. It was left to Clementine rather than Harris to decide that new yew plants were need to fill gaps in the hedges and in June she sent him a typical note instructing him to remove a privet hedge, reduce the size of the beds in the rose garden, replant some self-seeded tree lupins, move a honeysuckle and (though not an ideal time of year to do it) take rosemary cuttings for planting round the house.[7] It was certainly a year of active re-stocking and work. A fine selection of Asiatic Primula species was ordered from Hilliers along with numerous bulbs from Vanderschoot, clematis and a collection of standard hybrid tea roses from Whiteleggs. Roses, and border perennials were being bought almost every year from a number of leading nurseries right into and through the nineteen fifties. The Michaelmas daisy variety 'Winston

Churchill' arrived in a small collection as a gift from Gayborders nursery in 1954. The variety is still obtainable along with a cypress, dahlia, fuchsia, geranium, narcissus, peony, pelargonium, rhododendron and saxifrage that bear his name. There is also a fuchsia 'Mrs Churchill', a pelargonium 'Lady Churchill' and a kalmia 'Clementine Churchill'.

No sooner had they returned from the United States than Churchill was rekindling his interest in butterflies and believing the Kent butterfly farm was being restarted, his secretary Lettice Marston wrote to the owner, Newman in March 1946 asking what species could be supplied. Newman was quick to point out that 'like the Windmill' the farm had never closed and offered to give advice on how a frame could be constructed to place over a garden border so the butterflies would not stray next door.[8] Like many enthusiasts, entirely absorbed with their subjects, Newman was clearly quite blinkered to the fact that draping the Chartwell flower borders with muslin frames would rather detract from the visual delights Clementine had being working so hard to create. But in the event Churchill had other plans.

Newman visited Chartwell on 20 May, Jenner collecting him from the station, and brought swallowtail and silver-washed fritillary pupae and live adults of swallowtail and small tortoiseshell butterflies together with scarlet tiger and cinnabar moths, for which Churchill was later charged £1 15s 4d. They had a 'whirlwind' tour of the garden and as they returned, Churchill stopped by the small brick building close to the south-west corner of the house and suggested to Newman that it be used for butterflies. It had been built sometime between 1869 and 1896 as a game larder. In 1924, Tilden had converted it to a summerhouse by removing the East wall 'to allow the rays of the sun to penetrate into its recesses'. He constructed oak seats on three sides, and added brick and York stone steps and paving; Wallace, the Westerham joiner, rendered and painted it. After the war, Churchill referred to the building for a time as the peach house. He suggested to Newman that the roof could be replaced with a glass cover but eventually followed Newman's advice simply to use the existing seats as supports for butterfly cages and place a wooden framework covered in fine black mosquito netting over the top, with a small door at the front.

By mid-June, the insects seemed to be thriving but despite Newman's urgings, Churchill had rather little passion for scientific entomology. He regarded the butterfly house merely as a nursery[9] and Newman later wrote that he would sometimes sit inside it watching the adults emerge before drawing back the muslin to set them free. Churchill's main interest was not in breeding the things but in seeing them fluttering across his garden and he wondered if placing a little pot of honey among the flowers might help to attract them.

Newman continued to send butterflies through the summer, with varying

The butterfly house at Chartwell.

success – green-veined whites, speckled woods, peacocks, some of which arrived safely, some dead. Reviewing the year's efforts in October, Newman thought they could do better and in 1947, sent Churchill some more, although following the viciously cold winter, butterfly breeding in general had had a bad time.[10]

Unwittingly, however, Churchill had now become involved in a highly controversial practice. There was and remains much dispute among naturalists about the wisdom of attempting to introduce butterflies – or any other creature – to live and breed in parts of the country where they have died out or have never occurred naturally; or of reintroducing foreign stock of species that have become extinct in Britain. Today, under the 1981 Wildlife and Countryside Act, it would be illegal. During the summer of 1946, Newman had encouraged gardener Harris to plant some fennel, the food plant of the swallowtail butterfly's caterpillars, by the lake at Chartwell in the hope of establishing a colony there. It was an improbable and irresponsible notion, doomed to failure – and at Churchill's expense, because he paid for the larvae. In Britain, the magnificent swallowtail is a butterfly of the fenland marshes of East Anglia and has been restricted there for a very long time, although it once occurred in the Thames valley, on the Somerset levels and in a few other wetlands. It has almost certainly never lived naturally on the Weald of Kent. But Churchill in his naïve enthusiasm was not to know that and this giant of a man in his declining years had been sucked in to a scheme that was totally dotty. He even found time in a busy week, to write personally and tell Newman that some of his fennel was actually growing.[11]

The following year, Newman was extending his enthusiasm for reintroductions and persuaded Churchill to part with £10 for some caterpillars of the black-veined white, an insect that had died out in Britain in the 1920s. It was at least a species that had once occurred in Kent but Newman was clearly aware that he was treading on controversial territory by asking Churchill to keep confidential their records of the releases. The first attempt having failed, the following year they were at it again although at least Newman had the good grace to provide the caterpillars free of charge[12] and then went public in publishing his experiments in the magazine 'The Entomologist'. Today, attempting to reintroduce black-veined whites to Britain is considered 'futile'.[13]

Newman's enthusiasm nonetheless was undiminished and in 1949, he was collecting and sending Churchill pupae of the clouded yellow, a species that migrated in prodigious numbers to southern England from the Continent that year. In 1950, bizarrely he even offered Churchill live adults of a continental butterfly, the cleopatra, for liberation at Chartwell despite it being a species that has never been recorded in Britain, even as a stray;[14] but by then, it was all over. Churchill's secretary Chips Gemmell wrote to Newman on 20 June telling him the butterfly house had been done away with and they never corresponded again.[15] What prompted the end of the exercise can only be guessed at but having an attractive and rather prominent little building so close to the main house at Chartwell semi-permanently draped in black muslin may understandably have offended Clementine's sense of the chic.

The Churchills had only owned 28 Hyde Park Gate for a few months when it become apparent that although elegant and in an excellent location, it really was not an ideal house because there just was not enough space for the necessary office accommodation. Throughout his life, Churchill had received voluminous correspondence and now, despite being out of office, he was still 'number one world hero' and the flow of paper seemed to increase rather than diminish. He employed three full time secretaries while Clementine had a fourth, the much loved Grace Hamblin from Westerham who had worked for her since 1932. While they were in the United States in the early part of 1946, a solution fortuitously presented itself when the neighbouring property, No 27, a house of comparable age and size came onto the market, although Clementine's' initial response was that buying another house and garden simply to provide office space was somewhat extravagant.[16]

Churchill was staying with Jacques Balsan in Miami Beach in February when the news reached him and he cabled his agents Knight Frank & Rutley asking if the freehold of No 27 could be bought for £6,000 or 'at worst' £7,000. They responded that the property was in the hands of three trustees, only one of whom was in England. He would agree to £7,000 and would cable his fellow trustees for consent if Churchill would confirm the higher offer, which he did.[17] Moreover Clementine had now seen a way to make the purchase more attractive by converting part of the property into self-contained flats but unfortunately a restrictive covenant initially precluded this. After lengthy negotiations which continued well after they returned from the United States and were not completed until late summer, the owners agreed to modify the covenant but only for Churchill personally; the arrangement would simply hold as long as he owned the house. They also agreed to his use of part of the ground floor as offices, to making an internal doorway, the construction of new dormer windows and the removal of the garden wall to create a single unified garden.[18] The deal was done. Churchill paid £7,000 and the purchase was completed in August. The two houses were in due course linked together to provide Churchill with increased office space and also to create three apartments for letting: a basement flat, a maisonette and a studio flat/office. The garden was now twice the size of course although still only around one thousand square metres so no resident gardener was employed and a contract gardener visited regularly to maintain it.[19] There was certainly no space for a kitchen garden but regular consignments of fruit and vegetables were sent from Chartwell and Mrs Georgina Landemare, the Churchill's long-time cook who began working for them in the nineteen thirties and only finally retired in 1953-4 could never have enough of this fresh kitchen garden produce. Gardener Harris sent a consignment by car every Monday and a hamper by train on Thursdays.[20]

At the end of 1944, Churchill had rejected the approach from Knight Frank & Rutley for Chartwell to be sold for use as a hotel saying that it was not on the market. Strictly, that was true but the future of the property after the war had indeed been exercising his mind. He was already over 70 and although thanks to his writing, he could at last afford to run the estate properly; even at the best of times it had never been anything less than a worry for Clementine. It has been calculated that he had between £110,000 and £120,000 in the bank at the time[21] and he still felt financially insecure, although within a few years, the sale of literary works, most importantly *World War II*, would bring handsome rewards. The possibility of selling Chartwell, which he had entertained several times, therefore never really went away but before he could bring himself to make a serious decision, matters were generously and fortuitously taken out of his hands.

For some ten years, Churchill had known the newspaper proprietor William Berry, who became Baron Camrose in 1929 and then, in 1941, 1st Viscount Camrose. As owner of the *Daily Telegraph* he had backed Churchill in the debate about air parity in the mid-nineteen thirties and then, as a supporter of Chamberlain (who recruited him for a time to the Ministry of Information) had urged that Churchill be brought into the Government. He and his newspaper continued as staunch supporters of Churchill throughout the war and he later obtained a highly lucrative deal for him in the serialisation of *World War II* and its publication in the United States. When the two men met in London on 7 August 1946, Churchill told Camrose that he thought he needed £12,000 a year on which to live.[22] This tallied well with figures produced by his accountants at the end of 1946, which showed his actual and anticipated general annual expenses were around £6,500. This included overheads of £749 for Chartwell, £633 for 28 Hyde Park Gate and £159 for the Chartwell cottages. There were also costs of £300 for the Chartwell garden (of which £250 was wages), £52 for the garden in London, £3,217 for general housekeeping and £1,375 for wines, spirits, cigars and cigarettes.[23]

Churchill told Camrose that he felt he really should sell Chartwell to boost his capital. Camrose was dismayed and then had the imaginative idea of gathering together a group of like-minded and wealthy individuals who would collectively buy Chartwell and donate it to the National Trust while allowing Churchill to remain there for his lifetime. Churchill was most enthusiastic and when Camrose asked him if he would accept an offer of £50,000, the answer was 'Yes – and throw in the corpse as well'.[24]

After having its fingers burned with some early acquisitions, the National Trust had a general policy of only accepting houses for which there was an adequate maintenance endowment and in the case of Chartwell, this would amount to a further £35,000. Camrose approached sixteen individuals and was insistent that his identity and that of the donors would remain totally confidential. He gave £15,000 himself and received £5,000 each from all the others he approached: Viscount Bearsted (art collector and philanthropist), Lord Bicester (merchant banker), Sir James Caird (ship owner), Sir Hugo-Cunliffe-Owen (businessman – British-American Tobacco), Lord Catto (merchant banker), Lord Glendyne (stockbroker), Lord Kenilworth (motor manufacturer), Lord Leathers (shipping), Sir James Lithgow (shipbuilder), Sir Edward Mountain (underwriter), Viscount Nuffield (motor manufacturer and philanthropist), Sir Edward Peacock (merchant banker), Viscount Portal of Laverstoke (paper manufacturer), Mr J. Arthur Rank (flour miller and film maker), Mr James de Rothschild (Liberal politician and philanthropist who later bequeathed Waddesdon Manor to the National Trust), and Sir Frederick Stewart (engineer). It was many years later in a letter from Lord Camrose's son Lord Hartwell, published in the Sunday Times on 9 July 1989 that the identity of the benefactors was finally disclosed and a circular slate plaque on the East wall at Chartwell now records their names and the National Trust's gratitude.

Churchill formally sold Chartwell to the National Trust on 29 November 1946 for £50,000 and on the same day took from the Trust a rather complex 50-year lease. He had the right to terminate the lease (and thus hand over the property to the Trust) at any time on three months notice. According to Anthony Moir, Churchill's solicitor, the National Trust in turn had a right to terminate the lease on six months notice at any time after his death. Clementine therefore had in theory only six months guaranteed tenure after Churchill died although Mary Soames wrote that she believed her mother could stay there for her lifetime. Churchill would pay an annual rent of £350 and would be responsible for fire insurance, rates and other outgoings, internal redecoration (though not for keeping it 'in a better condition than it was in 1946'), cultivating the land and maintaining the trees. The property could be used 'only for private residential purposes or for the purposes of agriculture or horticulture'.[25]

A lunch at Chartwell was planned the following summer for as many as possible of the benefactors and their wives although the original intended date, 11 July was postponed for a fortnight as Churchill was unwell. Eventually, on 25 July, twenty two guests attended and Clementine thoughtfully send cards entitling all the chauffeurs to have lunch at the Wolfe Café in Westerham.

Gardener Harris died in 1947 after he had been at Chartwell for only three years, and in the autumn Clementine placed an advertisement anonymously in the trade magazine, *The Gardener's Chronicle.* Among a number of repliers to PO Box 46 was Victor Vincent. Like Albert Hill, he was a Norfolk man, born at Rackheath near Norwich in 1905, the son of a gamekeeper, and he began work

Victor Vincent in the garden at Chartwell (1977).

WESTERHAM 93.

CHARTWELL,
WESTERHAM,
KENT.

28th. October, 1947.

Dear Mr. Vincent,

I have to thank you for your letter in reply to the advertisement under Box 46 in the Gardener's Chronicle. This was inserted by Mr. and Mrs. Churchill who require a head gardener of three for the gardens here.

Mrs. Churchill is interested in your letter, and wishes me to send you a few particulars of the position. The wages offered are £5 a week, and a good bungalow-type cottage with three bedrooms.

However if the matter should go forward you will naturally be paid what you ask.

Mrs. Churchill wishes you to know that we are 2½ miles from Westerham itself but that from Westerham there are good bus and train services to London.

There is only one small heated green-house in this garden, and a slightly larger cold one. Mr. and Mrs. Churchill are anxious to obtain the services of someone who is particularly good with flowers, because as you may know, at Mr. Churchill's death the place will go to the National Trust, and it is their wish to beautify it as much as possible before that time comes.

It is a much smaller place than your present situation but if, because of the above mentioned facts, you are at all interested perhaps you will communicate with me.

Yours truly,

G. Hamblin
Private Secretary.

Letter received by Victor Vincent offering him appointment at Chartwell.

at the age of fourteen on the same local estate, Keswick, as his father. He then moved to Somerleyton Hall near Lowestoft where he served his apprenticeship and met his future wife Gwendoline, before moving to Yattenden in Berkshire, Sedgebrook Hall in Northamptonshire, Bedales at Haywards Heath and then

Muncaster Castle in Cumberland which he hated.[26] Unsettled enough to apply for the anonymous vacancy, his surprise must have been considerable when he received a letter from Grace Hamblin on behalf of Clementine saying she was interested in his application. The wages offered were £5 a week with a good bungalow-type three-bedroomed cottage. 'However', she added, with an unexpected gesture, 'if the matter should go forward, you will naturally be paid what you ask'.[27] Grace Hamblin went on to explain that Mr and Mrs Churchill were anxious to obtain the services of someone who was particularly good with flowers because 'as you may know, at Mr. Churchill's death the place will go to the National Trust, and it is their wish to beautify it as much as possible before that time comes'. Vincent was a much more experienced and better gardener than Harris and was certainly well versed in flower growing as he was in most aspects of practical horticulture. He was a charming man, a much liked and admired member of the Chartwell staff although unfortunately, his taste in colour and style did not invariably coincide with Clementine's; in truth, it invariably did not. Mary Soames described Vincent's colour sense to me as 'dreadful'.

Once the rearrangements to the house had been made at the end of the war, there were few material changes to the buildings at Chartwell although a lift, a present from Max Beaverbrook, was later installed close to the drawing room entrance on the ground floor and rose to the first floor and Churchill's study and bedroom. Some consideration was given towards the end of the nineteen forties to creating a museum to display Churchill's life and work and plans were drawn up for a building in the meadow to the north of the house. Sir Howard Robertson was suggested as the architect but it came to nothing.[28] A notable alteration did come however in 1949 to mark the occasion of Churchill's seventy fifth birthday. The Marlborough Pavilion that Philip Tilden had built in the twenties and Johnny Spencer Churchill had painted in 1934 had fallen into a state of disrepair. Clementine asked Johnny to repaint it as a birthday gift to his uncle but rather than simply re-do what he done fifteen years earlier, Johnny took advice about creating something more durable. He chose to concentrate on the Battle of Blenheim and create a frieze which was incised on twelve slabs of Welsh slate and then painted, a duality of artistic media that Churchill had never seen or heard of and about which he was extremely sceptical. The thirty feet long creation took several months with the aid of four helpers and, as in 1934, there were regular interruptions at 11 each morning from Uncle Winston en route to feed the golden orfe. There were also the inevitable Churchillian criticisms of the way the battle was depicted and even the way a French officer sat his bottom on his horse but eventually, on its completion in the spring of 1950 the work did receive the seal of approval and following the purchase of Chartwell for the Nation, Churchill said the frieze was assured of 'a place in history'.[29]

Around 1949, Clementine moved her bedroom from the 'Tower' to the ground floor where she converted the old blue sitting room at the rear and this led out onto the 'pink terrace' where large wooden planting troughs were filled by Vincent every spring with white tulips, forget-me-nots and polyanthus which gave way in the summer to white verbenas, fuchsias, single pelargoniums and heliotrope. She loved sitting here with her guests and this terrace, along with the rose garden and croquet lawn were among her favourite areas. What Mary Soames has called her mother's 'reconciliation with Chartwell'[30] was now almost complete, her former anxieties about their financial security and the drain the place had been on their resources now finally lifted with the knowledge that the house and garden were secure in perpetuity for the Nation. It was indeed she, rather than Churchill, who now sought to innovate and bring changes to

Chartwell croquet lawn.

the gardens. As a member of the Royal Horticultural Society, she called on the Society's expertise to advise her on pest problems with the Chartwell trees[31] and she became an Associate Member of East Malling, the fruit research institute in Kent in order to obtain professional advice on strawberries.[32]

In late 1949 and unbeknown to Churchill, Clementine attempted to obtain some timbers from the old warship HMS *Implacable* – a survivor of Trafalgar which the Navy had decided was rotten beyond salvation and was about to scuttle – for incorporating into new wooden gates.[33] But the first of her really big changes to the Chartwell garden had come in the previous year, 1948, the only time a major outside contractor was involved and the only time a serious outside designer had a proper professional influence at Chartwell.

Clementine went with her cousin Sylvia Henley (Venetia Montagu's sister) to the Chelsea Flower Show in May 1948, only the second Chelsea show after the war, and was much taken with a rock garden display by the Gavin Jones nursery. Gavin Jones DSO was an unlikely gardener. He retired from the Indian army in 1921 with the rank of Lt.-Colonel and he and his wife then bought a small horticultural holding in Letchworth which they developed as an alpine nursery. They subsequently expanded into landscaping and during the 1920s and 1930s acquired a high reputation for many large landscaping projects in the Home Counties. He staged one of many successful exhibits at Chelsea in 1948 where his rock garden won a Gold Medal. It is not at all unusual for Chelsea Flower Show exhibits, especially the more durable ones like rock gardens, to be bought wholesale and transferred to a customer's own garden. This is partly what seems to have happened when Clementine placed her order. Jones first took her to see a garden he had created near Nutley in Surrey and then adapted and enlarged the Chelsea garden to suit Chartwell.[34]

The design was a semi-circular wall comprising massive vertical lumps of Forest of Dean sandstone – an unusual medium for Jones who usually worked in granite. Johnny Spencer Churchill saw it being built as 'Monstrous lorries panted in from the depths of Wales carrying colossal chunks of mountainside'.[35] Water cascaded over the rock face and into a pool below and was intended to represent a natural stone outcrop with the strata dipping below the water. Jones sent a sketch by his manager Geoffrey Chalk, a professional artist, of the proposal for the finished garden showing stepping stones across the pool with an existing Japanese maple incorporated at the top of the design. Planting was to be minimal because Jones

Gavin Jones' rock garden at Chartwell.

wanted the rocks themselves to make the picture. Churchill watched as the rock garden was installed in October 1948, initially being wary of allowing Jones' foreman to undertake the work but eventually agreeing although Chartwell workers, including the German prisoners gave assistance. The following year, Churchill added some more rocks supplied by Jones and Clementine ordered thyme plants to embellish the display. When around eighteen months years later, Churchill built yet another fish pool – which became known as the reservoir – the water flow over the rock garden dwindled and Churchill had a prolonged correspondence with Jones to try and ascertain where the water had gone. Jones' conclusion was that in building the reservoir, Churchill had blocked the passage of some of the springs which had then found an outlet elsewhere.

Clementine's second big change came ten years later around 1960 when she had the dilapidated old greenhouses and cold frames swept away from the top terrace above the kitchen garden. New greenhouses were built out of sight in a much better position on the south side of the boundary wall to the new orchard. The wide terrace area, sometimes called the white terrace then became

Chartwell new greenhouses outside the walled garden.

Pet graves at Chartwell: Rufus II (left), Rufus (centre), Jock (right).

an attractive and appealing vantage point from where views stretch away across Chartwell Farm over the garden boundary and to the Weald beyond. Close by are the pet graves where much-loved family animals are buried. Churchill's favourite dogs were not, as might be imagined, British bulldogs, but brown poodles. He had two, Rufus who accompanied him throughout World War II and died in 1947 and his successor Rufus II who died at the age of fifteen in 1962. They were buried here under marked flagstones, together with the last of Churchill's cats, the marmalade cat Jock who died in 1974. He was a gift from Churchill's private secretary Jock Colville and there remains a tradition of having a marmalade cat at Chartwell.

Although it had always been intended that the main house at Chartwell would accommodate Churchill's painting studio, it became clear that space was limiting and in 1949, Churchill was minded to build a small out-house to accommodate his canvasses and frames. Clementine urged him to desist from such an 'unsightly and expensive addition'[36] although she was probably anxious to see his painting activities moved out of the house – oil paint on the carpet was not an unusual occurrence. The problem was resolved when between 1950 and 1952 a single storey studio extension was built on the east end of the small single storied nineteenth century building now called Stable Cottage, linking it to the old Chauffeur's Cottage. In 1967 it was refurbished to display some of Churchill's paintings.

Clement Atlee first called an election in February 1950. His Labour Party was returned with its majority slashed to only five and its continuation in power was clearly unsustainable for long. The post-war Labour government, like so many administrations forged in the heat of tumultuous events, had been unable to fulfil all the electorate's high expectations; a pattern that became so familiar forty years later when the Soviet Eastern European empire crumbled. So, inevitably, in 1951 came the event that once more dictated a Churchill house move. Attlee called a further election for 25 October and after a three week campaign, Churchill and his Conservatives triumphed with a majority over Labour of 26 seats. In an outcome that today in retrospect seems extraordinary, Churchill, a tiring man in relatively poor health and at the age of seventy-six, was Prime Minister again.

Churchill and Clementine were back in Downing Street and back at Chequers. The accommodation at No 10 had changed considerably since their departure in 1945. The first floor State rooms in which earlier Prime Ministers had lived were being used for large official functions and entertaining and work had been completed under Attlee's direction on the creation on the second floor of a Prime Ministerial flat and it was this comfortable although not opulent residence – 'our poor little attic' Churchill called it – that the family made home.[37] They moved in on 19 November but it soon became evident that the arrangement really was not good enough and a return to the provision of accommodation on the first floor was really impelled by the death on 6 February 1952 of King George VI. A Coronation was looming and the Prime Minister would be hosting many distinguished visitors for whom rather more splendid surroundings were needed. In consultation with the Ministry of Works, a return to something like the original arrangement was devised and executed although later still, after Churchill left office, a major rebuilding of 10 Downing Street was undertaken because the entire structure was essentially unsound with defective foundations.

Although Churchill spent less time at Chequers during his second term as Prime Minister than he had during the war, he made his mark. It was at Chequers that he sat for the infamous Graham Sutherland portrait, commissioned by the House of Commons for his eightieth birthday in November 1954, a portrait that both he and Clementine loathed and that she later had destroyed – almost certainly at the hands of Victor Vincent, the Chartwell gardener. And Churchill himself reputedly embellished the house's own most famous painting, Rubens' The Lion and the Mouse, deciding that the mouse needed a little highlighting and touching it up with own brushes.[38]

One of the most elegant rooms at Chequers is the small White Parlour beneath the gallery of the Great Hall. Norma Major called it one the few really 'feminine' rooms in the house and Neville Chamberlain's wife Annie first made it her own private retreat. Clementine too saw it as her special domain and during Churchill's second term as Prime Minister, her patience with male intrusions into it found an outlet in a polite but firm note to her husband: 'The 'White Parlour' is the lady's Bower & the private Sitting Room of the wife of the Prime Minister. Would it be possible when he confabulates with men to use: – 1. The Prime Minister's Study (opposite dining room) or 2. The Long gallery upstairs?'[39]

The Hyde Park Gate houses were now surplus to requirements but rather than sell them (even Churchill could not have imagined staying at Downing Street indefinitely and realised they would be needed again), they were let, the principal tenant being His Excellency Robert Mendoza, the Cuban Ambassador. Initially he paid 45 guineas a week to Clementine for the flat – the properties were run and managed in her name – but this was later increased by £25 a month to cover an additional room and finally, when he took over most of the furnished ground floor of No 27, a further £300 per annum.[40] Then in early 1954, 28 Hyde Park Gate was let furnished to the Earl of Mansfield. Clementine's shrewd business sense was paying dividends.

Churchill continued to keep a close watch on work in the garden at Chartwell in the post-war years, although he was conscious that he could not do as much personally as he had in the thirties and once he was back in Government, time was seriously limited. '…I must superintend things at Chartwell' he told his doctor Lord Moran in June 1952. 'I do not mean I am going to cut down trees – I promise you I won't do anything foolish – but I can direct others cutting them down'.[41] Guests were invariably taken to see the fish. Malcolm Muggeridge recalled a visit in 1950 when Churchill sat in the chair he kept close to the golden orfe pool and began to call to the fish which however only appeared when he threw some maggots in the water. 'He said' wrote Muggeridge 'that his

The Golden Orfe pond at Chartwell with Churchill's chair.

whole standing with the goldfish depended on their associating the sound of his voice with the provision of maggots…'[42] Churchill had a standing order for the weekly delivery of fresh maggots for which his secretary sent a regular postal order for 22/6 to the Don Bait Company of Mexborough[43] and they created a great impression on Violet Bonham Carter too when she visited. 'I cannot thank you enough for my heavenly visit – so full of varied joys – the long-backed pigs – the gold-fish swirling in their pool to catch the ambrosial maggots, (would that we could scatter maggots in our leaden skies and conjure up that glory in the clouds!)….'[44]

The garden had slowly returned to its former self. In the summer of 1952, Churchill wrote to Clementine who was in Italy telling her how the rains had come and freshened the arid fields. The croquet lawn which Victor Vincent had constructed from the old tennis court in 1949 (when a small wooden pavilion was purchased from Boulton and Paul) was 'the greenest spot for miles'. 'Yr garden is looking lovely & so is yr terrace' he wrote.[45] The lemon scented magnolia was in flower and the fish were well, both indoors and out – Churchill had acquired a fondness for tropical fish after the war and when he became Prime Minister in 1951, the whole tank was moved from Chartwell to Chequers.

A new fish expert named Douglas Parbury had appeared on the scene after the war, and was summoned to advise on the best way to handle Churchill's highly pregnant goldfish and also procured for him some red Higoi carp. Like Plater before him, he had worked for Harrods and also like Plater, clung with ferocious tenacity to Churchill who could be, and frequently was, aggressive, impatient and unrelentingly intolerant with his professional colleagues but equally could show generosity, patience and understanding beyond the call of duty to lesser mortals and innocents. He was in truth astonishingly kind and courteous when Parbury urged him to buy some second-hand government pontoons for his lakes at £15 each and asked if he could come with his friends to fish for roach ('vermin') at Chartwell while his wife went to a hen party and attended a 'Kiddies school treat'. He then sent Churchill a birthday card of surpassing tastelessness showing a picture of a fountain over the words 'May happiness like a fountain spread joy around on your birthday'.[46] Churchill even responded kindly to this (although called it a Christmas card) but did however draw the line at endorsing Parbury's new business venture selling plaques, explaining that he never allowed his name to be used in any sort of promotion.

The year 1953 was signal for Churchill. He oversaw the Coronation of Queen Elizabeth II, a monarch to whom he became devoted, he was created a Knight of the Garter and he was awarded the Nobel Prize for Literature; the latter however the only one of the events to improve his bank balance which swelled by £12,100 in consequence; '…free of tax. Not so bad!' he told Clementine.[47] And in the summer, shortly after the Coronation, he suffered a stroke, an event astonishingly kept secret from the public although one that made certain the reality of a final retirement before too long. Nonetheless an autumn stay in the warmth of the Mediterranean at Max Beaverbrook's villa La Capponcina at Cap d'Ail at least temporarily renewed his energies. Retirement was postponed, the interest in Chartwell was invigorated and the following spring Churchill was concerning himself once more with swans, goldfish and the rich pattern of country life – and death. Following the cold spring, he reported the garden and the lawns were looking lovely, '…but the poor pink rhody was sold a pup by that unnatural spring in February which brought so many of its buds to premature life' and the gunnera would probably be half its ordinary size. Clementine's wisterias however were magnificent.[48] But sadly, the black swan cygnets were killed by carrion crows and myxomatosis had cleared off the rabbits so the local foxes turned their attention to the pheasants and piglets.

But not even Churchill himself and the adrenaline that Chartwell injected into his veins could forever postpone the inevitable. He finally tendered his resignation as Prime Minister and announced that he would leave office on Thursday 5 April 1955, afterwards going initially to Chartwell where he would 'remain in strict privacy' before he and Clementine took a holiday in Sicily. Plans were carefully laid and Churchill said that while their possessions at 10 Downing Street could be labelled during the week, nothing must be moved before the 5th, although the house would be cleared by the following Friday.[49] There are only a few tangible reminders of Churchill's time at 10 Downing Street. In accordance with tradition, he presented a book to the library; a signed copy of his life of his father. Framed photographs of all past Prime Ministers line the walls of the main staircase. Churchill of course is among them but he alone has a second photograph, not because he served twice – he was not unique in that – but as a special tribute to his role in World War II. The second picture, the famous Karsh portrait, takes pride of place at the top of the stairs. In the room behind the entrance hall at No 10 Downing Street is a battered armchair known as Winston

Churchill's Reading Chair but quite what he read in it and when no-one seems able to explain.

As well as departing from Downing Street, Churchill also departed from Chequers where too there are reminders of his time. All Prime Ministers who have occupied the house are remembered by a framed photograph and also a stained glass window bearing their coat of arms. (The absentee from the list is Andrew Bonar Law, the shortest serving of twentieth century Prime Ministers who chose never to live at Chequers). But there has also grown up a custom of Prime Ministers planting a tree in the grounds before leaving office. Some choices have been fairly predictable though many are slightly strange – Ramsay MacDonald for instance planted a cedar and Neville Chamberlain a tulip tree. Churchill's was frankly bizarre. Sometime in March 1955, shortly before his departure – perhaps on Tuesday 27th when he and Clementine were at the house together – Churchill planted on the east lawn a specimen of *Quercus ithaburensis macrolepis,* the Valonia oak. An oak tree, a native English oak, either *Quercus petraea* the sessile oak or *Quercus robur* the pedunculate oak would truly have been an apt and enduring choice, the embodiment of national fortitude and solidity for which Churchill himself always stood. Indeed, later the same year, acorns were

The Valonia oak planted by Churchill at Chequers.

Commemorative plaque at Chequers.

requested from Chartwell for planting on the oak lawn at the Melbourne Botanic Garden in Australia.[50] But whoever suggested to him that at Chequers he should plant a species that is one of the most characteristic forest trees of Gallipoli and the area around the Dardanelles has a good deal to answer for. A rather more apt reminder of the Churchills at Chequers is the avenue of beech trees they presented in commemoration of their time there. When the Australian request for acorns was received, Clementine had commented 'we specialise in beech'. In later years and after Churchill's death, Clementine was invited back to Chequers by her close friend the then Prime Minister Edward Heath and was able to see with much interest the progress in the growth of the trees.[51]

The most charming and poignant floral addition to the garden at Chartwell came in 1958 as the initiative of the children; although the idea for it originated, unexpectedly not with Mary but with Randolph. He had been considering ways to mark their parents' impending Golden Wedding anniversary and although there had already been discussion of a family party, he had another, more imaginative suggestion. Aware of Winston and Clementine's joint love of roses, he conceived the gift of an avenue planting of golden flowered standard roses at Chartwell and wrote to his sisters in early July. They were all enthusiastic and Mary, ever the keen gardener, suggested that it might be sensible to have a few groups of floribunda roses too to balance the planting.

Randolph, if not as keen and knowledgeable a practical gardener as his sister, did nonetheless have his own inspiration. In the summer of 1955 he had bought a house at East Bergholt in Essex overlooking the Stour valley with wonderful views towards Dedham Church; rich John Constable country. He named the strikingly pink-painted house Stour and with help and advice from friends, including Xenia Field – later to become of gardening's few centenarians – he set about turning its overgrown seven acres into what became one of the finest gardens in the area. And he had practical rose growing help close at the hand too in the shape of the Essex family firm of Cants, founded as a general nursery in 1765, which claims to be the oldest rose growing business in the country. There had been a major Cant family rift at the end of the nineteenth century when the then owner, Ben Cant shared his rose breeding knowledge and skills with his nephew Frank on the understanding that he would not set himself up in competition locally. Frank however had other ideas and established a rival company, Frank Cant & Co. at Stanway, with rose fields close to Randolph's home and it was with this branch of Cants that he chose to work on the golden roses project.

But once Cants knew the date of the Golden Wedding – 12th September – they had to disappoint Randolph by telling him there was no possibility of having the rose avenue ready in time. Nothing could be planted until October unless the plants were to be completely stripped of all leaves and flowers; not exactly what he had in mind. Undaunted, Randolph dreamed up another complementary idea that would give his parents a 'taster' of the roses to come. He had the even more imaginative notion of creating a book of paintings depicting the roses that would be used for the avenue itself. In the early stages of the golden rose book, it was largely an East Anglian enterprise with several local artists contributing. Among them, and appropriately at his side throughout the whole project was another neighbour, a strikingly beautiful woman named Natalie Bevan who had become his lover and almost became his wife. She was married to a former naval officer and lived in the nearby village of Boxted. She and Randolph met by chance at his house in 1957 and it was love at first sight. He asked her onto the terrace within moments of their meeting, inviting her to 'smell the roses' and a memory of that fragrance stayed with her throughout their relationship – although Randolph, newly divorced, asked her to marry him, she declined but they remained lovers until his death.[52]

One wet and windy afternoon, Randolph and Natalie went to Frank Cant's rose fields behind the main London to Colchester road and selected twenty-eight varieties, taking an enormous bunch of the gold, yellow, honey and peach coloured blooms back to Stour. They drew up a list to be circulated to their selected artists. At first they approached local painters – Richard Chopping and Denis Wirth-Miller. It was Wirth-Miller who suggested that each rose should be painted by a different artist and as one artist suggested others, so the list grew. John Nash was the first to say yes and spotted 'Lydia' blooming in the garden at Stour and went off home to paint it – although grumbling that all the chosen roses were Hybrid Teas, not species or older varieties. Margaret, Lady Birkenhead, the eighty-two year old widow of Churchill's old friend F. E. Smith then rang to say she had some fine specimens of 'Mrs G. A. van Rossem' in bloom in own garden in Oxfordshire, so could she choose that. Richard Chopping opted for 'Peace', Dennis Wirth-Miller for 'Wheatcroft's Gold', promising 'something very startling'.[53]

Churchill's old friend Paul Maze visited Stour and was immediately dispatched to Colchester to buy some paints and start work. He was especially helpful in supplying other leads, suggesting Cathleen Mann (who did 'Sutter's Gold'), Alice Burton ('McGredy's Yellow'), John Barrow (who normally did abstracts but produced a conventional 'Barbara Richards'), Ivon Hitchens ('All Gold'), Cecil Beaton ('Phyllis Gold') and John Aldridge ('Moonbeam'). Adrian Daintrey stayed at Stour one weekend and in two hours on Sunday morning produced 'Golden Dawn'; only the previous week Lanning Roper's wife Primrose Harley ('Grand'mère Jenny') had told Daintrey she could not make an appointment with him because she was painting a 'special secret rose'. John Armstrong painted 'Beryl Ainger' against a background of soft rain, waiting patiently in his studio until the specimens arrived from Cants. Mary Potter ('Ethel Sanday') brought her rose specially from Aldeburgh. Duncan Grant ('Fantasia') and Vanessa Bell ('Golden Gleam') kept their telephone number secret and would only communicate with Randolph and Natalie by telegram. Dorothea Mclagan who had been seriously ill said that painting 'Golden Mainz' cured her completely and made her a new woman. The pièce de resistance, the real coup among the artists whom Randolph attracted came through the intervention of Cathleen Mann who persuaded Augustus John to do 'Golden Emblem'. Peter Norton, the naval officer turned painter put his 'Tawny Gold' in a jam jar; John O'Connor, head of the Colchester Art School filled the background of 'Quebec' with red thorns masquerading as poppies; Betty Churchill, the widow of Churchill's cousin, Ivor Spencer-Churchill produced a delicate little 'Honey Glow'; but Peggy Ramsay, sister in law of Admiral Sir Bertram Ramsay, Commander of the Allied fleets on D-day drew the short straw and had to paint the only misfit among the golden beauties in the uncommonly vulgar 'Masquerade' which really has no place in this hall of distinction. Other amateurs too made stirring contributions against the odds. W. G. Scott-Brown, a Harley Street laryngologist failed to satisfy the Randolph one-man selection committee at his first attempt and produced 'McGredy's Sunset' at the second. Rab Butler, the Home Secretary intended doing 'Andre le Troquer' in tempera but a tube of vermillion oil paint somehow strayed into the box and was incorporated – 'That's what comes of being an amateur'. 'Natalie Bevan herself did 'Lady Belper' at the fifth attempt, improving her technique on each occasion.

It was recognised that busy people were being asked to give of their valuable time without payment – and to do so almost instantly. First Randolph offered the list of varieties for the artists to choose their subjects. He then sent the actual flowers and asked that they be painted immediately as time was pressing. 'Some may choose to paint a bud and some a flower in bloom. Some may favour a strictly botanical exposition; some may prefer something more imaginative…' he said in his covering letter.[54] Without fail, the artists rose to the challenge; Cecil Beaton was the fastest of all although John Aldridge produced two paintings of 'Moonbeam' and 'Fantasia' within forty eight hours for Randolph to choose. The resulting volume is a triumph and a striking snapshot of mid-twentieth century British flower painting. The artists took Randolph at his word and the range of styles and approaches is legion, from the almost abstract 'All Gold' by Ivon Hitchens (which Augustus John thought 'flashy') through the exquisite flowing freedom of John's own vase of 'Golden Emblem' (his first watercolour for fifty years) to the botanically meticulous rendering of 'Peace' by Richard Chopping.

The Golden Rose book, however, contained more than simply paintings. It was through Richard Chopping and Denis Wirth-Miller that Randolph and Natalie met the calligrapher Denzil Reeves who worked as the book's illuminator from

'Golden Emblem' by Augustus John

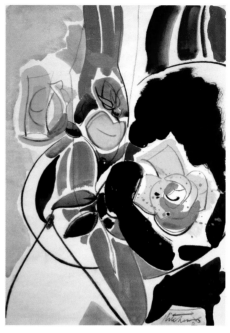

'Allgold' by Ivon Hitchens.

'Wheatcroft's Gold' by Dennis Wirth-Miller.

'Lady Belper' by Natalie Bevan.

his council house in Stratford St Mary. Through Paul Maze came the French engraver André Dunoyer de Segonzac whose contributions came via the British Embassy in Paris in a diplomatic bag. From some more obscure source came the inscription at the beginning: the writings of the Greek epigrammatist Meleager of Gadara and his description of the works of the Lesbian poetess Sappho as 'Few, but all roses'. Another East Bergholt neighbour, the humorous writer Paul Jennings contributed an apposite poem:

> *Once golden words transmuted leaden doom*
> *And fired all England to a golden age;*
> *Now golden roses for you two shall bloom*
> *Whose golden peace turns one more private page.*

The distinguished Oxford bookbinders Alfred Maltby & Sons worked closely with Randolph throughout, adapting and changing the magnificent binding as the contents themselves developed. At the very end of their involvement, they informed him that it was their pleasure to have undertaken the work and there would be no charge. The Garter King of Arms donated a special bookmarker though Cants, missing one of the greatest horticultural public relations opportunities of the century, sent in a bill. The Golden Wedding gift was completed by a specially made easel commissioned from John White & Sons and, from the grandchildren, a book of Augustus John drawings. Diana arranged for the purchase of this and then Randolph, with Churchillian precision, apportioned the cost of £21 between himself and his sisters according to the number of grandchildren they had produced. Mary with four paid most; Sarah with none, nothing.

The Golden Rose book presentation itself was carefully kept 'Press-free' although as many as possible of the artists together with the art critics of the Times, Telegraph, Manchester Guardian, Observer and Sunday Times were invited to a private view at 28 Hyde Park Gate in early September. The Golden Wedding day itself, 12 September, was spent at La Capponcina. Randolph and his nine year old daughter Arabella represented the family and presented the book which gave its recipients much pleasure. Arabella then delighted her grandparents by precociously reciting the Garland of Meleager. Following the celebrations, Churchill and Clementine enjoyed a cruise on Aristotle Onassis's' yacht *Christina*. The roses themselves were planted by Cants on 10 November in an avenue running east-west through the centre of the walled garden with the sundial and its Bali dove grave in the middle flanked by 'Peace' and 'Lydia'. It is a striking feature having survived the Lanning Roper plantings of the nineteen sixties and the recent kitchen garden restoration. Nonetheless, it is now barely recognisable as Randolph conceived it and the roses have been replaced several times over the years, sadly although perhaps of necessity with newer varieties. There is a commemorative wall plaque nearby by the distinguished engraver Reynolds Stone (1909–1979) that states: 'This Rose walk commemorates the golden wedding of Winston & Clementine Churchill & was the gift of their children Diana, Randolph, Sarah & Mary 12 September 1958'.

The later gardening years at Chartwell are well recorded in gardener Vincent's diaries and reveal an efficiently run but traditional English garden with little that is unexpected. Among the seeds being sown were China asters, sweet peas, stocks, wallflowers, sweet Williams, Canterbury bells, aquilegias, polyanthus and primula, petunias and verbenas, antirrhinums, cosmeas and nicotianas. Half hardy subjects such as pelargoniums, fuchsias, nepetas, solanums, penstemon, heliotrope, helichrysums, chrysanthemums and arctotis were routinely propagated by cuttings. There were, as there always had been, beds of cottage garden flowers for cutting – sweet Williams, Brompton stocks, Canterbury bells, aquilegias, cosmeas, irises, gladioli, stocks, asters, larkspur, dahlias and alstroemerias. In the spring daffodils and hyacinths were forced in the greenhouse followed by pot-grown freesias and then tulips and de Caen anemones from the garden. In late summer, specially grown choice or rare dahlias like the yellow 'Glorie Van Heemstede', white 'Wiegenlied' and peach coloured 'Corydon' were cut for vases while in November the house was filled with greenhouse grown chrysanthemums. The kitchen garden was highly productive and more or less self-sufficient. At last, in the declining years of her marriage, and after the pain and turmoil of unhappiness and broken relationships in the family – although with the greatest tragedy, Diana's suicide, still to come – Clementine had materially all she wanted. At Chartwell, she had roses in abundance, a country garden of gentle colour and fragrance in which she could relax and entertain; and one where the husband to whom she had devoted half a century too could rest, feed his treasured fish and reflect on a life of richness and service to Crown, country and wider world without parallel in modern times.

After retiring from office, Churchill made a number of overseas visits to relax and paint and enjoy the company of friends and he initially showed interest in the idea of buying a home in the South of France. He was sent particulars of many properties, especially near Cannes, Grasse, Villefranche sur Mer, Roqubrune, Cap Martin and Mougins (which Clementine was said particularly to favour) but Churchill himself remained non-committal and seems to have lost interest after 1957.[55] In the spring of 1963, he visited Monte Carlo where he stayed at the Hôtel de Paris. But the strain by then was palpable and he even declined an invitation to dine with his dear friend Max Beaverbrook at La Capponcina. On his return, he went to Chartwell where, on 1 May, he finally came to the decision, long pressed on him by the family, not to stand at the next General Election and the announcement was quickly made public. In June, he returned to Monte Carlo and the last of the several cruises he made after 1958 on Aristotle Onassis's yacht *Christina*.

Churchill saw his beloved Chartwell for the last time in mid-October 1964. He and Clementine had spent the best part of three months there before they withdrew as usual to London for the winter. The Hyde Park Gate houses had been altered to make life easier for Churchill as frailness and infirmity increasingly limited his mobility. Around 1962, a bedroom and bathroom were created for him on the ground floor at the rear of No 27 to avoid any necessity for him to use the stairs. The beautiful lower ground floor room at the back of No 28, which provides the main route to the garden was then a dining room and both it and the garden itself were made accessible by a wheel chair lift from the gallery/corridor above it. Although the lift itself has long gone, the access gate to it through the safety railings remains still, its survival officially protected by the local planning authority.

Increasingly, as Churchill remained in his London home, he withdrew to the company of his closest friends, his family and his thoughts. He often went for long periods without speaking and it was an ailing and forlorn figure, although one who could still summon up a 'V'-sign, that appeared at the drawing room window of 28 Hyde Park Gate on 30 November 1964, his ninetieth birthday. Then, within a few weeks, the world was waiting for the inevitable announcement as following a massive stroke on 10 January he passed into a coma. Well-wishers in their thousands sent tributes. On 14 January, Victor Vincent the Chartwell gardener, wrote in his diary 'Planted gift roses 25 'Mischief', 25 'Papa Meilland'. Tying in peaches'.[56] Then, ten days later, on Sunday 24 January 1965, it was Clementine's turn. Her diary records 'Winston died peacefully early this morning'.[57] He had died, not as the English Heritage blue plaque says, at 28, Hyde Park Gate but at 27 where the rear downstairs room had temporarily been his bedroom and his body remained there, in peace, until Tuesday evening.[58]

The nation mourned and, as with the death of other much loved public figures from the Duke of Wellington to Princess Diana, the nation, briefly, united. The Queen's wish that there should be a lying in state and a state funeral had been known to Churchill himself who was deeply touched by the honour. It was a funeral that had been long in the planning. For many years, it was Churchill's wish and intention that he should be buried at Chartwell but a few years before his death, he changed his mind after a visit to the small churchyard at Bladon, adjacent to Blenheim, and to the graves of his parents and his brother Jack, who had died in 1947. Following the funeral service at St Paul's Cathedral on Saturday 30th January 1965, Churchill's body was borne first by Thames launch and then north by train, finally to rest close by Blenheim Palace where, in another century, this remarkable life's story had begun. After his coffin had been lowered into the cold Oxfordshire earth, two wreaths were laid on the grave. From the Queen on behalf of the Nation and Commonwealth, there were spring flowers. From Clementine, there were tulips, carnations – and, like the gift from the Blenheim garden Churchill had given to her at their betrothal on a summer day long ago, English roses.

Endnotes

1 WSC to George Spencer-Churchill 30 Oct 1945 [cited in Churchill, R. S. and Gilbert. M. *Winston S. Churchill.* Vol. 8. p. 164; original not seen].

2 Soames, M. *Clementine Churchill. 2nd Ed.* p. 434.

3 Churchill, J. S. *Crowded Canvas.* p. 184.

4 CHAR 1/394/159–160. CSC to A. W. Southon & Sons. 12 Jun 1945.

5 CHUR 1/30. WSC to R. Southon. 5 Jan 1946.

6 CHUR 1/30/97. CSC to [?] Harris. 14 Jan 1946.

7 CHUR 1/33/47–48. CSC to [?] Harris 24 June 1946.

8 CHUR 1/30/17 L. H. Newman to Lettice Marston 3 Apr 1946.

9 CHUR 1/30/9. WSC to L. H. Newman. 13 Jun 1946.

10 CHUR 1/15/92. Kathleen Harris to WSC. 10 May 1947.

11 CHUR 1/17/19. WSC to L. H. Newman. 17 Oct 1946.

12 CHUR 1/20/127. L. H. Newman to WSC. 30 Apr 1949.

13 Asher, J. *et al.* The Millennium Atlas of Butterflies in Britain and Ireland. p. 295.

14 CHUR 1/22/38. L. H. Newman to WSC. 6 June 1950.

15 CHUR 1/22/36. Chips Gemmell to L. H. Newman. 20 Jun 1950.

16 Soames, M. *Clementine Churchill. 2nd Ed.* p. 437.

17 CHUR 1/17/116. Knight Frank & Rutley to WSC. n.d.

18 CHUR 1/17/172. Nicholl Manisty & Co. to WSC. 17 Oct 1946.

19 Mary Soames, conversation with the author, 2 Aug 2006.

20 CHUR 1/33/49. CSC to [?] Harris. 24 Jun 1946.

21 Churchill, R. S. and Gilbert. M. *Winston S. Churchill.* Vol. 8. p. 255.

22 Camrose papers. Chartwell 4 August 1946 [incorrect date] cited on p. 256; original not seen.

23 CHUR 1/17/369. Statement of account by Wood Willey & Co. n. d.

24 Churchill, R. S. and Gilbert. M. *Winston S. Churchill.* Vol. 8. p. 255.

25 CHUR 1/37/43–4. A. Moir to WSC. 7 Oct 1958.

26 John Vincent, conversation with the author, 27 Jul 2006.

27 Private papers. CSC to V. Vincent. 20 Oct 1946.

28 CSCT 3/72/14. CSC to [?] Alexander n.d.

29 Churchill, J. S. *Crowded Canvas.* p. 190.

30 Soames, M. *Clementine Churchill. 2nd Ed.* p. 513.

31 CHUR 1/33/104. Royal Horticultural Society to CSC. 24 May 1946.

32 CHUR 1/33/26. CSC to [?] Harris. 30 Nov 1945.

33 CSCT 3/72/13. CSC to Lord Hall. 4 Nov 1949.

34 NT Chartwell Archive. Grace Hamblin Files. Box 4. G. Jones to Grace Hamblin 8 Aug 1948.

35 Churchill, J. S. *Crowded Canvas.* p. 59.

36 CHUR 1/46/108. CSC to WSC. 14 Nov 1949.

37 CSCT 2/40/9–10. WSC to CSC. July 1952.

38   Major, Norma. Chequers. p. 200.

39   CSCT 1/32/1. CSC to WSC. n.d.

40   CHUR 1/27/119. Nichol Manisty & Co. to WSC. 4 Dec 1951.

41   Moran, Lord. *Churchill. The Struggle for Survival 1940–1965.* p. 391.

42   Muggeridge, M. *Like It Was.* Diary 23 Aug 1950.

43   CHUR 1/18/272. N. S. to Don Bait Co. 27 May 1948.

44   CHUR 2/181. Violet Bonham-Carter to WSC. 10 Aug 1954.

45   CSCT 2/40/11–13. WSC to CSC. 4 Aug 1952.

46   CHUR 1/20/138. D. Parbury to WSC. 23 Nov 1950.

47   CSCT 2/41/8–9. WSC to CSC. 16 Oct 1953.

48   CSCT 2/42/16–18. WSC to CSC. 31 May 1954.

49   CSCT 2/43/4–6. Note by WSC. 31 Mar 1955.

50   CHUR 1/37/5. M. V. Laurie to Grace Hamblin. 17 Oct 1955.

51   Soames, M. *Clementine Churchill. 2nd Ed.* p. 563.

52   Churchill, W. S. *His Father's Son. The Life of Randolph Churchill.* p. 393.

53   NT RDCH 2/9. Natalie Bevan. *Making the Golden Book.* n.d.

54   NT RDCH 2/7. Randolph Churchill notes. August 1958.

55   CHUR 1/29. File of correspondence Nov 1955 – May 1957.

56   NT Chartwell Archive, Diary of V. Vincent for 1965. 14 January.

57   CSCT 4/35. Diary of Clementine Churchill for 1965. 24 January.

58   Mary Soames, conversation with the author, 2 Aug 2006.

POSTSCRIPT
CHARTWELL AFTER CHURCHILL

The negotiations between the National Trust, Lord Camrose and Churchill and their respective solicitors during the drawing up of the lease were in large measure verbal and were also treated as highly confidential.[1] In written memos, Churchill was referred to as 'X' and Lord Camrose and his colleagues as 'the Group'. In December 1945, it was recorded that the original proposal was for the Group to buy the whole property from X for £50,000 and have it transferred to the Trustees [of the National Trust] upon trust to allow X and his widow to occupy it for their lives. The £10,000 which Lord Camrose had raised in excess of the purchase price should be handed over to the Trust and used, less costs, as the nucleus of an endowment fund.[2] By March 1946, it was being suggested that the lease might be for ninety years, determinable by the Trust on the death of the survivor of Mr and Mrs X and by either Mr or Mrs X at any time on three months notice.[3] After a number of further exchanges,[4] the Lease was eventually drawn up and dated 29 November 1946 for fifty years.[5] Chartwell was sold for £50,000.[6] The final document was however signed only by Churchill, not by Clementine. There was no mention of Clementine in the document and there were no papers transferring the lease to her. Legally therefore, it is evident that Clementine was obliged to leave Chartwell within six months of Churchill's death although a Memo from the National Trust's Secretary dated 3 February 1965 stated that the gift [of Chartwell by Lord Camrose's group] was made 'on the understanding that Lady Churchill would, if she wished, continue to live at Chartwell after her husbands death, after which it would be a permanent memorial to him'.[7] In practice, Clementine chose to leave more or less immediately. She also decided to sell the Hyde Park Gate houses and within a matter of weeks had found a flat only a short distance away at 7 Prince's Gate where she would spend her last years.

It was Clementine's wish (and had been Churchill's too) that the house at Chartwell should be returned as closely as possible to its appearance in the nineteen twenties and thirties; that it should be 'garnished and furnished as to be of interest to the public'[8] and this work was undertaken over the succeeding twelve months, Mary Soames and Clementine's secretary Grace Hamblin (who was to become the Trust's first Chartwell Administrator, a position she held until her retirement in 1973) liaising closely with the National Trust during this period. And although the agreement with the Trust had made no reference to the furniture and furnishings, it was Clementine's wish too that most of this should be handed over. In due course she loaned and then later gave many of Churchill's paintings to the house.

Churchill's grave at St Martin's church Bladon marked by a simple plain slab, (c.1968).

Clementine lived on into gracious old age, appearing at countless functions that honoured her husband – not least in being invited by the Queen to unveil the Ivor Roberts-Jones statue of Churchill in Parliament Square. She received honours too in her own right and greatly enjoyed the company of old friends and visiting and being visited by her family although like all those who live long, she found herself increasingly mourning the loss of close contemporaries. Clementine visited Chartwell for the last time in mid-June 1977, lunching in the restaurant and returning to London laden with flowers. She died peacefully in her Prince's Gate flat on 12 December of the same year at the age of ninety-three. Mary Soames wrote that she truly believed her mother had more real pleasure and satisfaction from Chartwell in the last twelve years of her life than in all the forty she had lived there before Churchill's death.[9] After a cremation Clementine's ashes were placed in Churchill's grave at Bladon at a private family service on 16 December.

The group of Churchill family graves at Bladon after refurbishment.

A meeting was held early in 1965 to plan ahead for the opening of Chartwell to the public and at this gathering, that included Clementine, Mary Soames, Grace Hamblin and Robin Fedden (Deputy Director-General of the National Trust), Clementine is said to have asked that the Belted Galloway herd be disposed of and shortly afterwards Churchill's home-bred bull, Chartwell Titus II, born 2 July 1963, along with eight Chartwell bred females who were all transferred into the ownership of the writer and poet Somerset de Chair of St Osyth, Essex. Regrettably, these distinctive and attractive black and white cattle have not been seen at Chartwell since – much to the sadness of the breed society. It was however agreed that the black swans should remain. It seems to have been at this meeting too that the idea of grassing over the kitchen garden was first proposed and Clementine expressed her wish of engaging the anglophile American garden designer Lanning Roper to oversee this. It was also decided around this time that the garden could not be opened to the public that year – apart from any other consideration, there was no proper car parking space. Discussions also took place on the transfer to the National Trust of Wellstreet Cottage and the new greenhouses, ownership of both of which had by then passed to Mary Soames. By the end of the year, these had been purchased by the Trust.

Following these preliminary discussions, the National Trust did engage Lanning Roper to advise both them and Mary Soames, and although initially this was simply to create a less labour intensive scheme for the Chartwell kitchen garden, in due course his influence grew well beyond that brief and he was responsible for dictating most of what happened in the Chartwell garden for the next fifteen years. Although he advised the National Trust on other gardens too he was a slightly strange choice, an instance perhaps of someone being chosen for a task because his was the name in vogue, regardless of whether they were the most appropriate. Born in New Jersey in 1912, the son of a banker, and having been stationed in England with the American navy during the Second World War, Roper acquired a love both of the country and its gardens and decided to stay on. He became a student at Kew and then joined the staff of the Royal Horticultural Society although as an Editor rather than a gardener. With his wife the artist Primrose Harley he developed a much lauded town garden at Park House, their home in Onslow Square and he soon became a consultant, advisor and garden designer for the rich and famous; including, later in 1981, HRH The Prince of Wales who had hoped he would work on his newly acquired garden at Highgrove although by then – fortunately for Highgrove – Roper's declining health made this impossible. He died in 1983.

Roper's first official visit to Chartwell was during 1965 and although his initial reports and appraisals are undated, it is evident he had made his first appraisal by 30 July. The following year, on 22 July 1966, Victor Vincent the gardener wrote in his diary, 'Lanning Roper coming'.[10] The entry was double underlined, indicative of the respect that Roper commanded at the time and Roper's first dated report was produced three days later. In due course he and Vincent came to like each other and worked well together.[11] Between 1965 and summer 1980, Roper produced around thirty-five reports on the Chartwell garden, based on his regular visits; after 1968 when most of his proposals were at least under way, he went two or three times each year.

Roper's first report describing what he had seen in 1965 and what he recommended indicated that he thought the park 'bare and lacking a setting' although he liked the contrast between the intimate enclosed areas and the broad expanse of water, woods and distant views.[12] Despite what must have been his plantsman's inclinations, he felt the 'sensitive and essentially pastel schemes and the concentration on roses, lavender and good flowering shrubs and the old fashioned border favourites' should remain, rather than shifting the emphasis to 'rarities and plant novelties'. No doubt to the National Trust's relief, he believed the maintenance should be simple and labour-saving; a philosophy that unfortunately in the context of the time meant in part the use of low growing, weed suppressing and generally depressing shrubs of the kind that became known as ground cover. But the practicality of the management was also recognised in the need to reduce the numbers of plants requiring staking and frequent division, to replace many of the annual plantings with perennials and to minimise bedding out to areas close to the house and the loggia to preserve the 'character and charm' of Clementine's own plantings. He was in truth stating no more than the obvious and in effect was defining the difference between almost any modern home garden and what had gone before. A recognition that many thousands of visitors would soon be tramping through what had hitherto been a private family garden was recognised in the need to add some more hard paving, replace some grass walks with stone and to undertake some resurfacing of steps. It was frankly something the Trust's own staff could just have easily produced.

It was important Roper felt to recognise such natural features as the lake, hillside and trees and the views towards them, and to preserve the atmosphere of Chartwell as a family home. He appreciated the intimacy of the enclosed areas such as the old greenhouse terrace, the rose garden and the croquet lawn and believed new planting should reflect what Clementine had in practice already discovered: that plants with fine silver and grey foliage and fragrance rather than harsh bold colours worked well in this green landscape. Roper's most important specific proposals for particular areas were:

- The area around the golden orfe pond should be kept as a secluded wild water garden.

- There should be 'comfortable benches in caved bays' and 'attractive shrub planting' in front of the house.

- The terraces close to the house at the rear should have paved steps and 'landings' and special attention should be given to the planting of the walls.

- The rose garden should retain its character but long-flowering floribundas should replace hybrid tea varieties. Roper's logic here is self-evident in wanting the plants to be attractive for as much of the season as possible; and as this was the nineteen sixties, another option apparent to the modern gardener, that of using long flowering New English roses (hybrids between old and modern varieties that combine the attributes of both) was unavailable.

- On the main lawn between the house and the lake, Roper suggested that a few forest trees should be planted to create an attractive setting for the lake itself and a few trees should also be used to screen the fence that protected the water fowl. The need for this fence continued to present a seemingly insurmountable aesthetic problem at Chartwell and only recently has a way been found to dispense with it.

- The orchard should be under-planted with drifts of single daffodil varieties. Like most good plantsmen, Roper recognised how much more attractive are plantings of single varieties rather than the mixtures that were becoming so poplar at the time but with which the impact is diminished by the later flowering varieties appearing among the dying flowers of the earlier ones.

- The shrubbery beds alongside the croquet lawn should be 'revised'.

- The terrace garden should be improved by widening and straightening the back border and filling all borders with mixed plantings of shrubs and a few sun-loving herbaceous perennials.

- The walled kitchen garden was to be completely altered and it was here that Roper sadly created his most depressing change. In recognising the labour-intensive nature of the kitchen garden he agreed it should be grassed but then dotted it with island beds (this was the nineteen sixties after all when such things were almost *de rigueur*) containing specimen trees 'such as medlars, mulberries, quinces and magnolias'. In practice, the area was planted with quince, *Malus* 'Golden Hornet', *Malus hupehensis, Sorbus hupehensis, Sorbus aucuparia* 'Aspleniifolia', *Sorbus vilmorinii, Robinia pseudoacacia* var. *coluteoides, Robinia viscosa* (= *Robinia x ambigua*) and *Crataegus orientalis*, all supplied by Hilliers. Roper proposed that Churchill's 'harsh brick walls' should be masked with 'shrubs and climbers, including clematis, roses, silver buddleias [*sic*], escallonias, actinidias, hoherias, robinias'. Mercifully he resisted interfering with the golden rose border, recognising its exceptional interest; although it is probable that both Clementine and Mary Soames would in any event have made serious objection to any significant alteration.

Opening Chartwell to the public necessitated significant building development. After some initial temporary accommodation (a shop for instance was created in the old rear entrance to the house), a car park, lavatories, shop, ticket office and restaurant (designed by Philip Jebb, the grandson of Hilaire Belloc)) were built in the field to the north of the house where there had once been the intention of creating a Churchill museum. A new entrance path was constructed from the car park, across the ha-ha ditch and below the fish ponds and the Gavin Davies rock garden, then along the path outside the rose garden to the west front entrance to the house. Access to the fish pools area was then excluded from the public and the water garden in consequence became more enclosed. The newly developed area was planted with vast swathes of ground cover shrubs, including that miserable nineteen sixties trademark, the prostrate juniper. The Gavin Jones nursery undertook much of the work.

In May 1966, the National Trust hosted a large lunch party at Chartwell in honour of Clementine and those who had generously donated towards the house's purchase. Then, a month later it first opened to the public under the Trust's ownership. The admission price for the house was fixed at 2/- for adults and 1/- for children, with the same charges for the garden, a modest eight page information booklet was produced and Green Line coaches introduced an additional stop for their route 706 which ran from Aylesbury via Victoria and Croydon to Westerham and now, continued on to Chartwell. In the first year, the house and garden were open until the end of November on Saturdays, Sundays, Wednesdays and Thursdays, with special additional openings for pre-arranged parties on Tuesdays. In the following year, the pattern was set of the house being open from March to November and the garden from April to mid-October.

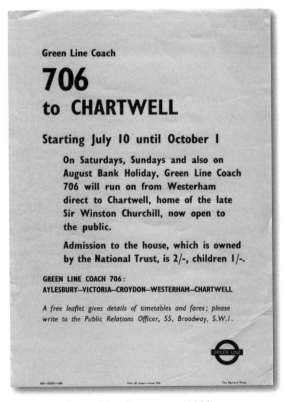

Green Line bus poster (1966).

In the first season, between the June opening and October, 150,000 visitors came; and many came in the rain as it was a wet summer. The infrastructure creaked. It was evident that much more hard paving would be needed and further extensive areas of grass path were replaced with stone while the car park path was laid with tarmac.

Over the succeeding years of Roper's influence, most of his original ideas were executed and expanded. A beech hedge was planted around the studio, a small cottage garden was created around Marycot, trees were planted between the lake and the studio to screen the farm, many thousands of spring bulbs were planted each year – the fine white daffodil 'Mount Hood' for instance was introduced to the slope below the croquet lawn – even more ground cover planting was introduced, the long steps known as Jacob's ladder south of the terraced lawn (the Marlborough Terrace) were built in 1967 and ever more hard paths were laid, including in 1969, a gravel and tarmac path across the orchard. As in any garden, large or small, worn-out, inappropriate or outmoded plants were replaced with others while old and damaged trees were felled and new

Jacob's Ladder, Chartwell.

young stock brought in. Borders come, are widened, then narrowed, then go again. New paths are created or old ones moved to where common sense reveals a more logical course.

In 1955 the National Trust had appointed its own first full-time gardens advisor in the shape of Graham Stuart Thomas, one of the most distinguished plantsmen and gardeners this country has ever produced. Born in 1909, Stuart Thomas learned both practical and academic horticulture and botany and his experience was prodigious, his knowledge encyclopaedic and his judgment impeccable. There is no evidence that either he or Roper ever indicated they felt they were treading on each other's toes and I have seen no relevant correspondence between them. Nonetheless, it is telling that in 1974, the last year of his full-time involvement with the Trust (although he continued as consultant), Stuart Thomas wrote following a visit to Chartwell 'It is pointless here to say that I find many small borders rather out of scale in so large a garden and landscape and the colour groupings rather repetitious. The garden has obviously grown piecemeal, but it is what we inherited and is different from any other. I am however very concerned to know what sort of views are envisaged as maturing in, say, fifty years time from the dotting of large trees growing on the lawns sloping to the water below the top terrace'.[13]

Lanning Roper's last official visit to Chartwell was on 24 September 1980 and from thence the guiding hand has been that of the Trust's incumbent gardens advisor. John Sales took over in this capacity from Graham Stuart Thomas and by and large continued to exercise what was primarily a maintenance role, though removing the more excessive expanses of Roper's tarmac until, in 1987, nature again set the agenda. The great storm of the night of 15–16 October has passed into the folklore of southern England and of especially of southern English gardens. Fortunately many of the Campbell Colquhoun trees survived and although a total of twenty-three trees in the garden were blown over, some were rescued by re-righting; the great Japanese cedar was largely unscathed. More recent trees however were lost, including nine of Churchill's 1930s apples and four yews and two sycamores from the screen against Chartwell Farm. Much more serious however was the loss of the wider landscape and the 'heavenly tree-crowned Hill' that had so entranced Clementine on her first visit largely vanished.[14] A claim for grant aid was made to English Heritage for £16,500 to make good the storm damage. Following the storm, Sales commissioned surveys of the history of the garden, estate and woodlands including an important study by John Meehan, and on the basis of what these told him, he set out a policy for re-planting. It was widely recognised as imaginative and sympathetic.[15]

The restoration of the woodlands was to be in accordance with their late eighteenth and early nineteenth century origins allowing some replanting and some natural regeneration of oak and beech and other natural associates of these species. Victorian style planting was to continue in the garden and across the Mapleton Road to the Common land. Significantly, Sales said 'The most important period at Chartwell was Churchill's and his influence must remain dominant in the garden, as in the house'. In the area around the lakes, the grass was to remain grazed as open parkland with trees confined to the late-Mediaeval field boundaries except where needed for shelter. They would be dotted irregularly as hedgerow trees – not in clumps in the 'Capability' Brown style with which Churchill grew up at Blenheim. The trees would be positioned to try and minimise the impact of the dreadful swan fence. The low-level screening along the Chartwell Farm boundary, lost in the storm would be replaced but clearly mindful of Stuart Thomas's warning, he added 'The important views from the house and formal garden will be maintained'.

The northern garden area would be maintained as an informal adjunct to the terrace gardens and large specimen trees, now so readily and reliably available, were planted around the car park to give 'instant maturity'. The ha-ha would remain clear of planting and the character of the trees and other plantings would become progressively more exotic towards the west while the lower part would merge with the park. Conifers would remain confined mainly to the western roadside area linking with the similar Victorian planting on the steep slope of the Common. The 'dreaded' rhododendrons would alone remain on the steep slope immediately behind the house.

Sales ruled out however much interference with the Roper plantings on the upper terraces to the south of the house and made a commitment to maintain and strengthen Roper's replanting of the south walled kitchen garden with broad shrub borders and climbers on the walls. The attractive top terrace where the old greenhouses had been located would remain as a pleasant seated area. Sales also pointed out that the boundaries to the south of the estate were 'uncomfortably close' and felt it would be a great advantage for the Trust to obtain control of Buddles Wood, the Oast Houses, buildings and surroundings of Chartwell farm.[16] Some fifteen years later, the Trust sadly failed in an attempt to purchase Chartwell Farm.

Whilst neither Clementine nor her children (which in practice meant Mary Soames) ever had any official veto over anything the Trust wished to do at Chartwell, great care was taken to involve them in all significant changes and to keep them informed of plans and developments. It is clear however that Mary Soames and the National Trust, especially in the person of John Sales, did not always see eye to eye about the garden. In September 1989 Mary Soames wrote to the Trust expressing her views with considerable trenchancy.[17] She was depressed she said to receive the impression that the maintenance and planning of the garden did not seem to be urgent and that John Sales had no plans to visit until the end of the following summer (he tended to make one visit per calendar year which could mean an interval of up to eighteen months). The Grey Walled Garden (the rose garden) she believed required the most urgent attention and she felt most upset by the way it had been allowed to deteriorate. In her mother's time it was her pride and joy and the part of the gardens she liked best. Although Clementine never had the benefit of four or five gardeners, Mary Soames said, this part of the garden was always ravishing and immaculate and she felt it should be restored to that state. She concluded that anyone with even a medium amount of gardening knowledge and taste would find the choice of roses in the Golden Rose Border to be banal and their arrangement poor. She thought the plantings around the Marycot (not 'Wendy house' she pointed out) were totally out of character and felt she would very much like to meet Mr Sales face to face.

In some respects, Sales was taking the brunt of criticism for features he had inherited from Lanning Roper but the letter had the desired effect and Mary Soames and John Sales first met at Chartwell two months later when she expressed the view to him that the Golden Rose walk needed renewal. She pointed out that the original planting was put together hurriedly and had been continually modified since. She was in favour of starting effectively from scratch with a new master plan – a wider colour range, more structure, fewer standards ('if any!'), and groups of shrub roses at the ends. She also suggested that the walled Rose Garden might be re-titled Lady Churchill's garden; a name that has been used ever since. Sales' view as expressed in his notes was that, like her mother, Mary Soames was interested more in detail and small-scale effect than in structure and the general layout.[18]

The Golden Rose Walk, Chartwell.

Golden Rose Walk commemorative plaque.

Thereafter, relations seem to have improved although Mary Soames continued to take a close interest in the planting and to visit Chartwell from time to time. At a meeting in March 1995 she was instrumental in having more 'ephemeral' planting introduced in Lady Churchill's Rose garden – summer flowering annuals followed by groups of spring flowering plants.[19] Then in March 1999, the Trust acceded to her wish to see roses in her mother's garden with softer colours, more to her mother's taste.[20]

The Golden Rose walk has continued to evolve and was extensively replanted in 1990[21] when 'Peace' and 'Sutter's Gold' became the only old varieties still represented – mainly because of the difficulty of obtaining stocks of the others that are vigorous enough to give a satisfactory display. Since then however, every effort has been made to return to the original layout and the Golden Rose walk was completely restored in the winter of 2015 and over two thirds of the roses there now match the original varieties while the remainder are all varieties older than the nineteen seventies to keep the feature as authentic as possible.

Following an unsuccessful attempt in 1992 by the Worshipful Company of Fruiterers, a new orchard of notable old apple varieties (including, appropriately, 'American Mother') was planted in front of the greenhouses – outside the main garden – in 1995 by the Kent Men of the Trees, the inspiration for the orchard being the public concern expressed about replacing Chartwell trees lost in the great storm. The last survivor of Churchill's 1930s apple planting – the area informally called the Studio orchard – an old 'Newton Wonder', was finally taken down in 2004 and replanting of the old orchard which had begun some years previously was completed.

Although Chartwell has never been a garden of ornaments – Churchill himself after all was not even very enthusiatic about garden buildings – there are two significant exceptions. There is the old sundial in the centre of the Golden Rose walk that bisects the kitchen garden and beneath which the Bali dove is buried, and at the lower end of the lower lake a massive statue of Churchill and Clementine by the Yugoslavian-born sculptor Oscar Nemon. This was unveiled by HM Queen Elizabeth the Queen Mother on 13 November 1990 and matches one in Kansas City USA. There is another Nemon stature of Churchill in the centre of Westerham.

John Sales retired as gardens advisor in 1998, to be succeeded by Jim Marshall and then, under a changed National Trust management system by the South-

Statue of Churchill and Clementine at Chartwell by Oscar Nemon

East regional gardens and parks advisor Mike Buffin based at Polesden Lacey and the national Head of Parks and Gardens Mike Calnan who later became head of horticulture for the entire National Trust. Emma McNamara, a National Trust gardens advisor has been working with the Chartwell team since 2015.

The largest and most unfortunate of Lanning Roper's changes was finally undone when in 2003 a master plan was prepared for the reinstatement of the kitchen garden, something to which Mary Soames gave her enthusiatic support.[22] The area was cleared in 2004 and splendidly restored to its original purpose. Using Victor Vincent's old diaries, surviving invoices and Churchill's own paintings as guides, the National Trust has re-created something like the appearance of the productive kitchen garden as the Churchills knew it.

In 1977, consideration was being given to Victor Vincent's retirement as Chartwell head gardener. This took place two years later and it was agreed his position would be filled by his deputy Mick Boakes who had been at Chartwell, apart from a short break, since 1962. This proved a successful appointment although some doubts about his suitability had been expressed at the time as he had little glasshouse experience, this being the prerogative of Vincent as head gardener.[23] It was largely because of this that an experienced assistant was appointed at the same time in the person of Mary Digby who had spent nine years at Sissinghurst. She remained at Chartwell until her retirement in 2006. Boakes himself retired in 2001 when his place was taken by Jon Simons who had begun his career at Chartwell in 1986 before going to another National Trust property nearby, Ightham Mote. He in turn left Chartwell in 2013 and was replaced by Tim Parker in a redefined role as Gardens and Countryside Manager for the entire Chartwell portfolio. In addition to Parker, there are now two full time senior gardeners, one other full time gardener and three part-time staff. Just as in the house and at all National Trust properties, they can call on the invaluable assistance of volunteers.

Long-time Chartwell gardener Mary Digby in the restored kitchen garden at Chartwell (2005).

Clementine's long-time secretary Grace Hamblin was succeeded as Chartwell Administrator or Property Manager by Jean Broome in 1973 and she in 1996 by Carole Kenwright and then in 2006 by Philippa Rawlinson who in turn was succeeded in 2013 by Zoë Colbeck. Wellstreet Cottage, now called Well Cottage was used until recently as the Manager's residence. Chartwell Cottage was sold on a long lease.

Chartwell lost its remaining direct contact with Churchill when Mary Soames died at her London home on 31 May 2014, having last visited Chartwell the previous year. Her death was greatly mourned nationally and the loss felt by the National Trust in a very practical way. I recall the Chartwell staff saying to me on several occasions that if they ever had a query about some aspect of the house or garden's history, the solution was simple: 'Ask Mary'.

Chartwell has been used by the National Trust to stage several high profile events, including a number of sons et lumières centred on the Marlborough Terrace lawn. The most celebrated in 1976 included a performance of a specially written production called A Man and his House by John Julius Norwich in which Nigel Stock played Churchill, Barbara Jefford Clementine and Garry Watson Philip Tilden while Sarah Churchill and, unbelievably, Harold Macmillan (although only by voice from his hospital bed) played themselves in cameo roles. Its author did not consider it a success.[24] The lighting presented a particular problem because Norwich thought the house far from beautiful and discovered that 'the more light you throw at it, the worse it looks'. The favoured illumination source was wartime searchlights but these would have been prohibitively expensive to hire and accompanied by their own deafening generators and the cheap substitutes used instead were frankly pathetic, little better than hand-held spotlights. But there was worse and Norwich thought 'The son was even more of a catastrophe than the lumière' because Churchill's speeches were taken from his post-war recordings which lacked energy and drama while the production's rough wartime songs were sung angelically by choirboys. The author said he buried his face in his hands. A further son et lumière was staged in 1982 but this was the last, the events being discontinued because of unacceptable wear to the lawns.

The Chartwell lawns have long been recognised by the Trusts' advisors as problematic. In 1984 John Sales wrote that '...the lawns at Chartwell do not do justice to the place as a whole'[25] and in 1992 he urged that the annual dance held on the terrace be discontinued. This was a celebrated local occasion when guests would dress in 1940's fashions with music of the period. 'The property does not need the additional visitors, the income does not make up for the damage and upheaval caused. Our major concern should be with conservation' he wrote.[26] He was dismayed in 1998, shortly before his retirement when he learned that a marquee was to be pitched on the main terrace for a major event. Nonetheless, other big events have been held at Chartwell – an open air opera in 2001, a recording of the BBC television programme *The Antiques Roadshow* in 2002, the launch of the new £5 note, commemorations for the 50th anniversary of Churchill's death, the end of the Second World War anniversary, exhibition launches and so forth. Increasingly events that might involve hot liquids (cups of tea) have been discouraged and more use has been made of the grassy slopes below the Terrace Lawn for the celebrations. These unavoidable conflicts between what is best for horticulture and what is best for marketing will be familiar to anyone running a large public garden; not least to the National Trust which owns more gardens in this country than anyone else has ever done.

The Chartwell house and grounds have been used for filming, most notably two BBC television drama productions, *Winston Churchill – the Wilderness Years* in 1983 with Robert Hardy as Churchill and *The Gathering Storm* filmed in October 2001 in which Albert Finney memorably played the part and some modest attempts were made to cover up more modern aspects of the property and to give it a closer appearance to that in the nineteen thirties. The most recent major drama filming was in 2016 for *Churchill's Secret* starring Michael Gambon, an Anglo-American production shown in Britain on ITV. In addition, a few scenes were shot in 2017 for the British film *Darkest Hour* starring Gary Oldman as Churchill, for which he received an Oscar in 2018, but all were filmed outdoors and any inclusion of the house was the result of recreated sets. The National Trust at Chartwell has a policy of most carefully vetting any proposal and as is evident will normally only allow filming that is directly related to Churchill or his times or the house itself.[27]

Chartwell is now one of the most visited of all National Trust properties receiving on average 230,000 visitors a year, so many that entry to the house is on timed tickets. Apart from two staff flats and offices, most of the main rooms of the house are open to the public and it has an English Heritage Grade 1 listing (a building of outstanding National importance). The front garden wall has a separate Grade II listing while the gardens have a Grade II* listing in the English Heritage Register of important gardens, having 'exceptional historic interest'. The National Trust denotes the garden Grade 5 – one of 'special location or national importance because of historical association or plant collection'. In 2016 A Conservation and Management Plan was produced by consultants Caroe Architecture and recommendations made for the ongoing care of the property and for the careful and sensitive opening of additional rooms by 2020 including for the first time Churchill's bedroom and bathroom and the secretaries' room.

The house is open seven days a week from around the end of February to the end of October plus weekends for part of December and there are always Churchill themed exhibitions for the public to see. The Chartwell garden, like any other, is never static and has inevitably evolved under the hand of the National Trust just as it had done under Churchill's ownership. The challenges facing today's gardeners are familiar ones. Their work has to be tailored to the presence of the public because the gardens are open seven days a week for the whole year. And like other gardeners in England and elsewhere in the global warming of the twenty first century, they face the problems of operating in a climate that is increasingly different from that in which the garden was created. A garden is not a museum and the skill and art of the National Trust as Chartwell's guardians lie and will lie in their ability to retain the essence of the site as Churchill and Clementine knew it while responding to the changes that nature and time impose. The risk of course lie in attempts to try and second guess what Churchill and Clementine themselves would have done.

Endnotes

1   NT Internal memorandum, 3 Feb 1965.
2   NT Internal memorandum, 20 Dec 1945.
3   NT Internal letter, 13 Mar 1946.
4   NT Minutes, Finance Committee 12 Apr 1946 and 14 Feb 1947; Minutes, Executive Committee 15 Mar 1946 and 11 Oct 1946.
5   NT Lease, National Trust to WSC 29 Nov 1946.
6   NT Conveyance, WSC to National Trust, 29 Nov 1946.
7   NT Internal Memorandum, 3 Feb 1965.
8   CHUR 1/27. WSC to Nicholl, Manisty & Few. 12 Apr 1946.
9   Soames, M. *Clementine Churchill. 2nd Ed.* p. 535.
10 NT Chartwell Archive. Diary of V. Vincent for 1966. 22 July.
11 John Vincent, conversation with the author, 27 Jul 2006.

[12] NT Reports on Chartwell by Lanning Roper. 1966-1980.

[13] NT G. Stuart Thomas to W. A. Kingston, 16 Aug 1974.

[14] NT Box No CIR/05/612. Chartwell 1988 to 2003 415727. Storm Damage 1987 Chartwell – Grant Aid Application to English Heritage, March 1990.

[15] NT Meehan, J. *Chartwell – an historical development of Chartwell Garden and Landscape.* June 1988.

[16] NT Sales, J. Outline Policy for the Conservation of the Garden and Park, 1989.

[17] NT Mary Soames to J. E. T. Cooper. 22 Sep 1989.

[18] NT Box No CIR/05/612. Reports of Visits by Gardens Advisor. Meeting with Mary Soames at Chartwell. 14 Nov 1989.

[19] NT Box No CIR/05/612. Reports of Visits by Gardens Advisor. Meeting at Chartwell. 13 Mar 1995.

[20] NT Box No CIR/05/612. Reports of Visits by Gardens Advisor. Meeting at Chartwell. 15 Mar 1999.

[21] Jon Simons, conversation with the author, 17 Jan 2007.

[22] Mary Soames, conversation with the author, 2 Aug 2006.

[23] NT Reports on Chartwell by Lanning Roper. 1966-1980. 14 Mar 1977.

[24] John Julius Norwich, personal communication, 7 Nov 2006.

[25] NT Box No CIR/05/612. Reports of Visits by Gardens Advisor. [?] 1984.

[26] NT Box No CIR/05/612. Reports of Visits by Gardens Advisor. 15 Jun 1992.

[27] Judith Seaward, conversation with the author, 17 Jan 2007.

Flowers left on Churchill's grave (May 2007); he is never forgotten.

Sources

CHAR	Chartwell Papers, Churchill Archive Centre, Churchill College, Cambridge
CHUR	Churchill Papers, Churchill Archive Centre, Churchill College, Cambridge
CSCT	Clementine Spencer Churchill Papers, Churchill Archive Centre, Churchill College, Cambridge
GU	Glasgow University Library, Special Collections.
HP	Hamilton Papers, Liddell Hart Centre for Military Archives, King's College London
K	Royal Botanic Gardens, Kew, Letters to Sir William Hooker.
KS	Centre for Kentish Studies, Maidstone
LP	Labour Party Papers, Labour History and Archive Centre, John Rylands Library, Manchester
NT	National Trust Archives, Chartwell and Swindon
RA	Royal Archives, Windsor
SLH	Sevenoaks Local History Library.
TP	Philip Tilden Papers, Private Collection
UL	University of Leicester Library, Transport Collection,
WCA	Westminster City Archives
WCHL	Churchill Additional Collections, Churchill Archive Centre, Churchill College, Cambridge
WSB	Wilfrid Scawen Blunt Papers, Fitzwilliam Museum, Cambridge
WU	Archives of the Amalgamated Union of Building Trade Workers, Warwick University Modern Records Centre.

SELECT BIBLIOGRAPHY

Anon. *Painting as a Pastime. Winston Churchill – his life as a painter.* (London, Sotheby's, 1998).

Anon. *Chartwell Son et Lumière.* (Lamberhurst, National Trust, 1976).

Asher, J., Warren, M., Fox, R., Harding, P., Jeffcoate, G. and Jeffcoate, S. *The Millennium Atlas of Butterflies in Britain and Ireland.* (Oxford, Oxford University Press, 2001).

Asquith, H. H. *Letters to Venetia Stanley.* (Oxford, Oxford University Press, 1982).

Asquith, M. *The Autobiography of Margot Asquith.* (London, Eyre & Spottiswoode, 1962).

Barty-King, H. *Maples: Fine Furnishers.* (London, Quiller Press, 1992).

Benton, A. *Cheals of Crawley: the family firm at Lowfield Nurseries 1860s to 1960s.* (Uckfield. Moira Publications, 2002).

Bettley, J. *Lush and luxurious. The Life and Work of Philip Tilden 1887–1956.* (London, Royal Institute of British Architects, 1987).

Binney, M. *The Ritz Hotel, London,* (London, Thames & Hudson, 1999).

Blackburn, R. *The Electoral System in Britain.* (London, Macmillan, 1995).

Bond, J. and Tiller, K. *Blenheim: Landscape for a Palace. 2nd Ed.* (Stroud, Budding Books, 2000).

Bonham-Carter, V. *Winston Churchill as I knew him.* (London, Eyre & Spottiswoode, 1965).

Booth, C. *The Goldfish Bowl. Married to the Prime Minister 1955–1997.* (London, Chatto & Windus, 1994).

Brown, J. *Lutyens and the Edwardians.* (London, Viking, 1996).

Brown, J. *Eminent Gardeners.* (London, Viking, 1990).

Buczacki, S. *A Short Guide to Chartwell Garden.* (London, National Trust, 2007).

Buczacki, S. *My darling Mr Asquith: the extraordinary life and times of Venetia Stanley.* (Stratford-upon-Avon, Cato & Clarke, 2016).

Churchill, J. S. *Crowded Canvas.* (London, Odhams, 1961).

Churchill, P. and Mitchell, J. *Jennie: Lady Randolph Churchill.* (London, Collins, 1974).

Churchill, R. S. *Twenty-one Years.* (London, Weidenfeld & Nicolson, 1964–1965).

Churchill, R. S. and Gilbert. M. *Winston S. Churchill.* 8 vols. (London, Heinemann, 1966–1988).

Churchill, S. *A Thread in the Tapestry.* (London, Andre Deutsch, 1977).

Churchill, W. S. *Lord Randolph Churchill.* 2 vols. (London, Macmillan, 1906).

Churchill, W. S. *My African Journey.* (London, Icon 1964 [1908]).

Churchill, W. S. *The World Crisis.* 5 vols. (London, Thornton Butterworth, 1923–1929).

Churchill, W. S. *My Early Life; A Roving Commission.* (London, Macmillan, 1942 [1930]).

Churchill, W. S. *The Second World War.* 6 Vols. (London, Cassell & Co. 1948–1954).

Churchill, W. S. *His Father's Son. The Life of Randolph Churchill.* (London, Weidenfeld & Nicolson, 1996).

Cilcennin, Viscount. *Admiralty House, Whitehall.* (London, Country Life, 1960).

Cleverdon, F. W. *A History of Mells.* (Frome, Frome Society for Local Study, 1974).

Collier, B. *The Defence of the United Kingdom.* (London, Her Majesty's Stationery Office, 1957).

Colville, J. *Footprints in Time. Memories.* (London, Collins, 1976).

Colville, J. *The Fringes of Power: Downing Street Diaries 1939–1955.* (London, Sceptre, 1986).

Coombs, D. *Sir Winston Churchill's Life through his Paintings.* (London, Chaucer, 2003).

Cooper, P. *Building Relationships. The history of Bovis 1885–2000.* (London, Cassell, 2000).

Dasent, A. I. *Piccadilly in three centuries.* (London, Macmillan, 1920).

Ditchley Foundation. *Ditchley Park Official Guide.* (Ditchley, Ditchley Foundation, 1995).

Ernle, Lord. *English farming – past and present. 5th Ed.* (London, Longmans, Green, 1936).

Fedden, R. *Churchill and Chartwell.* (London, National Trust, 1968).

Fedden, R. *Churchill at Chartwell.* (Oxford, Pergamon, 1969).

Fitzgibbon, C. *The Blitz.* (London, MacDonald, 1957).

Fletcher, J. *Sutton Courtenay. The History of a Thames-side Village.* (Sutton Courtenay, The Friends of All Saints Church, 1990).

Fretwell, K. *Chartwell: Historical Development of Garden and Landscape.* (Unpublished, Chartwell, National Trust, 2002).

Gilbert, M. *Churchill. A Life.* (London, Heinemann, 1991).

Gilbert. M. *In Search of Churchill.* (London, HarperCollins, 1994).

Gilbert. M. *Winston Churchill. The Wilderness Years.* (London, Book Club Associates, 1981).

Green, D. *Sir Winston Churchill at Blenheim Palace. 2nd Ed.* (Oxford, Alden Press, 1965).

Hamilton, I. *Listening for the Drums.* (London, Faber & Faber, 1944).

Hamilton, I. B. M. *The Happy Warrior.* (London, Cassell, 1966).

Hassall, C. *Edward Marsh. A Biography.* (London, Longmans, 1959).

Hasted, E. *The history and topographical survey of the county of Kent.* (Canterbury, Simmons and Kirkby for the author, 1778–1779).

Horner, F. *Time Remembered.* (London, Heinemann, 1933).

Hyam, R. *Elgin and Churchill at the Colonial Office.* (London, Macmillan, 1968).

Ingram, B. [Ed.]. *Winston Churchill. The Greatest Figure of our Time.* (London, Illustrated London News, 1954).

James, R. R. [Ed.] *Chips: The Diaries of Sir Henry Channon.* (London, Weidenfeld and Nicolson. 1967).

James, R. R. *Churchill: A study in failure 1900–1939.* (London, Weidenfeld & Nicolson, 1970).

Jenkins, R. *Churchill.* (London, Macmillan, 2001).

Jenkins, R. *Asquith.* (London, Collins, 1964).

Johnson, B. *The Churchill Factor.* (London, Hodder & Stoughton, 2014).

Julyan, H. E. *Sixty Years of Yachts.* (London, Hutchinson, n.d).

Landemare, G. *Recipes from No. 10.* (London, Collins, 1958).

Lee, C. *Jean, Lady Hamilton 1861–1941. A Soldier's Wife.* (London, Author, 2001).

Lee, J. *A Soldier's Life: General Sir Ian Hamilton 1853–1947.* (London, Macmillan, 2000).

Leslie. A. *The Fabulous Leonard Jerome.* (London, Hutchinson, 1954).

Lloyd George, F. *The Years that are Past.* (Hutchinson, London, 1967).

Longford, E. *A Pilgrimage of Passion. The Life of Wilfrid Scawen Blunt.* (London, Weidenfeld and Nicolson, 1979).

Longford, R. *Frances, Countess Lloyd George. More than a Mistress.* (Leominster, Gracewing, 1996).

Lough, D. *No More Champagne: Churchill and his Money.* (London, Picador, 2015).

Major, N. *Chequers.* (London, HarperCollins, 1996).

Marsh, E. *A number of people: a book of reminiscences.* (London, Heinemann, 1939).

Martin, R. *Lady Randolph Churchill. A Biography. Vol 1. 1854–1895.* (London, Cassell, 1969).

Martin, R. *Lady Randolph Churchill. A Biography. Vol 2. 1895–1921.* (London, Cassell, 1971).

Moran, Lord. *Churchill. The Struggle for Survival 1940–1965.* (London, Constable, 1966).

Morgan, T. *Churchill 1874–1915.* (London, Jonathan Cape, 1983).

Muggeridge, M. *Like It Was.* (London, HarperCollins, 1981).

Murray, W, J. C. *Stocking the garden with butterflies.* (Good Gardening, March, 1938).

Murray, W. J. C. *Copsford.* (London, George Allen & Unwin, 1948).

Newman, L. H. *A reintroduction of* Aporia crataegi *in Kent.* (The Entomologist. **82**, 140. 1949).

Newman, L. H. *Butterflies – Wings for Sir Winston.* (Country Life, December 3, 1987).

Newman, L. H. *Butterfly Farmer.* (London, Country Book Club, 1954).

Plummer, D. *Queer People.* (London, W. H. Allen, 1963).

Ponting. C. *Churchill.* (London, Sinclair-Stevenson, 1994).

Reid, P. G. *Churchill. Townsman of Westerham.* (Folkestone, Regency, 1969).

Robbins, K. *Sir Edward Grey: A Biography of Lord Grey of Falloden.* (London, Cassell, 1971).

Robinson, P. *Lincoln's Excavators – the Ruston Years 1875–1930.* (Wellington, Roundoak, 2003).

Sandys, C. *Chasing Churchill.* (London, HarperCollins, 2003).

Sandys, C. *From Winston with Love and Kisses.* (London, Sinclair-Stevenson, 1994).

Soames, M. *Speaking for Themselves. The Personal letters of Winston and Clementine Churchill.* (London, Doubleday, 1998).

Soames, M. *Clementine Churchill. 2nd Ed.* (London, Doubleday, 2002).

Soames. M. *A Churchill Family Album.* (London, Allen Lane, 1982).

Stanley of Alderley, Lord. *The Stanleys of Alderley 1927–2001.* (Anglesey, AMCD/Magma, 2004).

Stanley, P. E. *The House of Stanley.* (Bishop Auckland, Pentland Press, 1998).

Stansky, P. *Sassoon – The Worlds Of Philip & Sybil.* (New Haven and London, Yale University Press, 2003).

Sykes, C. *Nancy. The Life of Lady Astor.* (London, Collins, 1972).

Tilden, P. *True Remembrances – the memoirs of an architect.* (London, Country Life, 1954).

Tree, R. *When the Moon was High – Memoirs of Peace and War 1897–1942.* (London, Macmillan, 1975).

Welcome, J. *Neck or Nothing. The Extraordinary Life & Times of Bob Sievier.* (London, Faber & Faber, 1970).

Williams, J. G. *A Field Guide to the Butterflies of Africa.* (London, Collins, 1969).

Wood, M. *Nancy Lancaster – English Country House Style.* (London, Frances Lincoln, 2005).

Yates, J. A. *The butterflies of Bangalore and neighbourhood.* (Journal of the Bombay Natural History Society, **36**, 450–459, 1932).

Extensive reference was also made to:

Oxford Dictionary of National Biography. (Oxford, Oxford University Press, 2004).
Pevsner, N and others. *The Buildings of England.* (London, Penguin, 1951–1974).
Victoria County History. (London, 1899–).
Finest Hour, (Washington DC, The Churchill Centre, 1968–)

Picture Credits

Numbers refer to pages; t = top, b = bottom, l = left, r = right

The Publishers have made every effort to contact holders of copyright works. Any copyright holders we have been unable to reach are invited to contact the Publishers so that a full acknowledgment may be given in subsequent editions. For permission to reproduce the following photographs and illustrations, and for supplying images, the Publishers thank those listed below.

© Stefan Buczacki: 6, 14 tl, 14 tr, 16, 22, 23, 25, 27, 28, 32, 38, 46, 48, 58, 62, 63, 64, 66, 69, 75, 81, 85, 91, 97, 101 l, 103, 104, 111 t, 116, 120, 122 b, 130, 131, 132, 139, 142 t, 145 t, 145 b, 155 t, 155 b, 159, 177 t, 177 b, 188, 191, 208, 213 t, 229 t, 229 b, 238, 241 t, 241 b, 246, 252, 254, 256, 264, 266, 274, 275, 281, 283, 288 t, 288 b, 289, 296, 302 b, 307, 311, 330, 331, 337, 358, 365, 373, 375, 376 t, 376 b, 379, 382, 383, 385, 396, 401, 402, 406 t, 406 b, 408, 409, 412

Centre for Kentish Studies and East Kent Archive Centre: 179, 180, 181

By permission of the Chequers Trust: 313

Churchill Archives Centre at Churchill College, Cambridge: 184, 185 (WCHL 8/92), 213 b (BRDW 1-1-105), 142 (BRDW 1-2-98), 250 (BRDW 1-1-294), 251 (BRDW 1-2-89), (BRDW 1-2-141), 255 (BRDW 1-2-158), 335 (CHUR 1/32B/338), 339 (CHUR 1/32B/347), 350 (BRDW 1-1-349); also 196 (CHAR 1/139/86-87) [© Lady Soames]; and 322 (CHAR 1/167/30), (CHAR 20/32/17) [© expired]

Photographs from the Broadwater Collection [BRDW] are reproduced by permission of Curtis Brown Group Ltd., on behalf of Winston S. Churchill

Extracts from and facsimiles of the Churchill Papers CHUR 1/32B/338 and CHUR 1/32B/347 are reproduced by permission of Curtis Brown Group Ltd., on behalf of the Estate of Winston S. Churchill © Winston S. Churchill

Copyright © Churchill Heritage Ltd (Reproduced with permission of Anthea Morton-Saner on behalf of Churchill Heritage Ltd): 74, 155, 284, 294, 299

City of Westminster Archives Centre: 271

By courtesy of the Ditchley Foundation: 317, 319, 320

© Dundee City Council/www.photopolis.org: 157

Gertrude Jekyll Collection, Environmental Design Archives, University of California, Berkeley: 99 b

By courtesy of Helen Hamilton: 343

Liddell Hart Centre for Military Archives, King's College London: 137

By courtesy of the Earl and Countess of Lytton: 70

By courtesy of His Grace the Duke of Marlborough (photographer Richard Cragg): 14 b, 18

By permission of The National Trust, Chartwell: 260, 387 tl (Photo Stefan Buczacki), 387 tr (Photo Stefan Buczacki), 387 bl (Photo Stefan Buczacki), 387 br (Photo Stefan Buczacki)

PA Photos: 67

Private Collection: 15 l; 15 r; 20, 24, 29, 30, 34 t, 34 b, 36, 39, 41, 43, 44, 49, 53, 54, 68, 71 (Photo Stefan Buczacki), 71 t, 71 b, 73, 77, 78, 80, 82, 83, 84, 86, 93 t, 93 b, 94, 99 t, 101 r, 109, 110, 111 b, 112, 122 t, 127, 129, 134, 138, 141, 142 b, 143, 147, 153, 162, 163, 164, 167, 169 t, 169 b, 170, 172, 173, 174, 175 t, 175 b, 176, 186, 187, 190 t, 190 b, 192, 193, 195, 197, 198, 199, 200, 203, 204, 205, 207, 214, 215, 222, 227, 228, 245, 300, 302 t, 351, 353 t, 353 b, 370, 371

Jacket illustrations:
Front top: Blenheim Place, Nathaniel Gonzales / Alamy Stock Photo
Front bottom: Chartwell, Iconotec / Alamy Stock Photo
Back top: Winston Churchill with children Randolph and Diana, Wikimedia Commons
Back bottom: Churchill bricklaying, Churchill Archives Centre at Churchill College, Cambridge

$\mathcal{I}$NDEX

Reader's Note: page numbers in *italics* indicate a photograph.